JAZZ

THE ESSENTIAL GUIDE

JOHN FORDHAM

THIRD EDITION

John Fordham is a jazz critic, writer and broadcaster, who has been writing about jazz for nearly 20 years, initially for the London listings magazine, *Time Out*, and then for a variety of papers including *Melody Maker*, *Sounds*, *Zig-Zag*, *Wire* and *Q*. Since 1978 he has been a regular jazz correspondent for *The Guardian*, and more recently, for *The Listener*. His biography of Ronnie Scott, *Let's Join Hands and Contact the Living*, was published in 1986 to enthusiastic reviews; it was published in paperback in 1995 under the title *Jazz Man* by Kyle Cathie Limited. An illustrated jazz history, *The Sound of Jazz*, was published in 1989 and an extensive illustrated survey *Jazz* (Dorling Kindersley) in 1993. John Fordham has acted as a jazz adviser for the Arts Council of Great Britain, and the Greater London Arts, and was also editor of *Time Out* from 1978 to 1981, and co-editor of *City Limits* from 1981 to 1986. An anthology of his jazz writing over three decades, *Shooting From The Hip*, is also published by Kyle Cathie Limited.

This revised edition published in 1995 by
Kyle Cathie Limited
20 Vauxhall Bridge Road, London SW1V 2SA
First published in 1991, revised edition 1993

ISBN 1-85626-204-9
A CIP catalogue record for this book is available from
the British Library.

Typeset by DP Photosetting
Printed in Great Britain by Cox & Wyman Ltd, Reading, Berks

CONTENTS

PREFACE TO THE THIRD EDITION

W hen the first version of this guide was written, with its final entries creeping in under the wire in the early spring of 1991, the pattern of jazz record issue in a still unfamiliar format was growing fast but was distinctly unbalanced. Virtually all new sessions were emerging on CD by then, and so was a steady stream of reissues of the bebop music of the 1950s and early 1960s, which had become fashionable and saleable. But early jazz was still poorly represented, except for the work of the music's most legendary figures. Record companies weren't sure how large a group such a specialised cognoscenti was, or how tolerant customers would be toward the inevitably primitive sound quality of many of the pioneering recordings. Some crucial pieces in the pattern of twentieth century musical development were therefore missing – already deleted on vinyl in some cases, and not yet on the schedules for CD release.

In 1995, much has changed. Stuart Nicholson, in his book *Jazz: The Modern Resurgence* quoted a record company executive as commenting that virtually everything worth issuing from the jazz archives would have found its way on to CD by the early 1990s, and so it has proved. He might have added that what the majors wouldn't take care of, the small companies and crucial one-horse record labels would. The record industry's activities at all levels had turned to CD, and as the early 1990s controversies over the format's pricing proved, just about anyone could make a compact disc for a highly competitive price if they chose to represent anything like the real cost to the public.

The balance between pre-1940s and post World War II jazz is now much better, and I hope this second revision of *Jazz on CD* reflects some of those changes. New listeners will inevitably have to accept some compromises in the quality of reproduction they might be used to as the music goes further back. Leaving the originals more or less as they sounded when they were first sold is authentic, but distracting. Doctoring the sound by any of several reprocessing methods currently available, often helps to focus concentration on the essential momentum of the music, though in some cases it may subtly change the nuances of the originals. If it's been sensitively done it can invariably capture more of its spirit and energy.

The organisation of this book has changed little. I have persisted with prefacing each performer's entries with a brief biography, and short background commentaries about each period or style. This is not to suggest that the categories here are watertight, or that stages of history can be conveniently shelved like supermarket products, but simply to make the use of this book easier for those who have recently become acquainted with the captivating sounds of jazz and need some shortcuts through its mysteries and diversions. It should also be said that the behaviour of some of the record companies regarding entries and exits from their current catalogues can be capricious. But if what you are looking for has been recently deleted, specialist record shops are often very helpful with guidance toward an acceptable alternative.

To recycle a sentiment familiar to all authors, but one delivered with rare crispness by the musician and teacher Conrad Cork when he wrote, 'I owe everything to everybody,' gratitude to all those who helped to bring this book together is a theme for a chapter of its own. But I would venture to single out Eva and Jo at EMI, Ron Atkins, Richard Cook at Polygram, all at New Note, and *Q Magazine*, *The Guardian*, and Kyle, Beverley and Catherine at Kyle Cathie Publishing. And everlasting thanks, of course, to Ros, Fred and Leo.

John Fordham
London, 1995

NEW ORLEANS TO CHICAGO

New Orleans is usually taken to be the exclusive home of jazz, and it's a convenient simplification. But though it has become the shorthand way of accounting for this complex and dynamic music's evolution, sidestepping the many-stranded history of the southern United States in the 19th century, it's close enough. The seeds of jazz were borne on many winds, blown from the work songs and religious ritual of West Africa, from the psalmody of English Protestantism, from the village brass-band music of France, and from countless other places. But they coincided in New Orleans, and that was where the blooms of jazz burst open.

The geographical location of the town was crucial. It was a political bargaining chip for the French and Spanish (sometime landlords of the place) and for the emerging United States, and it had a multinational community of immigrants and itinerants embracing many cultures. It had two principal black populations – freed French-speaking slaves or Creoles, and African-Americans whose liberation had come only after the Civil War, and it turned out to have been a limited liberation for both. The French strand had inherited traditions of European classical music, popular songs, opera (New Orleans was an opera city earlier than anywhere else in the States, with blacks and whites attending the opera house) and dance.

From the American slaves came another musical line – the music of Africa, adapted by contact with church music in the States and the working conditions suffered under slavery. African music reversed the European supremacy of melody and harmony over rhythm, featured an elided, bent-note intonation (often attributed to a culture in which spoken language is dependent on pitch as well as vocabulary for meaning), had a tradition of songs accompanying everyday labours, and had a preference for grouping notes in threes over a single beat (triple time) rather than the European two-to-a-beat (duple) rhythms. Later graftings on to this tradition were two distinctive scales, somewhere between the five-note scales of African music and the seven-note European one, including some notes of variable pitch – quite unlike the 'tempered' scale of Western art music. These became the 'spiritual' and 'blue note' scales.

These various strands in the emerging music of America produced 'ragtime' – primarily a descendant of Creole culture – and the blues.

Ragtime became an obsession in the States in the late 19th century. The word meant what it said – ragged time. An even-tempo European-derived pulse would be played in a pianist's left hand while the right played the normally soft beats hard and softened the ones usually emphasised, in a 'syncopation' of the beat. The melodies were mutations of piano music that admirers of Chopin and Liszt would have easily recognised, and they became known across America before the century was out, played by saloon-bar pianists and on the 'piano-rolls' that activated automatic player-pianos. The most famous ragtime composer, Scott Joplin, wrote over 600 rags and two operas, including widely loved themes such as 'The Entertainer', 'Solace' and 'Maple Leaf Rag'. But ragtime – a wholly composed music – wasn't jazz, although the terms are sometimes thought of as interchangeable in early jazz history. Neither was the blues, though it too was a crucial part of the chemistry from which jazz erupted.

In the southlands of America these musics lived side by side, along with the work songs and spirituals of the plantations, the folk-blues of the travelling banjo players, the boogie-woogie piano style that drew on blues – and in New Orleans, the traditional songs of the French, the Spaniards, Africans, English, Italians and later Germans and Slavs. The southern European custom of playing dignified slow marches on the outward journey to a cemetery and celebrations on the way back survived into New Orleans life and provided an opportunity for collective and professional music-making in the locality. The other big employer of musicians was the red-light district, given a municipal go-ahead by Alderman Sidney Story in 1898 and thereafter immortalised as 'Storyville'.

The makeup of the proto-jazz band was a mixture of high-culture Creole influences (audible in the prominence of the clarinet) and military-band instrumentation. The ensemble playing of the early jazz bands suggested a louche mutation of European polyphony. There would normally be three melody lines combined, from the cornet, trombone and clarinet, though the intonation would be quite unlike the 'pure' pitching of conservatoire music. Rhythmically it was still primitive, resembling parade and circus music and rural French brass bands. And the New Orleans pioneers of the movement around the turn of the century were mostly black – bandleaders such as Charles 'Buddy' Bolden, Bunk Johnson and Freddie Keppard, all playing a distinctively phrased music of unusual tonality but largely pedestrian in rhythm. The style became popular musical currency around Louisiana in the early years of the 20th century. By 1913, the word 'jass' – usually taken to have a sexual meaning originally – was beginning to be associated with it. It was, however, a white group, the 'Original Dixieland Jass Band' that became the first jazz group to exploit the newly invented record-producing technology with 'Livery Stable Blues' and 'Dixieland Jass Band One-Step'. They were massive hits.

That a white jazz group should have made a world-wide craze out of the new ideas of only a few hundred southern States musicians, far more of them black than white, was a miscarriage of justice that reflected the race relations of the day. The ODJB, though it displayed a kind of frantic heat, was the vehicle for a palatable kind of jazz with little of the characteristic abrasiveness of the black bands like King Oliver's.

Joe 'King' Oliver was a cornettist who by 1910 had proved himself adaptable enough to work in the best of the New Orleans brass bands and dance outfits. Following the massive migration of southern African-Americans to work in northern factories galvanised by the war effort, Oliver went to Chicago to work in the predominantly black South Side clubs, and by 1922 he was running a band of his own. King Oliver's first Creole Jazz Band (with Johnny Dodds on clarinet, Baby Dodds on drums, Honore Dutrey on trombone, Lil Hardin on piano and Bill Johnson on bass) was a revelation for the emerging jazz audiences. It was raucous, exultant, witty and swinging, its polyphonic ensemble sound of multiple melody lines rolling and diving over a beat that was beginning to disengage itself from the regularities of street music. To add further variety, Oliver brought a young New Orleans discovery to Chicago to create a two-cornet front line.

The young man was Louis Daniel Armstrong, grandchild of slaves, raised in New Orleans slums, later recipient of a rudimentary musical training at the Colored Waifs' Home. Armstrong had learned about four-part harmony from singing in a vocal group on the streets, but his harmonic sense was such that he could improvise a counterpoint to melodies he was hearing for the first time, and he used this skill to devastating effect in improvising against Oliver's theme statements. Armstrong, Oliver and the Creole Jazz Band recorded for the first time in 1923, producing the first classics of jazz.

The Jazz Age began. Armstrong's genius soon led him to pursue a career of his own, and recordings of his Hot Five and Hot Seven bands rank among the most astonishing displays of spontaneous composition in jazz history. Under pressure from Armstrong's blazing virtuosity, the New Orleans contrapuntal ensemble style began to give way to jazz forms designed to highlight the soloist. But at the same time, more complex ensemble writing for improvisers to expand on was beginning to be developed by pianist Jelly Roll Morton with his Red Hot Peppers, and a larger ensemble for jazz was on the verge of being glimpsed by bandleaders such as Fletcher Henderson, Luis Russell and Duke Ellington.

The earliest period of jazz is now documented on CD. Though CD issuing of early jazz was slow at first, the tentative beginnings of the recorded history of the music are now easily available in the format, and reproduction standards are going up.

Ammons, Albert C.

(Born Chicago, September 23, 1907; died Chicago, December 2, 1949)

Boogie-woogie piano developed in the southlands. It was originally a highly rhythmic and rough-and-ready blues style based on a repeated ostinato eight-beat figure in the left hand, decorated by improvised blues melody in the right, and it existed in some primitive form in the railhead bars long before jazz as a recognisable idiom was born. Boogie was big in the 1920s, dipped in the 1930s and came back with the jazz revivalist movement in the 1940s.

One of boogie's most imposing later practitioners was Albert Ammons, the rock-steadiness and booming vigour of whose left-hand figures (lessons learned from an earlier boogie star, Jimmy Yancey) made him one of the most consistently exciting exponents of the style. Ammons was internationally known by the end of his life, having come to the fore in the 1920s, with François Moseley's Louisiana Stompers. He ran bands of his own between 1934 and 1938 in Chicago, and was taken up by the liberal impresario and talent scout John Hammond, who persuaded him to move to New York and work in partnership with two other blues pianists, Meade Lux Lewis and Pete Johnson. These musicians performing in duos and trios were a considerable hit with audiences, and the boogie idiom became something of a craze, figuring in the repertoires of several of the 1940s big bands. Ammons recorded with Lewis and Johnson for John Hammond's 'Spirituals to Swing' series, for the Library of Congress in 1938, and for the beginnings of the Blue Note label a year later. Between 1941 and 1944 Ammons' recording career was hampered by the Musicians' Union recording ban, but he returned to the studios extensively between 1944 and the end of his life, touring with the Lionel Hampton band in his final year, 1949.

Boogie Woogie and the Blues (Commodore 824 297)

Ammons' return to recording after the MU ban. This set features a mixture of strong solo performances and exchanges with a group of powerful partners, including Don Byas on tenor, Hot Lips Page on trumpet and Sid Catlett on drums. Tracks like 'Boogie Rocks' and 'Albert's Special Boogie', though not in the same league as earlier triumphs such as 'Boogie Woogie Stomp' and 'Suitcase Blues', confirm Ammons' steely touch and unflagging beat; and Big Sid Catlett's propulsive drumming mirrors the pianist's careering vigour on 'Bottom Blues'.

Armstrong, Louis Daniel

(Born New Orleans, July 4, 1900; died New York, July 6, 1971)
Louis Armstrong revolutionised the sound of jazz. His boldness, melodic audacity, technical range and spontaneous sense of structure was in a different league even to the work of a vigorous but more static performer such as his boss King Oliver. Armstrong's solos developed like well-told stories, full of sub-plots, diversions and grand finales, often with an integrating motif characteristic to the tune recurring with minor variations in chorus after chorus. He also played with equal fierceness in all registers and with astonishing volume – testified to in the now famous account of the Oliver band's early recording session in which Armstrong had to be distanced from his partners to avoid upsetting the sound balance. Armstrong's arrival had a lot to do with the transformation of jazz into a soloist's music in the later 1920s. Not only did the players of other instruments copy his phrasing, arrangers copied it for orchestras too, which did much to accelerate the evolution of polite dance outfits into the roaring big bands of the swing era.

Since his mother's paid employment in the New Orleans ghetto included domestic service and prostitution, the young Armstrong was raised by his grandmother in hard surroundings that appeared to dampen his characteristic amiability and optimism hardly at all. As a boy he raised money by singing in a harmony group on the streets, and when he fired a revolver into the air to help celebrate New Year's Day 1913 and was committed to the Colored Waifs' Home, his musical progress accelerated. From rapid promotion to the role of Waifs' Home bugler, Armstrong moved to being leader of its band, by now on cornet. This kind of progress made a mark even in a seething musical environment like New Orleans. The teenage Armstrong began to find work as a musician in Storyville, and at 18 joined the band led by local trombonist KID ORY. Through Ory he met King Oliver, who helped him further his education in the rudiments of jazz ensemble technique and the essentials of the repertoire.

Armstrong stayed home – sometimes gaining experience by working on the riverboats with Fate Marable – as the first migration of black musicians northwards followed an economic downturn in New Orleans. But when he got the call from

Chicago to join King Oliver, one of the most influential careers in jazz truly began. In 1923, when Armstrong was only 22, the Oliver band made its first historic recordings for the Gennett company of Richmond, Indiana, and the young Armstrong quickly demonstrated his incisive musical logic and often blistering sound despite the collective structure. After two years as 'second cornettist' to Oliver, Armstrong left to join the increasingly popular Fletcher Henderson dance band, and helped transform that organisation into a 'hot jazz' outfit, alongside other fast-rising stars such as saxophonist Coleman Hawkins. With Henderson, Armstrong began to record hair-raising solos that frequently carried the band more than its rhythm section, and his ability to listen creatively to another artist was also demonstrated in accompanying work with singers, most notably Bessie Smith.

The trumpeter's developing independence led him next to the formation of his Hot Fives and Hot Sevens, the bands that in the course of three years cut the most memorable music of the first phase of jazz. Armstrong also became celebrated as a singer, credited with inventing the wordless 'scat' style when he dropped his lyric sheet during a recording session. Though Armstrong's singing in later life shifted away from jazz in all but intonation, his early scatting technique was almost indistinguishable in phrasing and rhythm from his trumpet playing.

Armstrong toured extensively during the 1930s, captivating European as well as American audiences. But he began to suffer with lip problems that hampered his old blazing virtuosity, and his solos became more epigrammatic, though still demonstrating that characteristic shapeliness. These instrumental restrictions led Armstrong to sing more, but he was such an inimitable improviser in the role that it rarely seemed like second best. The collapse of the big-band era in the 1940s led Armstrong to continue his touring life with various lively small bands dubbed the All-Stars, the first edition memorably including cornettist Bobby Hackett, trombonist Jack Teagarden and drummer Sid Catlett. All-Stars tours could be routine affairs (driving away Teagarden and Earl Hines in 1951) but Armstrong proved he could still rise spectacularly to unique occasions, such as the 1953 and 1955 tributes to W.C. Handy and Fats Waller. In the 1950s and 1960s Armstrong, as one of American music's best-loved ambassadors, toured the world, appeared in over 30 movies, received awards and citations everywhere, and was the subject of many documentaries and books. In his later years ill-health forced him to replace much more of his trumpet playing with vocals, but the two major hits he had with these ('Hello Dolly' and 'What a Wonderful World') endeared him to a far bigger public than he could ever have reached with jazz alone. He died peacefully in 1971.

*Louis Armstrong – Great Original Performances 1923–1931 (BBC CD 597)

Tracks here include 'St Louis Blues', 'Muggles' and 'West End Blues' (with the most celebrated cadenza in jazz history in its opening bars), and the disc features all of Armstrong's timeless virtues crisply reproduced – urgent, declamatory tone, passionate blues feeling, immense audacity of phrasing. The compilation takes in King Oliver's band ('Snake Rag'), eight Hot Fives and Sevens (including the majestic but flawed 'Wild Man Blues', the flamboyant 'Muskrat Ramble', the perfectly poised 'Willie the Weeper' and 'Struttin' with Some Barbecue') and two tracks by the Savoy Ballroom Five ('Save It Pretty Mama' and 'St James' Infirmary'). The digital remastering technique pioneered by Robert Parker is in its early stages here.

*Louis Armstrong and the Blues Singers (Affinity AFS 1018-6 6CD)

A massive survey of Armstrong's work with the great blues singers of the 1920s, including Bessie Smith, Ma Rainey, Alberta Hunter and many other performers operating in a territory midway between blues and vaudeville. This is hardly a collection for casual listeners, but it's beautifully put together, very informative, and reveals the extent to which Armstrong – for all his almost offhand inventiveness and inevitable tendency to become the focus of every musical situation he found himself in – could constantly improvise utterly apposite music to burnish and reshape the work of the singers. Not only is it a series of fascinating insights into Armstrong, but also the music of an era in which blues recordings and the niche-marketing of 'race records' by the major companies was briefly big business.

★*Louis Armstrong Hot Fives and Sevens* Vols. 1, 2 & 3 (JSP 312/313/ 314)

'Wild Man Blues', 'Melancholy Blues', 'Willie the Weeper' and 'West End Blues', 'Cornet Chop Suey', 'Skid dat de dat' and 'I'm in the Barrel' are some of the most sensational improvisational displays of early jazz. 'Cornet Chop Suey' is one of Armstrong's first solos of purely independent improvisational virtuosity, partners JOHNNY DODDS and KID ORY merely nudging at the theme in the background – and it marks an emerging new era in jazz. 'Skid dat de dat' is a novelty song featuring the leader's scat singing as an effortlessly blended instrumental voice, and 'I'm in the Barrel' was one of the opening cuts of that historic first Hot Five session on November 12, 1925 – a blend on Armstrong's part of an initial minor mood transformed into a raucous blues, followed by poignant Johnny Dodds choruses on clarinet and resolved devastatingly by the trumpeter's final breaks. 'Potato Head Blues', with its roller-coaster of tension and resolution in Armstrong's solo, and his daring placing of accents on weak beats, is a display of genius at work. These JSP remasterings are among the best of a frequently reissued body of work.

★*Louis in New York* Vol. 5 (Columbia CK 46148)

Armstrong in full flight in 1929 and 1930, mostly backed by the Luis Russell band, and featuring excellent partners including trombonist Jack Teagarden, Albert Nicholas and Charlie Holmes on reeds. Though Russell's band had fire and life, these aren't remarkable arrangements, because the idea is to showcase a man who has by this time become the hottest property in African-American jazz. The material, too, reveals that the trumpeter has increasingly turned to Tin Pan Alley pop songs for material. Yet many of the solos are devastating, Armstrong's tone and sense of drama being at a peak – a track like 'Dallas Blues' is an example.

★*Laughin' Louis* (Bluebird/BMG ND 90404)

Orchestra recordings between 1932 and 1933, representing the final episode of Louis Armstrong's volcanic first creative period. Though the accompaniment is now more orderly and not prone to the occasional fluff, the sense of group endeavour is mostly gone and the pieces are showcases for the leader's by now utterly assured improvisation with trumpet or vocals. But Armstrong's solos are often breathtaking in their clarity of thought and panache, frequently on songs that have become mainstays of the standard repertoire – like 'I Got the World on a String' and 'I Gotta Right to Sing the Blues'.

Rhythm Saved the World 1935–36 (GRP/Decca GRD 602)

Armstrong with the Luis Russell band again, but later. Relaxed, swinging, inventive and amiable, this music comes from a period when Louis was settling into a role in the pop business, often covering the same material as Fats Waller – but though it has often been rejected by buffs as the point at which an improvising genius relaxed his grip, the material should not disguise the enduring quality of the playing. Not that the material is all that bad, either. Tracks here include 'Solitude' (with alternate takes) and 'I've Got My Fingers Crossed', and on 'Bran' New Suit' there's even a chance to catch a little more of Luis Russell's piano than usually remains on disc.

Pops: The 1940s Small Band Sides (Bluebird/BMG ND 86378)

The period during which Armstrong, like many other artists, found big-band company too expensive and opted for a stream-lined ensemble – and also the one in which early jazz styles enjoyed a revival as an antidote to bebop. Included is the music he recorded for the 1947 Arthur Lubin musical *New Orleans*, including the tune with which Billie Holiday made her only feature film role, 'Do You Know What It Means To Miss New Orleans'. Armstrong's delightful reunions with trombonist Jack Teagarden (from the first edition of the All-Stars) are the primary feature of the 1947 tracks, including exchanges with Teagarden of an intensity worthy of his earliest days on the justly celebrated Town Hall Concert material from May of that year.

★*Complete Louis Armstrong/Duke Ellington* (Roulette/EMI CDP 793 844-2)

A producer's idea of a good time rather than an artist's perhaps – this was Bob Thiele's attempt to find common ground between Armstrong and Ellington in 1961, and generally it can't be said to have been an unqualified success. But since Armstrong's reputation was mostly associated with pop hits after this, it's notable as one of his last unreservedly jazzy achievements, and for his scat vocal on 'Cotton Tail', embellishment of 'Mood Indigo' and nostalgically punchy treatment of 'Black and Tan Fantasy'.

★*Satch Plays Fats* (CBS 450 980-2)

Armstrong and the All-Stars in 1955, with Trummy Young having replaced Jack Teagarden and with Billy Kyle on piano following Earl Hines' departure. In a period in which touring pressure was leading Armstrong bands to sound a shade tired, a special stimulus was necessary to get a little extra – and this happened on the Fats Waller tribute, with the musicians appropriately reflecting Waller's bounce and the leader inspired in his performance of 'Blue Turning Grey Over You'.

★*What a Wonderful World* (Bluebird/BMG ND 88310)

By 1970 Louis Armstrong had stopped playing the trumpet, but his vocal style still transformed classic songs. He was by this point a much-loved institution, virtually beyond criticism, having influenced the course of 20th-century music more substantially in his most active years than anyone had a right to expect. These tracks were recorded for Armstrong's newer audience, some of whom may never even have known that he played the trumpet. The title song was a hit for Armstrong twice, once in 1961 and then again 20 years later with the success of the movie *Good Morning Vietnam*, in which it was featured.

Bechet, Sidney

(Born New Orleans, May 14, 1897; died Paris, May 14, 1959)
John Coltrane, listening to a soprano saxophone recording of
Sidney Bechet, is reputed to have said in wonderment, 'Did all
those old guys swing like that?' Bechet was, quite simply, *the* horn
virtuoso of the early jazz, with an ability to disrupt the rigid
accents that New Orleans had inherited from ragtime and to
deliver his rhythmically audacious solos with a blazing tone and
emotive vibrato equalled only by LOUIS ARMSTRONG. Bechet was the
only serious competitor to Armstrong for the title of supreme
architect of the early jazz. He established a substantial soloist's
role for the saxophone (shifting from the popular clarinet to the
rarely played soprano saxophone in 1919), his compositions were
probably better than Armstrong's, and he built an improvisers'
language for his chosen instrument virtually single-handed. But
unlike Armstrong, he was temperamentally fragile, lacked the
trumpeter's popular appeal, and spent the postwar years out of
America. In his adopted France in the 1950s he was treated with
much the same respect accorded to Maurice Chevalier.

Bechet grew up in the pre-jazz years in New Orleans, hearing
the powerful, assertive street-band trumpeters as well as the reed
players, and the experience may have helped him to cultivate his
fierce, incandescent sound. Bechet learned clarinet with a famous
local teacher, Lorenzo Tio; by 12 or 13 he was able to take on
virtually any kind of New Orleans band work and not long
afterwards was teaching the instrument himself. Like most New
Orleans jazz musicians, Bechet went to Chicago (in 1917), joined
the semi-classical orchestra of black composer Will Marion Cook,
and went with Cook to Europe with the Southern Syncopated
Orchestra. Ernest Ansermet, the Swiss conductor, heard Bechet
and instantly dubbed him a genius.

In J.F. Lafleur's Wardour Street music shop in London, Bechet
found his first soprano saxophone, had a double-octave key added
to it, and thereafter largely replaced the clarinet with it. He played
to royalty in London, but ended up being deported from Britain
after a fracas. Work with Duke Ellington and JAMES P. JOHNSON in
New York followed, and with the CLARENCE WILLIAMS Blue Five
from 1923 onwards (sometimes in partnership with Louis
Armstrong and various singers). Bechet had given early warning

of his violently ecstatic manner of playing. At the end of the 1920s Bechet travelled extensively in Europe again as a sideman with the Revue Nègre. By this point his improvising style was fully formed. He had subverted the rhythmic regularity of ragtime and was accenting notes in a wilful but deliberate manner, ideas seeming to tumble over each other in the effort to escape from the horn, and his tone was a colourful mixture of distortions, exultant and admonishing sounds, and massive, suspenseful vibrato. More so than Armstrong, he was prepared to abandon the tune and improvise on its harmonic foundations instead, occasionally improvising without a tune at all – developments that foreshadowed bebop. The New Orleans Feetwarmers, the band he formed in 1932 with trumpeter Tommy Ladnier, displayed Bechet in the full flood of this mature style.

Through the 1930s Bechet's fortunes were mixed (at one point he opened a New York tailor's shop with Ladnier) but he recorded some historic tracks in a competitive meeting with Louis Armstrong in 1940. Club work followed in the postwar years, but not enough of it to prevent him from having to teach for a living as well. Bechet did, however, record for the then new label Blue Note, his version of 'Summertime' (available on CD on the *From Boogie to Bop* disc of the Blue Note 50th Anniversary set, CDP 792 465-2) being a hit for the company. But when Bechet visited the Paris Jazz Festival in 1949 (on that occasion even performing with Charlie Parker) and was greeted rapturously, he decided to emigrate to a place that appreciated him. He remained in France until his death, a celebrated entertainer through hit records such as 'Les Oignons' and 'Petite Fleur' (allegedly composed while Bechet was seated on the lavatory) and toward the end of his life even the composer of a ballet, *La Nuit est une Sorcière*. A town square in Antibes was named after him.

★*The Chronological Sidney Bechet 1923–36* (Classics 583 CD)

Early Bechet is something of an enthusiast's territory because the recording circumstances in which he was working hampered his scope more than the Creole Band did for Armstrong – but the saxophonist's rivalry to Armstrong in improvising skill and penetrating tone is noticeable even in his first studio efforts. This collection includes work with the Noble Sissle Orchestra, and some spectacular early 1930s forays including a sweeping 'Maple Leaf Rag'.

★*The Bluebird Sessions 1932–1943* (BMG/Bluebird ND 90317)

A handsome documentation of a period of considerable change for Bechet, from prolific recording opportunities in the early 1930s, through semi-retirement by the end of the decade, and then resurgence with the New Orleans revival of the 1940s. It features 19 bands on 84 tracks, some of them represented in several takes, and it vibrates with Bechet's impassioned, impulsive sound, from the sultry, liquid clarinet on 'Blues in the Air', through the soaring, violin-like soprano sax high register with his 1941 New York trio on 'Strange Fruit'. On 'I Found a New Baby', Bechet's spine-chilling vibrato and sheer penetration provoke trumpeter Tommy Ladnier into almost desperate wailing, and 'Maple Leaf Rag' and 'Shag' are streams of lyrical consciousness, with the latter (based on the famous 'I Got Rhythm' sequence used by the beboppers) representing one of the first themeless jazz recordings. JELLY ROLL MORTON's 1939 band is featured too.

★*Salle Pleyel: 31 January 52* (Vogue 65001)

Bechet tended to play rather melodramatic rehearsed solos in the years following his emigration to France in 1949, sometimes in the effort to stimulate rhythm sections that were either lagging behind him or so respectful as to be walking on eggshells. But the American's recordings with French bandleader Claude Luter were often fruitful, particularly this somewhat rough and ready live occasion from 1952, introduced by the influential jazz commentator Charles Delaunay. There are plenty of jazz standards (such as 'St Louis Blues' and 'Sweet Georgia Brown') but also both the lyrical 'Les Oignons' and 'Petite Fleur', two big hits for Bechet in France.

★*Jazz Classics* Vol. 2 (Blue Note 7893852)

Blue Note sessions from the New Orleans revival period between 1939 and 1951 – an affectionate jaunt through a collection of raunchy blues and classic Dixieland vehicles like 'High Society'.

Bechet is older and not as full of beans as on the previous decade's Bluebird sessions, and he plays as much sonorous clarinet as soprano sax, but there's no doubting it's him. Good performances also from Max Kaminsky and a bluesy BUNK JOHNSON on trumpets.

Colyer, Kenneth 'Ken'

(Born Norfolk, April 18, 1928; died France, March 10, 1988)
Ken Colyer, the most unwavering and dedicated of British jazz traditionalists, doesn't really belong in a section devoted to the original New Orleans pioneers, but since he devoted his life to sounding like them, he doesn't belong anywhere else. His place seemed unshiftable by fashions, economics or mortality. Devoted to the New Orleans music that preceded Louis Armstrong, Colyer admired a collectively improvised contrapuntal music in which no-one stood in the spotlight. It was also rhythmically far closer to the marching bands and funeral bands of turn-of-the-century New Orleans than it was to the driving tempos and unpredictable placing of accents that coined the term 'swing'.

Colyer formed the Crane River Jazz Band in the early 1950s (which he named after a stream running near his home in Hounslow), was nicknamed 'The Guvnor' by all the serious adherents of the idiom, and rejoined his old service, the Merchant Navy, in order to wangle a trip to New Orleans. He deserted once he got there, played with many of the surviving veterans of the music, was jailed and deported back to England – to a hero's welcome from the cognoscenti. He rejected the convenient dilutions of the music that made money for many traditional jazz musicians in the 1950s, and though his mind was clearly closed to much of what was going on in jazz, his devotion to purely musical values and his indifference to compromise were an example even to players light years away from his style.

Marching Back To New Orleans (Lake LACD 21)

An unexpectedly mixed repertoire including the rickety recreation of a New Orleans marching band with the Omega Brass Band. Hot, rough, singleminded, and always held together by the firm, undemonstrative sound of the leader's cornet.

Dodds, Johnny

(Born Waverley, Louisiana, April 12, 1892; died Chicago, August 8, 1940)

Johnny Dodds was the most personal and imaginative of the first wave of jazz clarinettists, with a molten, pulsating sound and steamily controlled passion rarely moving far from the low register. Though he was not a technical virtuoso in the sense that SIDNEY BECHET was, Dodds had qualities that were hard to copy or teach. In the years when the clarinet's role was to weave the lightest and most fluent melody lines around the more rugged brasses in the New Orleans front line, Dodds' selflessness as a participant in the group, his sensitivity to the overall sound and the distinctive abrasiveness of his tone, and his moving variations on the blues made him a legend.

Like Bechet, Dodds was taught by the New Orleans Creole clarinet guru Lorenzo Tio. He worked the regular Louisiana circuit of riverboat jobs and marching bands, joined King Oliver, and also participated magnificently in the innumerable session opportunities with blues singers in the early 1920s. But as a member of LOUIS ARMSTRONG's Hot Fives and Sevens, Dodds' qualities blossomed – as a soloist at times, though Armstrong's light was all but blinding, but equally significantly as a group player. JELLY ROLL MORTON made use of the same qualities, hiring Dodds to participate in both the famous Red Hot Peppers sessions and some remarkable trio work with Morton and his drummer brother Warren 'Baby' Dodds.

Johnny Dodds remained active through the 1930s, even though the clarinet had been turned into a different instrument by swing stars such as Benny Goodman and Artie Shaw, and Dodds' New Orleans-based style had come to seem quaint. But the quality of his playing never faltered, and it was a sad irony that he died of a stroke just as the New Orleans revival was about to break.

Investigators of Johnny Dodds' early work should open their account by listening to him in one of the most exciting of all early jazz contexts, the Louis Armstrong Hot Fives and Sevens.

★*The Chronological Johnny Dodds 1926* (Classics 589)

Dodds' early work is now being systematically reissued by Classics, but this is one of the best of a growing bunch, including much of his finest work with the New Orleans Wanderers and Bootblacks. Musicians include KID ORY and George Mitchell, and there are some intriguing duets with a little-known clarinet partner, Junie Cobb. Dodds was already beginning to devote much of his playing time to lucrative work in the Mafia-run Chicago clubs, and turning into a highly disciplined pro, but much of this material demonstrates how musicianly he remains. Reprocessing isn't bad, retaining Dodds' characteristic glow.

★*Blue Clarinet Stomp* (RCA/Bluebird ND 82293)

A variety of Dodds-led bands, circumstances that didn't always get the best out of him. A 1928 trio featuring a rather erratic pianist, Charlie Alexander, is uneven, but the Washboard Band with bassist Bill Johnson displays a lot more bounce. Doubters of Lil Hardin Armstrong's keyboard qualities might be surprised by her work here in the 1929 Hot Six, but the piano star of the set is naturally Jelly Roll Morton, who is featured on 'Wolverine Blues' and 'Mister Jelly Lord'.

Johnson, Bunk

(Born New Orleans, December 27, 1889; died New Iberia, Louisiana, July 7, 1949)

With GEORGE LEWIS, Bunk Johnson hit the spotlight of the Dixieland jazz revival. But Johnson's moment didn't come until he was well into his fifties. He stayed in Louisiana when the more celebrated New Orleans jazz musicians moved north, he oscillated between music and labouring jobs, and dental problems hampered his trumpet playing in the 1930s. But Johnson had a feeling for the blues, considerable melodic inventiveness and a tantalising tendency to pull the beat back that gave his music a languid charm. In the early years of the 20th century, he was a sought-after second cornet player, even taking this role in a band led by the legendary first jazz star Buddy Bolden. Like Bolden, much of Johnson's work preceded the era of jazz discs.

By the early 1930s, Johnson was truck-driving and labouring in Louisiana. But at the end of the decade, jazz academics Frederick Ramsey and William Russell tracked him down, intrigued by references to him by LOUIS ARMSTRONG. Russell fixed Johnson up with new dentures, bought him a new trumpet, and recorded him in 1942. The music was like dropping into a jazz time-warp. It was not the floating swing or adventurous juggling with accents of post-Armstrong jazz, but a steady, chugging, street-parade music, infused with blues, brass-band ensemble sounds and avoidance of soloistic flourishes. Both the modern bebop and Johnson's archaic music were perceived as antitheses of the showbiz flash of the swing bands, and both gained a considerable following. But it wasn't until his final sessions – after dozens of recordings, many still likely to be reissued – that he found a band that suited him.

Bunk Johnson 1944 (American Music AMCD 3 CD)

Though this is music about as far removed as possible from a sophisticated jazz listener's perception of swing and improvisation – the ensemble connections are hazardous, the sharing of the melody line discreetly collectivised, the beat static – Johnson's bright tone and purposeful phrasing still emerges. Though he later had difficulties with a band that included clarinettist George Lewis and drummer Baby Dodds, it isn't apparent here. The repertoire inclines toward the quirky, though there are spirited renditions of standards, such as the indefatigable 'Panama'.

Johnson, James P.

(Born New Brunswick, New Jersey, February 1, 1894; died New York, November 17, 1955)
The finest of the early 'stride' pianists, a teacher of Fats Waller and inspiration to Count Basie, James Price Johnson was highly schooled in European art music but had immersed himself in the African-American music of the churches and the honky-tonks so completely that the traditions blended seamlessly in both his compositions and his improvising. 'Stride' was a piano develop-

ment of ragtime, with a choppy beat closely related to the earlier form, but a more spontaneously roving right hand, and its popularity boomed in Harlem during the early 1920s, when the black district of New York became a cultural centre for both locals and curious visitors during the African-American arts 'Renaissance'. Johnson was the most prominent of the performers who toured the clubs and rent parties, and some experts came to regard the precision, swing and invention of his playing as being superior to his famous pupil, Fats Waller.

Johnson's career was on a roll as early as 1912, by which time he was busy in the burgeoning New York dance halls and clubs. Four years later he was recording piano rolls, in 1917 he made his first disc, and in the 1920s he worked extensively with blues singers, even acting as musical director for Bessie Smith on the famous movie short *St Louis Blues*. In 1923 he put together the score for one of the most famous early black Broadway hits – *Runnin' Wild*, which launched the Charleston – and by the end of the decade he was also composing more extended works, though it was to be a long time before a black jazz composer would have his pieces endorsed as serious compositions by the arts establishment.

Snowy Morning Blues (GRP/Decca GRD 604)

Late recordings by Johnson, mingling some from 1930 and a majority from 1944, and dividing material between originals and features more usually associated with Fats Waller. By the later stage, Johnson's drive is slowing, but 'Snowy Morning Blues' is one of his most charming and poignant pieces. One of Johnson's most famous compositions, 'Carolina Shout', is on this set, but not 'The Charleston'.

Lewis, George

(Born New Orleans, July 13, 1900; died New Orleans, December 31, 1968)

Like BUNK JOHNSON, clarinettist George Lewis was discovered by the jazz researchers Frederick Ramsey and William Russell – a dockworker retired from music, recruited for the 1942 recording session that put Johnson on the map, and reappearing with him on and off through the 1940s.

Lewis' sound was much-copied during the revivalist era in the 1950s. A mixture of unaffected dignity, forthright, unvarnished lyricism and the blues, it seemed in the period to represent the honest, artless heart of jazz Bunk Johnson had represented until his death, and it brought Lewis considerable fame and a punishing touring schedule. From the mid-1950s he began touring the world, and the pressure sometimes exposed the limitations of his technique, for which he would then be rather unfairly castigated. But Lewis didn't come from a tradition for which pure tone or parade-ground precision made much sense, and it was the essence of his charm.

★*Trios and Bands* (American Music AMCD 4 CD)

Some of Lewis' most enduring work, particularly with a clarinet/banjo/bass trio, the simplicity of which revealed his easygoing inventiveness better than almost all his other playing circumstances.

★*Complete Blue Notes* (Mosaic MD3-132)

A wide spread of Lewis' material, from the first work for the recently launched Blue Note's Climax label in 1943, to the smoother and more knowing performances of 1955. On 'Climax Rag' or 'Just a Closer Walk with Thee', Lewis beautifully demonstrates how independent and flowing his lines can be, for all their empathy with the surroundings. 'Deep Bayou Blues' is a testament to Lewis' expressiveness as a blues player. The sound is good, the organisation clear, and for Lewis fans this is an essential set.

Morton, Ferdinand Le Menthe (or Lemott) 'Jelly Roll'

(Born New Orleans, October 20, 1890; died Los Angeles, July 10, 1941)
The great ragtime players – of whom the most fertile and creative was Scott Joplin – didn't really fall into even the widest definitions

of jazz because their music was primarily composed. Jelly Roll Morton was one of the most significant artists to have accelerated the evolution of ragtime into jazz, and it helped that his primary influences were both ragtime and the blues. A procurer, a vaudeville artist, a music publisher, boxing promoter and gambling-house manager, Morton nonetheless achieved more in his musical career (unappreciated though it was by the end of his life) than many early jazz figures who had pursued their craft with fewer diversions. The ragtime antecedents are clear in Morton's work, but he disrupts its even pulse and he improvises. And as a writer and arranger, he developed the resources of the standard New Orleans instrumentation, augmenting the lineup at times, creating a clarinet 'section', blending improvisation and composition and anticipating the future by the use of the repeated ensemble motif behind soloists (the 'riff') and the brief unaccompanied improvisation between abruptly stopped and started ensemble sections (the 'break'), both of which featured strongly in the big-band swing era.

Morton learned the piano as a child, being from a middle-class Creole background, though the fortunes of the family declined with the influx of northern commerce to Louisiana and an intensifying of discrimination against all people of colour. By his teens Morton was playing the piano in the 'sporting-houses' of Storyville and in 1923 he joined the exodus to Chicago. He began recording some sensational piano solos for Gennett (including classics such as 'King Porter Stomp', 'Kansas City Stomp' and 'The Pearls') followed up three years later by the first Red Hot Peppers sessions. The pieces are remarkable for their variation of pace and texture, for their interwoven and contrasting themes and for the blend of solo and ensemble energy – Morton being considerably assisted by the presence of excellent and understanding sidemen like trumpeter George Mitchell and clarinettist Omer Simeon.

But by the beginning of 1930, with the move towards more soloistic music and the demand for more elaborate jazz using bigger bands, Morton's fondness for elaborations on the old New Orleans style was going out of fashion. He attempted unsuccessfully to run a big band as the Depression hit; his record contract expired and he was soon scuffling for orchestra-pit work. Morton was eventually tracked down in Washington by the archivist Alan

Lomax and committed his thoughts and music to record for the Library of Congress in 1938.

★*The Pearls* (Bluebird/BMG ND 86588)

A compilation – and a good place to start – of brilliant Morton tracks from the Red Hot Pepper sessions, including classics such as 'Black Bottom Stomp', 'The Chant', 'Grandpa's Spells' and 'Doctor Jazz'. These sessions (more fully documented on a five-volume Bluebird set, *The Complete Victor Recordings* ND 82361) were high points of the most sophisticated early New Orleans music, and their blends of composition and improvisation, deft rhythmic shifts and subtle interweaving of the trumpet/clarinet/trombone front line give the music a constant brightness and vivacity. Morton skilfully avoids repeating devices within the same piece and engineers numerous shifts of tone colour to effect a previously unheard-of variety within the span of a three-minute recording. Trombonist KID ORY and clarinettist Omer Simeon are regular Peppers members, and on 'Steamboat Stomp' and 'Sidewalk Blues' two extra clarinettists are added (Darnell Howard and Barney Bigard) to produce Morton's revolutionary pre-big band reed 'section', albeit only briefly. The set also includes two tracks featuring Morton in collaboration with Sidney Bechet in 1939.

★*Jelly Roll Morton* Vol. 1 (JSP CD 321)

More of a specialist's set, part of a five-volume JSP survey. JSP uses John R. T. Davies' startlingly crisp transfer techniques, and the fidelity here is better than anything available on other labels. Volume 1 also features the first 1926 Peppers dates, the only sessions from this period – apart from Armstrong's unequivocally qualifying as an all-but-flawless set of jazz masterpieces.

★*The Library of Congress Recordings* (Rounder CDs 1091–4)

Morton's career was broken by the time these recordings were made. Always rooted in the New Orleans ensemble sound, Morton had seen swing absorb that history and even refashion some of his own classics ('King Porter Stomp' became a Benny Goodman staple) in the process. But Alan Lomax, for the Library of Congress, recorded both Morton's playing and his fascinating reminiscences in 1938, and they have become classics of jazz documentation. These recordings are a very good reappraisal of the famous Alan Lomax 1938 tapes with Morton, in which he sings, reminisces and recalls history he wrote, and rewrote. American jazz professor and pianist James Dapogny oversaw it all, and many of the vagaries of pitch caused by Lomax's primitive equipment have been compensated for. Much of the piano playing is wonderful, including accounts of 'The Pearls', 'Kansas City Stomp' and compelling tangos such as 'The Crave' and 'Creepy Feeling'. Only some of the anecdotal material has been trimmed.

Noone, Jimmie

(Born New Orleans, April 23, 1895; died Los Angeles, April 19, 1944)

A clarinet pupil of SIDNEY BECHET, Jimmie Noone was one of the most technically accomplished of all the instrument's practitioners in early jazz. His tone was delicate where that of many of the New Orleans players was ruggedly bluesy, and he had mastered the instrument throughout its range, rocketing through scales at blazing speed, effortlessly vaulting registers. The result was that a Noone solo was often a miniature masterpiece of balance and shape, sometimes contrasting sharply with its surroundings.

Noone worked first for cornettist/bandleader Freddie Keppard, and subsequently in an early KID ORY group that included a young King Oliver. He followed Keppard and Oliver to Chicago in 1917, and then spent six years with a fine jazzy dance band, Doc Cooke's Dreamland Orchestra. Noone's role mostly came second to the arrangements, but he let off steam in the Chicago clubs after hours, so emphatically that he eventually secured a residency for himself at the Apex Club, with Earl Hines as his pianist. Recording opportunities followed, and Noone quickly became the most celebrated clarinet star in the city – cultivating admirers as diverse as a teenaged Benny Goodman and the composer Maurice Ravel.

Noone didn't join the next jazz exodus, from Chicago to New York. Nor did he jump on the bandwagon of swing; instead he stayed with a robust, lively, expressive small-group jazz that recalled the styles of his early days.

★*Complete Recordings* Vol. 1 (Affinity CD AFS 1027-3)

Plenty of evidence of Noone's mastery on these sessions from 1926 to 1930, and of Earl Hines' revolutionary ability to sum up much of the progress of all New Orleans instrumentalists from the piano keyboard alone. But this is certainly a collection for serious students of early jazz and Noone's contribution to it, because the material is very uneven. Making it worse on some of these takes are the vocals of Lillie Delk Christian, a performer of nightmarish unmusicality. But Noone's clarinet still shines through it all, notably on the tremulous ballad 'Sweet Lorraine' and the smooth, almost urbane flow of 'Tight Like That'.

Original Dixieland Jazz Band

Justly or unjustly, the ODJB was where the Jazz Age began. Though musically the band was nowhere near the jazz equal of many of the black groups of the day (or some of the white ones) the mixture of fortuitousness and bravura that took it into Reisenweber's restaurant in New York in 1917 set the jazz message reverberating around the world.

The five founding members of the band were Nick LaRocca (cornet), Larry Shields (clarinet), Eddie Edwards (trombone), Henry Ragas (piano) and Tony Sbarbaro (drums). All of them were white, and had served a loose apprenticeship in the bands of local bandleader Papa Jack Laine, as well as closely attending to the work of King Oliver. LaRocca in particular, as well as being a cornettist of considerable force, was a ferociously energetic and ambitious man, and his application galvanised the ODJB's career. In 1916 LaRocca, Ragas and Edwards, plus drummer Johnny Stein and clarinettist Alcide Nunez, went to Chicago for a nightclub season, then moved to New York to Reisenweber's, helped by the encouragement of Al Jolson. With a mixture of virtuosic musicianship (Larry Shields, who replaced Nunez, was the most reliable exponent of it) and vaudevillian horseplay, the band provided diverting and engagingly anarchic entertainment and was soon a big commercial success. The enthusiasm it engendered resulted in the band entering the Victor studios in New York on

February 26, 1917 to cut the first jazz record. It sold over a million copies and jazz became a national craze.

The ODJB's overnight success led to a trip to Britain (it performed privately for members of the royal family), touring vaudeville theatres and holding down a nine-month residency at the Hammersmith Palais. Returning to the States in 1920, the ODJB continued to record and tour, but in 1921 Shields dropped out, followed in 1925 by LaRocca, at which point the group disbanded. It had sparked an enthusiasm for jazz in innumerable musicians (notably cornettists Red Nichols and Bix Beiderbecke) but was being overhauled not long after its arrival by the more spontaneous and vital playing of the black bands, and the more sophisticated ensemble sound of white groups such as Paul Whiteman's.

★*The 75th Anniversary* (RCA/Bluebird ND 90650 CD)

Most of the ODJB's successful early pieces are included on this set, and though much of it sounds archaic and clumsy today, the vitality and charging optimism of the group makes up for a lot. Clarinettist Larry Shields was a more than capable performer, and Sbarbaro, though he often sounds like a man stumbling around in a junk-shop in the dark, lends it all a wild, fervent quality. A disc of more historical than musical value maybe, but it covers all the Victor material recorded between 1917 and 1921, and as the starting point of recorded jazz, it has a special place.

Ory, Edward 'Kid'

(Born La Place, Louisiana, December 25, 1886; died Hawaii, January 23, 1973)

One of the most astute and successful of early New Orleans musicians, Kid Ory was also a basic but immensely powerful and effective trombonist in the gruff, relaxed manner required of the instrument in its collective-ensemble guise. He played with the very best of the first wave of musicians, including ARMSTRONG, JELLY ROLL MORTON and blues singer Ma Rainey, then dropped out of the business during the swing-band era of the 1930s, but returned

25

to become one of the most acclaimed defenders of New Orleans music in the revival that began in the 1940s.

Ory was a banjo player originally, and always believed that if there was a market for the increasingly popular idiom of jazz, it should be properly handled; that meant good presentation, and it also meant suitably profiting from the music's desirability. He had a talent for self-promotion, and was impatient with unsuitable musicians – but with those who did suit him (notably King Oliver and Louis Armstrong) he was a robust and sometimes enthralling performer. In California in 1922 Ory's band was the first New Orleans-style outfit to make a jazz record, and later in the 1920s the trombonist appeared on Louis Armstrong's Hot Fives and Sevens, as well as collaborating successfully with clarinettist JOHNNY DODDS and with Jelly Roll Morton's Red Hot Peppers. Though he retired to run a chicken farm in the 1930s he was back with a fine band of his own in the mid-1940s, appearing to great acclaim on the Orson Welles radio show. Ory toured Europe several times and his most famous composition, 'Muskrat Ramble', was a revivalist hit in the 1950s.

*Kid Ory's Creole Jazz Band 1954 (Good Time Jazz 12016)

Like many of the New Orleans originals who switched careers during the swing era, Kid Ory was sidelined and then came back in the revival, in his case to run one of the best bands of the entire phenomenon. Trumpeter Alvin Alcorn sustained the old collaborative trumpet sound of the original style better than most, and Ory's big, bleary trombone sound booms through all the music.

Williams, Clarence

(Born Plaquemine, Louisiana, October 8, 1893; died November 6, 1964)

Williams was a New Orleans pianist and composer who probably didn't receive his due recognition because the illustrious artists he performed with eclipsed him – most notably LOUIS ARMSTRONG and SIDNEY BECHET. But he wrote many of the most famous tunes of New Orleans music (including 'Baby Won't You Please Come Home', 'Everybody Loves My Baby' and 'Royal Garden Blues'), accompanied Bessie Smith on her recording debut, and was highly influential behind the scenes as well as on the bandstand in the difficult early days of recordiing black American music.

★*Jazz Classics in Digital Stereo* (BBC CD 721)

Wide selection of Williams' music with his celebrated Washboard Band, including such tunes as 'Organ Grinder Blues', 'Trouble' and 'I Can't Beat You Doin' What You're Doin' to Me'.

2

THE SECOND WAVE: SWING

L ouis Armstrong towered over jazz in the early 1920s, and his virtuosity and insight were the principal catalysts shifting the traditional New Orleans contrapuntal ensemble style towards jazz forms showcasing soloists. The result was that at the end of the 1920s jazz stood poised to develop on several fronts at once. Following Armstrong's lead, soloists on many instruments in the jazz band were developing styles that adapted his dramatic phrasing and refusal to be shackled by old-fashioned ragtime syncopation or the dictatorship of the regular beat. This crucial revolutionary movement towards an improvising style that unpredictably tightened and relaxed the relationship between the solo lines and the framework was echoed not only by instrumentalists, but by singers and by arrangers searching for bolder, hipper ensemble sounds.

Some of the most creative white musicians (most notably cornettist Bix Beiderbecke) took Armstrong's example but adapted it to more reflective moods. A pianistic genius, Art Tatum, was indicating new and richer resources for improvisation, using the underlying harmonic structures of songs rather than the melody lines themselves. Sidney Bechet's example on the saxophone, previously a vaudeville novelty instrument, was soon followed by an explosion of enthusiasm for these adaptable and expressive horns, and the first of jazz music's great saxophone stars emerged: Duke Ellington's Johnny Hodges, Fletcher Henderson's Coleman Hawkins (who developed a harmonic-improvising approach much like Tatum's on piano), Count Basie's Lester Young.

Pianist/arrangers Fletcher Henderson, Duke Ellington and Luis Russell started expanding the jazz ensemble, dividing the band into meshing blocks or 'sections'. This turned out to be the development that dominated the jazz scene for most of the 1930s. The economic slump of the early years of the decade hit the record industry hard, and all but sank the blues boom that had flourished through the 'race-records' outlets, but when the New Deal came, swing was just the big, brash, optimistic music for it. Bandleaders such as Benny Goodman, the Dorsey Brothers, Count Basie and Duke Ellington were front-runners in a big-band boom that at its height saw dozens of sizeable orchestras working flat out in every corner of the United States. From these bands emerged great instrumental soloists (saxophonists Hawkins and Young, trumpeter Roy Eldridge) and powerful improvising singers too (Billie Holiday, Ella Fitzgerald).

Duke Ellington, though he wasn't the most commercially popular of the orchestra leaders during the boom, was ultimately the artist who rewrote the book on what was possible for a large orchestra of jazz instrumentalists. Ellington's method of composition owed little or nothing to orthodox classical music or conservatoire methods, but drew its energies from the core of jazz, since his development of fragments of themes into rich tapestries of orchestral sound was often based on a trial-and-error exploration of harmonic options in rehearsal between him and his musicians. Sidemen of the creative quality of Johnny Hodges, Tricky Sam Nanton and Bubber Miley were therefore crucial to Ellington's conception, and timeless classics such as 'Creole Love Call', 'Mood Indigo' and 'Sophisticated Lady' came from such collaboration.

But Ellington's wasn't the only kind of big-band jazz, and less impressionistic versions of it than his tended to do better at the box-office. Bands such as Bennie Moten's and Count Basie's used the repeated, rhythmically insistent chordal figure behind soloists, a device that came to be known as the 'riff'. Clarinettist Benny Goodman's band drew on New Orleans music and the riff-dominated style associated with Kansas City musicians. Much of the appeal of the big bands depended on the quality of their soloists, and competition to be a bigger drawing card was intense.

The bottom fell out of the big-band business in the tough postwar economic climate. Leaner times required slimmed-down music production, one good material reason for the development of a predominantly small-band music – bebop – from the 1940s onward. By the mid-1950s, several strains of jazz were coexisting, not always amicably. Some big bands struggled to continue, if necessary in pared-down form, as Count Basie's was forced to do for a time. Some of the surviving musicians of the early New Orleans era enjoyed a comeback as those jazz fans who disliked the complexities of modernism embraced them again in a revivalism that was to result in a good deal of controversy between 'modern' and 'trad' fans. As younger musicians developed, they faced the choice of whether to burnish and develop the older styles or throw in their lot with bop. The result was a current of jazz that came to be known as the 'mainstream' (see page 239), involving both the original practitioners of earlier styles and subsequent generations of musicians who sought to protect them.

Allen, Henry 'Red'

(Born New Orleans, January 7, 1908; died New York, April 17, 1967)

By the end of the 1920s jazz was flourishing, and so was the record industry. For over a decade, new companies had been joining the early pioneers, and many of them already appreciated that jazz meant sales. But the labels specialising in jazz all wanted their own Louis Armstrong.

The Victor company's discovery was Henry 'Red' Allen, then barely 20. Allen's father had run a celebrated brass band in New Orleans since 1907, and the musical ingredients that had made Armstrong and Jelly Roll Morton such volatile talents were in the Allen family's background too. Red Allen quickly developed a spectacular technique, but where Armstrong's manner of improvising moved during the 1920s towards an almost classical purity and poise, the younger man retained the slurs, growls, whoops and bluesy sounds of the earliest roots of the music, qualities that he retained throughout his life.

Allen's career shadowed Armstrong's at many turns. He moved north from New Orleans in 1927 to join King Oliver, then returned to work with riverboat bandleader Fate Marable. During this time he was spotted by the Victor scouts, and recorded with LUIS RUSSELL's orchestra, eventually joining FLETCHER HENDERSON'S band in 1933. His boldness of conception and wild, exuberant effects were often ideal foils for the more stately and imperious manner of saxophonist COLEMAN HAWKINS. Allen had a hit with 'Ride Red Ride' in the company of the Lucky Millinder band, then returned to Luis Russell in the late 1930s, ironically to warm up the audience before Louis Armstrong's appearance.

Through the 1940s and into the 1950s, Allen ran his own highly progressive swing sextet (sometimes featuring Coleman Hawkins), and during this period his true originality blossomed. His solos were often masterpieces of contrast, surprise, colourful sound effects and ever-changing dynamics, and by the 1960s he was the star he always promised to be, described even by the wilful young progressive bandleader Don Ellis as 'the most avant-garde trumpet player in New York'.

Henry 'Red' Allen and His New York Orchestra 1929–1930 (JSP CD 332)

Allen with a boiled-down version of the Luis Russell Orchestra, featuring the takes that launched his career in 1929. Allen appears to be displaying a mature technique already fully formed, his solos a mixture of the earthy raucousness that always marked him out, and a shrewd and considered underpinning of logic and balance. For all the bravura of his style, Allen always displayed a musical intelligence that led him away from the most melodramatic effects, which gives his work an engagingly poetic quality.

Henry Allen/Coleman Hawkins (Hep CD 1028)

Allen in 1933, with the sessions that featured saxophonist Coleman Hawkins, when both men were partners in the Fletcher Henderson band. This is a more uneven set, with the commercial pressures of the period more apparent, but there are some classics on it, with the honours about equally shared between Allen and Hawkins. Hawkins plays with a jaunty urgency on 'The Day You Came Along', and Allen's rich repertoire of sounds is poignantly displayed on 'Heartbreak Blues'.

31

★*World on a String* (RCA/Bluebird ND 82497)

Beautiful Allen session from 1957, demonstrating just why he was held in such high regard by young musicians. 'I Cover the Waterfront' gets the full Allen treatment of slurs, squeals and rolling runs, and a renewed partnership with Coleman Hawkins is as eloquent as it ever was. Allen always sounded as if he'd invented his style in an utterly personal adaptation of what he heard around him as a child, and he disobeyed most guidelines about the cultivation of mood, switching from blasting bravura to sidelong, needling effects within seconds of each other. One of the best small-group sessions of the 1950s.

Barnet, Charles Daly 'Charlie'

(Born New York, October 26, 1913)

Saxophonist, singer, bandleader, sometime actor and eleven-times-married Charlie Barnet didn't believe in life passing him by. A white middle-class boy, destined for life as a lawyer, he opted to pursue the world opened up to him by the saxophone, which he had learned from the age of 12. Barnet became a fine, hard-swinging soloist influenced by COLEMAN HAWKINS and JOHNNY HODGES, but he also ran a series of very successful orchestras, working the territory between swing and 'jump' music. Like ARTIE SHAW, Barnet was committed to racial integration at a time when such convictions could make trouble for bandleaders, and the mixed-race stars of his various bands were an illustrious list of the prominent swing players of the 1930s and 1940s.

Barnet started his first band in 1931, already skilled on several reed instruments, but though his was one of the few white bands to succeed at Harlem's Apollo and to tour on the black theatre circuit, he quit four years later to change careers and act in two Hollywood movies. Barnet returned to bandleading however, and truly made his mark with the series of hit recordings for Bluebird, including 'Cherokee', 'Charleston Alley' and 'Redskin Rhumba'. Replacing COUNT BASIE at New York's Famous Door club in 1939 was Barnet's breakthrough, and he rode high in the big-band business until conscription to the Second World War shrank the lineup and young musicians in the postwar period only wanted to play orchestral music if it was based on bebop. Capitol Records attempted to encourage Barnet to pursue this hybrid and operate in similar territory to STAN KENTON. But Barnet disliked the idea, and was rich enough to say so. He wound up his band in 1949, and went into management and running a hotel chain, only returning occasionally to performance. *Those Swinging Years – The Autobiography of Charlie Barnet* is one of the most entertaining ever written about the swing era.

*Drop Me Off In Harlem (MCA/GRP 16122)

Terrific Barnet compilation from 1942 to 1946, when he'd begun to work for Decca, featuring many of his most celebrated pieces and his most celebrated partners as well. Barnet's orchestral inclinations were always towards DUKE ELLINGTON, and his own close resemblance to Johnny Hodges' sound on alto enhances the similarity. But Barnet's individuality is striking on 'Skyliner', his soaring biggest hit, and there's some superb trumpet work from ROY ELDRIDGE on the title track.

Basie, William 'Count'

(Born Red Bank, New Jersey, August 21, 1904; died April 26, 1984)

If the sound of any outfit came to define big-band jazz, it was the orchestra of William 'Count' Basie. Universally loved, it turned on succeeding generations to a way of making music that was quintessentially American. After Basie's death, when it was led by saxophonist Frank Foster, it still bristled with those classic Basie virtues of the blues: uninhibited soloing, simplicity, spontaneity, laid-back expertise and wit, and tireless capacity to swing.

William Basie, a one-time vaudeville pianist, got his jazz break with the successful BENNIE MOTEN band, one of the exciting Kansas City ensembles of the 1920s that showed New Orleans wasn't the only home of jazz. Basie displayed the 'stride' style of FATS WALLER, but unlike most young pianists preferred selectiveness, surprise and humour to technical fireworks. When Moten died unexpectedly during a tonsillectomy in 1935, Basie formed a new band out of the old one. Encouraged by the critic John Hammond to tighten up a rather haphazard collection of arrangements, the Basie band became by 1937 a brisk, disciplined and furiously rhythmic outfit, with players of the calibre of LESTER YOUNG and Herschel Evans on saxophones, BUCK CLAYTON on trumpet and a dazzling rhythm section (always the heart of a Basie band) with the leader on piano, Freddie Green on guitar, Walter Page on bass and Jo Jones on drums. Driving and purposeful but light as a feather, those musicians came to define the swing beat, and Basie's doodling fill-ins and sidelong introductions became a trademark. The simplicity of Basie's left-hand playing (he gradually downplayed thumping stride-style bass lines) became an influence on bop piano, and Jo Jones did the same for bop drums, lightening the sound by switching the beat to the cymbals. The even, inexorable, steady four beat of bassist Walter Page did much to liberate the piano and drums by taking on more of the rhythmic role, and it transformed jazz.

In the hard postwar years, Count Basie rebuilt his orchestra with more complex arrangements (featuring, among others, those of Neal Hefti and Johnny Mandel) but without sacrificing its characteristic punch. The revitalised Basie band also introduced a new tenor player in 1953, the Cincinnati-born Frank Foster. Foster stayed with Basie until 1964, and rejoined as keeper of the flame after the first inheritor of the Basie mantle, trumpeter Thad Jones, died a year into the job. A gifted arranger as well as a thrilling soloist, Foster wrote around 125 of the charts over the years, scored a Basie album all to himself with *Easin' It* in 1960, and wrote some of the ensemble's showpieces including 'Shiny Stockings' and 'Allright OK You Win' for the band's majestic blues singer of the day, Joe Williams.

★*The Original American Decca Recordings* (MCA/GRP 36112 3CD)

Absolutely essential early Basie from the period when his band had just arrived at the cutting edge, and beautifully packaged and presented too. This set features all of Basie's studio work between 1937 and early 1939, the point at which his overnight success had compelled him to expand a flexible mid-sized group into a big one – so the musicians were dealing with the problem of how to keep the same freewheeling qualities in a more demanding lineup without writing everything out. Lester Young, inevitably, is the most compelling soloist, but all of Basie's key players were so crucial to the way that the band evolved that they constantly grip the attention – notably the ever-consistent and poetic HARRY 'SWEETS' EDISON. As portraits of one of the finest of all jazz bands rapidly evolving to its most perfect incarnation, these are indispensable discs.

★*Best of the Roulette Years* ((Roulette CDP 7 97969-2)

When Count Basie moved to the Roulette label in the late 1950s it helped revitalise the enthusiasm of a bandleader who was then approaching 30 years on the road, and the sequence of recordings between 1958 and 1962 were among the best of his later years. The hit of the period was 'The Atomic Mr Basie' (as much a tribute to Neal Hefti's arrangements), and three tracks from that disc are featured here, including 'The Kid From Red Bank' and 'Whirly Bird'. Eddie 'Lockjaw' Davis lends his usual gravelly dynamism to the proceedings ('Battle of the Foo Birds') as do those crackling trumpeters Joe Newman and Thad Jones (major contributors to 'The Kid From Red Bank', though you wouldn't know it from the insert information). 'Jumpin at the Woodside', 'Lullaby of Bird-land' and 'Blue and Sentimental' are among the 20 cuts that will bring a tear to the eyes of Basie buffs. A good selection from a fruitful Basie period.

★*Complete Roulette Live Recordings* (Mosaic MD8-135)

Very much a luxuriously offbeat set for enthusiasts, this collec-tion features a high proportion of material never released before, and all 108 tracks date from a period between 1959 and 1962. Though several tunes make some inevitable reappearances as staples of Basie's live shows (the famous 'Whirly Birds' is in four versions here), repetition isn't an irritation and the recordings are intriguing representations of how this tireless orchestra worked, and how it constantly balanced tightness with spontaneity. SARAH VAUGHAN puts in one appearance, but otherwise the emphasis is on instrumental music, not singers.

★*Atomic Mr Basie* (Roulette/EMI CDP 793 273-2)

One of the later Basie band's greatest recordings, a session from 1959 that featured some of the best of the outfit's soloists on some of the most fitting material, its insistent rhythmic grace in full flow, its dynamic leaps constantly exhilarating. Eddie 'Lockjaw' Davis is grittily garrulous on 'Whirly Bird', Frank Wess on 'Splanky' and trumpeter Thad Jones and Basie himself make a delectable job of variations on 'The Kid From Red Bank'. State-of-the-art big-band music.

★*For the First Time* (Pablo J33J 20051)

Basie was a much better pianist than many of his listeners took him for, in a Waller-derived stride style that used space and prolonged silences with an audacity that made the pianist's eventual statements seem positively garrulous. Jazz impresario Norman Granz appreciated Basie's keyboard work, and set him with a vigorous trio (bassist Ray Brown and drummer Louis Bellson) for this attractive session, including 'Lady Be Good' and 'Royal Garden Blues'.

★*Count Basie – Compact Jazz* (Verve 831 364-2)

More of 'The Atomic Mr Basie', but generally a good-value 55 minutes or so of cuts from 1956 to 1964 with Thad Jones, Frank Wess and Frank Foster among the soloists and the band demonstrating much of its effortless swing. No Joe Williams, however, the blues singer who did much to restore the post war fortunes of the Basie outfit.

Beiderbecke, Leon Bix

(Born Davenport, USA, March 10, 1903; died August 7, 1931)
The legend of trumpeter Bix Beiderbecke is now hard to disentangle from Hollywood cliché. As the first white soloist to make a dent in the world of jazz, he set the legend in motion by dying young. Before that, his clean, precise and glistening sound on cornet had transfixed itself in the minds of all who heard it,

while his even-paced, almost stately phrasing held implications for the future that took decades to work through.

Beiderbecke's mother was a pianist, though the boy was a self-taught musician, originally inspired by the recordings of the Original Dixieland Jazz Band and its trumpeter Nick LaRocca, and also hearing Louis Armstrong during his riverboat-playing period before his move to Chicago. Beiderbecke's career on record began in 1923 with the Wolverines, a somewhat stodgy outfit that he pulled imperiously into shape during the ensembles. Comparing the band's version of 'Jazz Me Blues' and Beiderbecke's own 1927 recording reveals the extent to which he was developing a solo style more independent of the lead cornettist's role, and with more of an Armstrong influence in the dynamics. From the same year came the classic ballad 'Singin' the Blues', that places his tone in its most perfect setting. A few more sides from that year, including 'I'm Coming Virginia' and 'At the Jazz Band Ball' constitute the best of the Beiderbecke legend, not forgetting poignantly impressionist piano solos such as 'In a Mist', then derided as not jazzy enough. Beiderbecke joined the symphonic-jazz orchestra of bandleader Paul Whiteman in the later stages of his brief career, but alcoholism affected his consistency with the band. A sort of memorial to Beiderbecke exists in the form of one of the most popular of popular songs, 'Stardust' by his friend Hoagy Carmichael. The entire song, especially the verse, sounds like one gloriously extended melodic statement by Bix at his best.

★*Bix Beiderbecke - Jazz Classics in Digital Stereo* (BBC CD 601)

Beiderbecke recordings from 1924 to 1930. Where Armstrong approaches his solos like a man charging through a swing-door, a dreamer but with a pragmatic zest for life, Beiderbecke at his peak was like an illustrator able to draw a free-hand circle – his solos were as finely balanced as compositions, his tone like a chime, and his mood reflective, but reflective on an unattainable grace. Beiderbecke is sometimes found here in one of his most fruitful partnerships, with the equally wistful saxophone Frank Trumbauer, an influence on LESTER YOUNG. The disc features 'Jazz Me Blues' and 'At the Jazz Band Ball', but not 'I'm Coming Virginia'.

★*Bix Beiderbecke Vols. 1 & 2 – Singin' the Blues* and *At the Jazz Band Ball* (CBS 466309/460825)

Even better representation of the sublime Frank Trumbauer as well as Beiderbecke on the first of these sets, representing the work of both men during a fruitful period in 1927, and Beiderbecke's haunting piano solo and most famous composition, 'In a Mist'. The title track is one of Beiderbecke's most famous solos, an elegant example of the way his lines appear to drift away from the harmonic underpinning and his statuesque tone focuses the music while his spare and telling choice of notes provides the shape. The second disc also covers 1927 and work in the following year with his own small groups, and also includes 'Jazz Me Blues', 'At the Jazz Band Ball' and 'Sorry'.

Berigan, Rowland Bernart 'Bunny'

(Born Wisconsin, November 2, 1908; died New York, June 2, 1942)

Like BIX BEIDERBECKE, Bunny Berigan was a white trumpeter of prodigious talent who only partially developed as a jazz artist before drink and a diffidence about applying himself to details wrecked his career. Berigan lived longer than Beiderbecke, but not by much.

Berigan's sound at its best was both majestic and emotional, his dynamic range immense (he was one of the loudest players in the business, as well as one of the most melodically subtle) and his speed of thought such that much of his work seemed to consist of throwaway phrases that could have formed the start of innumerable trumpet solos on their own. His career began at the end of the 1920s when he joined Hal Kemp's dance band for a European tour and in 1931 he joined the prestigious Paul Whiteman outfit as a replacement for Beiderbecke, joining the fast-rising BENNY GOODMAN four years later. Berigan was restless in other people's groups and formed his own big band, with mixed results, in 1937. That year he also made a second recording of a classic song, perennially associated with him – 'I Can't Get Started'. Berigan's career went on the slide with the war years. TOMMY DORSEY paid for the trumpeter's funeral.

★*The Complete Bunny Berigan Vol. III* (Bluebird NL 90439)

A two-CD set of Berigan's work at the end of the 1930s, currently the only one of an original three-volume collection. What's striking is how much control Berigan exercises over his natural gifts and Armstrong-inspired technique. Though he could intimidate almost any trumpeter of his era on skill alone, he plays with measured authority on much of the music here. But exploring Berigan takes patience – not for any drawbacks in the trumpeter, but the tedious settings in which he was often to be found.

★*Bunny Berigan and the Rhythm Makers. Vol 1 – Sing! Sing! Sing!* (Jass CD 627)

More fine Berigan trumpet from 1936 and 1938, in the company of some equally forceful partners including Artie Shaw on clarinet and Georgie Auld on tenor. Once again, you have to take the surroundings with a pinch of salt, but some of Berigan's solos here reveal how advanced his thinking was, and how dramatic and resourceful his explorations of trumpet tonality.

Berry, Leon 'Chu'

(Born Wheeling, West Virginia, September 13, 1910; died Ohio, October 30, 1941)
If Chu Berry had not died in a road smash, he would almost certainly have gone down in the jazz histories as on close to equal footing with tenor saxophone giants such as COLEMAN HAWKINS, BEN WEBSTER and LESTER YOUNG. He had an opulent tone, mingled with a fragile high-register delicacy, he was fast, and – like Hawkins – it's likely that his technique and inclinations would have led him to embrace the development of bebop. Berry came to New York in 1930, joined BENNY CARTER's band and then rejected an offer from DUKE ELLINGTON in favour of FLETCHER HENDERSON, following that stretch with the period in CAB CALLOWAY's band that lasted until his death. It was with Calloway that Berry made some of his finest recordings, developing a productive relationship with the trumpeter ROY ELDRIDGE, and with pianist Teddy Wilson.

Berry's work on disc reveals him to be, if not independent of the inexorable Hawkins momentum, a gentler exponent of it.

★*Chu Berry Story* (Zeta ZET 738 CD)

Good Berry compilation from 1937 and 1938, but representation of this fine musician on CD is still pretty sparse. It indicates what a thrilling performer Berry must have been in the flesh, because his swing is relentless and his confidence in harmonic improvisation almost as assured as his model Coleman Hawkins. Berry could have been one of the most influential saxophonists of the postwar period had he lived and developed, and the company he kept often wasn't his equal. But until more Berry appears on CD, this creditable set will do.

Byas, Carlos Wesley 'Don'

(Born Oklahoma, October 21, 1912; died Amsterdam, August 24, 1972)

Like CHU BERRY, Don Byas was a supreme technician with a considerable debt to COLEMAN HAWKINS, but he was more of a modernist in conception than Berry, and his harmonic ear was very sophisticated, partly a result of absorption in the work of pianist ART TATUM. Byas took on the implications of bebop, although – like Hawkins – his 1930s notion of the even placement of accents didn't permit him to take the liberties the beboppers did. But Byas' big tone and deft construction made him an influence on both John Coltrane and Sonny Rollins, and his music almost always gave off energy and conviction. He was a violinist originally, but took up saxophone as a teenager and was appearing with mid-West big bands before he was 20. Moving to California, Byas worked with LIONEL HAMPTON, Ethel Waters, DON REDMAN and others before joining first Andy Kirk's band, then COUNT BASIE's. Byas played the 52nd Street bebop clubs in the 1940s, appearing on early bop record dates, then toured Europe with the Don Redman band in 1946, which led him to settle in France, and then in Holland. Byas was busy into the 1970s, working briefly with Art Blakey's Messengers on a 1971 Japanese tour.

★*Living My Life* (Vogue/Savoy VG 650122)

Some fine Byas material from the mid-1940s, including Max Roach on drums and Benny Harris on trumpet. The saxophonist's leanings towards bebop are apparent from these pieces, notably in the clarity and complexity of his work on 'Donby'. But his thick, lustrous tone made ballads his strongest card despite his fluency on uptempo music, and there's plenty of evidence of that side of him here.

★*Tenderly* (Savoy VG 655620)

Early to middle 1950s Byas, recorded in Paris with the likes of Martial Solal and Mary Lou Williams appearing in the piano chairs. Uneven sessions, but still representative of the saxophonist in his prime, and in the company of local players enthused by his roving imagination.

Calloway, Cabell 'Cab'

(Born Rochester, New York, December 25, 1907)
Bandleader Cab Calloway has had a remarkably sustained career in the jazz world, and on the fringes of it. His work has had as much in common with vaudeville as jazz, and he is best known to the public for a variety of novelty vocals that have become showbiz landmarks, most notably 'The Hi De Ho Man', a catchphrase that swept America in the 1930s. But, like many showmen with an interest in jazz, Calloway frequently hired excellent partners, his most illustrious soloist being saxophonist CHU BERRY. He began in vaudeville with his sister Blanche, and also worked as a sometime drummer and MC in clubs, but it was as a bandleader-singer that he made his mark, and 'Minnie the Moocher – the King of Hi De Ho' was the recording that has been associated with Calloway ever since. He worked at the Cotton Club successfully during the early 1930s, and he sustained a big band, a wild, unruly affair that included both Berry and a volatile Dizzy Gillespie, until 1948, after which the bandleader took to touring the world with a small group, playing a London Palladium season the same year. He was in the original cast of the musical

Porgy and Bess, played opposite Pearl Bailey in *Hello Dolly* and in more recent times featured in John Belushi and Dan Ackroyd's *Blues Brothers* as well as making regular appearances on *Sesame Street* and *The Muppet Show*.

★*Cab Calloway and the Missourians* (JSP CD 328)

As a guide to how long Cab Calloway has been delivering the mixture, here's the band he became big brother to in the late 1920s. This was the point at which Calloway joined the tough, hard-driving Missourians dance band and immediately impressed the jazz world that he was the new singer to watch. Blues plays a big part in this rugged, unrefined music, and some of the solos are surprisingly compelling.

Carter, Benny

(Born New York City, August 8, 1907)
Benny Carter has always been hugely admired for all-round musical ability by his peers, many of whom happily endorse his sobriquet of 'King Carter'. He is nearly as proficient on trumpet as on alto saxophone, he led a successful swing band and arranged most of the material as well; reissues of his early music today are still remarkable displays of the bandleader's overall command of resources, of strong themes put together with an innate sense of form. Carter's 'Symphony In Riffs', for instance, merges two contrasting melodies plus solos with superb aplomb, all within the three minutes available on a 78 rpm disc.

Benny Carter was brought up in New York City, and began as a trumpeter through his friendship with DUKE ELLINGTON's Bubber Miley. He formed his first band in 1928, and also worked and recorded with Charlie Johnson, McKINNEY's Cottonpickers, the Chocolate Dandies and others before travelling to Europe as COLEMAN HAWKINS did, spending the late 1930s there. This period included a spell in London as arranger to the BBC Dance Orchestra. On a recording from this period, Elizabeth Welch sings the original version of Carter's best-known song, 'When the Lights are Low'. And in Holland, Carter put together the first jazz orchestra that was both international and multiracial, with the Scots musician George Chisholm taking the trombone solos.

Carter returned to America and to bandleading, featuring emerging talents such as Max Roach, J.J. Johnson and Miles Davis alongside those from the swing era. Settling in Los Angeles, he became the first black musician to break into the lucrative field of film and television scores, and movie appearances include a shot of Carter serenading Gregory Peck in *Snows Of Kilimanjaro*. Carter still plays superbly, being much in demand for festivals and jazz cruises and generally getting the recognition he deserves.

★The Complete Recordings 1930–1940 Vol. 1
(Affinity CD AFS 1022-3)

Superb three-CD set covering Carter's prolific music-making in the 1930s, and spotlighting his remarkable adaptability – lovely arrangements for saxophone voicings, the occasional vocal, plus trumpet, alto and tenor sax, clarinet and piano. Displaying just about every size of jazz band in operation (some from his European travels), this set is certainly an extraordinary confirmation of Carter's relaxed command in a variety of settings, but eventually his alto-playing stays most indelibly in the memory, a mixture of warmth, easy swing and tightly edited eloquence. His duet with the singer Elizabeth Welch on 'When the Lights are Low' is a standout of the set, and of jazz history generally.

★Verve Small Group Sessions (Verve 849 395-2)

Carter's work with Norman Granz, putting the saxophonist in front of an assortment of crisp accompanists in more intimate settings than he was used to, but producing some elegant and spirited results. Carter seems tailor-made for the trio that also features pianist Teddy Wilson and drummer Jo Jones, though the group with Don Abney isn't thrilling. Three ballads with OSCAR PETERSON are unexpectedly affecting, considering Peterson's usual penchant for fireworks.

★*Jazz Giant* (Original Jazz Classics OJC 167)

Another small-group session for Carter, and one of his best. It dates from 1957 and 1958, and features that superbly knowing and witty accompanist Jimmy Rowles on piano (André Previn too, here and there) with BEN WEBSTER on tenor and Barney Kessel on guitar. Carter and Webster coexist so well, they sound as if they should have made a habit of the encounter. Drummer Shelly Manne drives the band with his usual fizz.

Christy, June (Shirley Luster)

(Born Springfield, Illinois, November 20, 1925; died 1990)
Singer June Christy has always been associated with the ambitious and idiom-stretching orchestra of STAN KENTON, though she made some convincing recordings of her own with small groups. Influenced primarily by ANITA O'DAY as a singer, Christy developed a cooler and more refined style as she grew older, and the appeal of her easy swing and distinctive phrasing brought her a new audience among younger jazz listeners. Christy worked as a teenager in bands around Chicago, and replaced Anita O'Day in the Kenton Orchestra in 1945. Through the 1950s she occasionally worked with reformed versions of the Kenton band, though more frequently with her husband, saxophonist Bob Cooper. She more or less retired at the end of the 1960s but returned in the mid-1980s to considerable acclaim.

★*Something Cool* (Capitol CDP 7 96329-2)

Rightly celebrated album from the mid-1950s, now expanded in CD form with 13 extra tracks, some previously unreleased. Stan Kenton's imaginative arranger Pete Rugolo provided the backing band and the arrangements, and for the most part they're a shrewd and sensitive exercise in unobtrusive enhancement of a soloist. 'Something Cool' and 'Midnight Sun' show Christy at her most assured and suggestive, but the set has very few slack moments anywhere.

★*Best of June Christy – the Capitol Years*
(Capitol/EMI CDEMS 1336)

Wider survey from several Capitol albums recorded with Kenton musicians, including some of the songs that made her one of the most popular of big-band singers. 'Something Cool' is there again, alongside a collection of standards including 'Give Me the Simple Life', 'They Can't Take That Away From Me' and 'Do Nothing Till You Hear From Me'.

Clayton, Wilbur Dorsey 'Buck'

(Born Kansas, November 12, 1911)
Consistently imaginative and rhythmically sparky, trumpeter Buck Clayton was long associated with the bands and the methods of COUNT BASIE, but he has worked in an immense variety of other settings and brings an amiable, easygoing musicality to all his work. Though forced to retire early from performance with health difficulties, he continued to work as an arranger and composer, imbuing his writing with much of the bounce he had displayed as a soloist.

Clayton's father was a brass player, and taught his son in the latter's mid-teens. The boy didn't take to a musical career at once, but by the mid-1930s his distinctive sound began to attract attention, and he joined Count Basie in 1936, as the Kansas band was about to break. Clayton's sound was perfect for Basie's sophisticated perception of swing. Though Louis Armstrong was his first inspiration, he was lighter and more oblique than Armstrong, very creative in the use of mutes, and put the essentials of a personal style in place before Basie's name became a coast-to-coast byword. As a soloist and as an accompanist to the band's blues singers, a graceful partner to BILLIE HOLIDAY, and a superb improviser within LESTER YOUNG's Kansas City Six band, Clayton was almost always in command of the situation. Even with the Jazz at the Philharmonic tours, celebrations of technical virtuosity, he rarely lost his charm. In the 1950s, Clayton devoted himself to many small-group recording sessions using the newly invented long-playing record to recreate the atmosphere of a jam session. The Basie style was never far away.

The Classic Swing of Buck Clayton
(Original Jazz Classics OJC 1709)

Sessions from 1946, the year Clayton left Count Basie, including trombonists Dickie Wells and Trummy Young, and drummer Cozy Cole. Precursors to the mainstream jazz of the 1950s, these sessions demonstrate the tireless inventiveness of Clayton, his melodic variations hardly ever formulaic. The two trombonists shimmer and slur deliciously behind it all.

Cole, Nat 'King' (Nathaniel Adams)

(Born Montgomery, Alabama, March 17, 1917; died February 15, 1965)
Through enduring interpretations of standard songs as a vocalist, and through a tradition that continues through the work of soul and funk vocalists such as George Benson, Nat 'King' Cole is largely remembered as an elegant romantic singer. But – just like Benson as a guitarist – Cole was a gifted improvising pianist before his pop successes, and it is this side of him that influenced subsequent pianists from OSCAR PETERSON to Bill Evans. Cole's style was derived from EARL HINES – using the right hand to approximate the melody lines of the increasingly virtuosic horn players of the 1930s, but in Cole's hands the process was smoother and less rhythmically disruptive. He recorded extensively with trios in the late 1940s, worked with LESTER YOUNG, and on Norman Granz' early Jazz at the Philharmonic tour packages. But from the 1950s onwards King was a pop star, and rarely worked in jazz contexts again. He was, however, the first black singer to dominate the pop market so successfully.

Best of the Nat King Cole Trio (Capitol CDP 7982882)

Eighteen tracks from 1943 to 1949, an instrumentals-only selection covering the heyday of the Cole piano trio and remarkable not only for the leader's silvery tone, unswervingly logical shapes and soft swing, but also for the guitar-playing of Oscar Moore, who often accompanies him with an empathy close to telepathy. This drummerless trio was a groundbreaking outfit –

many small groups copied it, including the duo of Bill Evans and Jim Hall – and *Best of* is a fine introduction to it.

★*The Complete Capitol Recordings* (Mosaic MD18-138)

For serious collectors, the full treatment of the Capitol years. Seventeen hours of music on 347 tracks, about a third of them never issued before. Cole sings on some of this material, and not all of it's perfect, but as a comprehensive assessment of a concentrated period in the life of a brilliant jazz musician who spent a lot of time not playing jazz, it can hold you for hours. But for those for whom Cole is divine, perhaps.

★*Jazz Encounters* (Capitol CDP 7 96693-2)

Cole the piano accompanist here, laying down fluttery intros and dewy arpeggios for a variety of performers including BENNY CARTER on alto, COLEMAN HAWKINS on heavyweight tenor, and the corner-of-the-mouth trumpet of Bill Coleman. A hesitant Kay Starr and a powerfully caressing Jo Stafford also make youthful appearances on three tracks. The collaboration with the STAN KENTON Orchestra misfires, and the vocals with WOODY HERMAN and Johnny Mercer are late vaudeville, but these unusual tracks are far from just curiosities for Cole fans.

★*The Billy May Sessions* (Capitol CDP 0777 89545/6 0/1 2CDs)

Not very much piano, but rather lots of big, sumptuous orchestral sound. However, as an insight into what pop music sounded like before Elvis turned up this 40-track, two-disc set is often fascinating. Cole is his usual glossy self, but arranger Billy May brilliantly deploys the saxophone section to curl sensuously around the music, and the brass to tell parallel stories to Cole's main theme. May treats the band as a palette of paint.

Crosby, George Robert 'Bob'

(Born Washington, August 25, 1913)
Bob Crosby was barely a musician – he had qualified as a lawyer and became a passable singer (though not in the same league as his brother Bing) but his bandleading career was launched when he took over a group of dissaffected musicians from the Ben Pollack Orchestra. Whatever his lack of technical skills, Crosby had an ear for a popular mix, and the band developed a repertoire of tight, breezy New Orleans music in the soloistic Dixieland style. Within the orchestra, Crosby also developed a sub-group, the Bobcats, which played the most spontaneous and flexible jazz material, and the music that has lasted best. Crosby's enterprise fell apart in the big-band slump of the 1940s; he became a TV and radio personality, and eventually left the music business altogether, though he has occasionally fronted Crosby revivals.

★*Bob Crosby – Jazz Classics in Digital Stereo* (BBC CD 688)

A mixture of novelty music and gimmicks and some driving Dixieland and thumping swing with fine soloists, this selection includes 'Fidgety Feet' and 'Honky Tonk Train Blues' among many others, and the classic vaudeville-jazz hit 'Big Noise From Winnetka', with drummer Ray Bauduc playing with sticks on the strings of Bob Haggart's bass. Haggart's playing is a cornerstone of much of this music, and Yank Lawson's powerful yet concise trumpet-playing suggests why Louis Armstrong chose him to play the King Oliver part on his own musical autobiography.

Davison, William Edward 'Wild Bill'

(Born Defiance, Ohio, January 5, 1906; died November 14, 1989)
Cornettist Wild Bill Davison, who on occasion played mellophone, banjo, guitar and mandolin as well as cornet, was one of the foremost white musicians of the 'Chicago school' of the 1920s, and continued to promote and by all appearances revel in that crisp and well-turned brand of jazz until into his eighties, as he proved in 1986 at the New York Jazz Festival, which had run a tribute concert in his honour.

Davison began picking up regular commercial work in Chicago around 1927. He was inspired by BIX BEIDERBECKE rather than Armstrong, though his clipped phraseology, full of spurting phrases and long pauses, owed a lot to a more primitive trumpet pioneer, Freddy Keppard. Davison's skills and forceful personality quickly made him a crucial part of the white Dixieland scene of the 1930s. But it was in New York in the 1940s that his reputation grew, partly through association with the influential white bandleader Eddie Condon. Working with pianist ART HODES and supporting the sublime saxophone voice of Sidney Bechet in 1945, Davison committed some of his most convincing performances to disc. Between this point and 1951, Davison also recorded other memorable performances at Eddie Condon's own club, including a version of the classic Beiderbecke vehicle, 'I'm Coming Virginia'. From 1960 onwards, feeling dislocated from the action by his move to California, Davison took to touring the globe, appearing with over 100 different bands between 1965 and 1975.

★*Allstars* (Timeless TTD 545 CD)

Davison at 80, but not apparently inconvenienced by it. A brisk Dixieland session in which enthusiasm, vigour and a gravelly irony in some places make up for accuracy not always apparent either instrumentally or vocally, but featuring an assorted European band including the fine British tenorist Danny Moss.

Dorsey, Thomas 'Tommy'

(Born Pennsylvania, November 19, 1905; died Connecticut, November 26, 1956)

A brilliant trombonist with an ethereal delicacy at the top end of the range, Tommy Dorsey was also one of the most successful of the swing-era bandleaders. Both he and his brother Jimmy led swing bands (originally they co-led one, but violent disagreements between them broke it up) and it was Tommy Dorsey's that retained the greater jazz content. Some of the finest jazz musicians spawned by that period came through Dorsey's group, including trumpeters CHARLIE SHAVERS and BUNNY BERIGAN, drummers BUDDY RICH, Gene Krupa and Louis Bellson, and singers

Frank Sinatra and Jo Stafford. Dorsey's band was orderly, his business and promotional sense was acute, and a string of hits including 'I'm Getting Sentimental Over You' and 'Sunny Side of the Street' followed his reunification with Jimmy in 1937.

★*Yes Indeed!* (BMG ND 904499)

Big-band music from Dorsey during the years of the Second World War, featuring some of the most explicitly jazz-based examples of his work and some good arrangements – notably Sy Oliver's recasting of 'Swanee River'.

★*Well Git It!* (Jass J CD-14 CD)

The title track is a typically hats-in-the-air celebration of Gene Krupa's drumming style, and Buddy Rich gets a look in as well. This compilation consists of airshots broadcast in the mid-1940s, and it's a better way of getting the measure of Dorsey's popularity than much of the rather sugary and passive studio work. Some excellent soloists, including clarinettist Buddy deFranco and the sidelong, foxy trumpet style of Charlie Shavers, improve the chemistry.

Eckstine, William Clarence 'Billy'

(Born Pittsburgh, Pennsylvania, July 8, 1914; died March 8, 1993) The first black American pop star, Billy Eckstine was one of the most copied singers of the 1940s, a romantic performer with a lustrous baritone voice, sultry vibrato and ability to get inside the lyrics of his songs. In the 1950s, both black and white youth followed Eckstine sartorially as well as musically, and he maintained a vigorous working schedule well into his seventies.

These would have been achievements enough for one lifetime, but Eckstine's musicianship extended beyond classy pop balladry. A competent trumpeter as well as a vocalist, Eckstine had developed an enthusiasm for jazz and jazz musicians around Washington, Buffalo and eventually Chicago in the 1930s, and became widely known through his association with EARL HINES in the early 1940s. During that period, he had a pop hit with the mid-tempo blues 'Jelly Jelly', and formed his own big band in 1944. Eckstine embraced the bebop revolution of the 1940s when most bandleaders in the mainstream were avoiding it, and hired the cream of the young players as sidemen – including Dizzy Gillespie, Charlie Parker, Dexter Gordon, Sonny Stitt, Miles Davis and Art Blakey. Eckstine's vocals provided the commercial appeal, the beboppers the fierce originality and verve, and the band was one of the most progressive of its kind.

With the big-band slump, Eckstine called it a day in 1947, however, and began touring with jazzy small groups, as he did until the 1990s.

*No Cover, No Minimum (Roulette CDP 7985832)

A CD-extended and remixed reissue of a 1961 session from Las Vegas, and an example of the timing and charisma of this fine singer in full flight, improved by some tweaking of the balance and 12 tracks not issued before. The latter include a sensitive Ellington medley and 'Little Mama', an obliquely suggestive centrepiece of Eckstine's stage act for years. From the rock-and-roll era to the 1980s, this elegant way of singing wasn't much sought after except on the supper-club circuit, but the resurgence of interest in jazz and swing and the popularity of young singers such as Harry Connick made it apparent just how good Eckstine was. The poignancy and the resignation in 'Lush Life' here is moving proof of it. One of the best accounts of Eckstine's craftsmanship currently around.

Edison, Harry 'Sweets'

(Born Columbus, Ohio, October 10, 1915)
An expressive player who has long been able to develop a solo as a story rather than a highwire act, Harry 'Sweets' Edison is also an uncannily empathetic accompanist whose lissome trumpet lines have wound around BILLIE HOLIDAY and Frank Sinatra among others. He has been so busy as a studio musician over the years that his originality as a soloist hasn't always been as widely exposed as it should have been. But enough good Edison material exists to demonstrate how an early Armstrong influence turned

into a striking tone of his own, a relaxed, nudging swing and delectable timing that has survived almost intact since the 1930s.

Edison was captivated by Louis Armstrong's sound as a child, took up trumpet at 12, and worked with the 'territory bands' in his native Ohio. Towards the end of the 1930s he joined the COUNT BASIE band just as its nationwide fame was beginning to spread, and remained with it until postwar hard times forced Basie to cut down the personnel. Edison's gleaming solos embellished dozens of Basie classics, including 'Jive at Five', 'Every Tub', 'Moten Swing' and 'Easy Does It', but after 1950 he joined the Jazz at the Philharmonic touring packages, was hired by BUDDY RICH, and took a job as Josephine Baker's musical director. Regular studio work followed, and Edison became famous for the apparently effortless scattering of pithy rejoinders and musical epigrams.

★Swing Summit (Candid CD 79050)

Though it's difficult for performers of Edison's experience not to canter through latter-day swing sessions in their sleep, this live set from Birdland in 1990 does give the trumpeter the chance to show what an evergreen he remains. It's an attractive lineup, with BUDDY TATE and Frank Wess on tenors, Wess in particular giving a frequently unambiguous idiom a touch of mystery with some delightfully oblique solos.

Eldridge, David 'Roy'

(Born Pittsburgh, USA, January 30, 1911; died February 26, 1989) It's doubtful if anyone called Roy Eldridge a missing link to his face, but some commentators imply his importance lay in being a kind of bridge between Louis Armstrong and Dizzy Gillespie. At least such neat categorisation does suggest he must have unearthed something new. He was, in fact, a soloist of tremendous character as well as originality, the most admired trumpet player of the later 1930s and one who could still turn it on almost up to his death.

Eldridge developed a more mobile style than his predecessors. He played high and with a scalding, sometimes abrasive sound into which he packed a barrelful of emotion – though the extremes of his playing were sometimes dismissed as poor tone and lack of taste. Much of Eldridge's inspiration came from saxophonists COLEMAN HAWKINS and BENNY CARTER, who were setting new levels of harmonic improvisation that Eldridge translated to the trumpet. He worked and recorded with FLETCHER HENDERSON and Teddy Hill, formed a band of his own from which came classics such as 'Heckler's Hop' and the feverish 'After You've Gone', and became one of the first black musicians to be featured with a white concert orchestra when he joined Gene Krupa. He later toured with Jazz at the Philharmonic, often forming an ebullient partnership with Coleman Hawkins, and spent the last of his playing years holding the fort at Jimmy Ryan's club in New York.

*Little Jazz (CBS 465684)

Sessions between 1935 and 1940, the point from Eldridge's emergence as a trumpet superstar to the arrival of bebop and the trumpet player whose muse he liberated – Dizzy Gillespie. For all his virtuosity, Eldridge was not a trumpet sideshow in his earlier years, but a musician who generated excitement by narrative logic and variation of pacing and accent as much as by squealing. He plays a superbly thoughtful solo on 'Blue Lou' with the Fletcher Henderson band here, a more traditionally skyrocketing one on his famous 'Heckler's Hop', and demonstrates what a good listener he could be in accompanying work with the likes of Mildred Bailey.

*After You've Gone (GRP 16052)

Eldridge's tone was taut and strong, his swing ecstatic and his phrasing agile, but it wasn't perfection but a sense of danger that made him such a charismatic performer. Much of the work here is from the 1940s, with the sound that helped bring Dizzy Gillespie to life written all over it, notably on Eldridge's own 'Sweet Georgia Brown' mutation called 'The Gasser'. The title track, a routine feature for Eldridge with Gene Krupa's band, gets a thunderous treatment from the trumpeter in 1943 here, so fast and bold in conception that a nervous record company held it back and originally released a more peaceable version. The last two of

Eldridge's big bands are featured on this disc too, on another account of 'After You've Gone' and a choppy 'Body and Soul'.

Ellington, Edward Kennedy 'Duke'

(Born Washington DC, April 29, 1899; died New York, May 24, 1974)

No orchestra leader in the history of jazz more imaginatively explored texture, idiomatic variety, the idiosyncrasies of soloists or the possibilities of art and pop as comprehensively as Duke Ellington. His compositions run to thousands, but unlike most composers he ran a band on the road at the same time. Ellington (dubbed 'Duke' for his snappy dress sense) was taught piano as a child, and though he had wanted to be a painter, by his late teens he was a musician specialising in rags and dance music. By the mid-1920s he had moved to New York and acquired the King Oliver-influenced growl-trumpet specialist James 'Bubber' Miley and saxophonist Sidney Bechet, two players who revealed much of the essence of jazz to Ellington, as did hearing the King Oliver band in Chicago.

Ellington's most important early engagement was a five-year apprenticeship at New York's Cotton Club, mostly backing the exotic 'jungle' routines so popular with white audiences. He had also learned from two black musicians with a profound understanding of composition: bandleader Will Vodery and composer Will Marion Cook, the latter the boss of the Southern Syncopated Orchestra which featured Sidney Bechet as a soloist.

Ellington, the man with the painter's perception of jazz, soon developed into a master of tone colour. His combinations of instrumental textures were richer and more subtle than anything previously attempted in jazz, his melodic sense was strong, and he would locate his themes in settings more variable in key centres and rhythmic patterns than was common in the music. During the Cotton Club years, Ellington recorded some of his best early pieces, including 'The Mooch', 'Rockin' in Rhythm', and 'Mood Indigo'. His was not as commercial an orchestra as BENNY GOODMAN's or the DORSEYS', but the romantic, balladeering side of pop music was strengthened in his band by the arrival of such luxuriously toned saxophonists as altoist JOHNNY HODGES (one of the most tremulously affecting instrumentalists in jazz history) and baritonist Harry Carney, and one of his finest songs, 'In a Sentimental Mood', was written during this period.

Ellington began to write concerto-like compositions devoted to members of his band. He would use the sound of the soloists – particularly Hodges, trumpeter Cootie Williams, trombonist Tricky Sam Nanton – as inspirations for compositions, or throw them a fragment of a melody in his head, hear the musicians spontaneously develop it and use this new stage as the basis of a composition. The 1940s represented Ellington's Golden Age. At precisely the point when the big-band movement was being undermined by wartime economics and the arrival of bebop, Ellington's rhythm section was strengthened by the addition of a double-bass genius in Jimmy Blanton (the pioneer of counter-melodic virtuoso bass-playing) and 'Concerto for Cootie', 'Harlem Air Shaft', 'Take the A Train' and 'Warm Valley' materialised during this period of intense, colourful, structurally elegant and moving work. Hodges left the band in 1951 and its progress stumbled from then until his return in 1955. The 1950s and 1960s saw Ellington become a cultural institution, and he even managed to confound listeners who thought that meant he was stagnating by staging a whirlwind performance at the 1956 Newport Jazz Festival which combined the frenetic drive of a rock concert with the richness that had made him famous. Tenorist PAUL GONSALVES' famous 27 blues choruses on 'Diminuendo and Crescendo in Blue' at Newport put the band back on the map and on to the cover of *Time* magazine.

Ellington began to compose again, prolifically. He wrote 'Such Sweet Thunder' as a dedication to Shakespeare, toyed with rearrangements of Tchaikovsky and Grieg, absorbed world music after extensive global touring with the 'Far East Suite' in 1956, and composed a good deal of religious music in his later years. He continued to work into his seventies, and was an ambassador for America's major art form all over the world.

★*Duke Ellington 1927–1929* (Classics 542, 550 and 559)

Now there's so much rivalry between majors and independents to issue the definitively chosen, definitively presented and defin-itively sound-enhanced version of Ellington's every move, there's no shortage of material from the early years of the band. For the sake of accurate documentation of the work of a giant of 20th-century music, this is only appropriate, but much of it is of passing interest to general listeners rather than collectors. Masters of Jazz have issued some giant CD sets of early Ellington, but these three separate Classics CDs, dealing with 1927–8, 1928 and 1928–9 respectively, are excellent places to start. Until 1928 Bubber Miley is clearly the primary source of the 'hot' New Orleans flavour in an otherwise largely orthodox dance band, with Tricky Sam Nanton's trombone not far behind. 'The Mooche', a swirling, wraith-like ensemble piece that breaks into a cruising mid-tempo dance and glows with the solo voices of Johnny Hodges and Barney Bigard, is an indication of the way the band finds itself – and so is 'East St Louis Toodle-Oo'. All three discs are valuable, though 559 might be a first port of call.

★*Jungle Nights in Harlem 1927–1932* (Bluebird ND 82499)

Jungle Nights covers the Cotton Club era from the angle of the rather self-conscious exotica that indirectly helped Ellington to cultivate his sensitivity to atmospherics and larger-scale pieces but which sound a little dated in their original form. Some originals such as 'Misty Morning' and the tantalising 'Mystery Song' show where he's headed, and Cootie Williams' showcase display on 'Hot Feet' is attractive. It gives you a strong sense of what the Cotton Club assignment required, though it doesn't play Ellington's strongest cards.

★*The Brunswick Sessions 1932–35*
Vol. 3 (Jazz Information CAH 3003)

Ellington's recordings for Brunswick, which ran concurrently with several for Victor and Columbia, are documented on three authoritative Jazz Information sets, but this one marks the debut of 'Sophisticated Lady' and the addition of the lyrical trumpeter REX STEWART to the lineup.

★*The Duke's Men – Small Groups* Vol. 1 (Columbia 468618 2CD)

A total contrast with the work Ellington was doing with his orchestra in the mid- to late 1930s, this magnificent set shows what the same set of musicians, in various combinations and mostly with Duke at the keyboards, could do if operating in far more open situations. Drummer Sonny Greer, not always accorded the praise heaped on Ellington's other sidemen, reveals his class here, and so does the man himself, constantly coaxing and tugging at the players in ways he usually let the charts take care of. Rex Stewart and Barney Bigard, originally among the nominal leaders of these sessions, get a lot of the solo work, 'Caravan' and 'Echoes of Harlem' are featured and the notes by Helen Oakley Dance have the clout of an expert.

★*The Blanton-Webster Band* (Bluebird/BMG PD 85659)

A three-disc boxed set covering the most exciting period in the life of Ellington's Orchestra, from the date in May 1940 when the astonishing bassist Jimmy Blanton stunned the jazz world both with his impact on the propulsion of the band as a whole, and his improvisational account of 'Jack the Bear', and over the next two years during which time some of the leader's finest achievements were captured on disc. There are 66 tracks, featuring the remarkable chemistry of Ben Webster on tenor, Blanton's bass, trumpeter Rex Stewart and the compositional talents of BILLY STRAYHORN. If there's an essential Ellington collection, this is it. Tracks include 'Ko-Ko', 'Cotton Tail' and 'Take the A Train'.

★*Duke Ellington – Solos, Duets and Trios* (Bluebird/BMG ND 82178)

Ellington's impact on orchestral jazz was so substantial that his piano-playing is sometimes sidelined by it. But though he was a peerless ensemble player, he was also a fine and often inspired stride-derived swing pianist. On this set, covering more than 30 years of his piano-playing, he is heard in partnership with Jimmy Blanton on nine memorable collaborations, with Earl Hines, and unaccompanied. The Hines meeting is fascinating for its display of different outlooks on similar raw materials, and a sense of competition between them gives the duet 'House of Lords' a tugging, no-holds-barred urgency.

★*Black, Brown and Beige* (RCA Bluebird 86641 3 CD)

In the mid-1940s, Ellington was steadily extending the range of an orchestra at the peak of its powers, and writing suite-like pieces that not only used the jazz vocabulary in ways never attempted by composers before but drew ever more poetic improvised contributions from the players. 'Black, Brown and Beige' was the first suite Ellington recorded, and trumpeters Cat Anderson and Taft Jordan, new additions to the lineup, give the brass section still more bite and impact.

★*At Newport* (Columbia 40587)

One of the most celebrated episodes in all Ellingtonia, when the band played the 1956 Newport Festival at a low point in its public esteem and dominated the entire proceedings with a ferociously swinging performance led by Paul Gonsalves' 27-chorus blues improvisation on 'Diminuendo and Crescendo in Blue', and a delectably measured account of 'Jeep's Blues' by Johnny Hodges.

★*Far East Suite* (Bluebird/BMG ND 87640)

Ellington's 1966 collection following an extensive period of world touring. Unlike many jazz journeys into unjazzlike territory, the 'Far East Suite' isn't precious or patronising, and Harry Carney's saxophone is a mixture of the majestic and the tremulous on 'Agra' while the great Johnny Hodges is at his rhapsodic best on the lacy 'Isfahan'.

★*Live at the Blue Note* (Roulette 7243 8 28637 2 4)

Ellington in a nightclub in 1959, a setting for him seldom offered on disc. The background noise is considerable, which explains why half of the material was never originally issued – but though some of the quiet passages suffer because of that, it doesn't swamp a delicate Johnny Hodges account of 'Passion Flower'. Harry Carney also plays beautifully on 'Sophisticated Lady' against the leader's prompting piano, and of course there are classics like 'A-Train', 'C-Jam Blues', 'Satin Doll' and the rest.

Fitzgerald, Ella

(Born Newport News, Virginia, April 25, 1918)

Ella Fitzgerald's popularity burst the definitions of 'jazz' a long time ago. She includes Bing Crosby, Frank Sinatra and Elton John among her fans, *Downbeat* magazine named her best female jazz singer for 18 consecutive years, and *Playboy* did the same for 13. She has set standards for the performance of popular song that expanded the meanings of good songs and camouflaged the weaknesses of bad ones. All this has been possible largely because of her remarkable range, and pitching of a certainty and accuracy rare among jazz singers attempting to emulate the flexibility and speed of instruments. She also understands harmony well enough to improvise freely around it, and has always swung furiously. But for all this expertise, she has nevertheless managed to retain an artless, relaxed innocence, an informality that instantly establishes a rapport with listeners.

Ella Fitzgerald was spotted as a 16-year-old singing in the amateur hour at the Apollo Theatre in Harlem, and shortly afterwards she began working for the drummer CHICK WEBB, a leading figure in the big-band business. Fitzgerald and the Webb band became internationally famous through their shows at the Savoy Ballroom, late night radio broadcasts and then recordings. Collaborating with arranger Van Alexander, Fitzgerald turned a children's song into a huge hit with 'A-Tisket A-Tasket'. Chick Webb died young, and Fitzgerald fronted the band for three years until the big-band boom ended and the singer became a solo star.

In 1946 Fitzgerald began working for impresario Norman Granz' early Jazz at the Philharmonic packages, as well as working in less populist circumstances with small groups, notably featuring the pianist Hank Jones. Her recordings on Granz' Verve label of the 'Song Books' series, dedicated to the greatest achievements of American popular songwriters, remains her best-loved and most ambitious work. They were celebrations of the best of Jerome Kern, Cole Porter, Rodgers and Hart, Irving Berlin, DUKE ELLINGTON, Johnny Mercer, Harold Arlen and Frank Loesser, and there were five volumes dedicated to the Gershwins. In more recent times, Ella Fitzgerald continued to perform and record, broadcasting on occasion with Frank Sinatra and Duke Ellington, performing with ensembles as different as symphony orchestras and COUNT BASIE's band – though by 1993 ill health had made public performances rare. She has also worked in small-scale but delicately detailed ensembles, with pianist Tommy Flanagan, often performing standards.

The Original Decca Recordings (GRP/Decca 26192 2CD)

As part of the 75th birthday tributes to Ella Fitzgerald in 1993, GRP assembled this book-format presentation package with 39 tracks covering the period from 1938 to 1955 – all the way from her unlikely hit with 'A-Tisket A-Tasket' to some elegant collaborations with the BENNY CARTER Orchestra and one revealing duo performance with the pianist Ellis Larkins. The fundamental Fitzgerald method is in place virtually from the beginning – no extremes of emotion but effortless command of intonation and ability to propel the beat, a forthright and unshowy approach to songs that makes the qualities of the best ones gleam. The Chick Webb band is also featured on 'Undecided', the versions Fitzgerald led after Webb's death appear on three takes, and there are interesting, though sometimes dated collaborations with the Ink Spots and the Delta Rhythm Boys. Fitzgerald's scat technique, extraordinarily agile but given to applause-milking quotation from other tunes, gets one of its best outings on 'Oh Lady Be Good'. She virtually becomes another trumpet behind Louis Armstrong's voice on 'Dream a Little Dream of Me', and 'Until the Real Thing Comes Along' with Ellis Larkins demands more reissues from one of her most fruitful but underrated partnerships.

Ella Fitzgerald on Verve (Verve 517 8982)

Polygram's task in sifting material for another book-style luxury package for the 75th birthday celebrations was probably harder. Fitzgerald's recordings for Norman Granz amounted to such a consistent body of work that some of the individual albums are virtually impossible to sample from, because the singer's performances and the quality of the original material match each other so ideally. This is the set for lovers of the great tradition of American popular song and show-tune writing. Granz was aiming Fitzgerald at a wider audience with the 'Songbooks' projects, and some of the results are a little more knowing, a little more routinised than the robust and jaunty music of the earlier period. A couple of live takes from her Berlin album of the 1960s exhausts the possibilities of prolonged scat, but a version of 'Lush Life' with an unexpectedly reserved OSCAR PETERSON, and some exuberant collaborations with Count Basie are among the highlights.

*_Sings the Duke Ellington Songbook_ (Verve 837035-2 2CD)

The Gershwin Songbook, a three-CD set, is a strong contender for any individual example of Fitzgerald's later work, but this 1956–7 collaboration with the Duke Ellington Orchestra perhaps noses ahead of it simply because the band still has an occasionally ragged expressiveness that gives it a jazzier informality missing from a Nelson Riddle arrangement. But it's an inspired collaboration, and it hauls Fitzgerald a little to the left of the mainstream.

*_Essential Ella_ (Verve/Polygram 523 990-2)

Twenty-five Verve tracks from the 1950s and 60s, including five from the 'Cole Porter Songbook', seven from Rogers and Hart. This set isn't really a substitute for the classic albums it's drawn from, but the music represents the singer in her exuberant prime, and as an introduction it would be invaluable.

Francis, David Albert 'Panama'

(Born Miami, Florida, December 21, 1918)
When BUDDY RICH and Jo Jones died, Panama Francis became the finest surviving swing-band drummer from the era of those heaving Harlem ballrooms, but the band with which he is associated, the Savoy Sultans, had been described in reverential tones by jazz musicians since 1937. Reputed to be the first to use the term 'jump music' to describe that riff-packed, highly rhyth-

mic idiom that was the precursor of rock 'n' roll, the Sultans were a peerless dance band, but they also featured soloists who could imaginatively bridge swing and bebop.

Panama Francis was originally a church musician, then a swing player who worked with trumpeter ROY ELDRIDGE from 1939 in New York. Working with Lucky Millinder at the Savoy Ballroom in the war years, Francis heard the Sultans at close range and loved their sound to the extent of trying to form a replica in the 1950s. It didn't work, and Francis retired to the studios, eventually becoming an r & b drummer and working with Ray Charles. But in 1974, anxious that his jazz past shouldn't be forgotten, Francis successfully re-formed a version of the Savoy Sultans.

★*Get Up and Dance* (Stash STCD 5)

Good Sultans set from the mid-1980s, featuring not just the band's old hits but material from other artists of the swing era. The band's emphasis has always been on the beat and on spirited delivery, and there's plenty of both here.

Freeman, Lawrence 'Bud'

(Born Chicago, April 13, 1906; died 1991)

Like Frankie Trumbauer on the C-melody saxophone, Bud Freeman was one of the rare white musicians in the early years of jazz to create a distinctive sound of his own and help to found a style. Though the development of the tenor saxophone's voice in jazz was dominated by COLEMAN HAWKINS from the 1920s on, Freeman imparted his own qualities to the instrument – a mixture of light, witty urbanity and unexpectedly savage power at times.

Like Trumbauer, Freeman began on the C-melody instrument but by 1925 he was playing tenor, and his progress was fast enough to bring him work in a variety of front-rank bands influenced by New Orleans music, including the excellent Red Nichols group, and Ben Pollack's. As the 'Chicago style' evolved in its brisk, more soloistic variations on the music from the south, the McKenzie-Condon Chicagoans became a lively hit-making unit and Freeman a key feature. His skill and fluency took him into the leading swing bands of the 1930s, notably TOMMY DORSEY's in

1936, and BENNY GOODMAN's for a stretch two years later. Settling on a sound somewhere between the buoyancy of LESTER YOUNG and the punch and rhythmic feel of Hawkins, Freeman abandoned the superstar swing bands because of their relentless schedules, and instead led the Summa Cum Laude Orchestra, a creation of Eddie Condon's, for 18 months in hotel jobs. The band also took part in the movie *Swingin' That Dream* with Louis Armstrong and Benny Goodman.

★*It's Got To Be The Eel* (Affinity CD AFS 1008)

Classic Freeman material drawn from the Summa Cum Laude era of 1939–40, and notable also for the crisp articulacy of Max Kaminsky on trumpet. The saxophonist sounds eager and commanding here, and PEE WEE RUSSELL's clarinet its usual foxy, idiosyncratic self. The tight and disciplined Chicago style had few better exponents than these performers, and the vitality of the band is remarkably well preserved.

Garner, Errol Louis

(Born Pittsburgh, June 15, 1923; died Los Angeles, January 2, 1977)
Errol Garner combined the rich orchestral self-sufficiency of the swing pianists with a broadmindedness of repertoire and a percussive technique that brought him commercial success he almost certainly never sought to engineer. The dancing rhythmic figures of his left hand and the churning melodic eloquence of his right made him one of the happiest-sounding pianists in jazz, and the impact of that vivacity on sales was inevitable.

Garner taught himself piano as a child, and appeared on a children's radio show playing piano at the age of ten. He moved to New York when he was 23 and began to work steadily in nightclubs. This was predominantly Garner's chosen setting for the rest of his career, though he made guest appearances on the recordings of others, notably an unsuitable but intriguing one with Charlie Parker on a Dial session in 1947. On his own or with a trio, Garner's performances unfolded with gleeful drama.

'Misty' was Garner's most famous composition, and 'Concert by the Sea' his best-known recording.

*Concert by the Sea (CBS 451042)

A massive seller, Garner's 'Concert by the Sea' album often appeared in the collections of people who didn't own a single other jazz record. Recorded in 1955, it's flat-out Garner operating all his unique talents for big crescendos, pounding chords, jackhammer left hand and drenching arpeggios, and even on this disc the treatment he metes out to tunes can seem rather routine after a while. But his introductions are lovely, and the repertoire includes 'Autumn Leaves', 'April in Paris' and 'I'll Remember April'.

Gonsalves, Paul

(Born Boston, Massachusetts, July 12, 1920; died London, May 14, 1974)

One of the most underrated of tenor saxophonists, Paul Gonsalves has largely been acknowledged for an astonishing single performance – 27 unbroken choruses on an uptempo blues at the 1956 Newport Jazz Festival – and for a 24-year membership of Duke Ellington's Orchestra. But Gonsalves was no passive sideman, any more than any other member of Ellington's band was allowed to be, nor did he just strike lucky on one show. Influenced by both BEN WEBSTER and DON BYAS, he was a harmonically advanced player who was even prepared to investigate aspects of dissonance that swing musicians usually avoided. His knowledge of chords gave him considerable improvisational agility and he could think his way through complex forms at speed – hence Ellington's use of him for extended solos. The 1956 Newport performance was an inspiration for the movement towards longer solos that characterised the jazz of the 1950s.

*Gettin' Together (Original Jazz Classics OJC 203)

A fine small-group showcase for Gonsalves from 1960, working with a boppish quartet featuring Wynton Kelly on piano and Nat Adderley on trumpet. There's hardly a slack moment on it, and as well as Gonsalves' fertility, there are some dazzlingly apposite interjections from Kelly.

Goodman, Benjamin David 'Benny'

(Born Chicago, May 30, 1909; died New York, June 13, 1986)
As most of the world knows, clarinettist and bandleader Benny Goodman's name was interchangeable with the title 'King of Swing', a contentious accolade that had come about because, in the period in the 1930s when big-band jazz received public endorsement on the scale of rock 'n' roll two decades later, Goodman did the best business. But he could also play more clarinet than almost anybody in jazz in the 1930s. A clarinet virtuoso, he was as comfortable with classical pieces as jazz, and often used the former in practice sessions.

Goodman was one of twelve children, descended from Russian Jews. His family was nearly always broke, and the children were encouraged towards music in the dance-band era as a possible route out of the ghetto. Benny learned so fast that he was a full-time professional by the age of 14 and his first big-time engagement, a year later, was with the briefly successful Ben Pollack Orchestra. But unlike many dance-band musicians, Goodman was fascinated by the seductive art of improvisation, and even in his early recordings he would quickly stray away from written themes. The tension between the adventure of improvising and the security of a popular repertoire, driven by the hustling, frantic quality that fuelled the swing craze, was Goodman's musical chemistry.

Goodman began leading his own big band in 1934 and by judicious purchase of swing arrangements (FLETCHER HENDERSON's, among others) and the aid of the fast-expanding radio networks and their growing army of DJs, his career took off. But though his big band was his most famous achievement, some of Goodman's most enduring jazz music was recording with small groups, the clarinet winging its way over the crisp insistence of accompanists such as pianist Teddy Wilson, drummer Gene Krupa, vibist Lionel Hampton and guitarist Charlie Christian. Goodman's authority and popularity were instrumental in the success of one of the legendary jazz events of the pre-war years, the 1938 concert at

Carnegie Hall, previously hallowed ground for classical music only. He became a jazz ambassador during the 1950s, touring extensively. He also maintained his relationships with classical composers: having worked with Hungarian modernist Bela Bartok, performed with the Chicago Symphony Orchestra, he eventually commissioned concertos for his clarinet from Aaron Copland and Paul Hindemith.

★*The Birth of Swing* (RCA Bluebird ND 90601 – 3 CDs)

Goodman's orchestra as the swing bandwagon began to roll in the mid-1930s – these takes were all made between spring 1935 and winter 1936. BUNNY BERIGAN, JACK TEAGARDEN, Gene Krupa and even occasionally ELLA FITZGERALD are featured, but it's the overall power of the band that stands out. Goodman's clarinet, both in solos and ensembles, has immense assurance and intelligence. Krupa's manic energy helps to give the whole ensemble its characteristic drive, but so do the arrangements, which create a swing that would still work even if Krupa had gone home. A well-presented and informative set, though uneven in sound quality.

★*After You've Gone* (Bluebird/BMG 85631)

Goodman's small-group recordings displayed his remarkable clarinet technique at its best, and his improviser's imagination as well. These sessions from the mid-1930s find Goodman in relaxed collaboration with the pearly-sounding Teddy Wilson on piano and Gene Krupa on drums, and the quartet tracks add the graceful sway of Lionel Hampton's vibes as well. 'China Boy' and 'Moonglow' are among the best-known tracks.

★*Carnegie Hall Concert* (Columbia C2K-40244 2CD)

One of the great jazz concerts, in which the significance of the venue being opened up to a music the arts establishment had previously sniffed at, brought exceptional performances from everybody present. As well as the Goodman orchestra, there were guest appearances from other jazz stars including Ellington's JOHNNY HODGES and Harry Carney, and COUNT BASIE at the piano. Krupa seems to turbo-charge his already considerable energies, and the jam-session atmosphere suggests much of the impact swing bands had in the 1930s.

★*Solo Flight* (Vintage Jazz Classics VJC-1021-2)

More live material, this time featuring the Goodman band of 1939 to 1941 with the leader's guitar prodigy Charlie Christian. On the studio recordings of this material, Christian's solos are short and sweet. Here he gets plenty of chance to stretch out, and his harmonic imagination and freedom from repetition are startling.

★*BG In Hi-Fi* (Capitol CDP 7 92864-2)

If earlier Goodman recordings recall the frantic furore that a swing band in full cry would have created in a 1930s dance hall, later ones present a smoothly oiled limousine of a band, playing to a reputation that precedes them. For all that, Goodman's clarinet-playing sounds as strong in 1954 as it did nearly two decades earlier, trumpeters Ruby Braff and CHARLIE SHAVERS provide completely different accounts of how swing trumpet might work, and the superb pianist Mel Powell almost carries the set away.

Grappelli, Stephane

(Born Paris, January 26, 1908)
A walking definition of grace, swing and orthodox tunefulness, violinist Stephane Grappelli has been entertaining audiences inside and outside the jazz fraternity since the 1920s. He took up the instrument at 12, went to the Paris Conservatoire as a teenager and soon after joined a jazz-influenced dance band (the Gregorians) first as a pianist, then as a violinist. Grappelli met the gypsy guitarist DJANGO REINHARDT, and began a casual improvising partnership with him that ended up as the Quintet du Hot Club de France – a band that became influential all over the world in the 1930s and 1940s, though its rhythmic rigidity hasn't aged well. Grappelli stayed in London during the war years and tried with mixed success to rebuild his always unsteady relationship with Reinhardt until the guitarist's death in 1953. During the 1960s Grappelli continued to tour in Europe, but it was the reconstruc-

tion of the Hot Club format with guitarist Denny Wright that led to Grappelli's resurgence in the next decade, appearing with artists such as vibraharpist Gary Burton and classical virtuoso Yehudi Menuhin among others.

★*Special* (Jazztime 251286 2 CDs)

Grappelli at work in France in the late 1940s and through the 1950s. The Hot Club atmosphere is strongly present, although Reinhardt is not among the guitarists and some of them depart inventively from his mannerisms. Grappelli's swooning romanticism is always countered by his own rhythmic momentum, sly wit and tight melodic intelligence, the sidemen are often excellent, and harpist Pierre Spiers band is a real jazz curiosity.

★*Tivoli Gardens, Copenhagen* (Original Jazz Classics OJC 441)

Excellent concert session for Grappelli with bassist Neils-Henning Ørsted Pedersen and guitarist Joe Pass. Grappelli demonstrates that the passage of the years seems to improve him and the interplay with Pass and Pedersen shows how flexible and accommodating his playing has remained. The bassist plays with his customary urge, and Pass, who can be a passive performer, takes on some of the leader's tirelessly tumbling loquacity.

Gray, Wardell

(Born Oklahoma City, February 13, 1921; died Las Vegas, May 25, 1955)
One of the key tenor players of the swing era who teetered on the brink of bebop, Gray was frequently associated with fellow-tenorist Dexter Gordon as a player inspired by LESTER YOUNG but tended towards a tougher and faster music rather than the romanticisms pursued by many Young admirers. Gray's achievements could have been more substantial than they were, but he died young – probably of a drug overdose – in Las Vegas.

Gray was raised in Detroit, worked with EARL HINES' band, and then appeared for brief stints with several leaders, including BILLY ECKSTINE, BENNY CARTER, BENNY GOODMAN and COUNT BASIE. But it was the partnership with Dexter Gordon, with whom Gray worked after he moved to the west coast in 1946, that was his most celebrated.

Gray was involved with some small Benny Goodman bands in 1948, his perceptions of a progressive form of swing helping the bandleader to incorporate some boppish elements, and at the end of that decade he worked successfully with both Count Basie and Tadd Dameron. In the last years of his life, Gray worked extensively on the west coast again, often in recorded recreations of jam sessions. He appears to have died of an overdose shortly after Charlie Parker.

Memorial – Vols. 1 & 2 (Original Jazz Classics OJC 050)

Interesting Gray material from 1949 and into the 1950s. The first disc includes the saxophonist's quirky blues 'Twisted' (later performed in a vocalese version by boppish singer Annie Ross) and finds Gray with a bop rhythm section of Al Haig on piano, Tommy Potter on bass and Roy Haynes on drums. But though Gray was comfortable in such a setting, he always hung back from bop as a player, and the disinclination to overcomplicate his work gave it considerable strength and shape. A sextet led by vibist Teddy Charles also supports Gray, and on the second disc Dexter Gordon lends some typical barging muscle to 'Move'.

Way Out Wardell (Crown CDBOP 014)

Gray in live performance with ERROL GARNER on piano in 1948, originally one of Gene Norman's 'Just Jazz' presentations. The credits were shared between Gray and Garner in the first version, and it's an appropriate way of dealing with their achievements on the session, because both of them play some of their most assertive and inventive music on 'Blue Lou'.

Hampton, Lionel

(Born Louisville, Kentucky, April 20, 1908)
Drummer, pianist, singer, vibraharpist and all-round showman, Lionel Hampton has led the longest-running jazz orchestra in the

music's history, and attained some of the most spectacular peaks of audience excitement with it. Hampton is often dismissed as showy to the point at which musicality evaporates, and his band's performances undoubtedly are celebrations of technique, volume, energy and the constant crescendo. But he has frequently turned in impressive performances of his own, and nurtured many excellent musicians, not to mention converting countless new jazz fans everywhere he has travelled over the years.

Hampton is probably unique among big-time jazz drummers for having been taught snare technique by a Dominican nun. He learned marimba later, but was a drummer when he backed Louis Armstrong in Los Angeles as a member of the Les Hite Orchestra. At his wife's recommendation, Hampton also took up vibes, and interrupted his career to study music at college. In 1936, while performing in an LA club, Hampton found himself backing BENNY GOODMAN and shortly afterwards he became a member of the Goodman band. Hampton was quickly popular, and secured a deal to record with whoever he liked. In 1940 Hampton formed his own big band and the likes of Charles Mingus, Art Farmer, Dexter Gordon, Wes Montgomery, Betty Carter and Dinah Washington passed through it.

★*Early Hamp* (Affinity CD AFS 1011)

Very little of Hampton the vibes specialist here, except for some indicative tracks with a 1936 Teddy Wilson group, but a lot of drumming and singing from a man who has always performed as if time is running out. With Eddie Condon, Hampton delivers some ferocious drum displays, and is even able to put some muscle behind rather ordinary groups such as Paul Howard's Quality Serenaders. A disc that satisfies curiosity about Hampton and the early stages of swing, though inconsistent musically.

★*Hot Mallets* Vol. 1 (Bluebird/BMG ND 86458)

Some of the results of Hampton's extraordinary record deal with Victor shortly after he was discovered, that enabled him to cut a series of small-band recordings with passing celebrities that amount to some of the best swing-playing of the entire period. Hampton gets an Ellingtonish ensemble sound on 'Buzzin'

Around With the Bee', with Ellington's trumpeter Cootie Williams and saxophonist JOHNNY HODGES in full flow. 'Hot Mallets' and 'One Sweet Letter From You' feature Dizzy Gillespie, BENNY CARTER, COLEMAN HAWKINS, Charlie Christian and many others. Beautiful soloing, and feline swing from Hampton himself.

★*Complete Paris Session* (Vogue VG 655609)

A spectacular Hampton big band (the one that included Clifford Brown, though he isn't heard here) toured Europe in 1953, and though there is a CD version of some of the full-scale results, these small group sessions involving both Hampton musicians and locals such as pianist Claude Bolling are less bombastic and more persuasive, notably in the leader's work on 'September in the Rain' and 'I Only Have Eyes for You'.

★*Newport 78* (Timeless CDSJP 142)

More recent and typical Hampton bravura, with emphasis on the tunes that became standbys with him, such as 'Flying Home' and 'Stompin' at the Savoy'. Noisy, blustering and uneven, but what marks it out is an excellent lineup including Doc Cheatham and Cat Anderson on trumpets, Charles MacPherson, Bob Wilber and Arnett Cobb on reeds, and Panama Francis on drums.

Hawkins, Coleman Randolph

(Born St Joseph, Missouri, November 21, 1901; died New York, May 19, 1969)
Though the expressiveness, tonal range and scalding intensity (in modernists' hands) of the tenor saxophone are now taken for granted, Coleman Hawkins picked up the instrument when it was used for little more than special effects, and brought it so reverberatingly to life that virtually every tenorist in the music's history either studied him directly or inherited part of his vision unawares. His sound was magisterial, deliberate, gruff and imposing, his melodic imagination more alert and fast-moving than any saxophone player in the pre-bop period.

Hawkins had a sophisticated musical education, which helped

him become such an ingenious exponent of harmonic improvising. He started young (playing in public by the age of 12), was a teenager as the migration from the south to Chicago got under way, went on the road at 20 with Mamie Smith's Jazz Hounds, and three years later was helping to build one of the most influential ensembles of the big-band era, FLETCHER HENDERSON's Orchestra. After the departure of Louis Armstrong, Hawkins was soon Henderson's brightest star, and he dominated saxophone-playing in America until he left for Europe in 1934, playing in England, France and Scandinavia for the next five years. On his return to the States in 1939 Hawkins recorded one of the most famous solos in jazz, a rhapsody on 'Body and Soul' that became both a hit and a model for both arrangers and improvisers.

Hawkins didn't reject bebop – his harmonic awareness helped him grasp its logic, though its timing and accents never entirely appealed to him – and he performed with many of the leaders of the movement, including Thelonious Monk in 1943. He continued to tour (both as a soloist and with Jazz at the Philharmonic), recorded with modernists such as Max Roach and Sonny Rollins, and remained on the road until shortly before his death.

★*Coleman Hawkins 1929–1934* (Classics 587)

The unsteady beginnings of Coleman Hawkins' independence, audible on the Fletcher Henderson discs of the mid-1920s, don't suggest anything of the abrupt arrival on the stage of jazz greatness that's soon to follow. The transition has already occurred by the time these sessions begin, and Hawkins is already rolling boldly away from the beat and has left the risible elements of his vaudeville-sax background behind. A famous Hawkins early triumph, 'Hello Lola' with the Mound City Blue Blowers, is here, and so is a wonderful Horace Henderson set from 1933.

★*Body and Soul* (RCA Bluebird ND 85717)

An excellent representation of the 'Body and Soul' session itself, including all the material from the two RCA sessions that spawned it. The disc then represents Hawkins' fascinating attempts to come to grips with bebop, in appearances with Fats

Navarro, J.J. Johnson and Max Roach. There is also material from a more variable 1956 session.

★*Bean and Ben 1944–45* (Harlequin HQ 2004)

Always an open-minded artist, Hawkins was aware of the changes in jazz in the 1940s, and part of the music on this set features the quartet he led with Thelonious Monk on piano in 1944. Often credited as being the first bebop recordings following the lifting of the union ban on the studios, these takes display Hawkins in full irrepressible flight on 'Drifting on a Reed' among others, and Monk is already his jangly, tangential self. Other takes include the early stages of a long association in the appearances of BEN WEBSTER.

★*The Hawk Flies High* (Original Jazz Classics OJC 027)

Hawkins was anxious to get back into the spotlight after the first wave of bop receded, and this session from 1957 with J.J. Johnson on trombone, Hank Jones on piano and Jo Jones on drums, among others, ranks among his very best. Though Hawkins' blues-playing has often been treated as secondary to his other achievements, there's not much missing in spirit and soulfulness about his performance on 'Blue Light'.

★*Bean and the Boys* (Fresh Sound FSCD-1013)

Live performances from 1959 and 1962, one a club appearance, the other a broadcast. Some of the best later examples of the way Hawkins could continue to attack his music in the right circumstances, featuring an unusual quantity of blues for this musician as well. Trombonist Jimmy Cleveland and tenorist Benny Golson take a guest spot on 'Perdido' and a blues jam.

★*The Hawk Swings* (Boplicity CDBOP 015)

Relaxed vigour from Hawkins and some fine sidemen on a 1960 session ideally suited to him. There are five originals by Hawkins on this open and amiable set, the rhythm section is ideal, and trumpeter Thad Jones turns out to be a provocative partner.

Henderson, Fletcher Hamilton

(Born Georgia, December 18, 1897; died New York, December 28, 1952)

For a man who made an immense (if eventually underrated) contribution to jazz, bandleader Fletcher Henderson's career was more accidental and idiosyncratic than most. A scientist by training, Henderson drifted into music, first as a record company demonstrator then as a bandleader, became a 1920s success with Louis Armstrong as his star sideman, then went broke, sold his best arrangements to BENNY GOODMAN, and watched Goodman become a wealthy celebrity.

Fletcher Henderson's mother was a music teacher, and the boy studied classical piano, but went to Atlanta University as a mathematician and chemist. Black graduates, however, found work they deserved hard to come by and Henderson wound up at a New York music publishing company, demonstrating new songs. He later became a fixer for Black Swan Records, finding musicians for studio sessions to showcase singers such as Bessie Smith, and when these aggregations started to perform live, Henderson found himself as a bandleader. His group won an audition to Harlem's Club Alabam in 1924, though at that time still performing in the genial, stolid plod of the period's dance music. Henderson's band for the Club Alabam included a then rather awkward-sounding COLEMAN HAWKINS, and a young clarinettist and arranger called DON REDMAN. When Henderson fell out with the management and moved to the nearby Roseland Ballroom he found the establishment that was to be his home for the next decade. Henderson also had the incalculable benefit of having hired Louis Armstrong. Henderson had heard the cornettist in 1922 when the King Oliver Creole Band had performed at Chicago's Lincoln Gardens. Initially reluctant to leave Oliver, Armstrong had answered Henderson's call two years later.

Louis Armstrong and Fletcher Henderson – The Complete Recordings 1924–25 (Forte Records F 38001/2/3)

These tracks, many of them alternate takes (four versions of 'Why Couldn't It Be Me', three of 'Alabamy Bound' and 'Swanee Butterfly') cover Louis Armstrong's work with the Fletcher

Henderson Orchestra in the mid-1920s, when the trumpeter's ability to float wilfully over the beat rather than cling to it brought a smooth dance-floor unit to life as a vividly swinging big jazz band. 'Shanghai Shuffle' and 'Copenhagen' are essential in any Armstrong or Henderson collection. The sound quality isn't great, despite some electronic manipulation, and the early Henderson band's arrangements with their sugary sax sound, raspberry-blowing trombones and frantic, strumming rhythms, hardly suggest the urbane power of the same band a few years on, or the originality of concept that led Benny Goodman to find much of his bandleader's inspiration in Henderson. But it's a jazz milestone for all that.

★*Hocus Pocus* (Bluebird/BMG ND 90413)

'Sugar Foot Stomp' and 'Singing the Blues' figure among the early Henderson milestones performed here by the likes of Coleman Hawkins, trumpeters REX STEWART, HENRY 'RED' ALLEN and ROY ELDRIDGE, saxophonist CHU BERRY and others in the high period of the band's life from 1927 to 1936. All the soloists are good but Eldridge is often sensational, and the arrangement on a swing classic like 'Sing Sing Sing' reveals the depth of the Goodman connection. Some of the material hasn't been previously issued (Rex Stewart's Beiderbeckian trumpet soliloquy on 'Singing the Blues', or the graceful vehicle for Coleman Hawkins' 'Phantom Phantasie').

Herman, Woodrow Charles 'Woody'

(Born Wisconsin, May 16, 1913; died Los Angeles, October 27, 1987)

Like BUDDY RICH, Woody Herman was a showbiz personality whose first appearances in the footlights had been as a child performer in vaudeville. He was billed as the 'Boy Wonder of the Clarinet' in his parents' act, and by the age of 23 he had become the leader of his own orchestra, three years later recording 'Woodchoppers' Ball', a million-selling disc that made his reputation. After the war, Herman formed the first of his famous Herds, broadcast with it, and became a household name. The result was that Herman survived the decline of the big-band era, an achievement partly due to his soloists, and partly because Herman was shrewd enough to perceive a potential in bebop. Herman's orchestras influenced young bop players all over the world who wanted to combine their adventurousness with dance-hall acceptability. Herman was a good clarinettist and alto saxophonist himself (performing on the latter in the honeyed style of Frankie Trumbauer) and the tenor saxophone style of LESTER YOUNG underpinned his reed section, notably in the hands of Stan Getz and Zoot Sims. It was a Getz recording with Herman, a brief, fluttering, feathery solo on a ballad called 'Early Autumn', that made Getz' name and made him the most emulated of white saxophonists.

Herman's 1950s Third Herd tried to stay afloat in bad times for the big bands. But by the 1960s, helped by the muscular style of tenorist Sal Nistico, and bending towards the sound of John Coltrane, Herman's orchestra came back. It used pop music to catch a younger audience, and relished combining it with the kind of blistering ensemble-playing (particularly from the brass) that a well-drilled jazz band could exhibit, but he never lost his enthusiasm for the kind of outfit that could still spring surprises.

★*The Thundering Herds 1945–47* (CBS 460825)

This set mostly features the First Herd of 1945, with a smattering of examples from the more boppish Second, including the young Stan Getz. The qualities of youthful energy and enthusiasm, virtuoso soloists plus arrangers Ralph Burns and Neal Hefti created a jazz orchestra to rival the best in the business. The arrangements and the tightly drilled ensemble-playing for the First Herd, particularly on uptempo pieces, concentrated on building excitement to a pitch of intensity before the soloists made their appearances – a habit that such fiery performers as tenorist Flip Phillips made trenchant use of. Trombonist Bill Harris adds his unique, ethereal gleam.

★*Live Featuring Bill Harris* Vols. 1 & 2 (Status STCD 107/110)

Like Count Basie and Duke Ellington, Woody Herman lived on the road. The band, with its precise, high-speed ensemble-playing and lustrous colours on ballads, was at its best on live shows, and these two discs catch it in flight in 1957, with more superb soloing from Bill Harris.

★*Woody and Friends* (Concord CCD 4170)

A lot better than the average guest-stars vehicle, this set from 1979 features Dizzy Gillespie, Woody Shaw and Stan Getz with the regulars. To stay in the game in the rock era, Herman had begun adapting pop songs for the band – as did Basie, Buddy Rich and others in the 1960s and 1970s – and his later discs weren't as fresh as the early ones, valuable mainly to no-questions-asked Herman devotees. But this set from the Monterey Festival draws some fine performances from the band and the guests, notably from Stan Getz on 'What Are You Doing the Rest of Your Life'.

Hines, Earl Kenneth

(Born Pennsylvania, December 28, 1903; died California, April 22, 1983)

Though Art Tatum's was a dominant name in piano jazz by the early 1930s, Earl 'Fatha' Hines was the instrument's first great virtuoso, and he retained the loyalty and admiration of a wide public and his fellow-musicians throughout six decades as an active performer. Hines developed his unique sound by listening to horn players – most notably Louis Armstrong – and evolving what became known as the 'trumpet style' on piano. Where the predominant jazz keyboard technique of the 1920s was the ragtime derivative known as 'stride', with its regular bass patterns and rocking chords, Hines loosened the left hand to play in a more free-ranging 'orchestral' manner and his right-hand runs closely emulated the wide leaps of intervals, tremolo effects and tempo-stretching ascents and descents of the New Orleans horn stars. It was a piano identity of such irrepressible, self-propelled energy that Hines, for all his collaborative exploits, became Tatum-like in a kind of glorious isolation. He sounded better on his own, and many of the recordings of the later stages of his career are preferable for just that reason.

Hines' family was musical, and he began on cornet, switching to piano and studying music formally. In the early 1920s he found work backing singers, played with Louis Armstrong's band in 1927, and then with the excellent clarinettist Jimmie Noone, producing some memorable recordings with him. But it was the collaboration with Armstrong in 1929 that produced the improvised duet 'Weatherbird' that revealed how far ahead of his contemporaries on piano Hines had come. The pianist led his own bands throughout the 1930s and into the 1940s, mostly at Chicago's mob-controlled Grand Terrace Club – and when bebop arrived, he formed a band that included Dizzy Gillespie, Charlie Parker and Wardell Gray, though his bop work was hardly recorded. In the 1950s, promoters sought to rebuild the Hines-Armstrong connection, but though the pianist played with the All-Stars from 1947 to 1951 it was an awkward period and Hines' natural exuberance was often stifled. The rest of the decade was a comparatively lean time for him but he resurfaced in the 1960s with some dazzling solo recordings.

*Earl Hines 1932–34 (Classics 514)

The perfect place to locate the first flowering of Earl Hines' talents is in his work with Louis Armstrong, but in the 1930s he not only led a highly creative orchestra but confirmed what a sensational ensemble player he was – unlike his pianistic rival Art Tatum. Walter Fuller, a crisp Armstrong-oriented performer, plays some taut and pithy trumpet solos, but it is Hines who constantly astonishes with offhand fills and introductions of dazzling complexity. Some of the best available representations of the mid-period work of the Grand Terrace band.

*Piano Man (Bluebird/BMG ND 86750)

The Grand Terrace band in the period from 1939–42 (a compilation of Victor material of the period), notably featuring the hit collaboration with singer BILLY ECKSTINE on 'Jelly Jelly' and the thunderous piano solo 'Boogie Woogie on St Louis Blues'. At times the ensemble resembles the big bands of both JIMMY LUNCEFORD and COUNT BASIE, but any routine qualities in the overall sound are despatched by Hines' own playing, some good

Armstrong-like Walter Fuller trumpet solos and the propulsive drumming of Alvin Burroughs.

★*The Legendary Little Theatre Concert of 1964* (Vogue 650139)

Hines' career had gone quiet by the early 1960s but 1964 was the year he came back, and to enormous acclaim. Listening to this disc, for all the uneven sound quality, it's not hard to hear why. Hines' use of the rocking right-hand tremolo to mimic brass vibrato was one of his trademarks in the 1920s, and he explores the device here (notably on 'Blues Jam') with a gleeful indulgence. The set is packed with Hines' audacious insights and thunderous, demanding style. Great live Hines.

Hodes, Arthur W. 'Art'

(Born Nikoliev, Russia, November 14, 1904)
A fine blues pianist and an unswerving traditionalist who has rarely strayed far from Chicago's South Side, Art Hodes has also been profoundly influenced by Jelly Roll Morton both as a soloist and an ensemble player, and he preserves vestiges of ragtime traditions that go back even further.

Hodes worked with Wingy Manone and other Dixieland-oriented bands in the early 1930s, but came to New York in 1938 to appear on 52nd Street. As well as playing, Hodes developed a sideline as a DJ and jazz journalist, working on the *Jazz Record*. He also began to lecture in the music, and his career within jazz was so varied by the end of the 1950s that he was enjoying a solo career back in the Chicago nightclubs, leading various bands, writing for *Downbeat*, hosting a TV show on the music and generally spreading the word.

Hodes began touring internationally in the 1970s, and his single-minded but colourful approach became more appreciated with time.

★*Sessions at Blue Note* (Dormouse International DMI CDX04)

The fledgling Blue Note Records adopted Hodes in 1944 and recorded him delivering his favourite proto-jazz materials with a jaunty Condon-esque band, even including such stalwarts of the genre as trumpeter Max Kaminsky. But some of the most evocative music on an interesting set principally showcases the pianist, in simple, moving and bluesy collaborations with Kaminsky again, and with clarinettist Leonard Centobie.

Hodges, Johnny

(Born Cambridge, Mass., July 25, 1907; died New York, May 11, 1970)

Though one of the most technically assured and opulent-toned alto saxophonists in jazz, Johnny Hodges is celebrated in the music's history as an inimitable conduit for the thoughts of DUKE ELLINGTON, with whom he worked from 1928 until his death with only a four-year break for a solo career. Hodges is often characterised as a romantic, and his ravishing sound seems to confirm it, but his rhythmic inventiveness and the originality with which he manages to be both poignant and avoid mawkishness gives his work far more bite and muscle. Hodges had many imitators, but his sound came from refinements of tone control that were much harder to replicate than fast note-spinning, so his work remains unmistakable.

Hodges was raised in Boston, and met Sidney Bechet when the great saxophonist was working there with a vaudeville show. Hodges took lessons from Bechet, eventually getting a job at a club run by the older man and frequently deputising for him. Duke Ellington heard Hodges in Boston, and signed him up. From then on, Hodges virtually ran Ellington's saxophone section, immensely enriching its textures and acting as a focus for Ellington's ideas on countless superb recordings.

Hodges left the Ellington band between 1951 and 1955, running a group of his own that briefly included John Coltrane. When he came back, it was to inspire Ellington still more and marked a return to the foreground for the Ellington band, symbolised by the sensational Newport 1956 show.

★*Used to be Duke* (Verve 849 394–2)

Superb Hodges music from 1954, with a band that includes a young and discreetly deployed John Coltrane, who doesn't solo. Several Ellington stars, including clarinettist Jimmy Hamilton and baritonist Harry Carney, are present on this set, which is one of the best under Hodges' leadership, though almost inevitably echoing the Ellington sound. Hodges' devastating slow playing is heard on the kind of extended ballad medley that sounds tailor-made for him.

★*Everybody Knows Johnny Hodges* (Impulse/GRP 11162)

More Ellington sidemen – Carney and Hamilton again, plus a vigorous PAUL GONSALVES among others – working in a mixture of small groups and full-sized bands in 1964. Hodges demonstrates his expressiveness with blues on 'Everybody Knows', and shares the honours with Gonsalves on '310 Blues', a composition for the session by BILLY STRAYHORN.

Holiday, Billie (Eleanora Fagan)

(Born Baltimore, April 7, 1915; died New York, July 17, 1959)
If ELLA FITZGERALD has been jazz singing's most popular and accessible artist, and SARAH VAUGHAN its most operatic and complete, Billie Holiday most intimately contacted the improvisational essence of jazz. Her timing, her delicate twists of intonation and phrasing, her ability to maintain intensity at low volumes and with the most measured and least histrionic of methods, amounted to a style that has defied imitation. If Holiday's significance to 20th-century western music is not as well understood as it should be, her vulnerability to myth-making as a troubled, narcotic-dependent artist whose slow decline happened in the glare of the spotlights hasn't helped. But on musical values alone, Holiday has never been rivalled in jazz. Though an 'instrumental' singer, she inhabited the lyrics of good songs with a poignancy – and earlier, with an exuberance – that integrated the meaning of the words with the movements of the music.

Billie Holiday was institutionalised at ten after being raped, and drifted into prostitution as a teenager, but a move to New York with her mother Sadie Fagan in 1929 resulted in work as a singer in the Harlem clubs. She immediately impressed listeners with a voice that was both youthful yet knowing, she was bluesy without explicitly featuring blues material, she strayed provocatively behind the beat giving her work a languid, sensual quality, and her sound had an imposing quality out of all proportion to its small volume. BENNY GOODMAN took an interest, and played on her first recordings – but when she appeared in a film featuring the DUKE ELLINGTON Orchestra (*Symphony In Black*) singing 'Big City Blues' her career took off, and a sensational appearance in April 1935 at the Apollo confirmed it. Holiday was soon finding favour with more top-flight instrumentalists than any other singer. Saxophonist LESTER YOUNG and pianist TEDDY WILSON became close friends, and Holiday's recordings with Young represented one of the finest recorded partnerships in jazz. Though the enduring image of Billie Holiday is one of a tragic victim, her work in the 1930s is constantly buoyant, if intimate, and quite out of line with the way she was typecast later.

Holiday also worked with bandleader ARTIE SHAW in the 1940s, and made occasional appearances with Benny Goodman and Duke Ellington but it was in small-band contexts that she was at her most incandescent. Her popularity increased when a liberal businessman, Barney Josephson, opened an integrated nightclub called Café Society in Greenwich Village – many clubs, tacitly or otherwise, still operated a colour bar – and encouraged Billie Holiday towards a repertoire including the treatment of racist oppression. The song 'Strange Fruit', its subject the southern lynchings, brought her a new audience. This was a mixed blessing, because the audience also favoured a good deal of material in which Holiday cast herself as a victim, and by the mid-1950s she was beginning to satisfy the demand for a tragic heroine. The effects of drugs and drink were increasingly audible in the rasping plaintiveness of her intonation, and though in some respects her communicating powers intensified as her technique broke, the change began to put audiences in a position of almost uncomfortable intimacy. She died at the Metropolitan Hospital in New York, facing a narcotics possession charge on her deathbed.

★*The Voice of Jazz: Complete Recordings 1933–1940*
(Affinity CD AFS 1019-8)

Eight CDs from the most productive and inventive period of Billie Holiday's life, featuring 189 songs, many of them the classic duets between Holiday and Lester Young. Young, a saxophonist with a musical temperament very similar to the singer's, was providing such a stream of seductive intros, nudging counterpoints and complementary solos that the voices of the two are inseparably entwined in a partnership that has very few rivals anywhere in jazz. Though it may come as a surprise to those who believe her to be permanently in despair, Holiday sounds as if she's enjoying herself on all the better material here, and her ease with the musicians is startling: she works as if her voice was an instrument, but without recourse to scatting or extravagant special effects, simply subtle and modest diversion of the melody and the ability to vibrate the hidden or underlying meanings of a lyric. This is an imposing set, though the sound quality isn't always ideal, and it has all the essentials for appreciating Holiday's early impact.

★*The Complete Original Decca Recordings* (GRP 26012)

Lady Day from 1944 to 1950, in the awkward period in which popular music was changing from songs performed by vocalists fronting jazz bands to vocalists working with anonymous orchestras and often with strings. Billie Holiday's success following 'Strange Fruit' shifted her towards a less casual and spontaneous studio approach. The Decca sessions were therefore some of the most elaborately arranged of her career, but include a good many classics just the same. 'Lover Man' was her Decca debut and one of her most revealing and saleable songs, and 'Don't Explain', 'Porgy' and 'T'aint Nobody's Business If I Do' (the latter a rare blues for Holiday) run it close. There's plenty of background information, and several takes in some cases.

★*Lady in Autumn* (Verve 849 434-2)

A two-CD set covering the period from the late 1940s to the end of her life in which Holiday's voice was certainly less reliable, but frequently as telling in its own way as it had been in earlier years.

Sometimes she sounds as if the demands of being a performing artist are unbearably wearying, sometimes as if they still offer unique returns – usually with empathetic musicians, such as BEN WEBSTER, HARRY EDISON and BENNY CARTER here. A few live takes include some shaky snatches from Norman Granz' Jazz at the Philharmonic shows featuring Holiday.

Humes, Helen

(Born Louisville, Kentucky, June 23, 1913; died Santa Monica, California, September 9, 1981)

A major jazz singer with a minor reputation, Helen Humes has latterly come to be recognised as a vocal talent of genuine character and distinction, working a personal territory poised between graceful jazz improvising and r & b. Long associated with COUNT BASIE, Humes was a singer of as much natural exuberance, clarity and easy swing as ELLA FITZGERALD, but often able to impart more spin to a song, and give each one an appropriate timbre, frequently heavily influenced by the blues. In the 1970s she was rediscovered following a successful appearance at the Newport Jazz Festival, and toured widely in her last years.

Helen Humes was influenced by Ethel Waters at first, and her career began precociously early, with a recording session for the Okeh label when she was just 14. Working with dance bands in the 1930s, she was discovered by Count Basie at the beginning of his band's upward curve in 1938, replacing a briefly employed Billie Holiday. Leaving Basie in 1941 Humes worked with leaders including TEDDY WILSON and ART TATUM, before joining the Norman Granz' Jazz at the Philharmonic tours and being featured as a rhythm and blues artist. Through the 1950s and 1960s she veered between blues shows with artists such as John Lee Hooker and T-Bone Walker, and elegant jazz with vibist RED NORVO. Following the successful 1973 Newport appearance celebrating Count Basie's music, she began to record extensively again.

★*Songs I Like to Sing* (Original Jazz Classics OJC 171)

Humes' best available recording, originally made for the Contemporary label in 1960. She effortlessly negotiates a sophisticated collection of Marty Paich scores for a band of sharp west coast session players including Art Pepper on alto (André Previn is the pianist), and responds to the musicians' relaxed streamlining of the swing idiom. Some of the tracks cut the backup down to a rhythm section plus BEN WEBSTER's tenor, good enough to sound like a dream setting for Humes' alert and supple performances.

Jacquet, Jean-Baptiste 'Illinois'

(Born Broussard, Louisiana, October 31, 1922)
On his night a tenor saxophonist of thrilling power and bluesy elementalism, Illinois Jacquet has always been the kind of musician more likely to drag an audience to its feet than induce it to speculate on the ambiguities of life. His sound is rooted in the blues, and he has the broad, shimmering tone often associated with mid-West horn players, but also a facility in the upper-register harmonics of the tenor that give his music an unexpectedly haunting quality beneath the turmoil. Jacquet is no mere crowd-pleaser. Given the right setting and the right partners, he can be a player of considerable subtle and tonal variety – and for all that his most characteristic sound has stereotyped him, he impressively avoids conveying the sensation that he has done it all a thousand nights before.

Jacquet was born in Louisiana but raised in Houston, Texas, and moved to the west coast in the early 1940s. His rugged approach was already formed, and made him ideal material for the big bands, a suitability that took him through LIONEL HAMPTON's, CAB CALLOWAY's and COUNT BASIE's ensembles inside five years in his early twenties. Jacquet's improvisation on the original recording of Hampton's 'Flying Home' entered jazz legend. Established as a solo star by the end of the 1940s, Jacquet took to touring – as a soloist, and sometimes with his own bands – and pursued this career for the next four decades, occasionally with reunion ensembles led by Hampton.

★*Soul Explosion* (Original Jazz Classics OJC 674)

Though Jacquet was by no means solely a blues performer, his technique and sound were perfectly suited to it and some of his best recordings have stayed close to the idiom. This set pitches him against a good studio band, including Milt Buckner on organ, Frank Foster on tenor and Al Foster on drums, and though the music doesn't break any barriers, it delivers some fundamentals of jazz with barging aplomb.

James, Harry

(Born Albany, Georgia, March 15, 1916; died Las Vegas, July 5, 1983)

In the 1940s there was no jazz musician doing better business than Harry James, not even Louis Armstrong. Having made his reputation with BENNY GOODMAN, James had begun a solo career showcasing his phenomenal technical displays, he had hired Frank Sinatra as his vocalist, married 1940s movie idol Betty Grable and the Columbia record label was unable to locate enough shellac to satisfy the demand for his records. James' shows at this time were built around virtuoso performances on manufactured vehicles such as 'Concerto for Trumpet' and 'Trumpet Rhapsody', and in 1940 his speed of execution was given its most testing exercise on a breakneck 'Flight of the Bumble Bee'.

But though Harry James was a circus act as much as a musician (he had been taught trumpet by his father, unsurprisingly a circus bandleader) he was an improviser too, and his skills and creativity were models to younger players. His talents were apparent as early as nine, when he began playing regularly in his father's band; when barely into his twenties, he had been hired by bandleader Ben Pollack, and was working the New York studios with a fiery style clearly indebted to Louis Armstrong. James had every piece of technical equipment a trumpeter needs – stamina, accuracy, penetrating tone – as well as the speed of thought and sense of shape essential to jazz. Initially arrogant about players with less agility than himself, James soon began to absorb the qualities of more expressive jazz musicians, such as BUCK CLAYTON. In 1937 he joined the booming Benny Goodman band, and stayed with it for two years, during which time he became its primary soloist apart from Goodman himself.

The 1940s was James' decade, and with his acceptance as a pop star, his trumpet sound broadened to include a warmer, more romantic ballad tone. But he refused to update swing with bebop, and if anything his bands of the 1950s turned back to earlier periods of jazz for inspiration, drawing on the materials of the Dixieland revival.

★*The Best of Harry James – The Capitol Years*
(Capitol CDP 798952-2)

James in the mid-1950s with a big studio orchestra and arrangements by Ray Conniff and Neal Hefti among others. The sound is often Basie-like for that reason, but James' playing has taken on a poise and restraint by this time as elegant as at any time in his career, and the contributions of singer Helen Forrest and the great alto saxophonist Willie Smith (the latter notably eloquent on 'In a Sentimental Mood') further enhance it.

Jordan, Louis

(Born Arkansas, July 8, 1908; died Los Angeles, February 4, 1975)
Saxophonist and singer Louis Jordan is most usually remembered now as a forerunner of rock and roll, and the 'jump music' he pioneered in the 1940s was revived in the 1980s in Britain by such bands as the Deep Sea Jivers and the Chevalier Brothers. The motive-power of the music is blues, but Jordan's personality was so strong, his timing so good and his feeling for dance music so commercial that he had a string of hit records in a rhythm and blues style throughout the 1940s and into the 1950s. Originally Jordan had been a swing saxophonist, working with the drummer Chick Webb, but he founded his first jazz-based r & b group, the Tympani Five, in 1938. The band sold a million copies of 'Choo Choo Ch'Boogie'. Jordan experimented with a big band in the 1950s but soon reverted to the Tympani Five lineup. When the rock and roll he had helped create left him behind, Jordan nevertheless continued to tour (working with the Chris Barber band in Britain in the 1960s) and he enjoyed something of a comeback in the 1970s.

★*Best of Louis Jordan* (MCA MCAD 4079)

Jordan's biggest hits from the beginnings of his success in the mid-1940s, featuring some distinctly wacky material and his uninhibited singing, and a lot of the hot, nervy alto style that endeared itself to many much jazzier saxophonists of the period. Energetic, funny, spirited music.

★*Five Guys Named Moe* (Bandstand BDCD 1531)

Late 1940s live material, taken from broadcasts and repackaged with good sound by an Italian label. Classic Tympani Five material such as 'Let the Good Times Roll' and 'Five Guys Named Moe' is featured the way the audiences heard it, and though the music is rougher, it's the best way to catch Jordan's wild impact.

Kenton, Stanley Newcomb 'Stan'

(Born Wichita, Kansas, February 19, 1912; died Los Angeles, August 25, 1979)

Bandleader Stan Kenton, by deciding to avoid most of the conventional ways of organising a jazz big band, wound up with a reputation for hyperbole and pretentiousness that he didn't deserve in his most creative period but probably earned in his later years. Kenton liked massive volume, complex and highly structured works, references to contemporary classical music, and orchestras in excess of 40 players when he could afford them. But he was still a commercial bandleader, and was obliged to reconcile his ambitions and his wilfulness with the regular big-band audience. In the 1940s, when he ran his first bands, the elements coexisted successfully – and by extensive radio broadcasting, Kenton became very popular, with fine sidemen such as drummer Shelly Manne and saxophonist Art Pepper reinforcing the impact. Towards the end of the decade the music became more impressionistic and influenced by the classics (explicit Stravinsky and Ravel), and Kenton began declaring his intentions to be 'progressive jazz', moving between dissonance and conventional resolution in a manner that infuriated the critics of the period.

These ambitious flights, for all their courage and audacity (years before the flowering of 'free jazz' and in a period when only pianist Lennie Tristano showed similar inclinations) did lack integration or musical logic and Kenton went back to more jazz-inclined material in 1952 with excellent soloists such as trombonist Frank Rosolino and saxophonist Lee Konitz. Despite occasional flights into Latin American music and neo-classical extravaganzas such as the Neophonic Orchestra, Kenton mostly maintained this side of his work for the rest of his life.

★*New Concepts of Artistry in Rhythm* (Capitol CDP7 92865-2)

One of the best of all Kenton bands, recorded in Chicago in 1952, and featuring Art Pepper, Maynard Ferguson, Frank Rosolino and others. Kenton had just ditched his flat-out 'progressive jazz' policy, but the 'Prologue' here finds him in typical hectoring mood, lecturing his public on his intentions and ham-fistedly emphasising them with illustrations from the players. After that things warm up, notably with excellent arrangements of 'Young Blood' and 'Swing House' by Gerry Mulligan, and a vivacious rendition of an Afro-Cuban piece, 'Taboo', as a feature for Frank Rosolino and Lee Konitz.

★*The Complete Holman and Russo Charts* (Mosaic MD4 136)

William Russo and Bill Holman were Stan Kenton's most creative arrangers and composers, bridging the territories of a dance-band-influenced jazz looking back to the swing era, and notions bordering on a Europeanised art-music. As such, this big set presents an intriguing survey of the curious chemistry of Kenton's success, with some of Russo's and Holman's adaptations of jazz-standard forms still sounding remarkably fresh. There's some fine soloing from Frank Rosolino, and more intelligent variations from Lee Konitz.

Lunceford, James Melvin 'Jimmie'

(Born Fulton, Mississippi, June 6, 1902; died Seaside, Oregon, July 12, 1947)

The star bandleading names of the swing era passed down by popular jazz history are ELLINGTON, BASIE and BENNY GOODMAN. Between them, the three embraced impressionistic art, solo-led energy and sheer well-drilled panache. But Jimmie Lunceford's band was in the same league at the height of the 1930s dance-hall era. Internal disputes over money within the band, which led to the departure of some of its most creative influences, and Lunceford's early death, denied it the historical prominence it deserved.

Lunceford's band was one of the most sought after and successful of the period. It was probably the best organised and most disciplined of any of the black bands of the first period of swing – not only musically, but in presentation as well, with a slick repertoire of coordinated movements, juggling with instruments, close-harmony singing and novelty routines. But Lunceford and his chief arranger Sy Oliver created dramatic contexts for a group of striking soloists, imparted highly original new twists to other bands' specialities (their treatments of some Ellington classics are particularly impressive) and gave the band a tightness and polish that nobody bettered. If its memory has not survived well, the fact that it was mostly locked rhythmically into the two-beat patterns of the earliest jazz, rather than Basie's gliding four-four, may have contributed to a dated sound today.

*Stomp It Off (GRP/MCA 16082)

The beginning of the Lunceford success story in 1934, when the band was hungry, enthusiastic, and drilled like a circus act. But all surviving notions that Lunceford simply played unoriginal music better than most of his rivals don't pass a listening to some of the arrangements, which were distinctly ahead of their time, particularly in the sax-section writing, which both entwines the players in vibrant and unexpected harmonies and catapults them soloistically. Sy Oliver's arranging skills were remarkably advanced, noticeably on the title track, and Willie Smith's alto-sax and clarinet-playing entitled him to a much bigger reputation as a 1930s alto star.

McKinney, William 'Bill'

(Born Cynthiana, Kentucky, September 17, 1895; died Cynthiana, October 14, 1969)

William McKinney didn't have a great deal to do with the considerable success of the band that bore his name in the 1920s – it came to be most regularly associated with the names of DON REDMAN and eventually BENNY CARTER. But McKinney's Cottonpickers was an early example of the emerging sophistication of jazz orchestra arrangement, as the urbane predictability of the early 1920s dance-band sound began to be displaced by charts driven by the rhythmic and melodic ideas of the New Orleans jazz soloists such as Armstrong. Though its life was short, it turned out to be a crucial element in a major transformation in jazz.

The primary influence from this direction in the McKinney band was arranger Don Redman, formerly with FLETCHER HENDERSON, though trumpeter John Nesbitt was an excellent and underrated writer for the band as well. Redman arrived in 1927, hired by Detroit bandleader and entrepreneur Jean Goldkette to reinvent the enterprising novelty dance band from Ohio led by William McKinney. The result was a string of pop hits including 'Four of Five Times' and 'Cherry', queues round the block at Goldkette's Graystone Ballroom, and a series of fine recordings with leading jazz solo artists including COLEMAN HAWKINS. When Redman formed his own band in 1931, trumpeter REX STEWART and saxophonist Benny Carter came to dominate it for a while. The Cottonpickers broke up in 1934, but McKinney continued in the music business.

★*The Band Don Redman Built (1928–1930)* (Bluebird ND 90517)

Cottonpickers material during the Redman years, displaying not only the sheen of that fine arranger's charts, but also the excellent Nesbitt's, on such glossy examples as 'Peggy' and 'Nobody's Sweetheart'. For the unwary, this certainly doesn't sound like any proto-COUNT BASIE outfit – the rhythm section still features a banjo and a tuba and it proceeds with a huffing deliberation, despite Cuba Austin's enterprising drumming. But the arrangements have energy and precision, and the impact of the young Benny Carter is a striking component of the later sessions. Despite Bluebird's NoNoise remastering system, however, some tracks here retain an irritating surface squeal.

McRae, Carmen

(Born New York, April 8, 1922)

Carmen McRae has displayed one of the most personal vocal styles in jazz for over 40 years, a disciple of Billie Holiday who nevertheless retains a characteristic brusque independence that marks her out. Like Holiday, she gets inside the lyrics of songs, her stage personality has the strength of Nina Simone's but with an acid wit in place of the defiance, and her rhythmic originality constantly changes the pace and spacing of standard songs.

Originally a pianist – and still a good one – she had a precocious start in the music business by writing the song 'Dream of Life' when she was 16, which Billie Holiday recorded. She then joined the bands of BENNY CARTER, COUNT BASIE and Mercer Ellington in rapid succession in the 1940s, briefly being married to the drummer Kenny Clarke during that period. After club jobs in the early 1950s, McRae began recording in 1953, and has worked with excellent piano trios (Ray Bryant and Duke Pearson have been among the pianists) ever since.

★Here to Stay (GRP/MCA 16102)

One of the best representations of earlier McRae material to have appeared recently, her recordings in the 1950s being generally neglected on reissues. This collection merges material from 'Special Request', a small-group session that included Kenny Clarke on drums, and 1959's 'Something to Swing About', in which she fronted an excellent studio band including sax-ophonists Zoot Sims and Phil Woods. McRae makes every sound count, and constantly and unpredictably shifts the emotional tone from the laid-back to the lapel-grabbing. Superb demonstrations of the jazz vocalist's art.

McShann, James Columbus 'Jay'

(Born Oklahoma, January 12, 1909)

McShann is principally known to younger jazz audiences as Charlie Parker's boss shortly before the saxophonist took the music world by storm. A bandleader with a strong enthusiasm for blues, McShann was both a powerful boogie-influenced pianist and a shrewd judge of his fellow-musicians, and his bands were excellent examples of Kansas City danceability and directness. McShann began touring with other leaders from the mid-1930s but formed his own quintet (with Charlie Parker on alto) in 1937, and a bigger band in 1940. This outfit displayed a good deal of unremarkable blues singing but the fascinating beginnings of Charlie Parker's mature alto style, as well as the other members of a first-class rhythm section in bassist Gene Ramey and drummer Gus Johnson. After the war McShann ran smaller bands, still blues-oriented, with BASIE's vocalist Jimmy Witherspoon making several appearances. McShann energetically defended the memory of Kansas City jazz at festivals and concert performances worldwide, and his talents became more widely known through his performance in the excellent 1978 jazz movie *Last of the Blue Devils.*

★*Jay McShann Orchestra. Blues From Kansas City*
(MCA/GRP 16142)

A good representation of both the McShann band in the late 1930s and the riffs-and-blues Kansas City big-band approach. The ensembles sound fine, punching out the chords in the Basie manner, but it's inevitably Charlie Parker's presence that holds the interest, particularly since Walter Brown's blues vocals are virtually indistinguishable from one another. Parker sounds in complete control, his tone and the shaping of his phrases still close to LESTER YOUNG, but beginning to brim with the passing notes and deceptively casual fills that upended jazz shortly afterwards.

Moten, Bennie

(Born Kansas City, November 13, 1894; died Kansas City, April 2, 1935)

Bennie Moten's contribution to jazz history is often demoted to the footnote that by prematurely dying he created the COUNT BASIE Orchestra. But Moten – a pianist and one-time baritone horn player – was a bandleader of considerable resourcefulness, and was leading a successful outfit of his own in Kansas City, a town that saw a busy, and often mobster-dominated nightclub scene emerge from the dance boom of the post-First World War years.

In the early 1920s the Moten band was an unsteady confection of ragtime and the special effects of the Original Dixieland Jazz Band. Later in the decade it became increasingly influenced by New Orleans music, and by 1925 the group was growing in size and blending east coast ensemble effects with an engaging earthy bluesiness, its repertoire designed for dancing. It first recorded for Okeh as a sextet, had grown to a ten-piece by the time of its first Victor recordings (1926) and by the end of the decade included pianist William 'Count' Basie from Walter Page's Blue Devils, a rival Kansas band that eventually merged with Moten's. Trumpeter Oran 'Hot Lips' Page, guitarist/composer Eddie Durham and singer Jimmy Rushing all followed, and eventually the then COLEMAN HAWKINS-like BEN WEBSTER. Moten's band thus changed from a down-to-earth dance band to a sophisticated larger orchestra, with complex arrangements being provided by Eddie Durham, plus additional material from saxophonist BENNY CARTER.

★*Basie Beginnings* (Bluebird ND 90403)

Recordings by the Moten Orchestra from 1929–1932, and featuring Count Basie, Ben Webster, Hot Lips Page and others. The disc includes classics of the larger Moten band's repertoire including 'Moten Swing' (which was later to be frequently featured by Basie), 'Toby', 'Blue Room' and 'Prince of Wails'. The last three demonstrate how far the Moten band's arrangements had progressed, with vigorous and intricate ensemble parts for the saxophones, and alternations of contrasting and unison writing for the brass and reeds together, as in 'Blue Room'. The sound of Ben Webster is already sumptuous and implacable.

South (1926–29) (Bluebird ND 83139)

Earlier Moten explorations, less well served by the passage of the years and more of a set for the determined enthusiast. There's a lot of approximate playing and the vaudeville influence is strong, though trumpeter Lammar Wright has his moments.

Norvo, Red (Kenneth Norville)

(Born Beardstown, Illinois, March 31, 1908)
For over 40 years various small bands led by the vibraharpist Red Norvo have been performing a concentrated distillation of elegant euphoria to reverential silences from the world's jazz audiences. Norvo is a pioneer of the use of the vibraharp in jazz, and has chosen musicians over the years who have helped him sustain a music-box world of glistening harmonies, sly quotes, and gently rippling pools of sound against all the odds from an increasingly amplified popular music. Norvo, who started his career in a marimba band in the mid-1920s, formed his first trio in 1949, assuming that even the sextet he led before was an uneconomic proposition in the music-business squeeze of the day. One of his early bassists was Charles Mingus, and that tempestuous individual still managed to fit with relative peace into Norvo's chosen formula which celebrated Broadway tunes, jazz classics and technical showpieces such as FATS WALLER's 'Jitterbug Waltz'.

Just a Mood (Bluebird/BMG ND 86278)

Material from two key Norvo dates in 1954 and 1957 on this classic Bluebird compilation, the latter being one of the best recording sessions the vibist ever participated in. The 1957 produced four long tracks ('The Night Is Blue', 'Easy on the Eye', 'Just a Mood', Sunrise Blues') in which a terrific band featuring Ben Webster on tenor, Harry Edison on trumpet and the delightful Jimmy Rowles on piano, not only empathised with Norvo's notions of restrained swing and melodic delicacy but also displayed their unique virtues to the full.

O'Day, Anita

(Born Chicago, December 18, 1919)

Anita O'Day, whose performance (and immense feathery hat) provided some of the most enduring musical episodes and 1950s imagery of the celebrated *Jazz on a Summer's Day* Newport movie, possessed at her peak a mixture of cool vivacity, immaculate technique (the most convoluted writing couldn't throw her) and original improviser's skills, both melodically and rhythmically. Though her influences included BILLIE HOLIDAY and ELLA FITZGERALD (and her best work is a remarkable blend of Holiday's subtlety of inflection and Fitzgerald's ebullience) she has remained a highly distinctive artist who has always rejected girl-singer stereotypes, even up to the point in recent times where her pitching has become more erratic and her stamina reduced – the belated consequences of early narcotic addiction that almost killed her. O'Day began in the entertainment business as a contestant in America's grisly 'dancethons' in the mid-1930s, then took various nightclub jobs in which singing was secondary. She joined drummer Gene Krupa's band as featured vocalist in 1941, and by the mid-1940s was highly regarded as the singer with Stan Kenton's demanding orchestra. O'Day influenced several subsequent Kenton vocalists, such as JUNE CHRISTY and Chris Connor.

★*Tea for Two* (Moon 023 CD)

Material from the 1950s and 1960s, featuring O'Day with trios, an ideal setting for her probing, detailed and ironic style. The title track is a tune long associated with the singer, following her improvisation on it in *Jazz on a Summer's Day*.

Redman, Donald Matthew 'Don'

(Born Piedmont, West Virginia, July 29, 1900; died New York, November 30, 1964)

Don Redman was a cornerstone of the swing era, but he disappeared into staff and studio work from the 1950s and more famous names of the big-band years eclipsed his. But Redman, a multi-instrumentalist and a singer as well as an arranger, was one of the first to appreciate that the characteristics of the jazz solo as developed by improvisers such as Louis Armstrong and Sidney Bechet could be adapted to arrangements for larger groups, completely transforming the rhythmic characteristics of dance-band charts and bringing the age of swing nearer.

Redman was a schooled musician who met FLETCHER HENDERSON in New York in 1923 when Henderson was beginning to put studio bands together for recording sessions. When a Henderson group was offered the Club Alabam for live shows, Redman came in as chief arranger, enriching and enlivening the sound of the band even before the arrival of COLEMAN HAWKINS and Louis Armstrong. Armstrong's presence gave Redman plenty to think about, and he developed his skills further with McKinney's Cottonpickers, an ordinary outfit that he and trumpeter/arranger John Nesbitt brought to life. Through the 1930s, Redman led his own bands, but in 1941 he began to operate a freelance arranging business, offering his services to many swing stars, including HARRY JAMES and JIMMIE LUNCEFORD. In the 1950s he arranged for innumerable session and theatre orchestras, as well as being musical director for Pearl Bailey.

The Chronological Don Redman 1931–33 and 1933–36
(Classics 543 and 553)

Two discs dealing with Redman's career after the Cottonpickers, the first featuring one of his all-time classics, 'Chant of the Weed'. Apart from discs under the McKinney band's name, these are the most revealing examples of Redman's talent at work in the 1930s, and the lineups feature such inventive performers as HENRY 'RED' ALLEN on trumpet, the underrated vocalist Harlan Lattimore and some tap-dancing from Bill 'Bojangles' Robinson.

Reinhardt, Jean Baptiste 'Django'

(Born Charleroi, Belgium, January 23, 1910; died Fontainebleau, May 16, 1953)
In a period in which European players were rarely commended by the pioneering Americans for much more than diligent plagiarism, Belgian gypsy guitarist Django Reinhardt impressed the

originators as the first European jazz artist of genius and his reputation has not dulled with time. Though self-taught and unable to read music, Reinhardt was the complete jazz guitarist. He executed singing fast lines with a precision that made the notes glitter, his driving chord-playing lifted his fellow-musicians with its swing and bounce, his playing of trills was like a pianist's, and his melodic construction was almost infallibly graceful. The fastest tempos could not unsettle Reinhardt, and he would launch into uptempo solos with a breakneck momentum that left him no room for coasting. But his ballad-playing, by total contrast, could be hypnotically poignant – rare for such a powerful technician.

Reinhardt was the son of a gypsy entertainer, and he learned both violin and guitar as a child. In one of jazz's most famous acts of fate, Reinhardt lost the use of two fingers of his left hand in a caravan fire, was forced to abandon the violin, and developed a technique for his second instrument better than that of all fully functioning jazz guitarists of his day. He loved Louis Armstrong's, Joe Venuti's and DUKE ELLINGTON's music from records, worked with various French semi-dance orchestras in the early 1930s, then formed his famous Quintet du Hot Club de France in 1934, with violinist STEPHANE GRAPPELLI. The QHCF recorded extensively, and Reinhardt's contribution to it was quickly recognised as ranking with the finest improvisation since the beginning of recorded jazz.

★*Swing In Paris* (Affinity AFS 1003)

A five-disc set, and a very comprehensive overview of Reinhardt's work from 1936 to 1940. Both BENNY CARTER and COLEMAN HAWKINS were working in Europe in the mid-1930s and appear on these discs in some of the most famous sessions involving Reinhardt, and trombonist Dicky Wells – then touring with the Teddy Hill band – plays some of his most telling solos on record. Violinist Eddie South, a more rugged player than Stephane Grappelli, also tantalisingly demonstrates why he was probably Reinhardt's true violin soul-mate. There is also plenty of the famous Hot Club group, Reinhardt's lines rocketing out of the amiable four-square backing. This is the set for serious students of Django, dealing with the era in which his powers were at their most blinding.

Bruxelles/Paris (Musidisc 403222)

A single disc covering later years, but putting Reinhardt in some interesting settings. Hot Club music gets its chance, with a re-formed version from 1947, there's broadcast material from the Club St Germain and some superb collaborations between Reinhardt and the excellent pianist Martial Solal, recorded only months before the guitarist's death.

Rich, Bernard 'Buddy'

(Born New York, June 30, 1917; died Los Angeles, April 2, 1987) Buddy Rich may have been one of jazz music's circus acts, but he was among its best ones. People who otherwise disliked his brash, frantic big-band style would watch his drumming mesmerised. His percussion introductions established a pitch of excitement that made the eventual arrival of the ensemble a climax rather than a beginning, his left-hand patterns were executed with the speed of two-hand rolls, and his solos were a blur. Rich's reputation in his later years was established by the big band he led from the mid-1960s to the end of his life – an ensemble tailored to please both older swing fans and younger audiences by including both traditional material and fusion music – but he could on occasion be a fine accompanist to good soloists, a role he wasn't often invited to play. Rich's career was a hangover from the dance-hall euphoria of the swing craze, and he never lost his commitment to direct, spectacular, pyrotechnical entertainment.

Rich was a vaudeville performer more or less as soon as he was weaned, and appeared onstage with his parents as a drumming toddler, dubbed 'Baby Traps'. He was dancing and playing on Broadway when he was four and was a bandleader at 11. Through his twenties, Rich occupied the drum chair in bands led by BUNNY BERIGAN, HARRY JAMES, ARTIE SHAW and TOMMY DORSEY, and decided to start his own big band in the 1940s when everyone else was giving up. Rich's outfit didn't last either, and until the end of the 1950s he played for Norman Granz' Jazz at the Philharmonic and almost became a Sinatra-inclined singer. Rich's second attempt at starting a big band at an inopportune time – in the mid-1960s rock renaissance – unexpectedly took off because of a wide-ranging repertoire, and it toured to enthusiastic audiences for the rest of Rich's life.

★*Illusion* (Sequel NXT CD 181)

A three-CD set, and a broad sweep of Rich's work from the mid-1940s to the 1970s, featuring some sensational musicians including Dizzy Gillespie, Charlie Parker, LESTER YOUNG, NAT COLE and COUNT BASIE and including examples of circus-act Rich (exchanges with Gene Krupa, Jazz at the Philharmonic shout-ups), guest-artist Rich (with a good British band) and Rich the sensitive musician. When Rich died, critic Whitney Balliett speculated on how much more respected the drummer's musicianship might have been had he recorded as a sideman with more small groups, and the tracks here with a 1954 Lionel Hampton ensemble reveal just how crisply propulsive and creative he could be in a more modest context.

★*Time Being* (Bluebird/BMG ND 86459)

Several items by a roaring Rich big band caught in motion at Ronnie Scott's Club, with both the strength of the arrangements and the leader's devastating drumming in evidence on a long workout on the title track and crisp versions of 'Straight No Chaser' and 'Dancing Men'. The rest is from a group of RCA albums of the late 1960s and early 1970s, and there are some rugged, early Coltraneish solos from Pat LaBarbara, about the only musician in the band who manages to surface above the leader's storming percussion.

★*No Jive* (BMG Novus 01241 66061-2)

A disc drawn from three RCA albums – *Plays and Plays and Plays*, *Speak No Evil* and *Different Drummer* – mostly dating from the later 1970s, including two fairly anonymous extended outings, 'Piece of the Road Suite' and a medley of 'Storm at Sunup' and 'Love Me Now'. Rich's band turned most music into a firecracker display without illuminating it, but Bob Mintzer's arrangements for the faster music here do deserve as much acclaim as Rich's own extraordinary drumming, and perform much the same job.

Russell, Luis

(Born Panama, August 6, 1902; died New York, December 11, 1963)

Luis Russell's long association with Louis Armstrong may have been his most commercially enterprising work, but he led one of the best jazz bands of the 1920s, a stylish blend of New Orleans earthiness and dance-band grace, featuring some memorable soloists including HENRY 'RED' ALLEN and clarinettist Albert Nicholas, and a superb drummer in Paul Barbarin.

Russell moved from Panama to New Orleans on a lottery win, and worked for several of the city's jazz soloists as a pianist. But it was in Harlem that Russell made his mark, bringing a group of leading New Orleans players, including Allen and Nicholas, to the Saratoga Club. Its millionaire owner Casper Holstein gave the club, lock, stock and barrel, to Russell on an impulse, and it supported Louis Armstrong on occasion, as well as augmenting its solo strength with trombonist J.C. Higginbotham and altoist Charlie Holmes. Russell also featured one of the most propulsive string bassists of early jazz in Pops Foster. Armstrong rediscovered the band in the mid-1930s and hired it as his backing group, but the commercial pressure to play more predictable material behind the star, and the ruthlessness of Armstrong's manager Joe Glaser led to it folding in the 1940s. By the end of that decade Russell retired from the business. He ran shops, chauffeured and taught music in his remaining years.

★Savoy Shout (JSP CD 308)

Excellent compilation of Russell material from 1929 and 1930. The characteristic feel of the ensembles still owes a lot to the New Orleans polyphonic front line, and the arrangements are basic. But Henry Allen's trumpet is a constant reminder of what a striking and original contemporary to Armstrong he was, J.C. Higginbotham is freewheeling and fast enough almost to suggest a bop trombonist, and Charlie Holmes and Albert Nicholas are thrilling reed players. Excellent and absorbing insights into 1920s jazz evolution.

Russell, Charles Elsworth 'Pee Wee'

(Born Maple Wood, Missouri, March 27, 1906; died Alexandria, Virginia, February 15, 1969)

Pee Wee Russell was one of the great jazz clarinet originals, with a deliberately disjointed, impressionistic style quite different to most of the practitioners of the instrument in either New Orleans music or swing. Usually associated with the various Chicago-style bands led by Eddie Condon, Russell delivered a music that seemed all the quirkier for being contained in such frequently formulaic settings, and he convincingly demonstrated his unconventionality towards the end of his career when he began recording far more modern material, lending it all his usual crabwise eloquence.

Russell was one of the busiest musicians in jazz in the late 1920s and early 1930s, recording extensively, working with Red Nichols' Five Pennies, and living hard in the nightclubs, to the extent of acquiring an alcohol addiction that changed both his physical appearance (his unique, tramlined physiognomy was commented on almost as often as his musicality) and his playing. By the end of the 1930s he was a regular performer in the Chicago small-band style, a living antithesis of the faultless, perfectly lubricated clarinet styles of stars such as BENNY GOODMAN and ARTIE SHAW. Russell's eccentric appearance seemed to sum up the offbeat jazz improviser in the 1950s, his picture appeared everywhere, and he became a minor celebrity, often for reasons that distressed him. As if to prove that if he could be physically typecast he would resist it musically, Russell formed a piano-less quartet in 1962 and also made a record with progressive arranger Oliver Nelson. But he returned to the Dixieland style in his last years.

★*Jazz Reunion* (Candid CS 9020)

Pee Wee Russell isn't represented well on CD so far, and he's such an oddity that his best work might still be a while coming. But this pairing with COLEMAN HAWKINS from 1961, beautifully driven by Jo Jones on drums, serves as a fine example of how creative Russell was, particularly in such stark contrast as that provided by the unswerving Hawkins. Russell squawks, pulls at notes like a bird trying to dislodge a worm, veers across registers and generally stamps his remarkable trademark all over the set.

Shavers, Charles James 'Charlie'

(Born New York, August 3, 1917; died New York, July 8, 1971)
Often regarded as the most technically complete trumpeter of the swing age, Charlie Shavers made many of his most effortlessly skilful contributions to the work of other leaders and never made the public impact ROY ELDRIDGE did. A humorous and easygoing man, he frequently clowned onstage, another idiosyncrasy that made his talent deceptive.

Shavers was a master trumpeter by his late teens, having worked as a dancer, banjoist and pianist in Harlem clubs in earlier years. He joined Lucky Millinder's band in 1937, and John Kirby a year later, writing several hits for the latter, including 'Undecided' and 'Pastel Blue'. After the Second World War Shavers joined TOMMY DORSEY and remained with him for 11 years, with breaks for the Jazz at the Philharmonic tours, in which Shavers and Roy Eldridge did their best to break the windows with implausible top notes. Shavers led bands of his own from 1956, but returned when a memorial band bearing Dorsey's name was formed, mixing his contribution between poised and shapely trumpet improvisations and vaudevillian antics. Shavers died the same week as Louis Armstrong, and he requested that his trumpet mouthpiece be buried with the older man.

★Live (Black and Blue 59 302)

Shavers' own small groups of the 1950s and 1960s aren't currently reissued, but this set from the year before his death captures a little of his old élan. The rhythm section is ordinary, and saxophonist Budd Johnson (with whom Shavers worked throughout the 1960s) is prominently featured, but until better material comes along, it'll do.

Shaw, Artie (Arthur Jacob Arshawsky)

(Born New York, May 23, 1910)
Clarinettist Artie Shaw produced some of the most substantial music of the swing era, but his contemporary BENNY GOODMAN diverted most of the limelight that this complex and gifted

musician might have attracted. Shaw's career was full of false starts because his commitment to the music business was ambivalent. A fine instrumentalist with a technique not far behind Goodman's and more originality of line at times, Shaw nevertheless constantly interrupted himself with sudden decisions to learn the guitar, write books, investigate psychoanalysis.

Shaw was a saxophonist originally, then worked in dance bands as a saxophonist and clarinettist in Cleveland, Ohio, returning to New York for recording sessions in the mid-1930s that led to highly successful collaborations with BILLIE HOLIDAY and BUNNY BERIGAN, appearing on Berigan's celebrated first recording of 'I Can't Get Started'. In 1937 Shaw put together a big band of his own, and had such a substantial hit with a tune called 'Begin the Beguine' that he began the first of several semi-retirements, occasioned by doubts about the hype attendant on showbusiness success. In 1940 he re-formed the band, and developed a small group within it called the Gramercy Five (featuring an excellent pianist who doubled on harpsichord, Johnny Guarnieri) with which he recorded some of his most creative playing. Shaw rebuilt the group after the war, with trumpeter ROY ELDRIDGE in a prominent role, but increasingly turned to literary work from the 1950s on. He has occasionally returned to bandleading since.

Shaw's intelligence and awareness of modernism marked him out among swing-band stars, and his courage in confronting the racial issue in the music business led to his hiring black artists (notably Billie Holiday) at a time when mixed bands were rare.

Begin the Beguine (Bluebird/BMG ND 86274)

The title track, Shaw's biggest hit, is featured on this compilation from his Victor recordings with four bands between 1938 and 1941. Quickly apparent is Shaw's disinclination to use the riff-packed crescendos and calculated hysteria common in the swing period, favouring instead more textured ensemble sounds and at times the use of strings, bordering on the 'symphonic jazz' explored by others later. Trumpeter Billy Butterfield, a strong and spirited performer, is a prominent feature of these recordings; the tunes also include 'Frenesi' (almost as big a hit as 'Begin the Beguine') and 'Stardust'. There are also appearances from Billie Holiday ('Any Old Time') and BUDDY RICH.

★*The Complete Gramercy Five Sessions* (Bluebird/BMG ND 87637)

The 1940 and 1945 versions of Shaw's Gramercy Five, confirming the general impression of Shaw that both his own playing and the jazz content of his music were at their most extended in these small groups. The compilation includes 'Summit Ridge Drive', which was a hit for Shaw and displays considerable imagination in the clarinet soloing, as well as the more modern-sounding 'Gentle Grifter' and 'Sad Sack' from a later session, featuring trumpeter Roy Eldridge, pianist Dodo Marmarosa (better known as a bop-oriented Parker disciple) and guitarist Barney Kessel. More punchy Butterfield playing, but a few of the pieces air contrivances that haven't lasted well.

★*The Last Recordings* (Musicmasters/Limelight 65071-2)

Interesting two-disc set from 1954, with uncharacteristic Shaw collaborators including bebop bassist Tommy Potter, guitarist Tal Farlow and pianist Hank Jones. Shaw's clarinet still sounds lissome and inventive, and though there's an unresolved quality to this music, it's a superior small-group session on the borders of swing and the music that displaced it.

Smith, Stuff (Hezekiah Leroy Gordon)

(Born Portsmouth, Ohio, August 14, 1909; died Munich, Germany, September 25, 1967)

Violinist Stuff Smith once announced that he didn't consider it amiss to hit a violin string the way a drummer hits a cymbal. That was the abiding impression his music left: a rough, assertive, percussive way of playing an instrument more usually performed in jazz with Stephane Grappelli's lilting lyricism. Smith brought far more of the forthright and unsentimental qualities of the origins of jazz to his playing, and he still sounds exuberant, good-humoured and forcefully rhythmic – as if he were a New Orleans trumpeter who had adapted the style to an unfamiliar instrument.

This wasn't always the characteristic of Smith's playing, because he emerged with the Alphonso Trent dance orchestra and was expected to play in a mellifluous manner. But Louis

Armstrong's sound greatly influenced Smith's conception, and as his style hardened he met trumpeter Jonah Jones, formed a band with him and in 1936 was playing the 52nd Street clubs in New York, where he was a considerable success. Smith was too temperamental and unpredictable to follow an orderly development of his career, but after a low period in the 1950s, he began to tour extensively the following decade.

★*Live in Paris* (France's Concert FCD 120)

The fine French pianist George Arvanitas turns out to be a perfect foil for Smith, as he has been for innumerable visiting Americans, on these takes from a European trip in 1965. Smith's baleful jauntiness is in full flow, though other ingredients in the compilation featuring some less than sparkling French performers blunt the edge here and there. Not enough Smith material has entered the catalogues yet.

Stewart, Rex William

(Born Philadelphia, February 22, 1907; died Los Angeles, September 7, 1967)

If one of the primary contributions of jazz to the music of the 20th century has been to break the stranglehold of European art-music's preoccupation with the 'pure' tempered scale on what's considered legitimate technique, cornettist Rex Stewart is a remarkable example of how expressive the jazz vocabulary is. A self-taught performer of considerable verve and fire, Stewart's speciality was the bent-note 'half-valve' effect, in which the register-shifting valve is only depressed for part of its proper distance, sometimes reducing regular intervals to quarter-tones. This device and his vivacious textural effects generally made Stewart a dramatic example of the 'vocalised' instrumental method. Colourful improvisers were rarely lost on DUKE ELLINGTON, who hired Stewart for his orchestra in 1934 and built a good deal of music around him.

Stewart began by shadowing Louis Armstrong's every move, and he replaced Armstrong in the mid-1920s FLETCHER HENDERSON Orchestra. But though he didn't possess Armstrong's command of the shape of an improvised line, he became a jazz character actor for a palette of special effects and with Ellington the cornettist and the musical setting struck an almost perfect balance. In the 1950s, when Stewart left Ellington, he worked extensively as a soloist, and also began a parallel career as an evocative jazz writer for *Downbeat*.

★*Finesse* (Affinity CD AFS 1029)

Though there isn't a great deal of Stewart material to be had on CD (outside of Ellington collections) this compilation from 1934, 1939 and 1940 is an excellent starting point. The 1939 takes find Stewart in Paris along with clarinettist Barney Bigard and guitarist DJANGO REINHARDT, all three reaching deep into their romantic imaginations for the slow title track. The 1940 tracks are Ellington small-group sessions with Billy Kyle on piano and Dave Tough at the drums. Stewart blasts as if trying to blow a fire out, and BEN WEBSTER's tenor and Bigard's clarinet balance his ferocity with calmly convoluted solos.

Strayhorn, William 'Billy'

(Born Dayton, Ohio, November 29, 1915; died New York, May 31, 1967)

One name takes care of Billy Strayhorn's musical career – DUKE ELLINGTON. But if Strayhorn devoted his life to working for Ellington, his contribution to some of the most enduring of all jazz has been incalculable; particularly so because from the point where 'Ellington-Strayhorn' began to be the regular credit for many of the band's pieces, it was almost impossible to tell where Ellington ended and Strayhorn began. Strayhorn compounded this mystery by staying out of the public eye, and refusing to divulge exactly his part in these collaborations. Several Strayhorn themes have joined the canon of jazz immortals, including 'Chelsea Bridge', 'Lush Life' and 'Take the A Train', and he was also a fine pianist in a style very similar to Ellington's.

Strayhorn began writing for Ellington in 1939, shortly after ending a substantial musical education that gave him a sophisticated grounding in composition, arrangement and piano-playing.

He submitted some work to the bandleader that impressed Ellington so much that he shortly afterwards became a member of the permanent staff – though as a lyric writer at first. Strayhorn's compositions regularly found their way into the band's repertoire after that, and 'Take the A Train' became its signature tune. Virtually all of Strayhorn's significant work with Ellington appears on Ellington-led records, though he occasionally led Ellington small groups on his own.

★Great Times (Original Jazz Classics OJC 108)

A 1950 set featuring both Ellington and Strayhorn at the keyboards, with a variety of bassists and the graceful Jo Jones on drums. 'Take the A Train' is there, and though Ellington dominates and Strayhorn proves that his ingenuity is more expressive on paper than at the keyboard, it's a genuine curiosity illuminating one of the most mysterious and magical relationships in music.

Tate, Buddy (George Holmes)

(Born Sherman, Texas, February 22, 1913)
Few of the swing giants who learned about life on the road with the big bands the hard way are still around to tell the tale now, much less play that music with the enthusiasm and casual lyricism that was so pivotal to its lasting charm. But Buddy Tate, a swing tenorist out of the mould of COLEMAN HAWKINS and Herschel Evans, still does it, and if his work has grown more tremulous with age, it continues to be a series of aural snapshots of a vanished era of jazz. Tate's sound in his prime was big and luxurious, his vibrato like a heat-haze, his beat imperious.

Like many southern saxophonists of the 1930s, Tate learned in the travelling territory bands, including those run by saxophonist Andy Kirk. Tate had originally met star BASIE saxophonist Herschel Evans on this circuit, and when Evans suddenly died in 1939, Basie called him in. Tate stayed with Basie for most of the 1940s, then in a variety of groups following the brief break-up of the Basie band, before he became resident musician at Harlem's Celebrity Club and held down the job for the next two decades.

Though tastes changed in the 1970s, Tate found work on the festival circuits in the States and in Europe, often with trombonist Al Grey.

Much of Buddy Tate's best playing can be heard on 1940s Basie discs, and some of his better subsequent work is on vinyl, but there are one or two solo exceptions.

★*Kansas City Joys* (Sonet SNTCD 716)

Tate in the mid-1970s, with a rhythm section including legendary Kansas bandleader/pianist JAY McSHANN, and a fine second tenor in Paul Quinichette. McShann's bands always owed a good deal to Basie, so there's a strong flavour of that outfit's horn voicing here, but everyone plays with the laid-back charm appropriate to veteran experts shuffling the pack once again.

Tatum, Arthur 'Art'

(Born Toledo, Ohio, October 13, 1909; died Los Angeles, November 5, 1956)

Very few jazz musicians have caused classical virtuosi to visit nightclubs and watch them open-mouthed (it's not self-evidently a recommendation anyway) but if nothing else it was certainly a testament to pianist Art Tatum's extraordinary technical command that concert artists such as Gieseking and Horowitz did exactly that. Tatum was the fastest and most elaborate jazz pianist there has ever been, with a style originally derived from stride musician FATS WALLER but which soon evolved into a shower of sound in which the harmonic basis of the song was spontaneously altered, there were constantly surprising key changes and eventual resolutions by the most circuitous of routes and the perpetual contrasts between left and right hand conveyed the impression of more than one improviser at work. Tatum was later criticised for sacrificing all material, good or bad, to the meat-mincer of his technique, but he remained within the spirit of the songs more often than he is given credit for.

Throughout the 1930s Tatum cut a succession of excellent recordings, and began sessions for Norman Granz in 1953 which were largely unaccompanied and among his most remarkable work. He also recorded with excellent sidemen in the mid-1950s and appeared to be performing at the peak of his own exacting standards right up to his death.

★*Classic Early Solos 1934–1937* (MCA/GRP 16072)

Twenty tracks recorded for Decca almost at the start of Tatum's studio career. Incomplete, because the precocious and extraordinary 'Tiger Rag' from his first recording session isn't present, but interesting for some of its alternate takes ('When a Woman Loves a Man', 'After You've Gone'), showing how many solutions he could present to the same problem. By the 1937 sessions (including the wonderful 'Gone With the Wind' and 'Sheik of Araby') the pianist's control and discipline are tightening. All this suggests how devastating Tatum's impact must have been when he first emerged. The clean-up on the sound quality is good.

★*Complete Capitol Recordings* Vols. 1 & 2
(Capitol CDP 792 866-2/867-2)

Tatum recorded both solo and trio work for Capitol in 1949, providing some good examples of his ability to break down the significant elements of a tune, rework them separately, build counter-melodies against them, alter the texture and then reassemble the whole lot in tumultuous resolutions. The pianist does exactly this in a version of 'Blue Skies' that nevertheless always retains the tune's identity and shape, and the ordinariness of 'Dancing in the Dark' is transformed by Tatum's treatment of it. Vol. 1 includes two of Tatum's most famous exploits, 'Aunt Hagar's Blues' and 'Willow Weep for Me'.

★*The Tatum Group Masterpieces* Vols. 1 & 8
(Pablo CD 2405-424 and 2405-432)

Tatum wasn't the perfect pianist to collaborate with others, but some of the situations that Norman Granz put him into in the 1950s were surprisingly fruitful. Vol. 8, a recording with BEN WEBSTER shortly before the pianist's death, was one of the best. The contrast between Webster's lazy lyricism and Tatum's energy worked perfectly, and on 'My Ideal' and 'Night and Day' they play well enough to make it a shame this unlikely meeting was such a rarity. Vol. 1, with BENNY CARTER is superb, the saxophonist unfazed in his meticulous polish by Tatum's tidal assault.

★*The Complete Pablo Solo Masterpieces* (Pablo 7PACD-4402-2)

The later group music is best taken in small doses, but the solo work Tatum produced for Norman Granz between 1953 and 1955 is so remarkable that it's hard to pick a winner, and the seven-CD, 125-track boxed set deserves full attention. Tatum cut over half of this material in two days at the beginning of the project, and although his approach to a piece of music had not substantially changed since his debut – he continued to treat any tune with a fine disregard for anybody's notion of what its 'mood' should be – his boldness with tempo has grown yet more cavalier, and the original stride technique has been modified so much that the pulse remains clear even when the vehicle for it changes tack or stops. Equally dramatic is Tatum's control of the timbres of the keyboard. The tunes are almost irrelevant, but the set includes 'Taboo', 'Blue Lou', 'Caravan', 'Aunt Hagar's Blues', 'Makin' Whoopee' and 'Sophisticated Lady'. There's no better Tatum than this, and not much better jazz piano in general.

Teagarden, Weldon John 'Jack'

(Born Vernon, Texas, August 29, 1905; died New Orleans, January 15, 1964)

Until Jack Teagarden and FLETCHER HENDERSON's Jimmy Harrison arrived, the jazz trombone was an invaluably supportive ensemble instrument of limited expressiveness for improvisers. Fluid but slow, its sound flowed thickly around the lighter instruments in the New Orleans ensemble, but if it was played fast, or with any attempt to emulate the sound of more agile horns, it often sounded (in Whitney Balliett's phrase) 'like a fat man trying to run uphill'.

Jack Teagarden was a colossus of early trombone-playing, and he did much to release the instrument's lazily garrulous lyricism, qualities now taken for granted. Teagarden took the blues, and the phrasing of Armstrong and Bechet as his model, not the ponderous brass-band approach. His tone was delicate, he could play more quietly than was thought possible, and with more agility. By 1928, when Teagarden joined Ben Pollack, his technique was formed, and an association with the commercially successful Paul Whiteman from 1933 shot him to prominence – for both his playing and his singing voice, which sounded like a man either just risen or about to retire, and brought him hits such as 'I Gotta Right to Sing the Blues'. Teagarden's success led him to try bandleading in the 1940s, but he wasn't at ease with the responsibilities and joined Louis Armstrong's All-Stars in 1947. The episode produced some fine performances, but Teagarden's gifts were downplayed in Armstrong's band and he returned to being his own man, touring and recording, until the end of his life.

*_That's a Serious Thing_ (RCA Bluebird ND 90440)

A long span of Teagarden's career, from the 1920s to the 1950s, covering the Whiteman band period, encounters with FATS WALLER, BUNNY BERIGAN and BENNY GOODMAN, and inevitably Louis Armstrong. Fine general introduction to Teagarden's magic.

*_I Gotta Right to Sing the Blues_ (ASV AJA 5059)

More of Teagarden's varied encounters but from a more concentrated period in the early 1930s. Fascinating for an early version of 'A Hundred Years From Today', the song which most instantly conjures up the sound of Teagarden's drooping-eyelids voice and which was his biggest hit, a robust encounter with another jazz maverick in violinist JOE VENUTI, and cuts from the Ben Pollack band in which Teagarden found his feet.

Terry, Clark

(Born St Louis, Missouri, December 14, 1920)
Enormously influential trumpeter, whose sound considerably affected the development of a St Louis brassman six years younger than him – Miles Davis. Terry brought the flugelhorn into jazz (it became a Davis trademark) and his playing is a

colourful mixture of half-valve slurs, muted effects, whimsical bebop and immense rhythmic bounce, with the voices of those idiosyncratic trumpeters CHARLIE SHAVERS, REX STEWART and Dizzy Gillespie at work on his style.

Terry came up in local St Louis bands but after the Second World War collected a string of illustrious employers including LIONEL HAMPTON, CHARLIE BARNET, COUNT BASIE, DUKE ELLINGTON (for eight years) and Quincy Jones. During the Ellington period (1951–9) Terry made several memorable contributions, notably to 'Up and Down' and 'Lady Mac' from *Such Sweet Thunder*. He was later employed as a staff musician by NBC for the *Johnny Carson Show* (one of the first blacks to be hired for a TV house band) and occasionally featured on the show, with his blues-scatting nonsense song 'Mumbles'. Terry has worked extensively as a jazz teacher since, though periodically he has partnered Johnny Griffin, Thelonious Monk, BEN WEBSTER, OSCAR PETERSON and others in a series of effervescent encounters, and has occasionally run his own big band.

★*Oscar Peterson Trio Plus One* (Emarcy 818 840-2)

One of the trumpeter's best-ever outings, and though it isn't marketed under his name but Peterson's, it's such a fine example of Terry's work that it deserves to figure in his discography. Terry saved many of his best recordings for other people's gigs, and he's outstanding on this 1964 Peterson date, with the pianist accompanied by Ray Brown on bass and Ed Thigpen on drums. It features Terry's celebrated technique of alternating phrases between the trumpet and flugelhorn (one in each hand, and applied here to the song 'Jim'), some bustling instrumental solos and Terry's hilarious form of vocal blues gibberish, 'Mumbles'.

★*Color Changes* (Candid 9009)

Another brilliant Terry display, this time assisted by a group of players of very distinctive personalities, including ex-Mingus trombonist Jimmy Knepper, multi-instrumentalist Yusef Lateef, and the resourceful Tommy Flanagan on piano. Lateef's use of the cor anglais and oboe as well as flute and saxophone extends the timbral range of this session immensely, and combined with

Terry's variations of texture between his two horns, the band sounds much bigger than it is. But for all that this is exactly the kind of exploration of tone the title says it is, there's plenty of flat-out swing jamming.

Thornhill, Claude

(Born Indiana, August 10, 1909; died New York, July 1, 1965)
Claude Thornhill was more of a dance-band arranger than a fully fledged jazz artist, yet his work was continually inflected with jazz and – as an inspiration to a truly great composer and arranger in Gil Evans – his influence filtered unmistakably into the mainstream of the music. Thornhill was a remarkable textural artist, whose avoidance of the percussive riffing technique of big jazz bands in favour of subtly coloured orchestral effects made tone-poems of the most mundane material. He constantly perceived new ways of organising regular jazz lineups (on one occasion turning his entire reed section into clarinettists) and he introduced the French horn into arrangement, a device unforgettably developed by Gil Evans later on. Thornhill's graceful methodology stood in the shadows of the famous Miles Davis/Gil Evans 'Birth of the Cool' recordings of 1949. Thornhill was a trained musician who had worked for Paul Whiteman, BENNY GOODMAN and then as a session arranger, before forming his own band in 1940, Gil Evans joining him a year later. His postwar band included altoist Lee Konitz. Thornhill's later career was hampered by personal difficulties, but his earlier music is excellent and his influence on jazz immense.

*_Tapestries_ (Charly CDCHARLY 82)

Excellent Thornhill compilation with most of his best work, including a good deal of material arranged by Gil Evans. Thornhill's manipulation of the dance-band repertoire is nowhere better represented than on 'Snowfall', the tune that became his theme song – a foxtrot turned into a piece of drifting impressionism. Reflecting the changes in the 1940s, 'Thrivin' on a Riff' and 'Yardbird Suite' also make fascinating appearances.

Vaughan, Sarah Lois

(Born New Jersey, March 27, 1924; died April 3, 1990)

Some artists transcend the technical demands of their craft. Sarah Vaughan was the jazz singer who made it sound easiest. Possessed of a four-octave voice, she could sound as fragile and wistful as a flute, or as luxurious and resonant as the low notes of a tenor saxophone. Her control of timbre, pitch, phrasing, dynamics and improvisation were extraordinary throughout her career. She was the operatic diva of jazz.

Sarah Vaughan began as a church singer at seven, and had piano and organ lessons at the same time. She won an amateur talent contest at the Apollo Theatre in Harlem when she was 16 (the song was 'Body and Soul') and joined EARL HINES' band shortly afterwards, following that up with fellow-singer BILLY ECKSTINE's bop-influenced orchestra. Vaughan understood bebop quickly, singing with Charlie Parker, Dizzy Gillespie, and the 'cool school' guru Lennie Tristano, and in the 1950s with Clifford Brown and Herbie Mann, but her material and her method remained closer to swing. She later worked with her own small groups, but also with organisations up to the size of symphony orchestras. Vaughan was *Downbeat* magazine's Best Female Vocalist for 18 consecutive years, and has recorded lyric writers as different as Stephen Sondheim and (on one memorable occasion) Pope John Paul II.

★The Divine Sarah Vaughan: The Columbia Years 1949–53
(Columbia 465597)

A good two-CD set dealing with early years, though not her debut or the period with the Billy Eckstine band. This was the period in which singers performing in sympathy with big-band improvisers was a fading fashion, replaced by the star vocalist in front of an anonymous orchestra, so a good many of these tracks are in that mould. But a small group featuring Miles Davis and Budd Johnson is in a different league, and there are enough examples of Vaughan's range and power to surprise to make this a valuable document of her apprenticeship.

★*After Hours* (Roulette CDP 7 93271-2)

Short weight for a CD at 32 minutes, but a lovely live recording by Vaughan from 1961, with Mundell Lowe on guitar and George Duvivier on bass. The spare support enhances the crystal clarity of the voice, and 'My Favourite Things', 'Every Time We Say Goodbye' and 'In a Sentimental Mood' are classic Vaughan.

★*Duke Ellington Song Books* 1 & 2 (Pablo 2312-111 and 2312-116)

Vaughan on an extended treatment of Ellington classics, with a good band featuring J.J. Johnson, Eddie 'Cleanhead' Vinson, Zoot Sims and Jimmy Rowles. These date from the late 1970s, and represent Vaughan pursuing the same contextual course as Ella Fitzgerald did two decades before for Norman Granz, an intriguing contrast of approaches. Vaughan can be so technically powerful as to flatten everything around her at times, including the emotions evoked by her materials, but on these sessions she is probing, revealing, sometimes alarming and they count among the best of her later work.

★*The Benny Carter Sessions* (Roulette 7243 8286-10 2 8)

Vaughan recordings for Roulette between 1962 and 1963. At this point in her career, Vaughan's extraordinary voice was becoming a showbiz hot property, so the playing isn't as spontaneously jazzy as some of the earlier work. But BENNY CARTER is an excellent and sympathetic arranger, and only a brief listening to 'The Man I Love' here shows why – the writing is economical, wry and stimulating to the band. The material is drawn from two Vaughan discs, 'Explosive Side of Sarah Vaughan' and 'The Lonely Hours' sessions. However, too little disc information is included.

Venuti, Giuseppe 'Joe'

(Born Lago di Como, Italy, September 16, 1903; died Seattle, August 14, 1978)
The first of the great jazz violinists, and to many the best of all, Joe Venuti attacked his music with a relish, humour, enthusiasm and

expressiveness that gave jazz violin a sound much closer in impact to horn and even vocal improvising. Venuti dismissed the silky, demure romanticism of the violin's use in popular music and created instead a style of rough seesawing figures, sudden bursts of strutting pizzicato, and long, skydiving phrasing. He even invented a technique whereby the bow was used upside down, with the gut curved over all four strings at once, producing unusual harmonies and a raw, aggressive sound.

Venuti brought the violin into the Jazz Age, but he was no prima donna about his artistic achievements and has entered jazz legend as much for his outrageous practical jokes (calling 70 bass players up for the same session just so he could watch them all congregating on the street, pouring flour into the Whiteman Orchestra's tuba during a movie shoot, occasionally playing nude) as for his cavalier performances. He admitted in his seventies he had been born in Italy – the earlier version was on board ship to the States – grew up in Philadelphia, and worked for bandleader Jean Goldkette with childhood friend and long-time guitar partner Eddie Lang. Lang and Venuti's recordings, made in the mid-1920s, are jazz classics, but the violinist worked for many leaders during the 1920s and 30s, briefly formed a big band, and was busy on Bing Crosby's radio show in the 1950s. Venuti's methods then went out of style, and a big drinking habit made matters worse, but he was rediscovered in the late 1960s and worked a punishing schedule, despite illness, until his death. Venuti was dubbed by his fellow-musicians 'the mad fiddler from Philly'.

Joe Venuti and Eddie Lang Vols. 1 & 2 (JSP 309 & 310)

Two delightful compilations of the work of Venuti and Lang from 1926 to 1931, music that sounds astonishingly fresh and contemporary even 60 years later. It's not simply a testament to the power of Venuti's tousled musical personality that these sessions charge along at the pace they do, but Lang's punchy guitar-work, confirming that until the arrival of Charlie Christian he was the finest guitarist in the music. There is a BBC version of this partnership (BBC CD 644) on one CD, but the music so brims with life that both of the above repay the investment.

Waller, Thomas Wright 'Fats'

(Born New York, May 21, 1904; died Kansas City, December 15, 1943)

As an all-round entertainer, Fats Waller is sometimes thought of as having sidelined his jazz talents, but he brought humdrum popular material to life throughout his career and it's been a particular virtue of jazz musicians to achieve such metamorphoses. He also turned the ragtime-derived 'stride' piano style – his first and biggest influence was James P. Johnson – into a dancing, witty and vivacious idiom that in turn influenced innumerable other pianists, as widely divergent as COUNT BASIE, ART TATUM, Thelonious Monk and Bud Powell. Waller was the son of a clergyman and learned organ first (an instrument he sometimes returned to later in his career) but he was a professional pianist by the age of 15, an accompanist to blues artists such as Bessie Smith in the 1920s, and a successful tunesmith for musicals as well. Waller made a series of pastiche recordings of popular songs in the 1930s that brought him wider popularity, but even these exhibited his usual swing and devastating piano flights. In 'Honeysuckle Rose' and 'Ain't Misbehavin'' Waller composed two of the best-loved tunes in popular music.

Turn on the Heat (Bluebird ND 82482)

Though Fats Waller was a superior all-round entertainer and much of his pop-oriented group material still stands up, his piano-playing is his real legacy and this fine two-CD set covers most of the significant material he recorded – except for some thrilling live takes – as a soloist between 1927 and 1941. One of the most controlled and richly shaded of all his solos, 'Handful of Keys', is here, and the only drawbacks of an excellent reissue are some deficiencies in the sound quality.

Fats Waller and his Rhythm (BBC CD 684)

Sessions from 1934 to 1936 by Waller and his Rhythm, the amiable showbiz band with which the pianist found the middle ground of the entertainment business. Much of the material is good, however, and it's a fair representation of this phase of Waller's career.

★*The Last Years* (Bluebird ND 90411)

Extensive survey of some of the best of showbiz Waller ('By the Light of the Silvery Moon', 'Your Socks Don't Match'), featuring good playing by regulars such as trumpeter Herman Autrey and clarinettist Gene Sedric, an excellent big-band session from 1941 and a final 'Ain't Misbehavin' featuring BENNY CARTER on trumpet. Vivacious, and sometimes inadvertently chastening music.

Waters, Benjamin 'Benny'

(Born Brighton, Maryland, January 23, 1902)
A squat, fervent, irrepressibly energetic man who continued to deliver swing sax with a youthful fire well into his eighties, Benny Waters is both a charismatic performer and a one-man jazz history lesson. A schooled musician in the 1920s who worked with King Oliver, FLETCHER HENDERSON and other jazz pioneers, Waters made Europe his base from the 1950s and was introduced to British audiences two decades later, after which he regularly toured the UK. Waters combines both the legato complexity of sophisticated swing-style runs, and a more unruly, blues-based expressiveness often using the outer reaches of the alto's top register, and frequently tenor and clarinet as well.

★*Hearing Is Convincing* (Muse M 5340)

Waters with a piano trio in 1987 – a little querulous at times, though still in assertive form as a singer, but retaining an awesome control of the internal logic of a solo. As with the octogenarian British tenorist Andy Hamilton, it's not that the age of the performer isn't apparent at times, but that jazz improvisation is an open enough form for Waters to make something fresh out of both his experience and the man he now is. The material mostly reworks standards, but with considerable charm.

Webb, William Henry 'Chick'

(Born Baltimore, Maryland, February 10, 1909; died Baltimore, June 16, 1939)

Bandleader and drummer Chick Webb's records are more usually investigated these days for examples of Ella Fitzgerald's early work: Webb was her mentor, and she took over his band after his early death from tuberculosis. But the small, hunchbacked drummer drove a big band in much the way Buddy Rich was to do in later years – sitting high on a dais, with a big, imposing kit, leading and punctuating the arrangements with a surging swing and crisp, staccato figures that propelled the music without breaking its flow.

Webb's break was the opportunity to bring a band to the Savoy Ballroom in 1927, its impact dependent on the leader's drumming and the excellent arrangements of Edgar Sampson for such hits as 'Blue Lou' and 'Stompin' at the Savoy'. As its experience grew, the band became almost unbeatable as a generator of seething dance-floor excitement, with novelty routines provided by trumpeter Taft Jordan's Louis Armstrong impressions. But it was Ella Fitzgerald's arrival – Webb spotted her at a talent contest – that provided a new focus for the band, and a new level of income with the pop success of 'A-Tisket, A-Tasket'. Illness interrupted Webb's career from 1938, but he had already done enough to show that his band was one of the finest of the swing era, and that as a drummer he deserved at least as much of the acclaim as went to Gene Krupa.

★*Chick Webb 1935–1938* (Classics 517)

The second of two Classics surveys of the early Webb band, and even via the limitations of transferred 1930s recordings the music indicates what a roof-raiser it must have been. Taft Jordan's trumpet solos are excellent Armstrong-inspired virtuoso displays, but Webb's drumming is the supercharged engine of the band and gives it an irresistible momentum.

Webster, Benjamin Francis 'Ben'

(Born Kansas City, March 27, 1909; died Amsterdam, September 20, 1973)

One of the supreme saxophone stylists in all jazz, Ben Webster's career divides neatly into two. The first period came to a climax during his stint with DUKE ELLINGTON's Orchestra, where his wide-brimmed sound transformed the reed section and where his driving solo on 'Cottontail' eventually became part of the arrangement. Webster has subsequently been thought of as primarily as a ballad specialist, in which the songs are remoulded, lightly bludgeoned but ultimately caressed by one of the most lustrous sounds ever to emerge from a tenor saxophone.

In the 1930s, Webster worked and recorded with most of the major swing bandleaders, including FLETCHER HENDERSON, BENNIE MOTEN, Andy Kirk and BENNY CARTER. When smaller groups became the fashion, he became one of the staples around 52nd Street, both as a leader and sideman. He later toured with Jazz at the Philharmonic, settled in Los Angeles and worked in the west coast studios and clubs. Webster spent his last decade or so in Europe, usually based in Copenhagen, from where he would periodically tour the continent. Never at his best at fast tempos, Webster in later years turned everything over medium pace into a glorified rasp. Putting over a romantic ballad, he combined a robustly opulent sound, controlled down to the last scoop and slur, with a deeply felt, deceptively casual sense of rhythm. He also had, like Armstrong, the knack of picking the choicest notes from the melody as written.

★*Ben and Sweets* (CBS 460613)

Perfect partners, one of the most languidly poetic of all jazz tenorists and one of the foxiest of trumpeters. Ben Webster and HARRY 'SWEETS' EDISON met in 1962 for this fine session, the sense of space and the apposite phrase (or lone, long-postponed note in Webster's case) being virtually unerring and a rhythm section including pianist Hank Jones taking care of the rest.

★Stormy Weather (Black Lion BLCD 760108)

Webster went to Europe for good shortly before this live recording was made in 1965, and it's a demonstration from Copenhagen's Café Montmartre of just why the saxophonist captivated European audiences for the next eight years – often for performances of a whispering minimalism that would look virtually inert if written down. Webster could make the sound of an outbreath curling slowly through the tube of the saxophone as eloquent as a stream of full-blown notes, and pieces demanding that kind of treatment are the most successful here. Pianist Kenny Drew supports superbly, and bassist Niels-Henning Ørsted-Pedersen lays down the kind of bass embrace that subsequently made him world-famous.

★For the Guvnor (Charly 15)

Ben Webster steadily improved with the years. Never an impulsive player, he grew into his reflectiveness and refinement of a handful of devices as recognisable as a smile. Here he performs with characteristic subtle resonance on an excellent selection including 'I Got It Bad and That Ain't Good', 'In a Sentimental Mood' and 'Rockin' In Rhythm' (recalling his Ellington associations) as well as Thelonious Monk's 'Straight No Chaser'.

★See You at the Fair (GRP 11212)

A fine 1964 session, made just before Webster's emigration to Europe, with the saxophonist's sumptuous sound thinning to a violin-like delicacy on high notes, humming like a bumble bee in the middle register. The upward-skidding slurs on 'In a Mellow Tone', the brittleness that undermines the sentiment of 'Our Love Is Here To Stay' and the romanticism of 'Stardust' make this a fine set, augmented by three tracks from the original LP.

Williams, Mary Lou

(Born Atlanta, Georgia, May 8, 1910; died Durham, North Carolina, May 28, 1981)

It may have been her willingness to perform in almost any context in periods in which eclecticism was unusual, periods of withdrawal from music, or simply the fact that she was a woman that resulted in the neglect of Mary Lou Williams' entitlement to the role of major jazz artist. A pianist, composer, arranger and teacher, Williams not only wrote pieces for some of the most influential of early jazz bandleaders – including DUKE ELLINGTON – but was a challenging, open-minded improviser developing the Earl Hines legacy, and the possessor of a probing intelligence about the development of African-American music. Her pieces were being presented in prestigious venues (sometimes with symphony orchestras) from the 1940s, she could perform in settings as different as gospel music or the 1960s avant-garde, and she was constantly preoccupied with demonstrating the music's roots. In her last years, Mary Lou Williams regularly gave lecture-demonstrations on jazz history.

★*The Greatest Lady Piano Player In Jazz* (Suisa JZCD 357)

Survey of Mary Lou Williams' early career from the mid-1930s to the mid-1940s, including some indications of the evolution of the Clouds of Joy under her adventurous streamlining influence. The Clouds of Joy's 'Walkin' and Swingin'' was such a modernised arrangement for a band that had started out as a rough-and-ready blues outfit that bits of it became bebop staples later on, including Thelonious Monk's 'Rhythm-a-ning'. Williams' piano skills are as evident as her arranging on the early takes, displayed on some revealing trio sessions from 1936 and 1938 and including a telling interpretation of Jelly Roll Morton's 'The Pearls'.

★*Free Spirits* (Steeplechase SCS 1043)

Excellent late Williams piano trio set, with a bop-oriented trio of Buster Williams (bass) and Mickey Roker (drums). The repertoire reflects her open-mindedness about all jazz, including Miles

Davis' 'All Blues', Bobby Timmons' 'Dat Dere' and even 'Surrey with a Fringe on Top'.

Wilson, Theodore Shaw 'Teddy'

(Born Austin, Texas, November 24, 1912; died New Britain, Connecticut, July 31, 1986)

If a good deal of swing music was raucous, spectacular and aimed at the dance floor, the fashion never diverted pianist Teddy Wilson from his imperturbable elegance. Wilson's music flowed as cool, clear and mellifluously as spring-water, and his meticulous orderliness and quietly pushing beat made him both a fine soloist and a superb accompanist. Wilson's most celebrated partner was BILLIE HOLIDAY on some of her best recordings of the 1930s, but he also worked successfully with BENNY CARTER and BENNY GOODMAN among many others.

The son of an academic and a librarian, studying music at university himself, Teddy Wilson discovered jazz in the Chicago clubs on a visit in 1928 and devoted himself to it from then on. Joining Speed Webb's dance band, Wilson became an arranger, mirroring DON REDMAN's methods in attempting to adapt the improvised solos of musicians such as BIX BEIDERBECKE to written ensemble parts. Wilson met the young ART TATUM and the two often performed as a duo, but it was a deputising job for EARL HINES that brought Wilson to the notice of recording executive John Hammond and then to his first recording date. A series of small-group recordings followed, often featuring an as-yet little-known Billie Holiday. Wilson picked the musicians and supplied just the right blend of support and restraint as her accompanist, and the sessions became classics. Wilson made every note count, forming each one as if it were jewel-like, and he swung hard without ever imparting the usual reverberating thump to the left hand.

Wilson soon became one of the first black musicians to join a white band when he joined Benny Goodman (to considerable controversy) in 1936, then briefly a big-band leader himself. During and after the Second World War he moved between club residencies, studio and teaching work, and the occasional Goodman reunion, and maintained his elegant keyboard touch to the end of his life.

★*Teddy Wilson* Vol. 1: *Too Hot for Words* (Hep 1012)

The beginnings of Wilson's maturity, in 1935, helping to shape bands including such star soloists as BEN WEBSTER and ROY ELDRIDGE and a fledgling Billie Holiday.

★*Teddy Wilson 1936–37* (Classics 521)

Though much of this material is also covered by reissues bearing Billie Holiday's name, they chart the growing absorption of Wilson's own delicate musical temperament into the sound of bands under his direction – and also the control he unobtrusively exerted over musicians such as Eldridge, who could always teeter on the edge of the inappropriate in a setting like this. Other fine soloists include Buck Clayton and Benny Goodman, and Holiday is sublime.

★*Teddy Wilson* Vol. 4: *Fine and Dandy* (Hep 1029)

Twelve Holiday takes here, with the singer and Wilson even putting a shine on some pop material outwardly too tawdry to be revived. Other singers, including Helen Ward and Boots Castle, don't really compare but Wilson's stealthily joyous settings make up for everything.

Young, Lester Willis 'Prez'

(Born Mississippi, August 27, 1909; died New York, March 15, 1959)

If any musician was the first model for the restrained 'cool school' of improvisation that became fashionable in the 1950s it was tenor saxophonist Lester Young. Yet Young's style, though delicate, displayed none of the chilly remoteness that some exponents of the 1950s method adopted. The diametric opposite of COLEMAN HAWKINS, his chief rival for pre-eminence in the saxophone world in the 1930s, Young not only became a primary influence on the developing Charlie Parker but later on Sonny Rollins and John Coltrane as well – all players whose styles were worlds away from 'cool' music. Young's tone on the saxophone was once memorably described as 'soundless laughter' and he brought to the tenor some of the gentler effervescence of the clarinet, which he also played. Unlike Hawkins, he was not a harmonic improviser (working off the related scales to chords) but a player who constantly remoulded the original theme, extracting motifs from it, manipulating them, relating them to the overall picture and, in his words, 'telling a story'. Young therefore placed much of his emphasis on tone, and his vocabulary of timbre was immense, from vibrant, singing sounds to wistful sighs.

Young was the son of a vaudeville entertainer, and he was strongly influenced by both BIX BEIDERBECKE's saxophone partner Frankie Trumbauer and by Jimmy Dorsey in his early development. He replaced Coleman Hawkins in the FLETCHER HENDERSON band in 1934 but was an insufficiently aggressive performer for Henderson, and left. Young's tenure with the COUNT BASIE band made his reputation – it ended all attempts by potential employers to harden his style – and in the late 1930s he also recorded memorable duo improvisations in jazz with BILLIE HOLIDAY.

Most of the best pre-Second World War work by Young is to be heard on recordings under the names of Billie Holiday and Count Basie.

★*Live at the Royal Roost 1948* (Jazz Anthology 550092)

Though Lester Young is often portrayed as a man increasingly disheartened by being out of step, sidelined by younger musicians who borrowed his methods, these postwar sessions are both energetic and curious about new jazz forms. In his own way, Young was rebuilding his style, and this group with Roy Haynes on drums has a distinctively bebop feel, notably on 'Bebop Boogie' in which Haynes leans relentlessly on him and a bop remake of 'Just You Just Me'. Elsewhere the classic Young virtues are in evidence on such standards as 'These Foolish Things'.

★*Lester Young and the Piano Giants* (Verve 835316)

Compilation from several Young albums pairing him with pianists OSCAR PETERSON, TEDDY WILSON, Hank Jones and John Lewis. The Wilson band also features ROY ELDRIDGE, who supplies a sharp contrast to Young's dreaminess, and this material –

though it covers the decade from 1946 to 1956, often superficially dismissed as Young's 'decline' – confirms that though his methods were becoming less ethereally lyrical and by his standards more experimental, he was still capable of being in command, and even exuberant, almost to the end.

★*Lester Young Trio* (Verve 521 650-2)

Lester Young in 1946 with NAT KING COLE on piano and BUDDY RICH on drums – a combination that works better than might be expected, not least because Cole's dandyish sound contrasts so sharply with Young's poetic languour. This is sometimes thought of as the beginning of the end for Young, but much of it is far more vivacious than popular mythology maintains, and tracks like 'Somebody Loves Me', and 'I Want To Be Happy' are terrific.

3

BEBOP

S WING WAS SUCH big business for a while in the 1930s that its major beneficiaries were anxious not to rock the boat. But because jazz is fundamentally a spontaneous music, it was inevitable that a good many of the musicians in the swing bands – particularly the younger ones – would resist pressures to play to a formula. The problem cost the energetic and imaginative young drummer Kenny Clarke his job with the popular Teddy Hill band at the end of the 1930s.

Clarke's offence was changing the beat, and the beat was the essence of swing. Teddy Hill believed that Clarke's methods would simply mean that the dancers wouldn't know where to put their feet. The rhythm of swing tended to be four beats to the bar, with the emphasis on the first and third, and the signpost of the beat was usually the bass drum so that nobody could possibly miss it. Clarke switched the marking of the beat to his cymbals and began using the bass drum for scattered accents. It wasn't the best way to stay in work at the time.

But Clarke's separation from Hill was amicable enough, and in 1940 the drummer was asked by his old employer to find some young and preferably inexpensive players to form a house band at a 108th Street club called Minton's Playhouse, a Harlem establishment setting up as an after-hours jamming joint for jazz stars looking for some off-duty excitement. Clarke came up with a band that included an eccentric young stride pianist called Thelonious Monk. John Birks 'Dizzy' Gillespie, a boisterous, technically adroit swing-band trumpeter came too, as did Benny Goodman's star guitarist Charlie Christian. Down the road, at Monroe's Uptown House, as well as toying with orthodox jazz rhythms, the musicians were exploring more complex and ambiguous harmonies to improvise on than the old Tin Pan Alley pop hits. Jay McShann's young altoist Charlie Parker seemed to be exploring similar variations on the orthodox harmonies of swing as the Minton's players were.

Charlie Parker had worshipped the work of Count Basie's saxophonist Lester Young and had learned a good many of Young's light and lyrical methods. But as the 1940s progressed, Parker made the impact on jazz development that Louis Armstrong had 20 years before. He could play in all keys (he had never been taught that it wasn't necessary to), he was a brilliant blues performer and he comprehensively transformed the received materials of jazz in melody, harmony and rhythm.

Parker, Gillespie, Monk, Clarke and others began increasingly to play together, to share ideas and deconstruct swing. The new idiom was first called (probably after its characteristic accents and jumpy melodies) 'rebop' and then 'bebop'. Its characteristics were fast tempos, harmonic progressions augmented by added notes on the chords, and a shift in phrasing and accents that made it seem at first to the unwary as if it began and ended in the wrong places. Chord changes usually began on strong beats in swing, resolutions ended on them. Charlie Christian, Gillespie and Parker used offbeats more and more. Eventually Parker's adventures with accents became so ambitious that he would appear to be in another world to his accompanists, if it weren't for the fact that he virtually always ended up where he meant to.

Bebop provoked sharp reactions. Many older musicians disliked it and felt that it neither swung, nor told a story. Even some of its practitioners found it too frenetic, notably Miles Davis, who quickly adapted its phrasing and intonation to a much more muted style. Davis brought an orchestra of his own to New York's Royal Roost in 1948, performing an unexpectedly soft and velvety arranged music, which was nevertheless embroidered on by a diffident form of bop soloing from the leader and from prominent white musicians such as Lee Konitz and Gerry Mulligan. A Canadian arranger called Gil Evans was instrumental in bringing about this change, but it wasn't the only form that 'cool' music took. A scholarly, single-minded Chicago pianist called Lennie Tristano developed a more ascetic version (saxophonists Konitz, Warne Marsh and others studied with him), which pursued the goal of melodic variation above all else. Tristano rhythm sections were timekeepers, not active participants, and bravura climaxes were considered cheap thrills and to be avoided. Another kind of cool style was explored by bored Hollywood studio players on the west coast – but though the emotional temperature of some of the music produced by players such as trumpeter Shorty Rogers and drummer Shelly Manne was a few degrees down on New York bop, it is often unfairly saddled with the 'cool' tag.

Through the 1950s groups led by drummers Max Roach and Art Blakey, by pianist Horace Silver, and featuring powerful soloists such as Lee Morgan, Clifford Brown and the young John Coltrane, performed a mutation usually called 'hard bop'. This was a version of bebop that had emerged as an antidote to cool music, restoring the earlier explicit emotionalism of jazz, a wider dynamic range and a powerful independent role for the rhythm sections. Max Roach and Clifford Brown, Art Blakey and Horace Silver, and harder-swinging Miles Davis (with partners including trombonist J.J. Johnson and saxophonist Lucky Thompson) were all forming groups of a loosely similar character in 1954. The success of hard bop was also aided by the invention of the long-playing microgroove record and 'high fidelity' reproduction, opening up the jazz club atmosphere of extended solos and in-person charisma on disc.

Hard bop and cool music vied with each other during the 1950s. Some writers described cool as the archetypal Cold War music: intellectual, pessimistic, repressed, mistrustful of emotional commitment. But it was undoubtedly the dominant jazz form with the public for a brief period, during which it made bop sound ill-disciplined and excessive. But by the end of the 1950s the expressions 'cool' or 'west coast' had taken on a pejorative ring. Only later was the work of Tristano, Lee Konitz, Chet Baker or Gerry Mulligan to recover its proper due.

But even hard bop didn't lead jazz musicians to smile all the way to the bank. Rock and roll was under way by the mid-1950s, sprung from a mixture of jazz-oriented 'jump music', blues and country music. To be commercially popular, jazz needed to emphasise its blues content, and provide a new version of a danceable beat. It was therefore the jazz groups that plainly featured the most pop-oriented material – tunes such as Lee Morgan's 'The Sidewinder' and Bobby Timmons' 'Moanin' – (for Art Blakey) – that made the charts. One of

Silver's song titles from the 1950s, 'Opus de Funk', brought a word into common currency that was soon to become an idiom of its own.

Miles Davis' music had become hotter and more urgent (John Coltrane was in his post-1954 band), but he still felt comfortable with a jazz of more oblique effects. He was also getting bored with the inexorable succession of chord changes underneath orthodox jazz improvisation (the restless Tristano had felt the same way at the end of the 1940s) and began to explore modes – cycles of scales – instead, as in Indian music. *Kind of Blue*, Davis' most famous exploration of this method, became one of the most influential jazz records of all time. Since the 1970s a revivalist interest in bop by many young musicians has dominated both jazz playing, and the economics of jazz recording.

Categorisation is often unhelpful, but the performers in this section are in general those who developed bebop, and whose work has remained closer to it than to anything else. Bebop-oriented players of more recent times are covered in Chapter 6.

Adams, Park 'Pepper'

(Born Highland Park, Illinois, October 8, 1930; died New York, September 10, 1986)

The baritone saxophone, a big, foghorn-toned instrument, principally featured in jazz in the years before bebop as a textural device – except in the hands of Duke Ellington's Harry Carney, but even that saxophone master didn't like to hurry with it. With SERGE CHALOFF, GERRY MULLIGAN and, most ferociously, Pepper Adams came a way of playing the unwieldy horn that reflected bop's mercurial mobility.

Adams' first serious jazz opportunities arose in a partnership he had as a teenager with tenorist LUCKY THOMPSON, and in the same year (1947) he toured with Lionel Hampton's Orchestra. After army service, Adams worked with DONALD BYRD and Elvin Jones, then with Stan Kenton, during which period he made some albums of his own with members of the west coast 'cool school'. Adams mixed stints with Charles Mingus, Donald Byrd and studio assignments during the 1960s, and was a founder of the bop-oriented THAD JONES-Mel Lewis big band.

★*Pepper Adams Plays Charles Mingus* (Fresh Sound FCR-CD 117)

Though Adams was usually a sure-footed and authoritative performer, some of his sessions suffered from the traditional hard-bop blight of sounding stubbornly formulaic. Partly because of the material (all Charles Mingus') and partly because of an odd mixture of partners (Zoot Sims appears on it) this set is significantly different from the usual machinations, and Dannie Richmond's drums help the whole thing to sound very much like a Mingus operation. Adams drives resolutely through 'Fables of Faubus', 'Haitian Fight Song' and others, and the contrast of his guttural sound with Zoot Sims' airy one is very attractive.

Adderley, Julian Edwin 'Cannonball'

(Born Florida, September 15, 1928; died Indiana, August 8, 1975) Virtuosic alto and soprano saxophonist, originally an army music instructor. Initially played in a style strongly flavoured with the ideas of CHARLIE PARKER, but affected by the more raucous and bluesier styles of Eddie Vinson and Louis Jordan too. Adderley's mature method was glossier and more self-conscious than Parker's, the notes more rounded, the accents more predictable and the inclination to leave very little space in the music at times fatiguing to the ear. But Adderley exhibited infectious swing, and his sensitivity to gospel and blues-influenced music made him a significant figure in the 'soul-jazz' movement of the 1960s that pre-dated funk.

★*Somethin' Else* (Blue Note CDP 746338-2)

Somethin' Else is one of Adderley's most famous albums, cut in 1958 with the MILES DAVIS rhythm section of the period. Adderley's Charlie Parker allegiances are strongly apparent here, as is his tendency to play all over everything – a torrent of notes that makes the discreet, offhand presence of Miles Davis here seem almost an admonition. Hank Jones is on piano, a steamy ART BLAKEY on drums.

Albany, Joe (Joseph Albani)

(Born Atlantic City, January 24, 1924; died New York, January 11, 1988)

A superb and much-neglected pianist of the early bop movement, Albany was an utterly idiosyncratic mixture. His full technique allowed him to interweave lines more resourcefully than many bop pianists could, and his rhythmic feel was almost as unpredictable as that of THELONIOUS MONK.

Albany worked with saxophonists Benny Carter, Lester Young and Stan Getz in the 1940s, meeting CHARLIE PARKER in 1944 and becoming one of the bop genius' favourite pianists. Yet he recorded hardly at all, save for a handful of takes with Young. Drug-addiction and stretches in prison meant that Albany was virtually unheard of in jazz for 25 years. But in the 1970s he resurfaced, and embarked on the only active recording period of his life.

★The Right Combination (Original Jazz Classics OJC 1749)

A celebrated occasion, a rough-and-ready document of a rehearsal featuring Albany with the great Tristanoite saxophonist WARNE MARSH and a bassist in 1957. Albany could be a superb, and unsettling, ballad performer, as he reveals on 'Angel Eyes'.

★Bird Lives (Storyville STCD 4164)

Albany with bassist Art Davis and drummer Roy Haynes in the late 1970s, performing some probing variations on a set of Parker originals. For anyone for whom Albany became a cult (and there were many after the 1970s) all of his meagre output is interesting, but this is one of the most focused and intense.

Bailey, Ernest Harold 'Benny'

(Born Cleveland, Ohio, August 13, 1925)

Both an imperious big-band section leader and an unusual bop-driven soloist, trumpeter Benny Bailey has recently grown more active as a small-group bandleader. Though his phrasing and attack belong to bebop, his sense of melodic shape is full of sharp angles and his most characteristic device is to allow a note to free-fall suddenly through the registers.

Bailey was a rhythm & blues musician as a teenager, but worked as a section player and soloist with a high-class succession of big bands in the 1940s, beginning with Jay McShann's and passing through DIZZY GILLESPIE's and Lionel Hampton's. Through the 1950s Bailey extensively worked in the studios, but when the American drummer Kenny Clarke and Belgian pianist Francy Boland formed their fine multinational big band in the 1960s, Bailey was a regular member.

Big Brass (Candid CS 9011)

Good bop-oriented Bailey session from 1960, featuring such fine exponents of the idiom as saxophonist Phil Woods and pianist TOMMY FLANAGAN. Not so impassive as a good many boppish dates of the era, beginning to be influenced by the changes in jazz construction pioneered by MILES DAVIS and others around the same time. It gives the music a less inevitable atmosphere.

Baker, Chesney H. 'Chet'

(Born Oklahoma, December 23, 1929; died Amsterdam, May 13, 1988)
Baker's popular image was as the James Dean of jazz (his combination of smouldering youthfulness and seductive balla-deer's singing voice couldn't miss in the 1950s, when cool jazz was big) but he was both a poignant and obliquely emotional trumpeter and when roused a fleet and imaginative player of fast bop. Baker came to prominence in the 1950s when he formed a groundbreaking piano-less quartet with fellow-saxophonist GERRY MULLIGAN.

From the late 1950s to the 1970s Baker was more often than not out of action with drug problems and some of his performan-ces drifted purposelessly, but the last decade of his life saw many performances of bruised and bruising tenderness, often captured on record. Baker's singing voice is often described as an 'acquired taste', and though its later manifestations obey no known rules of pitching accuracy, its battered sound could be highly communicative and its rhythmic momentum as effective as a drummer.

★*Chet Baker in Paris* (Emarcy 837474/5/6/7-2)

Four-volume CD set of Baker in the 1950s, sometimes languid or sentimental to the point of inactivity, but often delicately vivid – notably on the Vol. 1 tracks with pianist Dick Twardzik, a collection of memorable themes alternately illuminated by Baker's fragile and unsteady lyricism and Twardzik's archetypal cool-style ambiguity and reserve.

★*Cools Out* (Boplicity CDBOP 013)

A reconstituted 1956 Chet Baker session nearly all originally released as a Pacific album called *Chet Baker and Crew*. The sound is classic west coast, full of sliding chordal movements, elegant counterpoint and narrow dynamic range. The best track is the opener (and the one that wasn't on the original *Crew* session), a cruising blues called 'The Route' and featuring a typically seductive ART PEPPER.

★*The Italian Sessions* (Bluebird BMG ND 82001)

Baker in unusually bustling mood on a European session from 1962, with an excellent band including guitarist Rene Thomas and drummer Daniel Humair. This is bop fans' Baker, bristling and bludgeoning over SONNY ROLLINS' fast 'Pent Up House' (Humair's cymbals rattling relentlessly behind him) and delivering clean, ringing lines on the mid-tempo blues 'Ballata In Forma Di Blues', over the stalking bass of Benoit Quersin.

★*The Pacific Jazz Years* (Pacific Jazz CDP 0777 7 89292 2 2)

A magnificent four-disc special, celebrating Baker's career in both music and William Claxton's famous young-man-with-a-horn photography. There are 49 tracks covering the period from 1952 to 1957, Baker's most productive years – and a lot of material is included that doesn't usually see the light of day. These include the fine collaborations with pianist Russ Freeman, and stars like

ART PEPPER, ANNIE ROSS and BOBBY TIMMONS appear, as well as plenty of GERRY MULLIGAN. There's a good essay by critic Ted Gioia and a full Pacific discography, and only some indecipherably fancy graphics spoil it. An essential Baker set, if you or somebody else can afford it.

Blakey, Arthur 'Art'

(Born Pennsylvania, October 11, 1919; died October 16, 1990)
Originally a pianist, and a bandleader at 15; but his own story is that hiring Errol Garner made him redundant on piano and a promoter with a revolver persuaded him to play drums instead. In the 1940s Blakey worked both with Fletcher Henderson and singer Billy Eckstine's big bands, contributing a steaming cymbal beat and volcanic press-rolls capable of catapulting the most laid-back soloist into space.

THELONIOUS MONK, MILES DAVIS, Lucky Millinder and Buddy DeFranco all hired Blakey, but it was a 1954 studio date with the pianist HORACE SILVER that set the pattern for the drummer's career into irrepressible old age. Blakey and Silver established a cooper-atively run band under the name of the Jazz Messengers, that laid the foundation stone for three and a half decades of unfailingly swinging and bluesy 'hard bop' outfits. As well as being an inspired propellant of jazz musicians, Blakey has always been a remarkable talent scout and many of the finest musicians now at work – JACKIE McLEAN, Wayne Shorter, Bobby Watson, LEE MORGAN, FREDDIE HUBBARD, Joanne Brackeen and Wynton Marsalis – have all been Messengers at one time or another.

A Night in Tunisia (Blue Note CDP 7465322)

Blakey in 1960, sounding like an express train coming out of a tunnel, with a band including trumpeter Lee Morgan and the saxophonist Wayne Shorter, one of the most original Coltrane disciples. The clarity of CDs intensifies the heated, fervent style and Blakey's classic drum intro – galloping uptempo playing, punched through with wild cymbal splashes against a background cymbal beat like rain on an iron roof – which opens the title track here makes you leap out of your seat. Shorter is succinct and gritty, Morgan closes 'A Night in Tunisia' with some delicious half-valve warped notes and pianist Bobby Timmons sustains the pressure.

★*Night at Birdland*, Vols. 1 & 2. *With Clifford Brown*
(Blue Note CDP 7456519-2; 7456520-2)

Classic 1954 Blakey, featuring the drummer plus Horace Silver, CLIFFORD BROWN and LOU DONALDSON. The playing is constantly on an improvisational razor-edge and the material is excellent, including pieces that became bebop standbys, such as 'Wee Dot', 'Now's the Time' and 'Night in Tunisia'.

★*The History of Art Blakey and the Jazz Messengers*
(Blue Note CDP 7 97190-2)

A fine three-volume survey. There's a youthful Blakey (1947) in a bebop band with Kenny Dorham, WALTER BISHOP and others, the 1954 beginnings of the Messengers with Horace Silver, and on up to the band that included the Marsalises and Bobby Watson (on 'Wheel Within a Wheel') , which was probably the drummer's last classic outfit. Blakey's celebrated burst-boiler snare drum sound on 'Free For All', with the sensational 1964 group that included a pre-Miles Wayne Shorter (guttural and sinewy) and Freddie Hubbard (bright and blistering) is one of his freest, fiercest performances.

★*Art Blakey. Paris 1958*. (RCA Bluebird 74321101522)

Art Blakey and the Jazz Messengers stitched together from three sessions that went out on French RCA in the 1950s. This is a favourite Messengers for many, with Lee Morgan's robust bluesiness and BENNY GOLSON's earthy audacity and fine arrangements, all constantly nagged and galvanised by the leader's erupting volcano at the drums. The repertoire is classic Blakey, including 'Blues March', a ferocious 'Moanin'' and Parker's 'Now's the Time'.

Brookmeyer, Robert 'Bob'

(Born Kansas City, December 1929)

A valve trombonist and arranger associated with the white 'cool school' of the 1950s. Brookmeyer originally worked as a pianist in the 1950s, before joining Stan Getz, GERRY MULLIGAN and then Jimmy Guiffre as a trombonist, displaying a mixture of busy and fluent but dynamically subdued solos, and an occasional scattering of refreshing backward glances towards the more uninhibited trombone styles of earlier jazz. A founder-member of the THAD JONES-Mel Lewis band of the 1960s and a prolific arranger, Brookmeyer is a far more resourceful artist than his ostensibly offhand style might suggest.

★Back Again (Sonet SNTCD 778)

Very good representation of Brookmeyer's range as a valve trombonist, all the way from airy delicacy to the more traditional palette of grouchy or bucolic sounds at the instrument's lower reaches. The band is excellent, including the delightful JIMMY ROWLES on piano and trumpeter THAD JONES. Everybody mingles as conversationally as if they worked together every night.

Brown, Clifford

(Born Delaware, October 30, 1930, died Pennsylvania, June 26, 1956)

One of the great jazz trumpeters, whose impact on the music was blunted by his early death in a road accident at the age of 25. Educated in jazz theory, Brown was a professional by 18, his style principally founded on the quicksilver brass techniques of DIZZY DILLESPIE and FATS NAVARRO. He worked for a while in a rhythm & blues band (Chris Powell and the Blue Flames), then with arranger TADD DAMERON, with Lionel Hampton, briefly with ART BLAKEY, and then joined drummer MAX ROACH in the quintet – at times including SONNY ROLLINS, SONNY STITT and HAROLD LAND – for which both he and Roach are most fondly remembered. Brown's sound was polished and full-blooded at any speed, however audacious his improvising, and his influence on contemporary trumpet stars such as FREDDIE HUBBARD and Wynton Marsalis is incalculable.

★*Clifford Brown Memorial Album* (Blue Note CDP 781526)

Brown in 1953, with two bands – one featuring the fascinating but neglected bop pianist ELMO HOPE – performing both uptempo music and ballads such as 'You Go To My Head'. Brown's poise and breathtaking melodic construction are beautifully unfolded on 'Minor Mood', and the disc as a whole is an admirable introduction to a young trumpet master.

★*At Basin Street* (Emarcy 814 648-2)

Sonny Rollins was 26 when this record was made, and the partnership between Rollins and Brown (caught here on one of the only two studio sets linking them) is close to its briefly incandescent best. Though the Roach/Brown band was always perceived as a hard-bop group, Rollins and Brown took it to the limits of the preoccupation with chords. The saxophonist is astonishing on 'Gertrude's Bounce' (with its smoothly descending two-octave opener) and on 'I'll Remember April'.

★*Study In Brown* (Emarcy 814 646-2)

A crucial 1954 recording with Brown and the west coast tenorist Harold Land. Land is featured here in some of his best recorded playing, neck and neck and at headlong pace with Brown on 'Cherokee', attractively furnishing the whistle to Richie Powell's churning piano traction on 'Take the A Train'. Roach's cymbal work on the same track is a momentous piece of precise, apposite, scene-setting percussion.

★*Brownie* (Emarcy 838 306-16)

Clifford Brown's sound is one of the most captivating in jazz, but though you would have to be very seriously captivated to explore this ten-CD set, it magnificently wraps up two years' worth of material Brown recorded for this label between 1954 and 1956, including the above Emarcy albums and others such as 'Brown and Roach Incorporated', 'Best Coast Jazz' and 'Clifford Brown with Strings'. Vocalists Dinah Washington, Sarah Vaughan and Helen Merrill appear. For those pondering the level of invest-ment, Emarcy has issued a useful single compilation album (*Compact Jazz: Clifford Brown* – Emarcy 842933) from this set.

Brubeck, David Warren 'Dave'

(Born Concord, California, December 6, 1920)
The pianist and composer Dave Brubeck has had a controversial career, like many jazz musicians who find material success with the non-specialist public. Brubeck's records were in the pop album charts in the 1960s (he cut the first jazz instrumental to sell a million copies with his saxophonist Paul Desmond's composition 'Take Five' – still widely played); he mixed genres freely in a period in which musical sectarianism was widespread, he deliberately deployed complex devices (several of his most popular pieces were set to time signatures unusual for jazz, and he used classical structures like rondos and fugues).

Latterly Brubeck's career has been assessed more rationally, and his achievements as a composer and as a genuine original in rhythmic innovation are increasingly appreciated. Brubeck doesn't see himself as a star soloist, but his clunky block-chord playing (a piano parallel to the punch of orchestral sections) and rather refined *arpeggios* make him a recognisable stylist. The method was appropriate to his materials, which blended European compositional ideas, sophisticated rhythmic structures, jazz song-forms and improvisation in ways that could still be hummed in the bath.

Dave Brubeck was born in Concord, California, in 1920, and was originally trained in classical music. He was a jazz bandleader as a student in the 1940s, but also studied with the classical composer Darius Milhaud, a major influence. After World War II (in which he led an army band), Brubeck founded the Jazz Workshop Ensemble to explore new ideas in jazz, followed in 1951 by his first quartet, including the fine Cool-School altoist Paul Desmond. The best Brubeck quartet was completed later when a technically astonishing drummer, Joe Morello, and bassist Gene Wright joined. Into the syncopated hustle of regular jazz time came such metres as 9/8 (the Mozartian 'Blue Rondo à la Turk') and 11/4, though orthodox swing was often used for the solos.

After the biggest fuss died down, Brubeck began working on more classically-oriented projects, and with bigger groups – including work on ballets, a mass, and various cantatas. He has also worked extensively with his children Darius (a keyboard player), Chris (a trombonist/bassist) and Danny (a drummer).

★*The Essential Dave Brubeck* Vol. 1 (Sony/CBS 467 148 2)

Good span of Brubeck material from the 1950s to the 1970s, including the hits 'Take Five', 'Blue Rondo à la Turk' and 'Unsquare Dance', plus some standards including 'Someday My Prince Will Come' – in two time signatures, of course.

★*Time Out* (Sony/CBS 460 611 2)

One of the best Brubeck albums, dating from 1959. It includes 'Take Five' and 'Blue Rondo', but also the waltzes 'Three to Get Ready' and 'Kathy's Waltz', with some typically subdued but highly moving performances from Paul Desmond throughout.

Burrell, Kenneth Earl 'Kenny'

(Born Detroit, July 31, 1931)
Classy and incisive inheritor of the guitar style of CHARLIE CHRISTIAN and Django Reinhardt, Burrell worked around Detroit in the early 1950s, then moved to New York, and joined the Benny Goodman band in 1957. He recorded extensively under his own name in the 1960s, but was often to be found in the company of partners who played with a strong and danceable beat and were never far from the blues – such as organist Jimmy Smith and soul saxophonist Grover Washington.

★*Guitar Forms* (Verve 825 576-2)

One of Burrell's finest albums, with charts arranged by Gil Evans, in 1965. On five of the tracks the guitarist is accompanied by an illustrious big band including Lee Konitz and Steve Lacy, and the balance between soloing and atmospheric Spanish-flavoured band dynamics on 'Lotus Land' is perfect. Elvin Jones is on drums.

Byrd, Donald

(Born Detroit, December 9, 1932)
College-educated musician who hit the headlines with ART BLAKEY's Jazz Messengers. Byrd's sound is hot and full-bodied, and though his primary influences, unsurprisingly, were GILLESPIE, MILES DAVIS and CLIFFORD BROWN, he managed to evolve a genuine lyricism of his own. Byrd has been both an active educator and self-educator, studying with Nadia Boulanger in Paris, acquiring a string of degrees, and becoming chair of the Black Music Department at Washington's Howard University for a period in the 1970s. He became a successful crossover artist in this period, with some of the early jazz-funk hits. Byrd's best-selling fusion album *Black Byrd* (Blue Note) is not yet available on CD.

★*Fuego* (Blue Note CDP 746 534-2)

Good late 1950s Byrd set, with the title track and 'Lament' owing something to the Miles Davis' *Kind of Blue* manner, but with fine soloing from JACKIE McLEAN on alto.

★*Groovin' For Nat* (Black Lion BL 760132)

Byrd in 1962 with the uninhibited and unconventional Mingus trumpeter Johnny Coles and a piano trio led by Duke Pearson. The two-trumpet front line works unexpectedly well because the contrast between them is so sharp.

Chaloff, Serge

(Born Boston, November 24, 1923; died Boston, July 16, 1957)
As a contemporary with GERRY MULLIGAN, Serge Chaloff was overlooked as a pioneering influence on the development of the baritone saxophone and its use in bebop, and since illness took him from the jazz scene early, his significant work was more or less

concentrated on a decade from the mid-1940s to the mid-1950s. Chaloff avoided the pressure on bop musicians to play the instrument too fast, sustaining its rich, emphatic sound instead, and absorbing bop melodic construction at his own pace. Chaloff came from a musical family (his father was a classical player, his mother a piano teacher), and as a young man he worked with most of the influential big bands, including Jimmy Dorsey's, Woody Herman's and Count Basie's. But narcotics had all but ended Chaloff's career as he entered his thirties.

The Fable of Mabel (Black Lion BLCD 760923)

One of very few current representations of Chaloff's skills on CD, this is a mixture of two 1954 sessions, one featuring a quintet, the other a larger group. Apart from Chaloff's deceptively restrained playing and occasional eruptions into the instrument's extremes, this set is impressive for the work of the young saxophonist Charlie Mariano, already displaying the tonal quirks that were to mark him out later with Charles Mingus and beyond.

Christian, Charles 'Charlie'

(Born Texas, July 29, 1916; died New York, March 2, 1942)
A key member of that coterie of frustrated big-band soloists of the late 1930s who forged the harmonically adventurous bebop out of the standards and standbys of the swing repertoire, Charlie Christian inspired the methods of virtually all bop guitarists until the invasion of jazz guitar-playing by the more elemental sounds of rock. One of the first to make extensive use of the recently invented electric amplification in the swing era, Christian had worked with a variety of Oklahoma touring bands before the impresario John Hammond smuggled him onstage at a Benny Goodman gig and the guitarist established one of jazz music's indelible legends by improvising 90 minutes' worth of dazzling solos on 'Rose Room'. Christian became a celebrity through work with Goodman's bands, but it was during his after-hours visits to Minton's Playhouse that his reputation as a bebop pioneer was established. Aside from his work with Goodman, Christian played and experimented endlessly, but by 1940 tuberculosis and a

reluctance to rein in his fast-lane lifestyle contributed to his death at 25. KENNY BURRELL, JIM HALL, WES MONTGOMERY, BARNEY KESSEL and many other guitarists are in his debt.

★*Live Sessions at Minton's Playhouse* (Jazz Anthology/Musidisc France 550012)

Variable in sound quality and with plenty of background ambience, these recordings made by enthusiast Jerry Newman in the Harlem bebop clubs are nevertheless classic Christian. Driven on by Thelonious Monk and Kenny Clarke on drums, the guitarist cuts loose at length with beautifully built guitar solos, notably on the 'Topsy' remould, 'Swing to Bop'. The flow of Christian's ideas recalls Parker in flight, though the guitarist didn't live long enough to free himself completely from the evenness of swing.

★*Genius of the Electric Guitar* (Giants of Jazz GOJCD53049)

Christian's Columbia recordings with various Benny Goodman bands. Included is the famous 'Solo Flight', but Christian's blues roots are distinctly audible on 'Blues in B', the informal jam on 'Waiting for Benny', the proto-bop phrasing on 'Till Tom Special' and the movement away from swing-style on-the-beat accenting in 'Air Mail Special'.

Clark, Conrad Yeatis 'Sonny'

(Born Herminie, Pennsylvania, July 21, 1931; died New York, January 13, 1963)
A regular performer on Blue Note studio sessions of the 1950s (and DEXTER GORDON's favourite accompanist), Clark was a performer whose directness, percussive style and sympathy for attractive themes based on crisp rhythmic motifs made him a natural for the label's no-nonsense house style of the period. The ten albums he made with Blue Note testify to his consistency and outgoing imagination.

Leapin' and Lopin' (Blue Note 784091)

The BUD POWELL touch, and that of Hampton Hawes, combined with Clark's particular rigorous logic, and with a first-class band including Tommy Turrentine on trumpet, CHARLIE ROUSE on tenor, and the great Billy Higgins on drums. The soul-sax sound of Ike Quebec makes an appearance on one track, but Clark's interpretation of 'Deep in a Dream' is the standout track of an excellent and representative disc.

Coleman, George

(Born Memphis, Tennessee, March 8, 1935)
One of the fastest and most tireless of hard bop saxophonists and a virtual definition of the style – big, beefy tone, blues-steeped intonation, crafty quotation from other songs, almost constant use of double-time and harmonic inspiration even at the most breakneck tempos. Coleman's deep affection for blues came from early experience in bands devoted to the idiom, notably B.B. King's in the early 1950s, before his all-round technical assurance and penetrative, unsentimental style won him the tenorist's job in jazz groups led by MAX ROACH, Slide Hampton, Wild Bill Davis, Lionel Hampton, Elvin Jones and many others. Coleman was briefly a member of the MILES DAVIS quintet in the 1960s and in more recent times has led a variety of bands of his own.

Big George (Charly CDCHARLY 83)

A Coleman octet recording from 1977, including two other excellent Memphis musicians in pianist Harold Mabern and altoist Frank Strozier. It's a lesson in witty, unostentatious arrangement tailor-made for the idiom and the methods of the players, with a variety of tempos and ensemble voicings used in 'Body and Soul' (Coleman's fingers are too restless ever to settle for Coleman Hawkins' inexorable gravitas on such a tune) winding up with the Woody Herman 'Four Brothers' group-sax sound.

Cowell, Stanley

(Born Toledo, Ohio, May 5, 1941)
Classically trained pianist and composer who studied both in Europe and the States, and whose early associations in jazz in the early 1960s were with Rahsaan Roland Kirk and Yusef Lateef. Cowell performed through the latter part of that decade with a variety of powerful modernists including MAX ROACH, BOBBY HUTCHERSON and MILES DAVIS, and became a regular accompanist for Roach and his singer wife Abbey Lincoln. Cowell's breadth of view enables him to play in early stride styles, free-music or funk, and bebop with equal conviction.

★*Close to You Alone* (DIW 603E)

Superb 1990 Cowell session with Cecil McBee on bass and Ronnie Burrage on drums – and a genuine trio session it is, with no single voice absolutely dominant, though Cowell's sweeping range and intelligence give it its ultimate authority. In an era in which 'eclectic musicians' are all but commonplace, Cowell reveals throughout this disc how the jazz tradition can be both recalled and reshaped.

Criss, William 'Sonny'

(Born Memphis, Tennessee, October 23, 1927; died Los Angeles, November 19, 1977)
Like most young instrumentalists in the 1940s, Sonny Criss was profoundly influenced by CHARLIE PARKER. But Criss found his own route rhythmically: the earlier swing players went on influencing him late into his development, but he retained Parker's urgency.

In the late 1940s Criss worked in California with Billy Eckstine and HOWARD McGHEE, and appeared in a Buddy Rich small group in the 1950s. Personal difficulties led to long layoffs. In the 1970s he returned to playing after a period of social work with juvenile alcoholics in Watts, and he was by now a little influenced by Coltrane. Criss did not recapture his old fire though, and in 1977 he took his own life.

Portrait of Sonny Criss (Original Jazz Classics OJC 655)

Boppish set from 1966, with Walter Davis on piano, Paul Chambers on bass and Alan Dawson on drums, and featuring some classic jazz vehicles revitalised, including 'God Bless the Child', 'On a Clear Day', and an old 52nd Street standby, 'Wee'.

Sonny's Dream (Original Jazz Classics OJC 707)

Unusual setting for Criss as the principal soloist against a set of fascinating orchestral backdrops furnished by Horace Tapscott in 1968. Tapscott, an underrated and ingenious west coast composer, proves his class on this session, and Criss soars over the inspiring settings, loosely influenced by the cool school sound and dedicated to the civil rights movement.

Curson, Theodore 'Ted'

(Born Philadelphia, June 3, 1935)
A true original, influenced in his thinking by Rex Stewart, CLIFFORD BROWN and Charles Mingus (with whom he worked for a year) about equally, Curson is a musician of broad allegiances who nevertheless has an intensely focused style. As well as the trumpet and flugelhorn he favours the piccolo trumpet's high range. Curson studied music formally, and with saxophonist Jimmy Heath, then worked in New York with forward-looking performers including Mal Waldron and Cecil Taylor. The year in the Mingus band (1959–60) was a significant influence on Curson's thinking about uniting the blues and gospel associations of jazz with progressive forms.

Fire Plays Down Below (Original Jazz Classics OJC 1744)

There's little enough Curson material available, but this 1962 set is a reasonable representation of his outlook and sound. The dynamic Roy Haynes is on drums.

Dameron, Tadd (Tadley Ewing Peake)

(Born Cleveland, Ohio, February 21, 1917; died New York, March 8, 1965)

Tadd Dameron, one of the composers whose pieces in the 1940s were commonly associated with bop (such as 'Hot House' and 'Good Bait'), was nevertheless still close to swing, as was DIZZY GILLESPIE's big band of that decade. But Dameron was able to adapt the harmonic implications of the new music to an orchestra in innovative ways, though he's undervalued now.

Dameron worked first as a pianist, performing with territory bands around Ohio and working with trumpeter Freddie Webster, an influence on MILES DAVIS. In New York from 1939, opportunities expanded to include Jimmie Lunceford, Billy Eckstine and Count Basie. Dameron wrote 'Good Bait' for Basie, at the time when swing bandleaders began to realise that some elements of bebop might be good for their image. Dameron began performing informally with the boppers, including Dizzy Gillespie and CHARLIE PARKER, worked as pianist with the jazz/vaudeville group Three Bips and a Bop, and recorded both with his own band and FATS NAVARRO's. Into the 1950s, Dameron worked for both modern and swing outfits, led a larger group including trumpeter CLIFFORD BROWN in 1953, and wrote pieces for both the MAX ROACH/ Clifford Brown band and for singer Carmen McRae. Some significant Tadd Dameron work appears under Fats Navarro's entry.

*_Fontainebleu_ (Original Jazz Classics OJC 055)

A Dameron band in 1956, a mid-sized ensemble of exactly the scope he wrote his most memorable pieces for, and featuring trumpeter KENNY DORHAM and alto saxophonist Sahib Shihab. The leader determines the shape of this set very explicitly – 'Fontaine-bleu' itself is completely notated – but Dameron's subtle methods, almost disguising his melody lines within the lustrous movement of chords, establish a jazz feeling that all but implies improvisation is present when it isn't. On the other pieces the band relaxes, notably Kenny Dorham who plays with characteristic panache.

Davis, Eddie 'Lockjaw'

(Born New York, March 2, 1921; died Culver City, November 3, 1986)

Immensely attractive blend of the broad, affable style of the swing tenorists (Davis worked with the big band of Andy Kirk in the 1940s, and then began a long on-off relationship with the Count Basie band in 1952) and the speedier mannerisms of bebop. A powerful, emphatic performer whose early style had a distinct connection with the booming, bluesy authority of Illinois Jacquet, Davis came from a school that believed in raising the temperature as early as possible and keeping it on the boil. But some of his most engaging work as an improviser was to be heard in the partnership with fellow-tenorist JOHNNY GRIFFIN, an association that ran intermittently for over two decades.

Griff and Lock (Original Jazz Classics OJC 264)

Davis and Johnny Griffin together in 1960, with Junior Mance on piano in a hard-swinging band. Davis furnishes his customary mixture of admonishing squeals, headlong charges and an attractive contrast of cantankerous wildness and a reassuringly rumbling vibrato, and Griffin's fleet virtuosity fills every chink.

Davis, Miles Dewey

(Born Alton, Illinois, May 26, 1926; died Santa Monica, California, September 28, 1991)

'Miles,' once said the composer and arranger GIL EVANS, 'is aware of his complete surroundings ... the quality of a certain chord, its tension or lack of tension, can cause him to create a sound appropriate to it. He can put his own substance, his own flesh, on a note, and then put that note exactly where it belongs.' Alto saxophonist JACKIE McLEAN said, 'Miles can play three notes and say as much as someone playing thirty.'

Over a career spanning more than 40 years Davis not only developed one of the most evocative solo voices in the history of jazz but also made the music sound different to the way it sounded before on at least four major occasions. His innovations began with the haunting orchestral *Birth of the Cool* recordings of 1949, in collaboration with the gifted Canadian arranger Gil Evans. In the 1950s he ran one of the finest post-bop bands, with John Coltrane as his front-line partner. In 1960, with one of the all-time jazz classics, *Kind of Blue*, he explored modal playing on scales rather than chords, and at one stroke removed much of the monotony that accompanied endless improvisation on chord patterns in all but the most inventive hands. With Gil Evans (*Sketches of Spain*, *Porgy and Bess*) he used his poignant trumpet sound as the only solo voice against lustrous orchestral textures. In the middle 1960s, when many adventurous jazz players were turning to the tumult of free-form, Davis loosened bebop still further and brought back a collective interplay reminiscent of the earliest jazz in one of his finest quintets with Wayne Shorter, Tony Williams, Ron Carter and Herbie Hancock. The band became the nucleus of Miles' moves into the electronic age and with *In a Silent Way* and *Bitches' Brew* he gave jazz-rock fusion a rare sting and flavour.

Miles Davis was that rare entity in earlier jazz, the offspring of a middle-class black family who paid for a formal musical education. By the time he went to the Juilliard School of Music at 18, he had already played trumpet extensively in high-school bands, and soon began playing hookey from the college to hang out on bebop's boulevard, 52nd Street, New York. He joined CHARLIE PARKER in 1945, quickly establishing himself as a bop trumpeter quite different from DIZZY GILLESPIE, his very hesitancy imparting a tremulous delicacy to his music. Davis was preoccupied with timbre and texture while most of his colleagues were obsessed with speed.

In 1948 Davis began collaborating with arranger Gil Evans and saxophonists GERRY MULLIGAN and Lee Konitz, three white musicians who had been working in a superior dance band (Claude Thornhill's) using instrumentation unusual for jazz, including French horn and tuba.

The *Birth of the Cool* nine-piece was an artistic success but a commercial failure. Partly through narcotics problems, Davis' career declined until 1954, but he made a startling comeback that year with a fully formed style mingling minimalism with tightly edited bursts of boppish bravura, sketching ideas with incisive brush-strokes, hanging tantalisingly behind the beat, giving himself an entirely new palette of trumpet contemplativeness through the use of the metal harmon mute. A brilliant quintet followed – including John Coltrane – and Davis also took up work with Gil Evans again on three groundbreaking orchestral albums. With *Kind of Blue*, Davis led a 1960 session featuring Coltrane, pianist BILL EVANS and saxophonist CANNONBALL ADDERLEY, one of the most inspirational jazz recording sessions ever. It was a rippling, sometimes raga-like exploration of modified blues and cycles of scales that – despite its restraint – still burned with jazz's traditional heat. It was Davis' response to the emerging free-jazz movement.

In the mid-1960s Miles Davis (always possessed of a BLAKEY-like shrewdness for spotting new talent) re-formed his quintet with the new generation of post-bop players such as Wayne Shorter (saxophones), Herbie Hancock (piano), Ron Carter (bass) and Tony Williams (drums). This was perhaps Davis' most flexible and improvisationally agile small group, demonstrating on a sequence of albums in the mid-1960s a one-touch responsiveness and collective ingenuity that remains unsurpassed and is still widely imitated by young players. Never inclined to rest on his laurels, Davis began to be attracted by the textural and rhythmic possibilities of rock and funk in the late 1960s (as well as by the increased audience potential and income) and began incorporating electronics and rock percussion techniques into his music. But, like everything else he touched, Miles Davis' rock music bore a distinct trademark. (For further developments in Davis' career, see page 329.)

★*Birth of the Cool* (Capitol CDP7 92862-2)

The revolutionary nine-piece that Davis led for two weeks in 1948, but which had an impact out of all proportion to its lifetime through these later recordings. The *Birth of the Cool* sessions resulted from the blending of such unconventional ensemble methods with low-key, unhurried bop-based improvisation, inflected with the even sounds of the cool school players, particularly the fragile high sounds of Lee Konitz' alto and the plush mid-range of Mulligan. Davis himself sounds less than happy – more tremulous and Gillespie-like, and trying to play too fast. A historic event, nonetheless.

★*Miles Davis* Vols. 1 & 2 (Blue Note CDP 781 501-2/502-2)

Miles Davis, recording here with MILT JACKSON, Jimmy Heath and others in 1953, delivering some of his best recorded improvising from any era of his playing. The arrangements owe a lot to the graceful, velvety *Birth of the Cool* manner. Much of the dynamism of the session is also down to the presence of Art Blakey at the drums, who often sounds engagingly like a man in a bad temper doing the washing-up in the background.

★*Workin' and Steamin'* (Original Jazz Classics OJC 296/391)

The band that formed after Miles Davis' 'comeback' performance in 1954 at the Newport Festival. Nothing to choose between these two discs since the group that made them could have played nursery rhymes and made them swing (Davis even manages to make music both mysterious and vivacious out of 'Surrey with a Fringe on Top'), the rhythm section being RED GARLAND on piano, Paul Chambers on bass and Philly Joe Jones on drums, and John Coltrane on saxophone. Coltrane's contrast with Davis, terrifying bursting-dams of sound against the trumpeter's terse restraint, was part of the charm.

★*Kind of Blue* (CBS 32109)

Kind of Blue, recorded in 1959, is one of the most enduring of all postwar jazz recordings. In its use of sequences of scales rather than chords, *Kind of Blue* found the meditative spaciousness of a structure close to Indian music. Bill Evans' piano (sharpened and polished by the tempo stability of CDs) sounds like spring rain, and Davis' trumpet is able to create infectious swing with a handful of notes.

★*E.S.P.* (CBS 467899)

One of the best of a limited span of mid-1960s Davis sessions, with Shorter, Hancock et al, that are still available. The themes burn with energy and originality, Wayne Shorter's saxophone solos have a throaty, indirect grandiloquence and the rhythm section is one of the best jazz has known.

★*Porgy and Bess* (CBS 450985)

Miles Davis is the only soloist on this trumpet concerto for which the brooding arrangements were conceived by Gil Evans. Miles' 'Summertime', which is played with a piquant muted sound over an unexpected mid-tempo clip, and a devastating 'Gone' (performed fast against shattering Philly Joe Jones drum breaks in its later stages) are unforgettable.

★*Sketches of Spain* (CBS 460604)

A Gil Evans orchestral piece, using Spanish folk motifs and Davis' trumpet as a solo singer. The subtlety of Evans' writing for the percussion, the brass and the low sounds enriches the backdrop behind Davis' haunting trumpet. Rodrigues' 'Concierto D'Aranjuez' is a major feature of the album (an interpretation which classical listeners sometimes find trite, and the section playing isn't all that steady at times) but Davis' performance on the glowing 'Solea' is hypnotic.

Desmond, Paul

(Born San Francisco, November 25, 1924; died May 30, 1977)
Excellent cool school alto saxophonist whose originality was often obscured by his subsidiary role in various bands led by Dave Brubeck. Desmond began working with Brubeck in 1948 and remained in close association with the pianist until the late 1960s. His most famous contribution to the Brubeck band was the perennially popular tune 'Take Five', a theme of playful grace and catchiness that has become a modern jazz classic. A dedicated improviser whose roots were in Lester Young and the variations on that style explored by Lee Konitz, Desmond's music never hardened into mannerism despite the Brubeck years, and his advanced techniques on the alto even endeared him to an uncompromising *enfant terrible* of free-music, the saxophonist Anthony Braxton.

★*Polka Dots and Moonbeams* (Bluebird ND 90637)

Compilation of various solo outings for Desmond on RCA in the early 1960s, featuring the leader's feathery alto style against the utterly apposite guitarist Jim Hall, an assortment of bassists, and MJQ drummer Connie Kay, an appropriately tiptoeing performer for Desmond's hushed style.

Donaldson, Lou

(Born Badin, North Carolina, November 1, 1926)
As with most alto saxophonists forming their style in the early 1950s, Donaldson fell under the influence of CHARLIE PARKER, but his dislike of overt experimentalism and his enthusiasm for the spirited, blues-oriented simplicity of early jazz led him increasingly towards soul-jazz and funk in the 1960s after brief periods with ART BLAKEY and Charles Mingus. More declamatory and unambiguous in style than Parker, Donaldson brought rhythm & blues ideas to his improvising, and often compounded the effect with the use of an organ in his bands.

★*Blues Walk* (Blue Note B21Y-46525)

One of the better-known Donaldson discs from the late 1950s, it's a good example of the way that some of the early funk-oriented Blue Note sessions could swing hard without the dominating presence of major soloists. This is Donaldson's second album as a leader, made in 1958, and features the great conga player Ray Barretto in addition to Dave Bailey on drums. The dynamic rhythm section generates considerable heat on the title track, 'Play Ray' and 'Callin' All Cats'.

★*Quartet Quintet and Sextet* (Blue Note CDP 7815372)

Quintessential Blue Note recording material from the early 1950s, with an excellent roster of bop and prospective soul-jazz musicians between 1952 and 1954 – including trumpeter Blue Mitchell, pianists Horace Silver and Elmo Hope, and appearances from Art Blakey on drums. Donaldson had yet to discover a style beyond a more rhapsodic version of Charlie Parker's at this point, but the bands swing hard.

Dorham, McKinley Howard 'Kenny'

(Born Fairfield, Texas, August 30, 1924; died New York, December 5, 1972)
Kenny Dorham had a meteoric early career, replacing MILES DAVIS in the CHARLIE PARKER quintet in 1948 after stints with DIZZY GILLESPIE, Billy Eckstine and Lionel Hampton, becoming a founder member of the ART BLAKEY/HORACE SILVER Jazz Messengers in 1954, then replacing Clifford Brown in the MAX ROACH quintet after Brown's fatal road accident in 1956. Like LEE MORGAN, Dorham has been rediscovered in the hard-bop and dance-jazz renaissance of the 1980s, his appeal to the latter audience being related to his enthusiasm for Latin-American music.

★Jazz Contemporary (Time BCD 1048)

Dorham in 1960 with a superb and frequently overlooked pianist, Steve Kuhn, and featuring an interesting mix of material including 'Monk's Mood' and Dave Brubeck's 'In Your Own Sweet Way'. The trumpeter is in adventurous form technically here, and the group sound takes more chances than is common on hard-bop sessions of the era.

Edwards, Theodore Marcus 'Teddy'

(Born Jackson, Mississippi, April 26, 1924)
An intriguing combination of influences, Teddy Edwards has the big, bluesy sound of many southern tenor saxophonists and a warm and mellow approach to ballads – and though his inclinations are towards bebop, his solidity and timing recall the swing era. Edwards was one of the first significant bebop musicians to work on the west coast in the 1940s after stretches in the territory swing bands, and frequently worked there with the trumpeter HOWARD McGHEE, and occasionally DEXTER GORDON. Edwards' most fruitful collaboration in the 1950s was with MAX ROACH and

CLIFFORD BROWN, and he has spent the subsequent period recording extensively with other leaders (including Benny Carter, Gerald Wilson, Benny Goodman and singers Sarah Vaughan and Tom Waits) and occasionally leading groups of his own.

★*Together Again!* (Original Jazz Classics OJC 424)

One of Edwards' best-ever recordings – apart from the relaxed and elegant 'Teddy's Ready', which demands reissue – a reunion with Howard McGhee from 1961, its boppish atmosphere reinforced by the rugged bass of Ray Brown and such ingredients as CHARLIE PARKER's blues 'Perhaps'. Edwards the ballad player makes a delightful account of the much-played 'Misty'.

Ervin, Booker Telleferro Jr

(Born Denison, Texas, October 31, 1930; died New York, July 31, 1970)
One of the most distinctive of tenor saxophone voices, as gravelly a sound as Lee Marvin singing, a musician whom Charles Mingus described as 'one of the trance players' who inhabit their music totally. Ervin worked extensively in the mid-west in the 1950s until recommended to Mingus, whose band he joined in 1958. A player of deliberation and intelligent austerity, Ervin's selective approach in his solos led to a remarkable improvisational appropriateness whatever the time signature or theme. Though he was influenced by the work of DEXTER GORDON and John Coltrane, his tone was harder and – unlike either of those voluble performers – he preferred to mould and manipulate a handful of phrases in each solo rather than hurtle feverishly over the chord changes.

★*That's It* (Candid 9014)

Ervin's best session as a leader, largely comprising his own pieces. Sinuously reflective on spacey ballads such as 'Uranus', the saxophonist is nevertheless at his strongest over the testing changes of 'Speak Low', accelerating through them to stretches of sustained, surging passion.

Evans, Ian Ernest Gilmore 'Gil'

(Born Toronto, May 13, 1912; died Mexico, March 20, 1988)

One of the best-loved figures in jazz, a man whose youthfulness, broadmindedness and constant endorsement of living vibrantly in the present won him every kind of accolade, from honorary doctorates and fellowships from conservatoires, Grammy awards and pollwinners' prizes to performance of his work at the White House. He had the lightest touch of any jazz writer, and could infuse a band with his personality by means that were barely perceptible.

Evans moved to New York at the beginning of the 1940s. With dance-band leader Claude Thornhill in the late 1940s, Evans developed a new sound for the jazz lineup. It augmented the usual instrumentation with French horns, tuba and woodwinds. It often sounded poignant and reflective and replaced the super-heated quality of both bebop and its predecessor swing with a light, floating lyricism that explored texture and timbre more than explicit beat or the conversational call-and-response 'riffing' technique common to 1930s swing orchestras. Some dubbed the effect 'clouds of sound'.

The ideas appealed to the young MILES DAVIS. In 1949 Davis, pianist John Lewis (later of the Modern Jazz Quartet), saxophonists GERRY MULLIGAN and Lee Konitz joined with Gil Evans to form a ground-breaking but short-lived jazz orchestra. Its recordings came to be known as *The Birth of the Cool*.

Evans' collaborations with Miles Davis continued into the 1960s. The arranger's touch enriched the simplest materials with arrangements that made the most threadbare phrases glow, and imparted new subtleties to already complex work – as he did with Gershwin's *Porgy and Bess* and a remake of Rodrigues' 'Concierto D'Aranjuez' for Miles Davis' *Sketches of Spain*. Later, Evans increasingly made the arrangements flexible enough in interpretation for the ensemble sections as well as the solos to sound improvised.

Though Evans had, like Ellington, introduced some of the vertical richness of symphonic music to jazz – the strongest suits of which had hitherto been melodic inventiveness and rhythmic audacity – his open-mindedness frequently led him to pop music for new ideas. The inspired rhythm & blues guitarist Jimi Hendrix was much admired by Evans, who always kept a place for some of Hendrix' themes in his band's repertoire.

★*Out of the Cool* (MCACD 5653)

A 1960 album that provided an opportunity for Evans – who had reached a wide public with his sumptuous orchestral interplay with Miles Davis – to reveal that his own bands could sound as sensuous, surprising and light on their feet. Principal trumpeter here is the underrated Johnny Coles, whose subtlety of inflection is striking on the mood piece 'Sunken Treasure' and whose double-time ingenuity intensifies a vigorous adaptation of George Russell's 'Stratusphunk'. Trombonist Jimmy Knepper also makes his mark, grippingly desolate on 'Where Flamingoes Fly'.

★*Priestess* (Antilles (ANCD 8717)

A terrific live session from Evans' looser and more pop-oriented phase, including a sensational blues saxophone performance from Dave Sanborn on 'Short Visit', but with horn-playing hardly less animated from George Adams and Arthur Blythe, Lew Soloff and Hannibal Marvin Peterson.

★*Live at Sweet Basil* (Electric Bird K23P 6355/6)

Gil Evans' famous 'Monday Night Orchestra', which played at Sweet Basil's under Evans' leadership until his death, and continued afterwards as a tribute to him. A typical exhilarating night's work, featuring tunes by Jimi Hendrix, Charles Mingus ('Orange Was the Colour of Her Dress, Then Blue Silk'), Herbie Hancock and others, and featuring powerful soloists such as tenorist George Adams and the guitarist Hiram Bullock.

★*Rhythm-a-ning* (Emarcy 836401)

Unexpectedly impressive session featuring Evans in 1987 with a French orchestra including British tenorist Andy Sheppard and Miles Davis' percussionist Marilyn Mazur. French arranger Laurent Cugny could hardly have delivered a more respectful account of Evans' charts and, freed from the responsibilities of watching over the band himself, Evans performs some fascinating low-profile piano. Not all the soloing is anything to write home about, but the quality of the ensemble sound is mostly immaculate.

★*Gil Evans/Lee Konitz. Heroes* (Verve 511 621-2)

Lee Konitz' notes to this disc declare of Evans, departed by the time of its release: 'Gil was not a composer in the usual sense of the word. He was not a piano player in the usual sense, either. In fact, Gil was not your usual kind of man. He was a poet all the way from morning to night.' This delightful duet between Konitz and Evans dates from 1980 and includes Wayne Shorter's 'Prince of Darkness', Mingus' 'Reincarnation of a Lovebird', 'Lover Man' and an inimitable Evans' blues. Konitz repeatedly proves he's just as poetic as Evans. No technical display, it's nevertheless beautiful improvisation, steeped in the resonances of the tunes.

Evans, William John 'Bill'

(Born Plainfield, New Jersey, August 16, 1929; died New York, September 15, 1980)
Evans has been one of the most influential pianists in postwar jazz, his methods audible in the music of McCoy Tyner, Herbie Hancock, Keith Jarrett and many others. One of the subtlest piano players in jazz history, Evans possessed the rare gift of being introspective without sacrificing strength; though he could play hynotically at very low volumes and was a master of ballads, there was a steely core to his improvising that made it commanding whatever the tempo or the mood.

Bill Evans was taught piano, violin and flute as a child, and his first contact with jazz piano was swing. But by the mid-1950s, through an absorption of BUD POWELL's approach to uptempo playing, Lennie Tristano's experiments with breaking the rigid bar-line structures of bop (a characteristic of Evans solos is the long improvised line that sweeps aside the hurdles of the chord changes) and rich harmonic variation in the left hand, Evans had become unique. He joined MILES DAVIS in 1958, a connection that only lasted eight months but which saw the making of a historic jazz record, *Kind of Blue*. At the beginning of the 1960s Evans was working with the guitar-like double-bass-playing of Scott LaFaro, and with the addition of Paul Motian on drums, the band developed an uncanny empathy. Evans' compositions 'Blue in Green' and 'Waltz For Debby' have become jazz standards.

★*Portrait in Jazz* (Original Jazz Classics OJC 088)

The first trio recording of Evans, LaFaro and Motian. By 1959 Evans had more or less fully absorbed his studies and experiments (notably drawn from Tristano) into a lyrically driven whole: his timing was immaculate, his shading of a note taking care of minutiae with an offhand grace. The disc contains a memorable version of 'Autumn Leaves' and a first thoughtful, then dancing and animated version of *Kind of Blue*'s 'Blue in Green'.

★*Everybody Digs Bill Evans* (Original Jazz Classics OJC 068)

Evans' second trio album, with Philly Joe Jones on drums, one of the pianist's most suitable partners. The pianist is punchy and purposeful after Jones' sensational drum intro to 'Night and Day', driving through a mixture of trickling, waterfall treble descents, abrupt pauses, sudden chiming chords, more pauses, fragments of right-hand phrases (the rhythmic implications of which are resolved by a hint of a dab in the left hand) and two-handed chordal reminders of the tune. By contrast, he performs with Debussy-like reflectiveness on the beautiful 'Peace Piece'.

★*Sunday at the Village Vanguard* (Original Jazz Classics OJC 140)

A stunning example of the Evans trio's virtues – by 1961 far more reflexive and collectivised – and the pianist's first live recording. The music boils with invention and empathy, with Evans' playing at its most intense synthesis of introspection and impulsiveness. Tracks include Miles Davis' 'Solar' and a sublime interpretation of Gershwin's poignant 'My Man's Gone Now'. This classic Evans trio was broken up by fate just ten days later – LaFaro was killed in a road crash.

★*The Brilliant* (Timeless CDSJP 329)

Evans' sudden death in 1980 stunned his fans, not least because within a few weeks of it he seemed to be playing as well as ever, or better. This trio set from the same year was recorded live at Keystone Korner in San Francisco and documents an Evans moving ever closer to the outer limits of his materials, with excellent partners in bassist Marc Johnson and drummer Joe LaBarbera.

★*Turn Out The Stars* (Dreyfus Jazz Line 191 063-2)

The same band in that last year, featuring seven tunes from the last night of his final season at Ronnie Scott's in 1980. Poorer sound quality, but some explosive playing from Evans on 'I Do It For Love', amid a good deal of reflective music, and slowly-crystallising themes like 'Laurie' and 'Two Lonely People'. Essential for anyone who was there during that unforgettable season.

Farlow, Talmage Holt 'Tal'

(Born Greensboro, North Carolina, June 7, 1921)
An excellent guitarist emerging from the CHARLIE CHRISTIAN stable in the 1940s but at times indicating (notably with the vibist Red Norvo's ingenious trio of 1949–51) a lyrical originality that substantially extended the Christian legacy. Farlow's faults could be over-embroidery but though his recent work doesn't match some of his earlier trio sessions, he is both a creative ensemble player and a musician aware (as Django Reinhardt was and many beboppers were not) of the most telling nuances and timbral effects of the guitar.

★*The Return of Tal Farlow* (Original Jazz Classics OJC 356)

Superb Farlow quartet session from 1969, featuring the guitarist with John Scully (piano), Jack Six (bass) and Alan Dawson (drums). Farlow was already into his extensive period of retirement from the music business by this time, but he has always been able to return with no apparent loss of his touch. 'My Romance' is a delectable example of his intelligence and taste.

Farmer, Arthur Stewart 'Art'

(Born Council Bluffs, Iowa, August 21, 1928)
Trumpeter and flugelhornist Farmer worked in the rhythm & blues band of Johnny Otis, the swing band of Benny Carter and the bebop band of Wardell Gray. This catholicity extended later to work with composers as different as George Russell and Quincy Jones, but his partnership with saxophonist BENNY GOLSON from 1959 (a band that included the young McCoy Tyner) gave jazz one of its most attractive bop-influenced small groups. Farmer's playing is often wistful, but his phrasing is unusual (he favours wide intervals and behind-the-beat accents) and he exhibits a poise and burnished tone that has given him a notable reputation among fellow-musicians, though less so with the public.

★*Blame It On My Youth* (Contemporary C 14042)

Exceptional warmth and poise on flugelhorn from Farmer, notably on the title track, which might have been written just for him. Though this session wasn't cut until 1988, when Farmer was approaching 60, it's one of the best of his life. Pianist James Williams leads a crisp and creative rhythm section including drummer Victor Lewis.

Feldman, Victor Stanley

(Born London, April 7, 1934; died Los Angeles, May 12, 1987)
Feldman was a child prodigy on the wartime London jazz scene, adept on piano, drums and vibes. By the time he was 20 he had worked with virtually all of the prominent British jazz and dance-band leaders, notably Ronnie Scott, John Dankworth and Ted Heath. Both Feldman and Scott had formed close contacts with the Woody Herman Orchestra in the early 1950s and in 1955 Feldman chose to make the connection permanent, moving to the States to join the band. The fertility of his ideas and the depth of

his knowledge made a lasting impression on front-rank American modernists such as MILES DAVIS and CANNONBALL ADDERLEY (he turned down a chance to join the former for a piano job that Herbie Hancock eventually took, and worked briefly with the latter) but Feldman worked largely in the west coast studios, nonetheless writing a lasting contribution to jazz's raw materials in the tune 'Seven Steps to Heaven', which became a Miles Davis' album title. Original Jazz Classics should issue his superb *Arrival of Victor Feldman* trio session on CD.

★*Suite Sixteen* (Original Jazz Classics OJC 1768)

Feldman in 1955, before his emigration to the States, with various British groups including Ronnie Scott, TUBBY HAYES, Jimmy Deuchar and others. As intriguing as a document of the 1950s British jazz scene as it is of Feldman, it nevertheless features the leader in some succinct vibes outings.

Ferguson, Maynard

(Born Montreal, May 4, 1928)
Canadian trumpeter, renowned for his stratospheric high notes, which he displayed to spectacular effect with the Stan Kenton Orchestra of 1950–3. Like many technically extraordinary performers, Ferguson has had difficulty subsuming his skills within a convincing musical structure when working on his own account – and his choice of unremarkable fusion and pop material for his own orchestras from the early 1970s onwards has made this transformation all the harder.

★*Birdland Dreamband* (Bluebird ND 86455)

The young trumpet star in action in 1956 before his style became too muscle-bound, with a cut-down big band strongly flavoured by the Kenton legacy, and showcasing excellent partners such as saxophonist Al Cohn and pianist Hank Jones. The band is unsurprisingly given to sustained, somewhat frantic intensity and enthusiasm for permanent climax, but Ferguson's own playing reveals a coherence and sensitivity he didn't often display later.

Flanagan, Tommy Lee

(Born Detroit, March 16, 1930)

Flanagan is a deft, upbeat, bop-derived pianist probably best known for his shrewd and sensitive accompanying work for Ella Fitzgerald, and as a musical director for Tony Bennett. He has, however, pursued a fruitful career as a leader and a creative improviser in his own right: in the 1940s and 1950s with bands led by MILES DAVIS, SONNY ROLLINS, John Coltrane ('Giant Steps') and Coleman Hawkins, and since the mid-1970s. Where the work of some bop pianists can be fast and intricate to the point of relentlessness, Flanagan always maintains a bounce and brightness that is his instant trademark.

★Giant Steps: In Memory of John Coltrane (Enja 4022)

Minor piano masterpiece of the 1980s, this trio session finds a revitalised Flanagan in partnership with George Mraz on bass and Al Foster on drums. Flanagan's treatment of Coltrane's classic ballad 'Naima' puts most of the innumerable interpretations of this theme into the shade, and after a decade of constant saxophone-blasting in pursuit of Coltrane's elusive muse, the pianist's intelligent investigations come as an immense relief.

Freeman, Earl Lavon 'Von'

(Born Chicago, October 3, 1922)

Earl Lavon 'Von' Freeman, the Chicagoan saxophonist, formerly partner to Sun Ra, Andrew Hill and DEXTER GORDON, and father of the powerful avant-bop musician Chico Freeman, is an energetic performer still in his distinctive prime. Freeman Sr sounds as if he has listened to a mixture of Lester Young, Coleman Hawkins, Ornette Coleman and John Coltrane – an unusual combination of influences for a musician of his generation. He has a legendarily curious tone, a querulous, sometimes squawky sound that blends fragments of bebop constructions, thematic variations running a clear line back to Lester Young, scatterings of the booming, expansive sound of the Coleman Hawkins school, and unexpected liberties of pitch and tuning that predate Ornette Coleman.

Freeman's father was a trombone-playing policeman and jazz-lover, his mother had been a church musician, and all the Freeman sons turned pro. Freeman performed around the Chicago clubs in the years after the war, when the city was full of exciting jazz, and joined the experimental and quirky early bands of composer/pianist Sun Ra. The experience thus made him a different caste of bebop player, able to anticipate the demands of the period between the spawning of bebop and the coming of free-form.

★*Serenade and Blues* (Chief CHIEFCD 3)

A 1975 trio set featuring Von Freeman with John Young on piano, and Wilbur Campbell on drums. Those who have heard Von Freeman in his son's band, with a more adventurous rhythm section, might find this relaxed breeze through blues and standard songs a little unassuming. But his appearances on record are rare enough, this is his only CD, and his sound and fluency make striking remoulds of some familiar material.

Garland, William M 'Red'

(Born Dallas, Texas, May 13, 1923; died Dallas, April 23, 1984)
A much-copied bebop pianist, distinctive for his characteristic percussive two-hand block-chord solos, which brought an informal, jangling, bar-piano forthrightness to an idiom sometimes inclined to inscrutability. Having worked in the late 1940s with the blues band of Eddie Vinson (a group that included the young John Coltrane), Red Garland took up his most celebrated employment between 1955 and 1958 as a member of the first great MILES DAVIS quintet, recording albums such as *Workin'* and *Steamin'*.

★*Soul Junction* (Original Jazz Classics OJC 481)

Effectively the Miles Davis band without Miles; trumpeter DONALD BYRD convincingly occupies the chair. Coltrane is forthright and emotional, and Garland bluesy in a manner that echoes much earlier jazz. His playing throughout the disc is a delight.

Gillespie, John Birks 'Dizzy'

(Born Cheraw, S Carolina, October 21, 1917; died New Jersey, January 6, 1993)

A colossus of modern trumpet-playing and crucial component of the informal group that helped found bebop as an idiom in the late 1930s. Gillespie was the son of a bricklayer and amateur musician, won a scholarship to Carolina's Laurinburg Institute and by the mid-1930s – then living in Philadelphia – he began to find regular work as a trumpeter in the style of the thrilling Roy Eldridge.

In 1937 Gillespie took his idol's place in the Teddy Hill band, establishing himself with an excellent technique and an advanced harmonic knowledge that led him beyond the basic song-forms of swing. Two years later he joined Cab Calloway but was soon sacked for a mixture of musical unconventionality and disruptive behaviour. He began sitting in with the band that drummer Kenny Clarke had put together at Minton's.

Like CHARLIE PARKER, Gillespie did not simply use in his improvisations notes explicitly related to the chord of the tune he was playing, but also those derived from momentarily sliding into another chord a semitone away. He would also mix major chord solos over minor key changes, or substitute new chords for those of standards.

In May 1945 Gillespie participated with Parker in the first full-blooded bebop recording session, making an impact almost as startling as Parker's with his mixture of early jazz bent notes and blues effects, breathtaking speed and constant variety and powers of surprise. The trumpeter formed a big band at the end of the 1940s which – though its overall ensemble sound was not as audaciously new as the impact of a bebop small group – nevertheless opened a new chapter in the history of jazz orchestration, and Gillespie compositions such as 'Night in Tunisia', 'Groovin' High' and 'Salt Peanuts' became modern standards. The trumpeter also revealed an interest in Latin (particularly Cuban) rhythms that stayed with him for life.

Dizzy Gillespie recorded and toured constantly with small groups and orchestras from the 1950s to the beginning of 1993, as well as encouraging promising newcomers (FATS NAVARRO, KENNY DORHAM, MILES DAVIS, CLIFFORD BROWN, LEE MORGAN, Jon Faddis, Arturo Sandoval), being feted by governments and arts foundations worldwide, and receiving innumerable awards, tributes and honorary doctorates. In the 1980s he spectacularly toured with his United Nations Orchestra, featuring some of the most illustrious jazz artists to have built their reputations a long way away from New York or Chicago or Kansas City.

★*Groovin' High* (Savoy SV 0152)

Compilation of music featuring Gillespie from 1945 and 1946, when the bebop revolution had already been under way for nearly five years. These takes feature both small groups and Gillespie's powerful bop-oriented big band and cover most of the trumpeter's significant work outside sessions under Charlie Parker's name during the period.

★*Pleyel Concert 1953* (Vogue 655608)

Gillespie began to resynthesise his early experiences in the swing bands with the insights of bop during the early 1950s, with the result that his music became more open and forthright and his solo playing more amiably imperious. On this set from Paris, Gillespie rolls through a mixed bebop and vaudeville repertoire with a relatively unexceptional group, but his own playing is magnificent.

★*Max + Dizzy, Paris 1989* (A & M 6404)

Co-founders of bebop in captivating communion in Paris in 1989. Gillespie was paired with MAX ROACH for this memorable get-together, and the sentiments aroused by the occasion brought the best out of the trumpeter despite his technique having slowed; as for Roach, he has seemed unmoved by the years and his drums still crackle like the old days. Some of the disc features some reminiscing and reflection by the two men.

Giuffre, James Peter 'Jimmy'

(Born Dallas, Texas, April 26, 1921)
Reed player and composer Jimmy Giuffre's name is most commonly associated with two themes: 'Four Brothers' for the Woody Herman Second Herd, and 'The Train and the River', the latter a compelling piece of cool jazz featured in the Newport Festival movie, *Jazz on a Summer's Day*. Giuffre worked with eminent white big bands in the 1940s (Buddy Rich's, Jimmy Dorsey's, Woody Herman's), and became associated with the west coast cool school in the next decade, frequently appearing in small combos with unconventional instrumentation. Giuffre continued these investigations with small ensembles (notably with pianist Paul Bley and bassist Steve Swallow) in the 1960s. A highly unusual clarinettist, Giuffre favours the mellow chalumeau middle and lower register of the instrument.

★*The Jimmy Giuffre 3* (Atlantic 90981)

Giuffre in the 'Train and the River' era, with that celebrated piece of subtle cool jazz featured prominently, plus other examples of just why this band represented a pooling of musical resources highly unusual for its time on several counts – dynamic subtlety, absence of cliché, and stretching of the boundaries of orthodox jazz structure. Giuffre is accompanied by JIM HALL's thoughtful guitar-playing and for the most part Ralph Pena's bass.

★*1961* (ECM 1438/9)

One of the best documents of Giuffre's work available, an imaginative package built out of his 1961 albums *Fusion* and *Thesis*, and featuring an all-but-free band with pianist Paul Bley and bassist Steve Swallow. All three musicians are immersed in the pursuit of taking jazz development beyond bop. At the time they made these records, modal jazz was offering one alternative, but much of what is happening here is closer to Ornette Coleman's reactive approach. Giuffre's foggy, predominantly low-register murmur is hypnotic, and some of the early Carla Bley tunes featured here sound as modern as when they were conceived.

★Quasar (Soul Note 1108)

A discreet but elegantly complex 1985 session. The lineup seems oddly balanced at first, the leader on flutes, clarinet and saxophones, with Pete Levin's electric keyboards and bass. But Giuffre's control over his materials and sense of texture doesn't fail him. Levin is more prominent, but his taste doesn't lapse. Giuffre's version of 'Shadows', on bass flute, is worth the disc.

Golson, Benny

(Born Philadelphia, January 25, 1929)
Golson's tenor-playing was close to the full, earthy sound of LUCKY THOMPSON, but also incorporated the harmonic audacity of Don Byas. For all that this repertoire made his instrumental contributions useful, Golson's talent was primarily as an inspired composer and arranger, classics such as 'I Remember Clifford' being among memorable work of his. Golson made an impact with the DIZZY GILLESPIE big band (1956–8) and then with ART BLAKEY's Jazz Messengers; he followed by forming a closely related outfit called the Jazztet, also featuring ART FARMER on trumpet, and McCoy Tyner on piano, shortly before Tyner joined John Coltrane. Though lucrative studio work took Golson out of sight for much of the 1970s, he returned in the next decade to re-form the Jazztet, when Coltrane's influence on him became apparent.

★The Other Side of Benny Golson (Original Jazz Classics OJC 1750)

Delightful Golson-led session from 1958, close to the form the Jazztet would take and featuring Barry Harris on piano, Curtis Fuller on trombone and Philly Joe Jones on drums. Golson, as usual, sounds forthright to the point of cantankerous, and Jones is in his element in a band of this kind.

★Stardust (Denon 33CY-1838)

Excellent 1980s Golson session in the imposing company of FREDDIE HUBBARD on trumpet and new-generation star sidemen of the quality of Mulgrew Miller (on piano) and Marvin 'Smitty'

Smith (on drums). Golson's deft arrangements sparkle every bit as strongly as the soloists.

★*Live* (Dreyfus Jazz Line 191057-2)

Golson's ability to sound as if he occupies several periods of jazz at the same time is convincingly borne out by this fine live set with a good band, including the erudite and agile pianist Mulgrew Miller. Golson repeatedly develops solos from the relaxed, offhand mood of a swing player to the boiling ferocity of a John Coltrane, and Miller shadows him everywhere. There's a powerful account of 'Sweet and Lovely', and a mid-tempo original called 'Along Came Betty' that resembles the baleful organ blues 'Killer Joe'. The classic 'I Remember Clifford' is the highlight, however – an improvisational masterpiece of droning sounds, cross-register skids, and soft, yielding notes.

Gordon, Dexter Keith

(Born Los Angeles, February 27, 1923; died August 1990)
Bertrand Tavernier's 1986 feature film *Round Midnight* brought Dexter Gordon into the movie theatres of the world, and then into its living rooms – but the sheer drama of his performances on the tenor saxophone are ultimately his real epitaph. He was first a clarinettist, then an alto saxophonist, and a tenorist by the age of 17, at which point he joined the Lionel Hampton band (featuring in scorching tenor dialogues with Illinois Jacquet) and not long afterwards the influential bop-oriented Billy Eckstine band. Lester Young was a major influence on his early playing, with his lyrical strength and sense of shape, but the structurally sophisticated and imperious Coleman Hawkins, and the mercurial Charlie Parker were inevitably others. Gordon sought a style that had Parker's dynamism, Hawkins' gravitas, and Young's delicacy. He explored these qualities further in energetic partnership with another tenorist, Wardell Gray.

By the end of the 1940s, Gordon's skills were consolidated into a style of immense melodic variety, freedom from cliché and repetition over even the most prolonged extemporisations, a mischievous enthusiasm for rampant quotation from other tunes, and an arsenal of boneshaking special effects – warbles, hoots, honks and hoarse, ascendant cries. John Coltrane, among others, always acknowledged the depth of his debt to Gordon.

★*Dexter Rides Again* (Savoy SV 0120)

A young Dexter Gordon, recorded between 1945 and 1947 in partnership with various alumni of the bebop movement, including ART BLAKEY and MAX ROACH. These sessions don't include Gordon's legendary exchanges with the lighter-toned but equally quick-thinking Wardell Gray, but though the other saxophonists present are by no means his equal, everyone keeps up, and Gordon himself already sounds like an improviser who doesn't let anything get in his way.

★*Go* (Blue Note CDP 746 094-2)

Gordon's own favourite album, recorded with his most suitable rhythm section of Sonny Clark (piano), Butch Warren (bass) and Billy Higgins (drums) on his return to New York in 1961 after the second prison sentence. *Go* features two sublime examples of Gordon's massive authority at slow tempos as well as fast, with reverberating renditions of 'Guess I'll Hang My Tears Out To Dry' and 'Where Are You?', but also displays the charging, flat-out bop horn king's clout on 'Second Balcony Jump'.

★*Our Man in Paris* (Blue Note CDP 7463942)

Another Blue Note classic, this time from 1963 in Paris, finding Gordon in exactly that tireless, seven-league-stride form that influenced Coltrane. Like ROLLINS, Gordon combines the weight and solidity of the early saxophonists with the alacrity of bebop and much of his playing here is the closest you can get to a musical version of a sculpture in granite. Even on the fast 'Scrapple from the Apple' Gordon retains this impact, and an added bonus is the presence of pianist BUD POWELL – not functioning on all cylinders by this time, but full of unexpected melodic twists.

Biting the Apple (Steeplechase 1080)

Gordon's homecoming to the States in 1976, the event taken by some to be the starting-gun fired on the 'neo-bop' movement. Both as a ballad player and as a thunderous uptempo performer Gordon is still in superb fettle, and an excellent band featuring Barry Harris on piano, Sam Jones on bass and Al Foster on drums are admirable foils.

Green, Grant

(Born St Louis, Missouri, June 6, 1931; died January 31, 1979)
Always close to the territory between bebop and the beginnings of jazz-funk in the 1950s and early 1960s, Grant Green recorded first with Elvin Jones (1959) and in the following two years appeared in bluesy organ groups led by Sam Lazar and Jack McDuff. By the mid-1960s Green was recording for Blue Note under his own name, in the company of excellent horn players such as Joe Henderson and HANK MOBLEY. With a mixture of organ-like punchy chord-playing and pure, gliding lead lines Green quickly became a popular sideman, his style looking towards the coming of jazz-fusion rather than being locked in CHARLIE CHRISTIAN-like bop playing. Drug problems led to long layoffs, and when he returned to playing in the early 1970s it was mostly to bland and routine funky sessions. Green's best Blue Note session, *Solid*, is currently unavailable in any format.

Idle Moments (Blue Note B21Y 84154)

Some of the best guitar-playing of the early 1960s documented here in Green's mixture of strength, confident attack and lyricism, with sustained improvisations that don't evaporate into the neutral repetition of funky licks that the guitarist was to go in for later. Apart from the title track, Green is thoughtful and inventive in his rendition of John Lewis' 'Django'.

Griffin, John Arnold III 'Johnny'

(Born Chicago, April 24, 1928)

A hard bopper to his fingertips, Griffin joined the Lionel Hampton band as a 17-year-old, began recording for Blue Note in the company of front-rank contemporaries such as John Coltrane and HANK MOBLEY, and was tailor-made for membership of ART BLAKEY's Jazz Messengers. When the 'soul-jazz' boom occurred at the end of the 1950s Griffin made some of the most distinctive and least formulaic contributions to the genre, notably with the compulsive 'Wade in the Water' from *Big Soul*. He then formed a two-tenor partnership in the mould of DEXTER GORDON/Wardell Gray when he began working regularly with the gritty swing saxophonist EDDIE 'LOCKJAW' DAVIS. Griffin moved to Europe in 1962 and joined the Kenny Clarke-Francy Boland band.

★*A Blowing Session* (Blue Note 781 559)

Griffin in breakneck partnership with John Coltrane and Hank Mobley, a situation in which the newcomer generally proved himself ahead for sheer explosive energy and speed.

★*The Man I Love* (Black Lion 60107)

The tenorist during his fertile European period of the 1960s, a CD featuring Griffin with two fine expatriate beboppers (Kenny Drew on piano and Albert 'Tootie' Heath on drums) plus bassist Niels-Henning Orsted-Pedersen. The title is deceptive. Though Griffin certainly plays the tune, he swarms all over it as if trying to block the romantic interpretation out of his mind.

★*The Cat* (Antilles 422 848 421-2)

At 63 the Little Giant had inevitably lost a little. No sensational tunes, but Griffin's use of space, ghostly trills, nudging notes, honks, and mixtures of drifting lyricism and dug-in grooving makes up for it. He's not so comfortable with fast bop now ('Hot Sake' almost trips him) but his breathy, faintly creaking ballad style, performed as if he can hardly bear to push the air out of the horn, makes 'Woe Is Me' hypnotic.

Haig, Allan W. 'Al'

(Born Newark, New Jersey, July 22, 1924; died November 16, 1982)

Haig was an excellent pianist of the first bebop wave in New York, influenced initially by Nat King Cole and Teddy Wilson and quickly developing a sense of order and logic of his own. Haig was the favourite piano accompanist of both CHARLIE PARKER and Stan Getz, and was a member of Parker's brilliant 1945 band that recorded for Dial. Haig worked with Parker again between 1948 and 1950 and with perfect calm appropriateness in partnership with Stan Getz in the early 1950s. Haig's sophisticated piano-playing is now extensively documented on vinyl on Britain's Spotlite label, but hardly at all on CD.

★*Live in Hollywood* (Xanadu 206)

Haig in the early 1950s, performing crisply and purposefully with a west coast band including trumpeter CHET BAKER and the fiery, emotional saxophonist SONNY CRISS.

Hall, James Stanley 'Jim'

(Born Buffalo, NY, December 12, 1930)

Because Jim Hall is a brilliant jazz guitarist who doesn't shower the listener with notes, his restrained gifts are easy to underestimate. Often dubbed the thinking fan's guitarist, Hall is a master of melodic subtlety and fresh statements delivered with a tightly edited succinctness, cool, plush tone and immense swing. He first came to public notice with the Chico Hamilton group of 1955, then worked with the JIMMY GIUFFRE trio (appearing on the famous *Jazz on a Summer's Day* Newport session), the Ella Fitzgerald trio of 1960-1, and in a duo with saxophonist Lee Konitz. Hall also worked memorably with pianist BILL EVANS, a musician after his own heart, and in the SONNY ROLLINS band of 1961 (see Sonny Rollins' *Quartets* on Bluebird).

★*Live At Village West* (Concord Jazz CCD 4245)

Another duo set for Hall and Carter, from the early 1980s. Hall still plays superbly as he enters his sixties, as a little listening to his solo here on 'All the Things You Are', with its casual Ellington quotes, vivid mingling of steady swing, jangly runs, jaunty trills and octave sequences reveals. There is a graceful Caribbean-flavoured piece, 'Down From Antigua', an offhand 'Bags' Groove', and perhaps slightly too fluffy versions of Blue Monk and Sonny Rollins' calypso 'St Thomas'. But it's consummate duo music.

★*Alone Together* (Original Jazz Classics OJC 467)

A 1972 live set with bassist Ron Carter, another improviser who shares Hall's grace, melodic resourcefulness and softness of touch. Though uptempo work on Sonny Rollins' 'St Thomas' and 'Whose Blues' display the guitarist's relaxed momentum, the atmosphere – inevitably, given the instrumentation and the perfectionist gloss of both men – is largely restrained.

Hayes, Edward Brian 'Tubby'

(Born London, January 30, 1935; died London, June 8, 1973)
British jazz is now firmly on the world map, but during Tubby Hayes' short life it wasn't. His own achievements are testament to the fact that this neglect was undeserved, as are those of saxophonist Peter King and pianist Stan Tracey. Hayes was comparable to Johnny Griffin for sheer speed and stamina in the 1950s and 1960s. He was also a fine vibes player and a talented composer.

Hayes learned violin first, but took up saxophone at 12, playing professionally three years later on the London dance band scene. At 20 he was leading his own band, and in 1957 – with Ronnie Scott – he formed the Jazz Couriers, a hard-bop band that was one of the most admired in the British jazz world of the day. No tempo could unsettle him, but though he was able to play with phenomenal dexterity, his imagination ran ahead of his fingers and his soloing had strength and logic.

After heart problems in the early 1970s, his playing noticeably slowed down but if anything it deepened.

★*For Members Only* (Mastermix CDCHE 10)

Twelve tracks from 1967 sessions mixing standards and originals (the former include standards-to-be like Herbie Hancock's 'Dolphin Dance') and hard-bop is the main agenda item. The Hancock inclusion and some echoes of Coltraneish implacability reveal that Hayes was open to the new music of his day, but the most boppish playing is the most forthright and relaxed, and a rhythm section including a fine young drummer, Tony Levin, is ideal company.

Hope, St Elmo Sylvester 'Elmo'

(Born New York, June 27, 1923; died New York, May 19, 1967) Now that the brilliant contemporary pianist Geri Allen mentions the work of Elmo Hope in her biographies, it may provide an additional incentive to explore the small but vivid achievements of one of the most intriguing of bop pianists. Hope was a conventional bopper in that his principal influences were Bud Powell (a childhood friend) and Thelonious Monk, but his phrasing was distinct and his openness to change able to embrace the loosening of jazz harmony that came with modalism and the rise of John Coltrane. Hope had an informed understanding of European classical music, and its methods surfaced in his jazz work.

Hope worked in r & b bands in the late 1940s, and his career briefly flowered in the mid-1950s with recording sessions he led featuring Sonny Rollins, Jackie McLean and others, culminating in a 1959 session with Harold Land (see p 191) that was one of his finest. But narcotics addiction hampered his development, and lost him his cabaret card, which prevented him working in New York. He worked little in the later years, though he did record again in 1966.

★*Trio and Quartet* (Blue Note CDP 784438)

These Blue Notes sides find Hope distracted a little by group roles that didn't suit him as an improviser, but they do feature a wonderful drummer in Frank Butler and convey Hope's harmonic intelligence and verve on a repertoire of brisk bop for the most part. Apart from Harold Land, an assortment of saxophonists and trumpeters don't add much, but the trio pieces are full of melodic surprises, and there's a delicious account of 'Sweet and Lovely'.

★*The Final Sessions* Vol. 1 (Original Jazz Classics OJC 1765)

Hope in creative trio settings in 1966, given an exceptional bounce and fire by the presence of Philly Joe Jones on drums on some tracks. For all that Hope neither courted public acclaim, had to wrestle with narcotics addiction, and couldn't find his way out of the accompanist's role he had for much of his life, the sureness of his touch is still clear and emphatic on these last recordings.

Hubbard, Frederick Dewayne 'Freddie'

(Born Indianapolis, Indiana, April 7, 1938)
In the 1960s, trumpeter Freddie Hubbard was one of jazz music's most dazzling prodigies. He had begun working around Indianapolis as a teenager, appearing with local guitar hero Wes Montgomery, and strongly influenced by a neighbourhood trumpeter, Booker Little. He then moved to New York in 1959, working with SONNY ROLLINS, Quincy Jones and others, and in 1961 – like many of the finest trumpeters in post-1950s jazz – received his most testing apprenticeship in ART BLAKEY's Jazz Messengers, sharing the front line with another remarkable youngster, saxophonist Wayne Shorter, who was soon to join MILES DAVIS. In 1961 Hubbard won the Downbeat New Star award and after the Blakey stint he began recording as a freelance for Blue Note, working with DEXTER GORDON, Herbie Hancock, JACKIE McLEAN and Shorter again.

Though he later gained a reputation for appearances in rather bland fusion surroundings, Hubbard was regarded as an adventurer as well as a virtuoso in 1960, appearing as part of the double quartet featured on avant-garde saxophonist Ornette Coleman's famous *Free Jazz* album on Eric Dolphy's *Out to Lunch* session, and Coltrane's *Ascension*.

★*Open Sesame* (Blue Note CDP 784040)

A young band – Hubbard just making his break, with McCoy Tyner on piano, Clifford Jarvis on drums – displaying energy and imagination. A good deal of the material here was written by the excellent saxophonist Tina Brooks, and the rhythm section drives the set enthusiastically. Classic hard bop.

★*Best of Freddie Hubbard* (Blue Note CDP 793202)

An assortment of Hubbard's Blue Note work, including the excellent 'Outer Forces' from the *Blue Spirit* album and the title tracks from *Open Sesame* and *Hub Tones*, the latter recorded by one of the trumpeter's most suitable bands, including James Spaulding on reeds and a young Herbie Hancock.

★*Topsy* (ENJA 7025-2)

Hubbard returned to the style he had grown famous with, and this Nineties disc of jazz standards (including 'Caravan', 'As Time Goes By' and 'Cherokee') finds him in majestic command of it, with effervescent assistance from Kenny Garrett on alto, Benny Green on piano and a buoyant Carl Allen on drums.

Hutcherson, Robert 'Bobby'

(Born Los Angeles, January 27, 1941)
Another member of the 1960s Blue Note stable, vibraharpist Hutcherson worked extensively with the rising musicians of that era – Herbie Hancock, Andrew Hill, Tony Williams – to develop a music exhibiting some of the freedoms of the then avant-garde, but within organised rhythm patterns and sophisticated explorations of counterpoint. He had come to New York from the west in 1961 with a boppish group featuring trombonist Al Grey, but his broadmindedness and distinctive tone led him to work on Eric Dolphy's classic *Out to Lunch* (see Eric Dolphy), then to freelance with a variety of New York modernists, and then to a series of challenging Blue Note albums under his own leadership. In more

recent times Hutcherson's fusion exploits made his sound more anonymous and his impact on jazz has lessened.

★*Dialogue* (Blue Note B21Y 46537)

Hutcherson on a brilliant early session as leader, exploring what he called 'a fusion of free counterpoint' – tougher music than much of the vibraharpist's later work, frequently involving parallel melody lines and exploration of rhythm and tone-colour rather than conventional bop harmony. Hutcherson's awareness of the avant-garde is apparent in the fierceness of 'Les Noirs Marchent'.

★*Happenings* (Blue Note B21Y 46530)

Hutcherson's third Blue Note session, more orthodox but featuring some of the most imaginative vibraharp improvisation to have emerged since the high points of Milt Jackson's work. Hutcherson's harmonic knowledge gave him immense range, which he resoundingly displayed in this session on the straight-ahead uptempo 'Aquarian Moon' (a glittering high-speed display) and the slow, harmonically subtle 'Bouquet'. All the tracks but one – Herbie Hancock's 'Maiden Voyage' – are Hutcherson originals.

★*In the Vanguard* (Landmark LM 1513)

Hutcherson's creative energies haven't slowed as he's moved into middle age – if anything his curiosity about new possibilities in music has grown stronger. This superb live session from 1986 finds the vibist with a piano trio, but though the repertoire is largely standards, the interpretations are more open than almost anything Hutcherson has previously recorded. Reworking of classics such as 'Some Day My Prince Will Come' and MONK's 'Well You Needn't' are definitions of how reconsiderations of the jazz past should be handled.

Jackson, Milton 'Bags'

(Born Detroit, January 1, 1923)
One of jazz music's greatest vibraharpists and a man who has maintained his standards of technical expertise, deceptive simplicity and powers of sympathetic listening through nearly a half-century at work. Some of Jackson's earliest outings involved collaborations with DIZZY GILLESPIE, through which he quickly proved himself to have been crucially influenced by the thinking of CHARLIE PARKER rather than by other vibists such as Red Norvo or Lionel Hampton. Jackson's conception of an extemporised line ran longer than the earlier vibists and the phrasing was more reminiscent of a horn than a keyboard instrument. His solos were instantly recognisable for an endlessly varied set of favourite devices – the percussive hammering of a repeated note, the deft double-time breaks between theme and solo, the use of the vibrato mechanism to extend a prolonged note – and he proved himself to be one of the few improvisers capable of exploring and enhancing the compositions of THELONIOUS MONK. Jackson has played with the best, but his most celebrated context is the Modern Jazz Quartet – launched in 1954 and, with minimal personnel changes, one of the longest surviving of all jazz groups – in which he shared the bulk of the solo responsibilities with pianist John Lewis.

Throughout this period Jackson continued to guest with many other artists (including WES MONTGOMERY, MILES DAVIS and Quincy Jones) and led his own bands. Jackson left the MJQ in 1974, but its legendary status has led to a series of reunions.

*Milt Jackson (Blue Note CDP 781 509-2)

An early Jackson classic – the 1948 recordings finding the 25-year-old vibist in a quartet setting – with Thelonious Monk on 'Mysterioso', 'Evidence', the brilliant 'Criss Cross' and three others, plus five tunes with his future MJQ partner John Lewis, including 'Willow Weep For Me' and a warm and fluid 'What's New', fascinatingly charting the prototypical MJQ.

★*From Opus De Jazz to Jazz Skyline* (Savoy 650103)

A combination of two albums from the mid-1950s, this disc features many of the reasons why some of Jackson's fans thought he played better out of the MJQ. Apart from the leader's understatements and delectable sense of melodic shape, particularly on blues, the other virtue of this set is the tenor-playing of LUCKY THOMPSON, who is as concise and swinging as Jackson.

Jamal, Ahmad (Fritz Jones)

(Born Pittsburgh, July 2, 1930)

One of the few musicians MILES DAVIS ever admitted to being an unqualified fan of, Ahmad Jamal is not only a unique piano improviser but also a composer capable of bridging the normally yawning gap between unconventional and exploratory music and the commercial record business. A child prodigy, strongly influenced by Art Tatum and later by Errol Garner, Jamal has retained an energy and independence of spirit that has rescued him from inclusion in any school. Fascinated by the resonances and timbres of the piano, he has explored them in wayward methods embracing both bebop and the orchestral styles of earlier swing. In the 1990s, Jamal has made a considerable comeback, his style an education in jazz piano history, and his urgency undimmed. Only an occasional tendency to lean on set-pieces hampers him.

★*At the Pershing* (Vogue VGCD 600049)

Live concert by Jamal from Chicago's Pershing Room, where so many of his memorable performances took place. Excellent jazz vehicles get the probing Jamal treatment, including 'Woody 'n' You' and a moving version of one of his most popular compositions, the sedate, atmospheric chamber-piece, 'Poinciana'.

★*Live at the Montreux Jazz Festival* (Atlantic 781699)

A good representation of Jamal's music of recent times, this live set was made at Montreux in 1986 and features the pianist in his familiar setting of bass, drums and percussion. The downside is still a slightly showy over-elaboration and dependence on pre-pared material, but on Wayne Shorter's 'Footprints' Jamal displays his class.

Johnson, James Louis 'J.J.'

(Born Indianapolis, Indiana, January 23, 1924)
The first truly convincing bebop trombonist, overcoming what seemed like the insuperable technical obstacles to playing this gruff and bulky instrument fast, accurately and with clean tone.

A member of both Benny Carter's and Count Basie's bands when barely past 20, and an occasional partner of DIZZY GILLESPIE and MILES DAVIS between 1949 and 1953, Johnson began a fruitful partnership with Scandinavian trombonist Kai Winding in 1954. Film-score and studio work occupied Johnson a good deal in the 1950s and 1960s, but he made several excellent albums, including appearing with SONNY ROLLINS and Stan Getz.

★*The Eminent* Vol. I (Blue Note B21Y 81505)

Johnson with his own sextet on two crucial dates in 1953 and 1954, the first including trumpeter CLIFFORD BROWN. Johnson virtually writes the book on bebop trombone technique with perfectly honed, flat-out performances on uptempo pieces such as 'Get Happy', and sustained-note displays on 'Lover Man'.

★*Things Are Getting Better All the Time* (Pablo 2312141)

Punchy 1983 collaboration between Johnson and fellow-trombonist Al Grey including 'Softly as in a Morning Sunrise', 'Paper Moon' and 'Things Ain't What They Used To Be'. This was the period in which Johnson resoundingly reminded the world that he hadn't gone away, and the contrast with the earthier, more orthodox Grey is ideal.

★*Let's Hang Out* (Gitanes Jazz/Emarcy 514 454-2)

The bop trombone pioneer with a bunch of skilled young postboppers, including trumpeter Terence Blanchard, saxophonist Ralph Moore and pianist Renee Rosnes. The repertoire mixes an original suite, and standards like 'It's You Or No-One' and 'I Got It Bad and That Ain't Good'. Bands that wrote hard-bop and soul-jazz house-style, like Art Blakey's, are echoed in Johnson's suite, and there's a Latin flavour as well. Johnson's contemporaries Jimmy Heath (tenor) and Stanley Cowell (piano) make some trenchant contributions, and the leader's slow playing often induces an intake of breath. Very high-class.

Jones, Thaddeus Joseph 'Thad'

(Born Pontiac, Michigan, March 28, 1923; died Copenhagen, August 21, 1986)
A superb trumpet improviser who was generally better known for his co-leadership (with drummer Mel Lewis) of a fine big band, Thad Jones developed Dizzy Gillespie's style in melodically original ways as a soloist, and Count Basie's with more modern rhythmic departures as a writer and arranger. The Jones-Lewis band displayed the punch and bravura of a 1930s big band but mixed it with progressive ingredients from post-bop harmony, and it became one of the most musical and creative large jazz ensembles in the 1960s and early 1970s, when most of the others were relying on pyrotechnics or rearrangements of pop.

Jones was Charles Mingus's favourite trumpeter, for his warmth and subtlety of timbre and his agility in straddling the extremes of the range. He learned about big bands in one of the best, working for Count Basie between 1954 and 1963, before leaving to freelance as an arranger and let off steam with a rehearsal band of leading studio musicians. This became the Jones-Lewis outfit, which gained worldwide acclaim.

★*Thad Jones/Mel Lewis* (LRC CDC 9004)

There are better examples of Jones as a straightforward brass virtuoso, but this set from the late 1960s is a fine example of the way the Jones-Lewis band sounded, with such excellent sidemen as saxophonist Joe Farrell and trombonist Jimmy Knepper. Jones plays flugelhorn throughout, with characteristic certainty of pitching and warmth of tone.

Kelly, Wynton

(Born New York, December 2, 1931; died Toronto, April 12, 1971)
Kelly, whose origins were in the blues bands of Cleanhead Vinson
and Ray Abrams, was a bop player of charm and a genial,
twinkling sprightliness that made him highly sought after in his
short career, notably by DIZZY GILLESPIE, Dinah Washington and
Lester Young in the early 1950s. Kelly's most famous employer
was MILES DAVIS, whose band he joined between 1959 and 1963.
Kelly's lightness of touch made him a perfect pianist for a band
devoted to loosening the bonds of bop, and he also recorded
extensively with a relaxed and bluesy late-bop band of his own,
sometimes accompanying other powerful soloists such as guitarist WES MONTGOMERY.

*Kelly Blue (Original Jazz Classics OJC 033)

More or less Miles Davis' classic Kind of Blue band, with Paul
Chambers on bass and Jimmy Cobb on drums. The soloists
include Nat Adderley on trumpet, the excellent Belgian-born
Lester Youngian Bobby Jaspar on tenor and on two tracks a
slightly over-vigorous BENNY GOLSON.

Kessel, Barney

(Born Muskogee, Oklahoma, October 17, 1923)
One of CHARLIE CHRISTIAN's most adept followers on guitar, Kessel
was self-taught and his first notable job was in a big band led by
Chico Marx. Big-band work with more plausible leaders followed
in 1944 and 1945, first with Charlie Barnet, then Artie Shaw,
leading to a prosperous career in the west coast studios with
intervals for recording with CHARLIE PARKER and performing with
the Oscar Peterson trio and in the Jazz at the Philharmonic
touring show. Under his own name Kessel recorded for the West
Coast Contemporary label in the 1950s and in recent times has
toured worldwide with Herb Ellis and Charlie Byrd as the package
Great Guitars.

★*To Swing Or Not To Swing* (Original Jazz Classics OJC 317)

Excellent early Kessel session, demonstrating how full the guitarist's tone is in all tempos but how tough and vigorous he can be in the firmly struck accents and busily accumulating runs. The band is a septet including trumpeter Harry Edison and saxophonist Georgie Auld, the whole effect reminiscent of a Count Basie small band.

Lambert, Hendricks and Ross

Lambert, David Alden 'Dave' (born Boston, June 19, 1917; died Westport, October 3, 1966)
Hendricks, John Carl 'Jon' (born Newark, Ohio, September 16, 1921)
Ross, Annabel Short Lynch 'Annie' (born Surrey, England, July 25, 1930)
Lambert, Hendricks and Ross were a popular multinational vocal trio who were among the most effective purveyors of the generally ill-advised art of concocting clever vocal equivalents to jazz instrumentals. They came together in 1959 to vocalise Count Basie hits for the album *Sing a Song of Basie*. The group had a short life in its original form despite the success of the Basie album; Annie Ross left in 1962 to be replaced by Yolande Bevan, and the trio disbanded two years later. 'Vocalese' frequently loses the rhythmic audacity and inflectional surprises of jazz, but LHR preserved a surprising amount of it, not least because of Annie Ross. Her understanding of jazz improvisation was spectacularly audible from 1952's remarkable hit based on Wardell Gray's 'Twisted' solo, through to her Buck Clayton 'Fiesta in Blue' impressions on *Sing a Song of Basie*.

★*Sing a Song of Basie* (Impulse/GRP 11122)

The original personnel on an excellent selection devoted to Count Basie's music in 1957. The trio was expanded by multi-tracking here, enabling it to cover all the instruments in the big band and though there's inevitably a novelty aspect to such astonishing vocal athletics – listen to Annie Ross' 'trumpet' effects – the depth of their immersion in jazz timing and intonation is so subtle and strong that the musicality never wavers. A remarkable record.

Land, Harold DeVance

(Born Houston, Texas, February 18, 1928)
Harold Land has been a shadowy jazz hero. His saxophone sound comes from a mixture of the circuitousness of bebop and the swagger of the swing tenorists, and his improvising inclinations are towards the neat and graceful, but not at the expense of surprise. Cultivating a spare and sometimes melancholic sound from a highly personal blend of sources and imagination, Land became affected by John Coltrane in the late 1950s, but not in obvious ways, and he retains a deceptive strength into his sixties, with a gruff lower range, remarkable purity of tone in the upper register, sparing use of Coltraneish technical devices (like harmonics) and a remarkable ability to sum up the substance of a tune and its improvisation in throwaway codas and fills.

Land was raised in California, and worked there in the late 1940s, before joining the superb Max Roach-Clifford Brown hard bop band in the next decade. He was active on the west coast with musicians such as Shorty Rogers and Red Mitchell, and worked in a challenging group with vibist Bobby Hutcherson in the late 1960s. Land still tours and performs, sometimes appearing with his pianist son, Harold Land Jnr.

★The Fox (Original Jazz Classics OJC 343)

One of the great small-group sessions of the 1950s, this fine band was remarkable for its independence from most of the obvious models of the time (Art Blakey's, or Miles Davis's), though the Max Roach-Clifford Brown band is certainly recalled by it. The music is challenging – four of the pieces are pianist Elmo Hope's – though loosely categorisable as hard bop, but Frank Butler's drumming gives it a looseness that even anticipates Elvin Jones. Hope's ambiguity and soft resilience underpins the session, and Land's tenor confirms the arrival of a major improvising talent.

Little, Booker Jr

Born Memphis, Tennessee, April 2, 1938; died New York, October 5, 1961)
Another precociously gifted 1950s trumpeter who died young (of uraemia at 23) and left the jazz world wondering what he might have achieved. Little's mercurial technique and razor-edged sound were perfectly adapted to the fast-moving idiom of hard bop that he seemed – like his contemporaries FREDDIE HUBBARD and LEE MORGAN – to be a natural exponent of, but he possessed a musical imagination that extended beyond bop and hinted at an audacity of the dimensions of Ornette Coleman or MILES DAVIS. Little grew up in 1950s Memphis with other dynamic jazz talents – GEORGE COLEMAN, Charles Lloyd, Phineas Newborn. He moved to Chicago in 1957 and joined drummer MAX ROACH.

Out Front (Candid 9027)

One of Little's final studio sessions, and the one that most sharply indicates the gathering potential cut off in 1961. It features two associates always linked with Little – Max Roach and Eric Dolphy – and though the prevailing atmosphere is often reflective and the compositional style ambiguous, the soloing of Little and Dolphy in particular are among their most moving and personal on disc.

McGhee, Howard B.

(Born Tulsa, Oklahoma, February 6, 1918; died New York, July 17, 1987)
A fine trumpeter who successfully bridged bebop and swing, working with the Charlie Barnet and Andy Kirk bands in the 1940s, then with Coleman Hawkins, and often including CHARLIE PARKER in groups he led in Los Angeles towards the end of that decade. With his crisp phrasing yet casual feel, sensitive use of the mute and intelligent adaptation of ideas drawn from earlier players such as Roy Eldridge and modernists such as DIZZY GILLESPIE and FATS NAVARRO, Howard McGhee was an improviser who could convey excitement without resorting to

bluster. Little of McGhee's best work (notably 'Maggie') is available on CD however.

★*The Bop Master* (Affinity AFF 765)

Highly representative McGhee sessions from 1955 and 1960, particularly commanding when Philly Joe Jones is at the drums. McGhee doesn't play at breakneck bebop trumpet speeds, but his construction is his own, and one of his best-ever recordings – 'Dusty Blue', with TOMMY FLANAGAN on piano and Ron Carter on bass – is here.

McLean, John Lenwood 'Jackie'

(Born New York, May 17, 1932)
Jackie McLean has frequently been regarded as a CHARLIE PARKER clone, an opinion that doesn't stand up to closer listening. McLean is less attentive to the details of harmony than Parker, in some respects more impressionistic and intense, like a forerunner of the 1960s avant-garde (with which, perhaps unsurprisingly, he eventually became involved), and his emotional qualities are starker and more strident. The pianist BUD POWELL was McLean's neighbour in youth and after the two studied together Powell recommended McLean to MILES DAVIS. In the 1950s the rapidly maturing McLean then found work with a succession of inspired leaders including pianists Paul Bley and George Wallington, then Charles Mingus and ART BLAKEY, the stint with Blakey's Jazz Messengers lasting three intense years.

★*Let Freedom Ring* (Blue Note CDP 746527-2)

Widely hailed as McLean's breakthrough to independence, 1963's *Let Freedom Ring* represented the saxophonist's inspiration, through the new music of Ornette Coleman, to loosen bebop's fetters. A highly influential album that opened the ears of some to looser possibilities for jazz in the 1960s, its energy is notably sustained by the delightful drumming of Billy Higgins.

★*One Step Beyond* (Blue Note B21Y 46821)

Development of McLean's concept from the sax-led piano trio to an augmented band featuring Grachan Moncur on trombone and BOBBY HUTCHERSON on vibes. This is also the recording debut of one of the most thrilling drummers of recent times – Tony Williams, then 17 and soon to become a dominant force.

★*Dynasty* (Triloka 181-2)

McLean began to work extensively with his saxophone-playing son Rene from the 1970s on, and his repertoire opened up to many of the elements from other musics – notably African and Asian – that began to enter jazz in the period. By the late 1980s, when this recording was made, McLean's reputation as one of the leading saxophone inspirations in jazz was secure.

Marmarosa, Michael 'Dodo'

(Born Pittsburgh, December 12, 1925)
An excellent first-wave bebop pianist whose accomplishments are barely known outside the coterie of pioneer bebop collectors. Improvisation is irresistible to Marmarosa – he is always embellishing and refining, in theme statements as well as in solos – and he possesses a joyous, singing tone and capacity to make each chorus of a solo take on its own rounded character that makes his work distinctive. Marmarosa's sense of improvisational shape was registered as early as 1943 in a beautiful extended solo on Charlie Barnet's 'The Moose', and after a stretch with Artie Shaw, Marmarosa moved to the west coast where he was busy as a freelance, working with CHARLIE PARKER (Dial recordings in 1946–7 including 'Moose the Mooche' and 'Ornithology') and Lester Young (1945 recordings of 'These Foolish Things' and 'DB Blues') among others. Marmarosa was ill for much of the 1950s, cut three albums in the early 1960s (of which the CD listed here was one), then returned to obscurity.

★*Chicago Sessions* (Affinity/Charly CDAFF 755)

Originally issued as 'Dodo's Back', this 1961 trio album with Richard Evans on bass and Marshall Thompson on drums was one of Marmarosa's few later recordings to stand serious comparison with the punch and elation of his 1940s playing. The soloing crackles with surprises – the unexpected mixture of bustling chords suddenly entering the single-note ripples on 'Why Do I Love You?', the brief stride-piano entrance on 'Green Dolphin Street' – and Marmarosa constantly gives the impression of playing nothing that isn't governed by his unerring sense of proportion.

Marsh, Warne Marion

(Born Los Angeles, October 26, 1927; died Hollywood, December 18, 1987)
Like Lee Konitz, a saxophonist member of the Lennie Tristano cool coterie, but undeservingly far more obscure than Konitz. Yet had Marsh played as much as the other Tristano adherents he might easily have gained the status in jazz that an improvisational flair at times close to genius entitled him to.

Marsh played with Hoagy Carmichael in 1944 and, after army service, with Buddy Rich and then Lennie Tristano following a move to New York in 1948. The debt to Tristano in Marsh's case is probably more audible than for any other saxophone player, his improvisations consisting of complex linear variations of great rhythmic subtlety, mostly delivered fast in a pale, glancing tone adapted from Lester Young. Marsh's tone, in fact, is one of the oddest in jazz saxophone-playing, cool to the point of chilliness in the mid-register, but turning into a wry, squawky sound on high notes. Marsh recorded with Lee Konitz and with ART PEPPER in the 1950s and there were reunions with Tristano until the mid-1960s and with Konitz in the 1970s. His best recorded work was hard to find until recently, although several good Storyville vinyl discs have emerged. CD availability is so far poor.

★*Ne Plus Ultra* (Hat Art 6063)

One of the only Marsh items of major significance to have been reissued on CD, this 1969 set finds him with a comparable alto saxophonist to Lee Konitz (Gary Foster) plus very discreet drums and bass. It's an object-lesson in the Tristano method, pursuing the melody line over everything else, as Marsh demonstrates with serpentine originality on 'Lennie's Pennies'.

★*Posthumous* (Interplay IP 8604)

Two years before Marsh died, he recorded some superb performances with a fairly ordinary rhythm section of pianist Susan Chen, bassist George Mraz and drummer Akira Tana – but his own powers of logic and foresight as an improviser were so developed, and the Tristanoite suspicion of active rhythm players so ingrained in him that it didn't matter. On 'My Romance' and 'Parisian Thoroughfare' his even, deliberate lyricism and avoidance of cliché – either his own, or any idiom's – sweeps new meaning into the music.

Merrill, Helen (Helen Milcetic)

(Born New York, July 21 1929 or 1930)
A singer of great precision, harmonic ingenuity and softness of touch, who sang with leading bop musicians including CHARLIE PARKER, MILES DAVIS and J.J. JOHNSON in the 1940s, and then with Earl Hines in 1952 – when she made her recording debut, with CLIFFORD BROWN making a guest appearance. Bebop influenced Merrill's time and intonation, but she has never pretended to be an instrument, or relied overmuch on scat.

Merrill moved to Europe after divorcing in 1959. She worked in Scandinavia with Stan Getz, and at festivals all over the world. She returned to the States in the 1960s, but her career ran erratically and her private style was often unappreciated – though there were successful sessions with THAD JONES and Elvin Jones, JIM HALL, Gary Peacock and even swing piano star Teddy Wilson. She went back to recording in the late 1970s, and her work has grown in authority and substance in her later years.

★*Jazz Round Midnight* (Verve 846011)

Very good collection of Merrill's work between 1954 and 1976, much of it unhurried and sometimes preoccupied, but a good demonstration of her insight and feeling for tone and time. Plenty of fine sidemen present, notably the MODERN JAZZ QUARTET's John Lewis, a tailor-made collaborator for this singer.

★*Brownie – Homage to Clifford Brown* (Verve 522 363-2)

No pretence from Merrill that water hasn't gone under the bridge – she sounds at times a little grouchy and uncertain – but a distinctive and expressive record, pitching her voice against four younger trumpet heroes all with dues to pay to Clifford Brown. The trumpeters are Lew Soloff, Roy Hargrove, Tom Harrell and Wallace Roney, and though the arranged unison-horn transcriptions of classic solos isn't the most spontaneous-sounding way of celebrating a great improvisor, Harrell's shy obliqueness ('Your Eyes') and Roney's clarity and strength ('Daahoud') reflect the magic. Pianist Kenny Barron is superb, and Merrill's slow exploration of 'Don't Explain' painfully exquisite.

Mobley, Henry 'Hank'

(Born Eastman, Georgia, July 7, 1930; died Philadelphia, May 30, 1986)
One of the Blue Note stable who was neither a legendary pioneer nor a fierce iconoclast, but a saxophonist of delicacy and poise who – in his own reflective and sidelong way – did much to soften the barrelling attack of hard bop with the bluesy poignancy of Lester Young. Another tenorist who cut his teeth in blues bands, Mobley worked with TADD DAMERON and DIZZY GILLESPIE. He then joined the Horace Silver group in 1954, soon to become ART BLAKEY's Jazz Messengers, where his unusual rhythmic ideas meshed productively with Blakey's drumming.

Mobley's talents then brought him a flood of illustrious jobs, and between 1957 and 1962 he was a member of bands led by MAX ROACH, Art Blakey and MILES DAVIS, delivering a beautiful version of 'I Thought About You' on the latter's *Some Day My Prince Will*

Come. Narcotics problems dogged him through the 1960s and 1970s, though he worked for two years with pianist Cedar Walton, and by 1975 he had virtually retired, eventually dying of pneumonia at 55. A player of restrained fire, with a sense of melodic shape and quirkiness rivalling that of SONNY ROLLINS, though with none of Rollins' bullish theatricality.

*Soul Station (Blue Note CDP 746 528-2)

One of the best, and best known of Mobley's high-quality Blue Note recordings, this 1960 session featured the saxophonist with WYNTON KELLY on piano, Paul Chambers on bass and Art Blakey on drums. Inaccurately named, to appeal to the soul-jazz fad of the time, it is far from a honking, gospelly session and instead reveals Mobley at his most ingenious. The plausibility of comparisons with Rollins are justified by the two labyrinthine unaccompanied choruses on the bluesy 'Dig Dis'.

*Roll Call (Blue Note B21Y-46823)

The follow-up to *Soul Station* and very nearly as good, featuring open-handed, almost aggressive Mobley on the title track (though still mobilised by subtly camouflaged rhythmic disruptions) but now in near-perfect balance with his ambivalent, shadowy lyricism on 'The More I See of You'. Trumpeter FREDDIE HUBBARD augments the lineup, very effectively.

Modern Jazz Quartet

Lewis, John Aaron (born La Grange, Illinois, May 3, 1920)
JACKSON, MILT (born Detroit, January 1, 1923)
Heath, Percy (born North Carolina, April 30, 1923)
Kay, Conrad Henry 'Connie' (born New York, April 27, 1927)
One of the best-loved and longest-lived of all modern jazz groups, the Modern Jazz Quartet has attracted mixed opinions from critics but its accessibility, melodic simplicity and fastidious romanticism has won it a big audience not restricted to jazz fans alone. It started life as DIZZY GILLESPIE's 1946 rhythm section, at that time featuring pianist John Lewis and vibraharpist MILT

JACKSON but with Ray Brown on bass and bebop pioneer Kenny Clarke on drums. In 1952 the quartet became an autonomous band, with Percy Heath having replaced Brown. Already the elements that were to make the MJQ so popular were audible in the repertoire. There was a strong allegiance to subtle, needling blues, occasionally ravishing displays on ballads, and considerable dependence on European classical forms (even on orthodox material the band frequently used sophisticated counterpoint) reflecting Lewis's classical training.

In 1955 Connie Kay replaced Clarke and one of the most famous lineups of all time was completed, Kay's presence giving the band its characteristic tiptoeing, chamber-jazz atmosphere. The years 1956 to 1960 were high points, with the criticism from some quarters that their music was anaemic and a waste of the talents of Jackson, in particular, being effectively countered by their intensity (despite low volumes) in collective improvisation, and some enduring compositions from Lewis including 'Django' and the vibrant 'Golden Striker'. But from then until Milt Jackson's resignation in 1974 the band produced increasingly colourless reworkings of past formulae, an elegant decline nevertheless rivetingly reversed on the urgent *Last Concert* album. Lucrative offers led to the re-forming of the band for concert tours in the early 1980s, but recordings of substance did not emerge from these reunions.

★*Concorde* (Original Jazz Classics OJC 002)

An excellent insight into early MJQ, Connie Kay's debut with the band recorded in New York in 1956. 'Concorde' itself is a fugue, glowingly displaying the conversational counterpoint between Lewis and Jackson, and there is a medley of four Gershwin tunes that has the same impact, possessed of both mutual improvisational glee and an abiding sense of form and order. Jackson is by now in his most relaxed prime, his playing a mixture of hair's-breadth accelerations and delays against the beat, his phrasing fluent and responsive to the overwhelming sense of collective responsibility within the band.

Lonely Woman (Atlantic SD 1381)

A double-CD set from recordings made in 1962, revealing among other things the depth of John Lewis' concern for the future of jazz – often overlooked in the dismissal of the MJQ as conservative – as exemplified in a superb treatment of the Ornette Coleman piece of the title. One of the best MJQ collections.

MJQ 40 (Atlantic 782330-2)

For serious admirers, this four-CD package edits imaginatively from the entire MJQ canon, not only featuring the regular band but various one-off projects involving other musicians, including the formal experiments with European contemporary music that came to be known as 'Third Stream'. The set is accompanied by an invaluable history and discography of the band.

Monk, Thelonious Sphere

(Born Rocky Mount, Carolina, October 11, 1917; died New Jersey, February 17, 1982)

Few jazz musicians can ever have expressed their disinterest in inessentials with more vinegary determination than the late Thelonious Monk. In the 1940s he and DIZZY GILLESPIE virtually embodied the bebop life – the behavioural eccentricities, the bizarre headgear – but Monk especially embodied it in music. Critics argue about whether or not he was actually a bebopper because much of his style revolved around a dismantled and dissonant stride piano technique (he was originally an admirer of Teddy Wilson, a surprisingly urbane and rational model), but in his thinking about harmony and in the constant surprises of his phrasing and timing he still sounds contemporary today.

As a child, Monk adapted early piano lessons to accompanying his mother's singing in church, and the music of evangelism played a big part in the formation of his unique approach. In New York in the 1940s, Monk played with a wide variety of musicians, including after-hours playing with Kenny Clarke at Minton's Playhouse, where many of the first experiments in bebop were shared. In 1943 he joined Coleman Hawkins – always a discriminating leader with an ear for originality – and made his recording debut with the saxophonist. By 1947 he was leading his own bands in some brilliant recordings but false imprisonment on a drug offence and a subsequent ban from New York clubs kept him out of public circulation until the mid-1950s. In any case his acerbic and uncompromising style was not universally popular either with his fellow-bebop musicians (many of whom adopted an even, multi-noted legato approach that foundered among the pianist's dissonant chords, sudden prolonged silences and hopping runs) or with the public, for whom his playing sometimes seemed too weird even by hipster standards.

The year 1957 represented Monk's ascent to the stature he deserved, and a residency at the Five Spot Club with the young John Coltrane led to the blossoming of his career through invitations to festivals and to European tours.

★*Genius of Modern Music* Vols. 1 & 2 (Blue Note CDP 781510 & 781511)

Thelonious Monk's Blue Note sessions of the late 1940s and early 1950s are, for sheer improvisational wilfulness, among the most compelling jazz ever to find its way on to that august label. They also contain (apart from early versions of his sharpest tunes such as 'Straight No Chaser', 'Well You Needn't' and 'Round Midnight') solo passages that provide a more comprehensive picture of all Monk's skills than simply the stabbing dissonance and long-pause style for which he's renowned. The second volume is later, better recorded, and features the more urbane though equally blues-derived influence of MILT JACKSON, a man who understood Monk's uniqueness well enough to play creatively with him.

★*Thelonious Monk and John Coltrane* (Original Jazz Classics OJC 039)

Long thought to have been the only tracks recorded by one of the most famous and short-lived of postwar jazz bands, the 1957 quartet with Monk, John Coltrane, Wilbur Ware on bass and Shadow Wilson on drums. Apart from Monk classics such as 'Ruby My Dear', 'Nutty' and 'Crepuscule with Nellie' the sessions are remarkable revelations of Monk's impact on even the most loquacious and ambitious of soloists. Coltrane is forced to explore space and delays in Monk's company, and the result is some of the saxophonist's quirkiest playing.

★With John Coltrane. *Live At The Five Spot* (Blue Note 0777 7 99786 2 5)

Lo-fi, but hi-energy. This material was recorded on Coltrane's own machine, and the sound quality is approximate, to say the least. But for all that, this is an invaluable representation of a period from which little remains. The saxophonist is much more unruly and heated, beckoning the coming years in his career, than he is on the studio set. The five tunes are all immortals, and Trane's whirlwind against the pianist's cobblestones momentum on 'I Mean You' is hypnotic.

★*Brilliant Corners* (Original Jazz Classics OJC 026)

A session with SONNY ROLLINS and MAX ROACH, and the beginnings of one of the most suitable regular Monk bands, that with tenorist Charlie Rouse. Rollins and Monk weren't a perfect partnership, despite some temperamental similarities, and the saxophonist's mild unease led him to simplify his soloing to a point that underused him, but cornettist THAD JONES turned out to be unexpectedly galvanised by Monk, responding vigorously to this music of gaping intervals and convoluted phrasing.

★*Misterioso* (Original Jazz Classics OJC 206)

Live recording of the 1958 Monk band that featured tenorist JOHNNY GRIFFIN, with Ahmed Abdul Malik on bass and Roy Haynes on drums. Griffin was less inclined to humour Monk than either Rollins or Coltrane, and roared through the repertoire largely oblivious to the leader's prickly nuances; but the band shouldn't be underrated for this alone because Griffin conveys a furious excitement that can be an attractive counterweight to Monk's proddings and needlings, and Roy Haynes balances suspense and inevitability with a poise worthy of the leader.

★*Alone in San Francisco* (Original Jazz Classics OJC 231)

Because he was so hard to partner, and because his use of dynamics is so personal, solo performances by Monk represent some of his most satisfying work. A more ruminative Monk is to be heard here, but the pianist's pared-down lyricism brings vim and muscle to 'Remember', and one of his best blues performances is to be heard in this version of the famous 'Blue Monk'.

★*Big Band And Quartet* (Columbia Jazz Masterpieces 476898-2)

Unusual Monk settings from 1963, a live recording featuring a ten-piece band as well as the quartet and some solo playing. All the usual suspects – 'I Mean You', 'Epistrophy', 'Misterioso', 'Evidence' – and Monk's characteristic interventions, plus some fine Phil Woods alto sax. Like all under-rehearsed horn sections that tried Monk's pieces in ensemble in those days, there's a certain amount of baffled groping around, but it gives a glimpse of how adaptable those extraordinary tunes are to almost any treatment.

★*The Complete Blue Note Recordings* (Blue Note CDP 7243 8 30363-2-5)

Definitive Blue Note Monk. It replaces the Blue Note Vols 1 & 2 sets, and adds live material with Coltrane, and a highly informative booklet. Blue Notes saw the first appearances of classic compositions like 'Epistrophy', 'Misterioso' and 'Evidence', and there are telling appearances by SONNY ROLLINS, ART BLAKEY and others. As a starting point to explore the work of a key figure in 20th century music, it's ideal.

Montgomery, John Leslie 'Wes'

(Born Indianapolis, March 6, 1925; died Indianapolis, June 15, 1968)
A powerful influence on the playing of contemporary guitar stars Pat Metheny (who took up the guitar in the year Montgomery died) and George Benson, Wes Montgomery had become a victim of the middle-of-the-road market by the end of his life, which

wanted his easy swing and soft, luxuriant sound but had no use for his sensational improvising skills.

Montgomery didn't start on the guitar until his late teens, but six months later he was busy on the Indianapolis jazz scene. A fan of CHARLIE CHRISTIAN, he learned Christian's solos note for note, and borrowed Django Reinhardt's technique of soloing in octaves too, developing the latter to a fluency belying its awkward fingering and creating a trademark relentlessly used by George Benson in the latter's funk career. Two years with the Lionel Hampton band from 1948 to 1950 might have launched Montgomery's career but he never liked straying far from Indianapolis and returned home to a day job and a punishing series of nightclub-playing assignments throughout the 1950s. At the end of that decade he was discovered by CANNONBALL ADDERLEY.

Montgomery's music was not portentous or self-consciously weighty. In addition to his lyricism and rhythmic momentum, he had a texture all his own because he plucked the strings with his thumb and never used a pick. In the most suitable settings these virtues conveyed a music of genial, athletic beauty; but they were also the qualities that the record business perceived as ideal raw material for the middle-of-the-road market. But, as the 1965 Paris CD reveals, he never lost his magic touch despite his soft-pop output from 1964 on.

★*Far Wes* (Pacific Jazz 94475)

Some excellent early Montgomery west coast sessions including the reliable, if unremarkable, skills of brother Monk on bass and Buddy on piano but with a distinguished and undervalued guest in the watchful, dry-toned HAROLD LAND on tenor. 'Leila' (also featuring altoist Pony Poindexter) includes some of Montgomery's most explicit tributes to the romanticism of Django Reinhardt. Unlike an earlier vinyl, *The Montgomery Story*, however, this doesn't include the bluesy 'Bock to Bock' or the Chicago recordings that featured Freddie Hubbard.

★*Incredible Jazz Guitar* (Original Jazz Classics OJC 036)

This album was one of Montgomery's best, an uncluttered and direct 1960 session that found him in excellent company with pianist TOMMY FLANAGAN, bassist Percy Heath and drummer Albert Heath. Though it softens into some rather meandering tunes in the end, the uptempo bop of SONNY ROLLINS' 'Airegin' and Montgomery's walking-riff theme 'Four on Six' finds the guitarist in full unquenchable flood, and Flanagan provides appropriately pearly, buoyant solos of his own.

*_Full House_ (Original Jazz Classics OJC 106)

Delightful, fast-moving session with Montgomery in the company of tenorist Johnny Griffin and the WYNTON KELLY trio. This album, coming after Montgomery's move towards MOR had begun, was proof to his admirers that in a club he was still the most joyous and freewheeling of improvisers.

*_Round Midnight_ (Charly CD13)

The band that Montgomery brought to Europe in 1965, including Harold Mabern on piano. The repertoire includes Coltrane's 'Impressions' (Montgomery had worked with the saxophonist on the west coast five years before), a driving 'Mister Walker' and a gentle 'Round Midnight' soon toughened by the unexpected arrival of Johnny Griffin.

Moody, James

(Born Savannah, Georgia, March 26, 1925)
A much-loved jazz club artist of continuing inventiveness on saxophones and flute, and irrepressible surrealism that sometimes finds its way out in song. Moody's delightful melodic unpredictability and fondness for mingling hard-bop complexities with earthy blues and gospelly sounds have served him well since the 1940s, with DIZZY GILLESPIE. His tenor sound is indebted to DEXTER GORDON, though without Gordon's sledgehammer weight, and he builds his solos from a rich palette of deftly chosen devices – wriggling slurred sounds, end-of-line accents like exclamation marks, constant tonal changes, and a gradual widening of the intervals in his phrasing.

*Hi-Fi Party (Original Jazz Classics OJC 1780)

Good Moody selection from 1954, confirming his insight into bebop, but mingling it with accessible and entertaining vocals and vaudeville just the way he has always done. Vocalese artist Eddie Jefferson joins Moody on one track here.

*Something Special (Novus/RCA PD 83008)

Well, it wasn't as special as all that, not really being comparable to the irrepressible Moody in person, but it remains the best of his Novus recordings so far and features an excellent band including Kirk Lightsey on piano, and Idrees Muhammad on drums. The leader is in amiable form on 'Moody's in the Mood for Love'.

Morgan, Frank

(Born Minneapolis, December 23, 1933)
The man ART PEPPER fans listened to after the master departed – but a player who should have had a massive reputation in his own right, save for years knocked out of his career by drug abuse and prison stretches. Pepper's fractured sound and poignant use of dynamics, bebop processed through the Cool School and an isolated sensibility are closely related to the way Morgan plays. In the 1980s, Morgan emerged from his years of troubles, and came back playing beautifully, creeping up on the implications of tunes like a cat shadowing prey.

Morgan plays alto and soprano saxophone. His father was a guitarist, and the boy first took up the clarinet, then the alto at ten. He won talent contests as a teenager, and recorded with visiting bop celebrities after the family's move to the West Coast – including Teddy Charles and Kenny Clarke. He made his album debut in 1954, but was in and out of jail from the mid-50s, playing with Art Pepper on one occasion in a prisoners' band.

*Listen To The Dawn (Antilles 314 518 979-2)

Very good current Morgan set, in the company of such inventive performers as guitarist Kenny Burrell, bassist Ron Carter and drummer Grady Tate. Morgan plays with biting economy on bluesy features like the fine composition 'Grooveyard', but it's his ballad performances that linger longest.

Morgan, Lee

(Born Philadelphia, July 10, 1938; died New York, February 19, 1972)

Trumpeter Lee Morgan was one of the early stars of the first wave of jazz-funk, but his involvement in a more commercial jazz didn't require him to alter a technique that was already deeply inflected with earthiness, blues and funky phrasing. Morgan displayed much of the robustness of the earliest jazz trumpeters, his solos peppered with half-valve slurs and bent notes, his tone bright and brassy, and such directness appealed to DIZZY GILLESPIE, one of the best judges of a trumpeter, who hired Morgan at 18 in 1956. He played in an alert and confident CLIFFORD BROWN-ish manner on John Coltrane's 1957 *Blue Train*, and was later a member of the 1958 Jazz Messengers with ART BLAKEY, his blazing solos on BENNY GOLSON's 'Blues March' regularly raising the roof. Morgan continued to develop as a colourful and often moving performer until he was shot outside the New York nightclub Slug's, following an argument with a woman friend.

★*The Sidewinder* (Blue Note 784157)

A hit in the 1960s, and a hit all over again, since 'The Sidewinder' became popular with the dance-jazz audience of the 1980s. The title track is a mid-tempo swinger with a driving beat, but so is the much brisker 'Boy What a Night', which bristles with Billy Higgins' buzzy cymbal sound and has a long, curling melody line ending in a tantalising break before a characteristically blurted, throaty tenor solo by Joe Henderson. Morgan's solo on 'Totem Pole' is one of his finest, and the presence of Higgins is a big plus for the disc, a man in Ed Blackwell's mould of furiously swinging moderation.

★*Search for the New Land* (Blue Note 784169)

Morgan could have sat back and replayed the formula of 'Sidewinder' for the rest of the 1960s (and Blue Note did get him back to repeat the mixture with the same band on *The Rumproller*) but this album was musically richer, the intense and complex extended title piece being atmospherically complemented by the work of Wayne Shorter on reeds and Herbie Hancock on piano.

★*Live at the Lighthouse* (Fresh Sound FSR CD 140/2)

Morgan at full stretch two years before he died on a two-CD live show, and in collaboration with musicians whose time was yet to come in the 1970s, including saxophonist Bennie Maupin. It's a ferocious, thrilling encounter, and gives considerable flavour of what Morgan in person was like – which compensates for some unevenness of sound.

Mulligan, Gerald Joseph 'Gerry'

(Born New York, April 6, 1927)

Just 21 when he worked in the august company of MILES DAVIS, Lee Konitz and GIL EVANS on the pathfinding 1948 *Birth of the Cool* sessions, Gerry Mulligan contributed some timeless tunes such as 'Jeru', 'Rocker' and 'Venus De Milo' to the band's roster, establishing an atmosphere of relaxed lyricism that has stayed with him to the present day. Mulligan had been a rapid developer, contributing arrangements to the dance bands of Claude Thornhill and Gene Krupa while still a teenager. Attracted, like his baritone model SERGE CHALOFF, to the graceful, airier saxophone sound of Lester Young, Mulligan developed a saxophone technique that combined speed and smoothness.

Gerry Mulligan was constantly searching for new forms and timbres for jazz, but balanced this curiosity with the 'classicism' of his attraction to the Basie-Young mainstream. In 1952 he formed a famous piano-less quartet with the late CHET BAKER on trumpet, a group that became famous for delicate traceries of counterpoint that set the tone for much that came to be dubbed the 'west coast' style. As his reputation grew, Mulligan's work extended to film scores, but he was also capable of relaxed participation in jam-sessions, with musicians as different as Stan Getz and THELONIOUS MONK. In the 1980s Mulligan frequently led a cut-down jazz orchestra playing his own subtle and elegant work. His extraordinarily empathetic meeting with altoist PAUL DESMOND in 1957 (*Blue in Time*) would be an attractive addition to the Mulligan CD roster.

★*California Concerts* Vol. 1 (Pacific Jazz CDP 746860)

The piano-less quartet in the early 1950s with Mulligan deft and assured, Jon Eardley on trumpet this time, on a sizeable scattering of blues and ballads.

★*The Best of the Gerry Mulligan Quartet with Chet Baker* (Pacific Jazz CDP 7 95481-2)

Various quartets between 1952 and 1957, some featuring Baker, some the sharper and less languid valve trombonist BOB BROOK-MEYER. 'My Funny Valentine', 'I'm Beginning to See the Light', 'Half Nelson' and many other classics by the band are all here, as well as one of its most famous explorations on 'Walkin' Shoes'.

★*Age of Steam* (A & M CDA 0804)

Mulligan's effective combination of breezy, laid-back swing, dynamic evenness and subtle harmonic mobility, at work on a set of pieces devoted to the leader's enthusiasm for steam railways, and bearing appropriate titles. The recording revitalised material he had written in the early 1970s for a 14-piece ensemble, and featured a fine band, including Bob Brookmeyer and trumpeter Harry Edison, that expertly polished his meticulous pieces.

★*Rebirth of the Cool* (GRP 96792)

Mulligan's resprayed version of the *Birth of the Cool* sessions of 1948, originally intended to involve MILES DAVIS, then continuing as a tribute after the trumpeter's death. Mulligan and pianist John Lewis are thus the only survivors of the original band, and trumpeter Wallace Roney takes the Miles part. It's better played than the first one was, and more amiably and warmly too, though Roney is a little too animated for the languid nature of some of the themes. Mulligan plays superbly, and Phil Woods recreation of the endless alto note (first delivered by the young Lee Konitz) over the floating harmonic movement of 'Moon Dreams' is delicious.

Navarro, Theodore 'Fats'

(Born Key West, Florida, September 24, 1923; died New York, July 7, 1950)
A trumpeter who would unquestionably have been a major influence on the evolution of bebop in the 1950s (what influence he did have came through the line of trumpeters who admired him, such as CLIFFORD BROWN and LEE MORGAN) if narcotics-addiction hadn't led to tuberculosis and his early death. Like CHARLIE PARKER, Navarro was intelligent, articulate and restless about the possibilities of the new jazz. Unlike either Parker or GILLESPIE, he was not attracted by unbroken fusillades of uptempo playing but maintained an utterly distinctive poise and shapeliness in all his work, balancing a spontaneous bite against the sensation that his solos had been written out beforehand. After early swing work with Andy Kirk, Navarro replaced Gillespie in the Billy Eckstine band in 1945, then recording with Coleman Hawkins, EDDIE 'LOCKJAW' DAVIS, Illinois Jacquet and others, before commencing a close association with composer TADD DAMERON, whose notions of larger-scale bebop were more suited to Navarro's style.

The Fabulous Fats Navarro Vols. 1 & 2 (Blue Note B21Y 81531/ B21Y 81532)

Essential Navarro, and essential bebop generally, featuring a string of dazzling themes illuminated by the trumpeter's glowing tone. A fascinating contrast of brass styles is to be heard in Navarro's alternating choruses with the more heated Howard McGhee on 'Boperation' and 'The Skunk' (Vol. 2), and Navarro's harmonic imagination on 'The Chase' and 'Lady Bird' at times rivals Parker's. Some key tracks from this period, involving pianist BUD POWELL and the young SONNY ROLLINS ('Wail', 'Bouncing with Bud', '52nd Street Theme' and 'Dance of the Infidels') are unfortunately missing from the CD, but what's here provides more than a flavour of an unfulfilled jazz genius.

Nelson, Oliver Edward

(Born St Louis, June 4, 1932; died Los Angeles, October 28, 1975) A gifted composer and arranger and a forceful alto saxophonist, Nelson's contribution to jazz development has been limited only by his choice of a life in the Hollywood studios, writing music for films and TV (*Ironside*, *The Six Million Dollar Man*), rather than on bandstands. In the 1960s, Nelson's most fruitful collaboration was with the adventurous saxophonist Eric Dolphy – a good match, since Dolphy's wide leaps of intervals and devious phrasing ideally balanced Nelson's pure sound, straighter conception and clean articulation in the upper register. Apart from his famous *Blues and the Abstract Truth* and a sophisticated seven-part suite (*Afro-American Sketches*) using a richly augmented big band, Nelson made the beautiful *Images* with Dolphy, part of which is available as Fantasy's *Straight Ahead* but not on CD.

Blues and the Abstract Truth (MCAD 5659)

Nelson's best session by a considerable distance, an astonishing re-profiling of some of the most familiar materials in jazz. The leader's harmonic imagination and manipulation of basic forms is the engine of its impact, but it helps to have soloists of the class of BILL EVANS and Eric Dolphy on hand.

Black Brown and Beautiful (Bluebird/BMG ND 86993)

A 1970 Nelson dedication to Ellington, augmented by the lustrous alto saxophone of a veteran Johnny Hodges on the leader's own 'Yearnin'' and on Ellington originals 'Creole Love Call' and 'Rockin' in Rhythm'. Vocalist Leon Thomas, a forceful and inventive singer who seemed a rising star in the 1970s but faded, appears briefly.

Nichols, Herbert Horatio 'Herbie'

(Born New York, January 3, 1919; died New York, April 12, 1963)
Herbie Nichols was a piano original whose insights were matched
by his neglect, and he didn't live long enough for belated
recognition despite the fact that some members of the 1960s
avant-garde were beginning to draw attention to him at the time
of his death from leukaemia. He was an uncategorisable performer, like THELONIOUS MONK, who also suffered from the baffled
neglect of the jazz world, but unlike Monk, he was never
welcomed back. Nichols' unfashionable preference was for
paraphrase and restatement of themes rather than a preoccupation with streams of new melody on the chords and he rarely
performed his extraordinary originals – including 'Lady Sings the
Blues' for Billie Holiday – in public, condemned to a supporting
career in r & b and Dixieland bands. Nichols led only six recording
sessions in his lifetime, and his brilliant early Blue Note work
(with MAX ROACH and ART BLAKEY sharing the drum duties) is
unfortunately not on CD.

★*Bethlehem Sessions* (Affinity/Charly CDAFF 759)

Nichols' last recordings, made in 1957: far more mixed and
uncertain than his earlier work, but full of insights into a
remarkable stylist nonetheless. Though there's a bland account of
'All the Way', and a disembodied treatment of Nichols' only love
song, 'Infatuation Eyes', his most personal quality, the ability to
evoke the particularity of places and emotional events, is still
audible on the ironic 'Love Gloom Cash Love' and the grotesque,
ricocheting 'S'Crazy Pad'.

Parker, Charles Christopher 'Charlie' (also 'Bird')

(Born Kansas City, August 29, 1920; died New York, March 12,
1955)
MILES DAVIS said that the history of jazz could be told in four words:
'Louis Armstrong, Charlie Parker'. Most assessments would tip
the hat to a few more artists than that, notably Davis himself, but
Parker's genius – despite the undoubted influence of other key

musicians of the bebop era – wrenched jazz into modernism and changed the way all subsequent players conceive of it. In the mid-1940s when he was at his creative peak, Parker constantly rewrote the rules of saxophone improvisation, riding over the natural starting points and pauses suggested by the bar-lines to produce phrases of quirky lengths and unexpectedly placed resolutions, interspersing long-note passages with flurries of sixteenths, constantly rising and falling in volume. It was a rewriting of saxophone law incorporating Lester Young's lightness and storytelling skill and Coleman Hawkins' clout, but within a modern harmonic framework incompatible with a swing-band repertoire.

Charlie Parker was the son of a Kansas song-and-dance man and a devoted mother, Addie Parker, who gave the boy his first saxophone. His early familiarity with it came through a little teaching and a lot of self-education, during which the young Parker departed from general jazz practice and learned the instrument in all the keys, subsequently the cornerstone of his remarkable spontaneous facility for drifting in and out of key without losing his place. The boy began to work with local Kansas bands and eventually joined the Jay McShann Orchestra in New York. Parker's first recordings reflect Lester Young, Johnny Hodges and Benny Carter, but the harmonic departures – augmenting the basic chords with higher related notes and using these as the materials of a new melody line – were already audible.

Parker left McShann in 1942, and began sharing his ideas with other radical musicians including DIZZY GILLESPIE, THELONIOUS MONK and the other habitués of the after-hours Minton's Playhouse. Though he took up jobs with the Earl Hines and then Billy Eckstine bands, Parker's addiction to narcotics and alcohol made him an unreliable sideman, and in any event his musical sympathies were elsewhere. In 1944 he began recording with his own groups, initially in a territory somewhere between modernism and swing (though on early recordings with McShann it's clear that his preparations were virtually complete by 1942) and with unsuitable partners, then a year later with the formidable prototype bebop band including Dizzy Gillespie and Miles Davis (trumpets) and MAX ROACH on drums. Classics of the bebop idiom emerged from these performances, such as 'Now's the Time' (a bristling blues containing three devastating Parker choruses, to which *Downbeat* magazine nevertheless awarded a no-star rating), 'Billie's Bounce' and 'Koko'.

Parker's music stunned the jazz world, and had the same impact on more perceptive listeners that the King Oliver/Louis Armstrong band had had on its arrival in Chicago over 20 years before. Many other classics, including 'Cheryl', 'Buzzy' and 'Parker's Mood', were recorded by Savoy over the next three years, as well as the brilliant 'Ornithology', 'Yardbird Suite' and 'Night in Tunisia' and later 'Cool Blues' for the west coast Dial label between 1946 and 1948. The Savoy takes of 1944–8 and the Dial recordings are generally taken to represent Parker's finest work.

★*The Charlie Parker Story* (Savoy SV 0105)

Though there are compilations of Charlie Parker's work for Savoy between 1945 and 1948 (*The Genius of Charlie Parker*, SV 0104) the session in November 1945 covered by this disc offers plenty of reasons to be considered the saxophonist's greatest single day in a recording studio, including 'Ko-Ko', 'Billie's Bounce' and 'Now's the Time'. The band featured Max Roach on drums, Curley Russell on bass, BUD POWELL on piano and alternations of Dizzy Gillespie and an unsteady Miles Davis on trumpet. This CD features retakes of many of the pieces, but Parker is consistently superb.

★*Charlie Parker on Dial: The Complete Sessions* (Spotlite SPJ CD-4 101)

Parker's celebrated Dial material, hitherto exhaustively surveyed by Tony Williams' Spotlite label on vinyl, now in a superb CD set with notes by Williams and Parker's biographer and ex-Dial boss, Ross Russell. Much of this material features the saxophonist at his devastating creative peak, and some of it imperfect performances that nevertheless retain an agonising beauty of their own – such as the famous tortured 'Loverman' when Parker was barely able to stand, let alone play but on which his searing tone slashed through the uncertainties of form and the blurted flurries of notes were as expressive as anything he recorded. Dial also recorded some scorching Parker blues, notably 'Cool Blues' (from a February 1947 session after Parker's six-month stretch in the

Camarillo mental hospital, with a surprisingly accommodating Errol Garner on piano) and a breezing, lyrical and supremely confident 'Relaxin' at Camarillo' with more appropriate partners a week later.

★*Rare Bird* (Recording Arts Reference Edition Rare 04/05)

Parker broadcasts (including the soundtrack of the only known movie of the saxophonist in action on 'Hot House') between 1947 and 1954. A collector's item, because the sound quality is about as good as current technology can make 1940s airshots, but featuring Parker with trumpeters Dizzy Gillespie, KENNY DORHAM and FATS NAVARRO, and various ensembles augmented by strings and woodwind. Five tracks are from the 1950 gig at New York's Birdland in which Fats Navarro – on his last public appearance a week before the end of his life at 27 – breezes through characteristically effortless solos on such tunes as 'Ornithology' and 'Out of Nowhere'.

★*Bird – The Complete Charlie Parker on Verve* (Verve 837 141-2. Ten-disc set)

A no-stone-unturned package of 137 selections featuring more or less everything from Parker's years with Norman Granz, including tours with Granz' travelling Jazz at the Philharmonic roadshow, the recordings with classical string sections and with Machito's Latin orchestra, the intriguing oddities such as the session with Monk, Dizzy and an ill-matched Buddy Rich on drums, and the floundering exploration with a GIL EVANS woodwind jazz ensemble and assorted vocalists that Granz himself pulled the plug on after four takes. All this material, endless retakes, false starts, studio banter and all, has been repackaged with a helpful booklet and includes the piquant 1946 occasion when Parker encountered his old (and by this time languorous-sounding) hero Lester Young onstage and produced a raw, slashing masterpiece of a solo on 'Love for Sale'.

★*The Quintet: Jazz at Massey Hall* (Original Jazz Classics OJC 044)

One of the bebop legends, this Toronto concert from 1953 demands a degree of tolerance for sound quality determined by the vagaries of Charles Mingus' tape recorder, but despite backstage wrangles between the musicians it's an astonishing live representation of Parker's and Gillespie's skills (notably on 'Hot House' and 'Perdido') and Bud Powell on TADD DAMERON's 'Wee'.

★*The Complete Dean Benedetti Recordings* (Mosaic MD7-129)

This massive Parker set (seven CDs) provides perhaps the most illuminating insights into the way he worked, not least because the way he worked (often presented in isolation and with considerable repetition of material, is virtually its only subject matter). Benedetti was a musician who idolised Parker, followed him everywhere, and recorded him extensively on a portable acetate-cutting machine during 1947 and 1948. There are 278 tracks on these discs, some of them very brief, but the opportunity to compare alternative approaches to the same tune is invaluable. The background information that comes with the set is as comprehensive as the material itself, though this is very definitely a collector's item.

Pepper, Arthur Edward 'Art'

(Born Gardenia, California, September 1, 1925; died California, June 15, 1982)

A devoted admirer of PARKER, but also influenced by the white west coast cool school scene of the 1950s, Los Angeles altoist Pepper was a fascinating mixture of bebop speediness and a kind of fragile, wounded introversion that made his solos recognisable from the first few notes. Pepper often began solos, particularly later in his troubled life, as if the notes were being wrung out of him; throughout his career an audacious use of space, fondness for remoulding a single phrase or fragment of a melody, and sudden bursts of raw emotion gave his music an unpredictability that suggested, in method, THELONIOUS MONK.

Pepper was a brisk starter in music, playing around the Los

Angeles clubs by the age of 17. In the early 1940s he briefly joined the bands of Benny Carter (whose alto-playing exerted a powerful influence on him) and Stan Kenton, and he was an early admirer of Charlie Parker. Pepper played a second stint with Kenton from 1947–52 and then began a series of prison sentences for drug offences that interrupted his career through to the late 1960s, when he was rehabilitated and made a dramatic comeback.

★*The Way It Was!* (Original Jazz Classics OJC 389)

The first of a sequence of remarkably inventive and consistent sessions Pepper originally cut for the Contemporary label in the 1950s. Though his health was poor and his application erratic, his life seemed unfailingly to come together with a jazz band; this compilation of music recorded between 1956 and 1960 extensively features the great Warne Marsh, a superb partner for Pepper, on careering encounters such as 'Tickle Toe'.

★*Meets the Rhythm Section* (Original Jazz Classics OJC 338)

This album was a hastily arranged session to take advantage of the presence in Los Angeles of the MILES DAVIS rhythm section of 1957. The saxophonist hadn't played within weeks of the date, was badly strung out and exhausted, but the rapport between the players is obvious, notably on the New Orleans standby 'Jazz Me Blues' and impassioned 'Star Eyes'.

★*Living Legend* (Original Jazz Classics OJC 408)

A 1975 session with Pepper's ideal form of accompaniment, the piano trio, and a highly compatible one with Hampton Hawes at the keys (the dynamic and bluesy pianist making his last recording), the darkly dramatic Charlie Haden on bass and Shelly Manne on drums. This is Pepper after a long layoff from recording and powerfully affected by a relatively recent influence – John Coltrane. He can be heard at his most fraught, heartfelt and brooding on the slow and sorrowful 'Lost Life', one of his great recorded performances.

Powell, Earl 'Bud'

(Born New York, September 27, 1924; died New York, July 31, 1966)

The most influential pianist of the bebop era and one of the most influential in all jazz, his sound still audible in the work of many young practitioners for whom his music is a subconscious or second-generation influence. Powell went as far as he could to give the piano the vocalised horn sound of CHARLIE PARKER: but not through primitivism, special-effects dissonances or any kind of gimmickry, rather by developing an equivalent to the harmonic complexity and ecstatic energy of Parker.

Powell was taught classically but in his late teens, fascinated by jazz, began hanging out on the New York bebop scene. His jazz piano inspirations were initially the dapper, dancing sound of Teddy Wilson, the fluency of Nat King Cole and the Wilsonesque (but punchier) manner of John Kirby's pianist, Billy Kyle. But the genial manner of these players was an unsuitable emotional timbre for bebop, particularly in its first wave, and Powell set about providing a piano equivalent for Parker's headlong flights.

Later in his life Powell became prone to periods of mental disturbance, but much of his work during the 1950s remains compelling as on the 1953 Massey Hall concert with Charlie Parker, Charles Mingus, DIZZY GILLESPIE and MAX ROACH.

★*The Genius of Bud Powell* (Verve 827901)

A revealing example of the complex and erratic Powell's work, featuring a trio (a slightly curious chemistry of Ray Brown and Buddy Rich), but largely the pianist's unaccompanied reflections. The quality of his thought and touch make the listener wish there were more opportunities to hear him alone. His own 'Parisian Thoroughfare' is here, and there's a heartfelt embrace of piano history beyond bebop in 'A Nightingale Sang in Berkeley Square'.

★*The Amazing Bud Powell* Vols. 1 & 2 (Blue Note 781503/781504)

Vol. 1 contains a Powell classic, 'Un Poco Loco', explored in several takes, and a group version of 'Parisian Thoroughfare'. The group includes a scything FATS NAVARRO on trumpet, and the gathering force of SONNY ROLLINS' tenor saxophone. Vol. 2 is notable for a sensational Powell original, 'Glass Enclosure' – a piece of constantly changing mood from the vivacious to the sinister – and a typhoon of exultant bebop on 'Ornithology'.

Raney, James Elbert 'Jimmy'

(Born Louisville, Kentucky, August 20, 1927; died May 1995)
Bebop led many guitar players to pretend they weren't playing guitars – the textures the instrument was capable of were lost in the rush to play speedy single-note lines and support other musicians with the sketchiest latticework of chords. Jimmy Raney is an electric guitarist whose melodic ear and empathy with the instrument helped bop to sound like a natural idiom on it, his methods lying somewhere between the song-like relaxation of Lester Young and the chunky drive of CHARLIE CHRISTIAN. Raney worked around Chicago and New York as a teenager, joining Woody Herman in 1948, then playing in small groups with excellent white beboppers such as pianist Al Haig before joining Stan Getz in 1951 (playing beautiful counterpoint with the tenorist on the *Getz at Storyville* CD on Vogue VGCD 600093) and replacing TAL FARLOW in the Red Norvo group a year later. The later 1950s found Raney in low-key supper-club jobs, rejoining Getz in 1962–3, then dropping out for much of the 1960s.

★*Two Jims and a Zoot* (Original Master Recordings MFCD 833)

Raney in partnership with another fine guitarist, JIM HALL, in a 1964 studio session that also involved the unfailingly swinging Zoot Sims on tenor. Raney and Hall intertwine beautifully on the contrapuntal theme statements of several Latin-tinged pieces (the bossa nova craze was still in evidence at the time), but the urge of all these improvisers is towards a straight bop four-four beat.

★*Duets* (Steeplechase SCS 1134)

Raney Sr with his son Doug on some of the most creative duo performances in recent jazz, a partnership between two musicians who seek to develop each other's ideas rather than bat them back and forth like tennis balls. The repertoire is standards, such as 'My Funny Valentine' and 'Have You Met Miss Jones'.

Roach, Maxwell 'Max'

(Born New Lane, North Carolina, January 10, 1924)

Max Roach is the quintessential modern jazz drummer, the most complex of all the percussionists to have emerged from the first wave of bebop and the first drum partner of CHARLIE PARKER not simply to stay afloat around him but actively push him to new heights. But he has almost as substantial a reputation as a campaigner, a teacher, and what Gary Giddins called 'a monitor of the music's best instincts', avoiding artistic compromise throughout his long career. Roach took his lead from Kenny Clarke, but went as far as to say that he wanted 'to do with rhythm what Bach did with melody'. Roach's playing often sounded like several drummers at work at the same time.

Roach was born in Carolina but was moved to New York at four. He rapidly took to music as a child and received his first drumkit at 12, eventually studying theory and composition at the Manhattan School of Music. He was good enough to replace Kenny Clarke in Coleman Hawkins' band at 19, then worked with DIZZY GILLESPIE, Benny Carter and Stan Getz before becoming Charlie Parker's regular drummer from 1947 to 1949. Roach thereafter became associated with Charles Mingus, recorded the celebrated 1953 Massey Hall concert with Mingus, BUD POWELL, Dizzy Gillespie and Parker, then formed one of the finest small groups of the mature phase of bop with the trumpeter CLIFFORD BROWN. Brown's death in a road crash shook Roach badly but he continued with a variety of fine brass players (DONALD BYRD, BOOKER LITTLE, FREDDIE HUBBARD and others), partnered SONNY ROLLINS on some of his strongest records, and in more recent times has experimented with choirs, with solo singers, including his wife Abbey Lincoln, string quartets and all-percussion ensembles with strong African connections. In the 1960s, Roach's vociferous civil-rights campaigning had him blacklisted from studio work, and also produced one of his most striking records, 'We Insist – Freedom Now Suite'.

★*Max Roach in Concert* (Vogue 655602)

Live recordings from two concerts in the early days of the Brown/ Roach unit, with guest performers TEDDY EDWARDS on saxophone and the percussive, metallic Carl Perkins on piano on four of the tracks. There's a thrilling extended version of Duke Jordan's 'Jordu', Bud Powell's 'Parisian Thoroughfare' and some memorable Clifford Brown trumpet on 'Tenderly'.

★*Deeds Not Words* (Original Jazz Classics OJC 304)

Two years after the accident that killed Clifford Brown and Richie Powell, this fine session featured young trumpeter Booker Little, with Ray Draper on tuba, GEORGE COLEMAN on tenor and Art Davis on bass. Coleman, who can sometimes sound over-elaborate, is magnificent here, and Little forms an intimate, and challenging, relationship with Roach. Some of the most direct and forceful jazz of the period immediately preceding the free era.

★*We Insist! Freedom Now Suite* (Candid CCD 9002)

A famous 1960 session, also featuring Booker Little, and with a larger band augmented by saxophone legend Coleman Hawkins. Apart from sensational trumpet performances from Booker Little on the furious 'Freedom Day' and 'Tears for Johannesburg', there's a rugged, magisterial performance from Hawkins over the whiplash of Roach's drums on 'Driva' Man'.

★*Birth and Rebirth* (Black Saint BSR 0024)

A duet between Roach and avant-garde saxophonist Anthony Braxton from 1978. Braxton is a multi-instrumentalist of superlative technique and theoretical interests that take in both jazz and contemporary straight music. Despite all their differences Roach and Braxton struck up a spectacular rapport, the drummer's polyrhythmic mastery complementing, pushing and echoing the saxophonist's labyrinthine runs and blurted, sharply accented dissonances at every turn.

★*To the Max!* (Enja 7021 22)

Double CD of Roach at work in the 1990s, just to prove that as he approaches his sixties he continues to investigate jazz as if he were just launching his career. A vast throng of performers inhabits this record, and it includes some of Roach's work with the Uptown String Quartet, the classical group featuring his violin-playing daughter Maxine. There is also an orchestral performance of a suite called 'Ghost Dance', part of which is performed by Roach's percussion band M'Boom, in one of the ensemble's rare surviving outings on record. If ever there was an example of eclecticism and musicality in balance, this is it.

Rodney Red (Robert Chudnick)

(Born Philadelphia, October 27, 1927)
Busy in the 1940s big bands (Jimmy Dorsey, Gene Krupa, Woody Herman) before his meeting with CHARLIE PARKER, Rodney discovered bebop while in the trumpet section of Woody Herman's Second Herd, and his admiration for Parker's music led him to follow the altoist around until he eventually won a coveted place in the quintet when Miles Davis left. Rodney worked effectively with Parker through 1949, and in the mid-1950s cut a memorable album displaying his vigorous and bustling style in partnership with multi-instrumentalist Ira Sullivan, *Modern Music from Chicago* (Fantasy), only available on vinyl. Rodney resurfaced in the mid-1970s with the renewal of interest in bop. A more recent collaboration with Ira Sullivan resulted in a captivating album, *Sprint!* (1982), which, surprisingly, is unavailable in any format.

★*Red Giant* (Steeplechase SCS 1233)

Ten tunes from a Copenhagen session in 1988, in which Rodney is teamed up with a trio of two hard-bitten local beboppers and an expatriate American pianist, Butch Lacey. As a group performance, it's variable, but Rodney's own playing is expressive, witty and thoughtful over a wide-ranging repertoire that includes 'Greensleeves', Coltrane's 'Giant Steps' (rather unwisely, but maybe inevitably, taken at a dragging mid-tempo) and Waller's 'Jitterbug Waltz'.

Rogers, Shorty (Milton Michael Rajonsky)

(Born Lee, Massachusetts, April 14, 1924)
Always identified with the cool west coast jazz scene of the 1950s, Shorty Rogers was a punchy boppish trumpeter but his reputation in jazz was made as an arranger. Rogers' big-band work of the 1950s has stood up well, through a combination of careful craftsmanship and determination to ensure that the cool style, however restrained, always swung. Rogers was raised in New York, attended the High School of Music and Arts (*Fame*) and began working with vibraharpist Red Norvo in his late teens. It was the second Woody Herman Herd of 1947 that expanded Rogers' horizons and he began producing effervescent large-scale charts such as 'Lemon Drop', 'More Moon' and 'Keeper of the Flame', including audaciously scoring a chunk of CHARLIE PARKER's 'Dark Shadows' saxophone solo as an ensemble figure for 'I've Got News'. Rogers left Herman for Stan Kenton's band in 1948 gaining valuable experience scoring for Kenton's exotic instrumentations and formed a rich creative relationship with saxophonist ART PEPPER.

★*Short Stops* (BMG/Bluebird ND 90209)

The essential compilation for Rogers fans. This set merges material from three recording sessions for RCA in the early 1950s, including the one that produced the *Cool and Crazy* material, and a set dedicated to Count Basie. The bands Rogers assembled for these encounters – including Art Pepper, Hampton Hawes and MAYNARD FERGUSON – were the pick of the west coast. Pepper is at his most rhapsodic on the ballad 'Bunny', Hawes is brisk and pearly on 'Diablo's Dance', the Herman 'Four Brothers' saxophone sound is recalled by 'Boar-Jibu' and 'Short Stop' is a blues. The buoyancy of much of this music firmly counters the common contention that the cool school was subdued, unemotional and never used driving rhythm sections.

Rollins, Theodore Walter 'Sonny'

(Born New York, September 7, 1930)

For four decades the irrepressible, garrulous and often subversive music of Sonny Rollins has dominated 'modern' jazz, and now that most of his powerful contemporaries have died he has become the most imposing survivor of the bebop era still fully functioning on the saxophone. Rollins' trademark from the mid-1950s was a muscular, vibrato-less, frequently ironic (rather than self-revelatory) style that in the course of a single unrehearsed solo could embrace blues, West Indian calypso (his parents came from the Virgin Islands), alternations of bleak, pebbly minimalism with mischievous manipulations of Tin Pan Alley doggerel, and episodes of broad, rolling swing highly reminiscent of Coleman Hawkins. The pianist THELONIOUS MONK, a childhood friend, was also a major influence.

Rollins also liked the popular pre-rock 'jump' music of the 1940s, an enthusiasm for pop and dance music that remains with him. By 1951 he was forging a unique saxophone style that had Hawkins' stately weight, Charlie Parker's intensity and Lester Young's melodic inventiveness – with more than a dash of the abrasive drive of DEXTER GORDON. The confection appealed to MILES DAVIS, who hired him. In 1956 Rollins began working in the definitive hard-bop group, that led by CLIFFORD BROWN and MAX ROACH, and it was with Roach (a drummer with as much musical curiosity as Rollins, and the technique to handle his cavalier displacements of the beat) that he recorded some of his most lasting work.

Rollins in more recent times has become less intractable, and though some of his recorded work of the past dozen years or so has veered towards the commercial (funk, gentler ballad-playing than formerly, soul), his mercurial musical mind has rarely slowed in live performance.

★*Sonny Rollins Plus Four* (Original Jazz Classics OJC 243)

Actually the Clifford Brown/Max Roach band in March 1956, but with Rollins taking the leadership credits for contractual reasons. This was Clifford Brown's last recording, and the young trumpeter is in scorching form on Rollins' bebop original, 'Pent-up

House'. Rollins and Roach demonstrate their almost arrogant comfort with rhythmic adventures on the waltz-time 'Valse Hot'.

★*Saxophone Colossus* (Original Jazz Classics OJC 291)

Probably Sonny Rollins' most famous album, June 1956's *Saxophone Colossus* is the apogee of the saxophonist's work with Max Roach and a masterpiece of spontaneous composition. In addition to the energetic, elbowing calypso 'St Thomas' and an imperious version of 'Mack the Knife' ('Moritat') there is the prolonged improvisation on the bleak, mid-tempo 'Blue Seven', an assembly of brooding, staccato variations that Rollins' control of shape and musical intelligence turns into one of the greatest episodes of recorded jazz.

★*Tenor Madness* (Original Jazz Classics OJC 124)

Miles Davis' rhythm section of 1956, including the fiery Philly Joe Jones, with Rollins and John Coltrane. The gig was a Rollins date, but Rollins had asked a spectating Coltrane to participate in the two-tenor blues chase of the title. Coltrane's music is still unsettled at this stage, and his dense, harmonically complex style is much more symmetrical than Rollins' – but as the only recorded encounter of the two tenor stars, a special session.

★*Way Out West* (Original Jazz Classics OJC 337)

An example of Rollins' ability during this period to pull even musicians unfamiliar with his methods into his own erratic orbit, on a meeting with west coast players in 1957. On two versions of the blistering uptempo 'Come Gone' – the first of which opens with Rollins swaying and curling over only Ray Brown's bass, accelerating to a mixture of boppish chord-running, blazing double-time and preoccupied toying with perplexing phrases – there is a tour de force running a close second to 'Blue Seven'.

★*Night at the Village Vanguard* Vols. 1 & 2 (Blue Note CDP 746 517-2, 518-2)

Despite his prolific recorded output, long-time connoisseurs agree that Rollins' most transported moments in live performance beat most of his studio work, and this is an occasion from 1957 that confirms the view. Freed by the absence of a piano from the inexorable march of the chords, Rollins is in roaring form with Wilbur Ware on bass and Elvin Jones – a player of comparable rhythmic unruliness to Rollins, though restraining himself here – on drums. Rollins' brand of muscular whimsy is fully unfurled for 'Old Devil Moon' and 'Softly as in a Morning Sunrise', with an outstanding debut for 'Sonnymoon for Two' on Vol. 2.

★*The Freedom Suite* (JVC/Fantasy VDJ 1520)

Another trio album, this time from 1958, with Max Roach back on drums and Oscar Pettiford on bass. The title is a dedication to black rights and the album is a mixture of concentrated and committed Rollins – magisterial on the 19-minute title piece, his farsightedness about the development and architecture of a spontaneous composition never more in control – and detached and ironic Rollins, on the doodling 'Shadow Waltz'.

★*Quartets* (RCA Bluebird ND 85643)

Rollins recorded six albums for RCA in the three years after his comeback in 1961, *The Bridge* being one of the best known for its associated anecdote about Rollins being given to practising on the catwalk of the Williamsburg Bridge during his sabbatical. This CD includes the title tune, the bustling and convoluted 'John S' and a quirkily considered 'God Bless the Child', all in the company of the gently lyrical guitarist JIM HALL. Good music, though the temperature is down compared to the 1957–8 work.

★*Sunny Days, Starry Nights* (Milestone 9122)

Rollins from the mid-1980s, after the saxophonist had modified the frequency of his furious improvisatory flights to suit his more mature years, and expanded the volume of pop and funk in pursuit of a non-purist audience. Though most of his records since the 1970s have had their moments, none of them have had his 1950s and 1960s panache – but *Sunny Days* gets close. 'Mava Mava' is a vintage Rollins calypso full of erratically bending and straightening notes and 'I'm Old Fashioned' is a delightful gutting and dissecting of the Jerome Kern standard.

Falling in Love With Jazz (Milestone 9179)

A 1989 session coupling Rollins with a variety of contemporary jazz stars, including saxophonist Branford Marsalis and drummers Jack DeJohnette and Jeff Watts. Not an unqualified success, and maybe proof that these days the more assertive the accompanists are the more intrusive Rollins finds their presence in his thoughts. But he's on his old form on a delightful account of 'Tennessee Waltz'.

Ross, Annie (Annabel Short Lynch)

(Born Surrey, July 25, 1930)
One of the few British jazz artists with careers beginning in the early postwar period to make an impact worldwide. Annie Ross possessed several qualities that were then uncommon among European jazz vocalists: she understood instrumental improvisation, she could be spontaneous and swinging yet faithful to the spirit of a song, and she had immense confidence, often expressed as a coolness to the point of diffidence. Yet with the Lambert/Hendricks/Ross vocal trio, she made a lasting, if minor, contribution to jazz history and the group spawned several imitators, notably the 'vocalese' ensemble Manhattan Transfer.

Born in England but raised in Los Angeles, Ross eventually studied acting in New York. She came to prominence in the States in 1952 with a set of lyrics of her own to accompany the lines of Wardell Gray's tenor improvisations on 'Twisted'. Through the 1950s, she was busy in Europe and America, forming LAMBERT, HENDRICKS AND ROSS at the end of the decade, originally for a single Basie-dedicated project. She left in 1962, freelanced and worked in TV (notably the early *That Was The Week That Was* mid-1960s satire shows for BBC), opened her own nightclub (Annie's Room), acted and sang in Brecht productions, and returned to New York in 1985 primarily as a singer.

★*A Gasser!* (Pacific Jazz CDP 746 854-2)

One of only two Ross-led CDs currently available (the other is with GERRY MULLIGAN), this 1959 album finds the singer in both her trademark mood of knowing resignation on an illuminating version of Ellington's 'I Didn't Know About You' and one of less familiar blazing directness – revealing her immense range and swing – on the aptly titled 'Everything I've Got'. Saxophonist Zoot Sims, always an inspiration, plus driving drummer Mel Lewis help to give this excellent session its sparkle.

Rouse, Charles 'Charlie'

(Born Washington DC, April 6, 1924; died November 30, 1988)
A tenor saxophonist of unusual tone and considerable rhythmic flexibility who managed to do what many more eminent saxophone players (including SONNY ROLLINS and John Coltrane) had struggled with – successfully play with THELONIOUS MONK, which he did from 1959 to 1970.

Like many talented bebop players of his generation, Rouse performed briefly in the saxophone sections of the Billy Eckstine and DIZZY GILLESPIE orchestras in the 1940s, and followed that with employment by TADD DAMERON, Duke Ellington and Count Basie. As the partnership with Monk developed, Rouse became an increasingly astute interpreter of some of the most pungent material in jazz. In the 1970s Rouse played with a quintet led by another forcefully independent pianist, Mal Waldron, and then in the group Sphere, which dedicated its activities to Monk when the originator had retired from playing.

★*Epistrophy* (Landmark 1521)

Rouse in action a month before his death. This October 1988 session was a birthday tribute to Monk, and Rouse's rugged style can be heard on five classic compositions including 'Nutty', 'Blue Monk' and 'Round Midnight'. The acerbic quality of the originals has faded a bit, but Don Cherry on trumpet is a musician whose structural quirkiness rivals Monk's own.

Rowles, James George 'Jimmy'

(Born Spokane, Washington, August 19, 1918)
For many years Rowles has been a walking encyclopaedia of jazz and American popular song, and an ingenious improviser. His sparkling, Tatumesque, offhand dominance of the keyboard ought to place him, if not alongside jazz music's great immortals, certainly not far behind.

Rowles was living on the west coast in the 1940s, where he worked with Lester Young, Benny Goodman and Woody Herman and later Tommy Dorsey. A virtually photographic memory for song-parts made him an inspired accompanist, in which role he contributed strikingly to several later recordings by Billie Holiday, but he then disappeared into studio work until a move to New York in 1973.

★*We Could Make Such Beautiful Music* (Xanadu 157/EPM 5152)

Jimmy Rowles in the late 1970s with a trio comprising George Mraz on bass and Leroy Williams on drums; not totally perfect ('I Can't Get Started' and 'In the Still of the Night' are unremarkable) but Rowles' wit, full-bodied technique and Lester Young-like sense of thematic improvisation are at their jaunty best on a bossa nova version of 'Stars and Stripes Forever', Errol Garner's 'Shake It Don't Break It' and a version of 'Here's That Rainy Day'.

Shank, Bud (Clifford Everett Jr)

(Born Dayton, Ohio, May 27, 1926)
One of many saxophonists who initially performed such a refined and seamless version of CHARLIE PARKER as to be written off as an insignificant imitator, reedman Bud Shank later toughened his style and became one of the most graceful and adept exponents of the difficult art of bebop flute as well. A clarinettist originally, Shank worked with Stan Kenton's gargantuan 1950 band, and with members of the west coast school of Kenton alumni. He appeared on early recordings led by trumpeter/arranger SHORTY ROGERS and appeared in the Lighthouse Allstars band; like Rogers, he also disappeared into studio work for long periods and

resurfaced with Rogers for joint tours in the 1980s. Shank's music often veers towards pop (his pop album *Michelle*, with CHET BAKER on trumpet, was a chart hit) but he remains capable of delightful playing in the right company. He was a founder member of the LA Four in 1974, a group devoted to smooth commercial bop.

★*At Jazz Alley* (JVC/Fantasy VDJ 1120)

Bud Shank's alto in its rougher, tougher, 1980s guise on a live quartet set from a Seattle club. Not a revelation about this complex, underrated performer exactly, but a fitful display of his bop roots and an occasionally successful struggle to throw off the habitual restraint of those studio years.

Shaw, Woody

(Born Laurinburg, North Carolina, December 24, 1944; died New York, May 10, 1989)
Though he worked with most of the bandleaders of consequence in modern jazz, it is with a cooperative group commemorating a departed jazz scene – the Paris Reunion Band, which united several of the fine American musicians who emigrated to France, including Kenny Clarke – that Woody Shaw is probably best remembered in Europe.

Woody Shaw was not a first-generation bebopper however. He was 11 and just taking up the trumpet when CHARLIE PARKER died. Hard bop was already firmly established when Shaw was a teenager. His father was a gospel singer, and the boy played extensively in high school bands and began working with a local Newark musician, organist Larry Young, whose interests lay in a territory between jazz, funk and rhythm & blues. The young Shaw worked around New York, variously with Chick Corea and Eric Dolphy, and after Dolphy's death in 1964, with Clarke, BUD POWELL, saxophonist JOHNNY GRIFFIN and pianist HORACE SILVER.

Like his contemporary FREDDIE HUBBARD, with whom he is often compared, Shaw possessed an immense technique, warm tone and imagination. But Shaw had been influenced enough by the 1960s free-scene to be convinced that judicious experiments with atonality could reveal new colours to songs, rather than simply negate or dismiss them. Shaw went into hibernation in San Francisco at the beginning of the jazz-rock era of the 1970s, but when the public interest in bop revived in the late 1970s so did Shaw, and his subtle blend of bop harmonic technique and free-music borrowings gave his music considerable bite.

Imagination (Muse MCD 5338)

Longer on expertise than atmosphere and it doesn't display much of the trumpeter's wilder side – but as a piece of neo-bop it's a good deal better than many of the more prominent recordings by less experienced artists. Shaw has an excellent band here (including the dramatic, intelligent Steve Turre on trombone and Kirk Lightsey on piano) and on such bop trumpet classics as 'If I Were a Bell' he intriguingly handles the tune with a mixture of its faintly cloying delicacy and sudden rocketing double-time.

Silver, Horace Ward Martin Tavares

(Born Norwalk, Connecticut, September 2, 1928)
'Funk' has been part of the language of music for a long time: pianist Horace Silver quoted it as far back as the mid-1950s with the tune 'Opus de Funk'. Silver is a classic example of an artist who energised a new way of playing jazz by astute rearrangement rather than subversion. Though a devotee of the work of BUD POWELL as well as THELONIOUS MONK, he avoided bebop's streams of notes, instead linking Monk's percussiveness to those more forthright relatives of jazz – rhythm & blues and gospel music.

Silver's first high-profile work was with Stan Getz in 1950, then with Coleman Hawkins, Lester Young, MILES DAVIS and Art Blakey. In 1954 Silver's first recording band (with Art Blakey on drums) became the first Jazz Messengers, and the departure of tenorist HANK MOBLEY and trumpeter DONALD BYRD for the Max Roach/Clifford Brown band encouraged Silver to form a new permanent quintet with Louis Hayes replacing Blakey. Silver wrote prodigiously, for the original Messengers and its successors, contributing to the jazz repertoire innumerable catchy blues (such as 'Home Cookin'', 'Filthy McNasty', 'Senor Blues'), ballads

('Calcutta Cutie' from *Song for my Father* is one of his best) and emphatic soul pieces such as 'The Preacher'.

★*Horace Silver Trio* (Blue Note B21Y 81520)

Silver's 1952 and 1953 sessions for Blue Note, and intriguing examples of his evolution from Bud Powell. But already Silver was turning away from the onward rush of Powell's music, preferring to lag slightly behind the beat, creating an air of laconic expectancy, hitting brusque single-note solos assembled out of short phrases against lazily banging chords in his left hand. 'Opus de Funk' is one of the disc's standout tracks.

★*Horace Silver and the Jazz Messengers* (Blue Note CDP 746 140-2)

The first edition of the Jazz Messengers in 1954, with the high-octane fuel provided by Silver's piano and Blakey's drums blasting an already vigorous band into space. 'Doodlin'', a Silver original whose r & b drive was given even greater emphasis on a Ray Charles recording, is featured here, as is the soulful, backbeat-driven Silver classic, 'The Preacher'. KENNY DORHAM is on trumpet and Doug Watkins on bass.

★*Finger Poppin'* (Blue Note B21Y 84008)

A 1959 recording by what's widely regarded as Silver's finest and most joyous band, featuring Blue Mitchell on trumpet and Junior Cook on tenor, with Gene Taylor on bass and Louis Hayes on drums. Mitchell and Cook meshed perfectly with Silver, their performances models of crackling economy and awareness of when not to get in the way of the beat, and in addition to 'Juicy Lucy' and 'Finger Poppin'' the fast blues 'Cookin' at the Continental' is one of the leader's most exciting performances.

★*Song for my Father* (Blue Note CDP 784 185-2)

One of Silver's best-known works, springing from a mid-1960s session that (though less taut and insistent than the earlier recordings) produced the blues of the title, and the evocative ballad 'Calcutta Cutie'.

★*The Jody Grind* (Blue Note CDP 784250-2)

One of Silver's most celebrated funky sessions, from 1966. The title track is a scalding 12-bar blues, founded on the pianist's hammer-and-anvil left-hand chordal vamp, and expanded dramatically by tenorist Tyrone Washington's spluttery, argumentative gestures to the methods of Sonny Rollins.

Smith, James Oscar ('Jimmy')

(Born Norristown, Pennsylvania, December 8, 1925)
For his theatrical mixture of rhythm 'n' blues, gospel and charging bebop, Hammond organist Jimmy Smith is still the guru in this forthright and exciting field. Now nearing 70, Smith still pumps out a mixture of jazz-funk and urban blues that attracts both his original audience and newcomers who have arrived via the dance-jazz and acid-jazz scene.

Smith learned piano first, then went to music college in Philadelphia, and took up the Hammond in 1951. He became a local hero on it, then took New York's Café Bohemia by storm in 1956. An appearance at Birdland followed, and his steaming show at the 1957 Newport Jazz Festival secured his international career. Smith rescued the organ from its role as an occasional special effect or a novelty, and turned it into a fully-fledged improvising machine, adapting a phraseology drawn from both bebop and rhythm 'n' blues. His feet provided a stomping bassline, his chordal style sounded like an orchestral brass section, his right hand like a bop horn. After years of touring, Smith went to live in Los Angeles in the mid-1970s, where he opened Jimmy Smith's Jazz Supper Club. He returned to touring in the 1980s, and, with the return of enthusiasm for the idiom he has always worked in, has enjoyed a renewed career. Almost all jazz organists acknowledge a debt to him.

★*The Master* (Blue Note CDP 7243 8 30451 2 9)

Recent Smith, running over all the usual ground, a disc that was issued before his rather too theatrical 1994 European tour. Smith's great hits are on it – 'Organ Grinder's Swing', 'Back At

The Chicken Shack', and 'The Cat' – as well as some relentless r & b like 'Got My Mojo Workin'. A big plus is the reunion with guitarist KENNY BURRELL, who plays as if he hadn't done all this stuff a million times.

Solal, Martial

(Born Algiers, August 23, 1927)
An explosive French pianist whose style can reflect the orchestral pianistics of Art Tatum, the boppish monologues of BUD POWELL, and at times the trio methods (though rarely the meticulous contemplativeness) of BILL EVANS. Solal has been one of the foremost jazz pianists in Europe since his emergence in the 1950s, with a technique, harmonic knowledge and dislike of cheap effects and well-worn licks that should have entitled him to a bigger reputation than he has.

Solal was born of French parents in Algiers and moved to Paris in the 1940s. In the following decade, he worked with the expatriate Americans living there, including drummer Kenny Clarke and the veteran genius Sidney Bechet; he also worked on Django Reinhardt's final recording session. The pianist also occasionally ran a big band, and has written much film music, for Jean-Luc Godard (*A Bout de Souffle*) and others.

★*Zo-Ko-So* (MPS 843107)

Solal with Hans Koller on tenor saxophone and the bluesy Attila Zoller on guitar in 1965. But though Solal engages in graceful duet with Zoller on 'Stella by Starlight', it's the unaccompanied performances that really establish his credentials, particularly the dynamic contrasts and harmonic shifts that create a sense of expectancy in every chorus.

Stitt, Edward 'Sonny'

(Born Boston, February 2, 1924; died Washington, July 22, 1982)
A brilliant saxophonist unfairly burdened with the reputation of being a PARKER imitator, Sonny Stitt was one of the fastest, most

accomplished and competitive of all bebop saxophonists. An altoist at first, he switched to tenor at the end of the 1940s to downplay the Parker comparisons, and for three decades proceeded to tour the jazz haunts of the globe firing fusillades of blistering improvisation at all comers, often with unfamiliar rhythm sections or on hastily arranged recording sessions.

Stitt served his apprenticeship in the 1940s big bands (Tiny Bradshaw's, Billy Eckstine's, DIZZY GILLESPIE's) and began leading his own groups at the end of that decade, recording with BUD POWELL, John Lewis, MAX ROACH, ART BLAKEY and many others. Between 1950 and 1952, after he had taken up the tenor, he co-led a band with fellow-tenorist Gene Ammons, and the two played with a demonstrative, conjuror-like virtuosity. Such skills made Stitt first choice for bands formed specifically as tributes to the achievements of beboppers.

★*Sonny Stitt/Bud Powell/J.J. Johnson* (Original Jazz Classics OJC 009)

Early days for Stitt – 1949 – but he was already shoulder to shoulder with the best beboppers on 52nd Street. This collection of oddments finds him imperiously in command of the fastest pieces, and displays some magnificent improvising from Bud Powell as well. Max Roach is on drums.

★*Sonny Stitt Sits in with the Oscar Peterson Trio* (Verve 849396)

Nearly ten years later, and if anything Stitt is faster still. He appears here on both alto and tenor saxophones, and in the company of a musician just as concerned to spray notes around like confetti. But instead of cancelling each other out, Stitt and Peterson develop an unexpectedly empathetic relationship.

★*Constellation* (Muse MCD 5323)

One of the best of the later Stitt sessions, a 1972 performance finding the saxophonist with a highly suitable pianist, Barry Harris. On the face of it, this could have been one of dozens of Stitt recording sessions, running down the chord changes against a routine trio backup. But Stitt isn't leaning back on his peerless skills here, but probing music such as the Parker composition of the title.

Thielemans, Jean Baptiste 'Toots'

(Born Brussels, April 29, 1922)

Toots Thielemans is a musician easily sidelined as a vaudeville act: he developed a bebop style for the harmonica and features a good deal of astonishingly accurate jazzy whistling in his performances as well. His career changed after his worldwide hit with the catchy composition 'Bluesette', and he played on the soundtracks to many TV shows and movies (notably *Midnight Cowboy*, *Sugarland Express*, *The Wiz* and the children's TV show *Sesame Street*). But Thielemans has an intimate understanding of bop, and a feeling for the harmonic intensity and fierce emotionalism of John Coltrane too. He is an unclassifiable performer.

He began his musical life on accordion, and took up harmonica when he was 17, but hearing Django Reinhardt turned him on to the guitar, and playing on American bases in Europe after the war brought an awareness of the new bop movement. Thielemans sat in on 52nd Street on a visit to America in 1947 and two years later met CHARLIE PARKER at the Paris Jazz Festival. He toured Europe with Benny Goodman in 1950, then went to the States to work with Dinah Washington and George Shearing as a guitarist. 'Bluesette', a lilting, lyrical and unjazzy theme, was the hit record that made constant studio and movie-score work compete with his continuing desire to tour as a jazz performer.

★*Only Trust Your Heart* (Concord CCD 4355)

Probably Thielemans' best record ever, made in 1988 and displaying an even wider sweep of his jazz allegiances, including compositions by THELONIOUS MONK and Wayne Shorter. The leader plays harmonica throughout, and demonstrates more convincingly than he ever has how fruitfully it can be transformed from a novelty instrument or a rhythm & blues device. The partnership with pianist and arranger Fred Hersch is a big plus.

Thompson, Eli 'Lucky'

(Born Detroit, Michigan, June 16, 1924)
Lucky Thompson is a musician of maturity, intelligence and fertility of phrasing – his principles founded on the methods of Don Byas, but his sound softer and more fluid.

Thompson's career began in New York, working with big bands including those of Don Redman, Lionel Hampton and Billy Eckstine, and recording on the bebop scene with Dizzy Gillespie and Charlie Parker. In the Fifties, after being active in r & b and constant studio work, Thompson worked with major jazz players including Milt Jackson, and briefly performed with the Stan Kenton band. He settled in Europe for long periods in the 1950s and 1960s, and was an early champion of the soprano saxophone.

Lucky Strikes (Original Jazz Classics OJC 194)

Thompson from 1964 with a good quartet featuring Hank Jones on piano. The leader's fast, unblinking tenor style and liquid sound are in full flow, and his improvising resourcefulness shines fascinating light on 'In A Sentimental Mood'. This disc is one of Thompson's best performances as a leader, and backs it up with one of his best bands.

Timmons, Robert Henry 'Bobby'

(Born Philadelphia, December 19, 1935; died New York, March 1, 1974)
Originally a BUD POWELL disciple, Bobby Timmons made his reputation by borrowing from both the clattering attack of HORACE SILVER and the pounding chordal style of RED GARLAND, a blend that he rarely seemed to forge into an entirely successful whole. But as a blend of urbanity and earthiness it was popular, and its roots lay explicitly in black church experience. Timmons did go down in jazz history for the creation of a number of archetypal hard-bop classics, suffused with gospel motifs, such as the insistent, playful 'Dat Dere' (which Oscar Brown Jr put words to) and the famous gospel-jazz theme 'Moanin''.

Timmons came to fame with Art Blakey at the end of the 1950s (having worked with KENNY DORHAM, CHET BAKER, SONNY STITT and CANNONBALL ADDERLEY previously) and recorded his brand of hard-driving and rather unsubtle music sporadically through the 1960s, usually with a trio – the setup he played with in Greenwich Village bars for most of the later years of his short life.

★*This Here's Bobby Timmons* (Original Jazz Classics OJC 104)

A 1960 trio recording, one of the best of the pianist's albums from the 1960s, and notable for a heated rendition of his trademark theme, 'Moanin".

Turrentine, Stanley William

(Born Pittsburgh, Pennsylvania, April 5, 1934)
A soul-jazz saxophonist who could also be a fine improviser, Stanley Turrentine has mostly occupied the musical territory his bluesy sound has invited. His father was Thomas Turrentine, a swing saxophonist with the original Savoy Sultans, and his older brother is a good trumpeter. Stanley Turrentine served his apprenticeship with rhythm & blues and soul bands, working in the early 1950s with a Lowell Fulson group that included Ray Charles on piano. Turrentine worked with MAX ROACH in the late 1950s, but during the next decade he moved increasingly towards more popular music, playing extensively with organist Jimmy Smith, ground that he has continued to inhabit since.

★*The Best of Stanley Turrentine: The Blue Note Years* (Blue Note B21Y 93201)

Over 20 years of Turrentine's work on Blue Note, and a highly suitable survey of his development, with partners including Herbie Hancock, George Benson, McCoy Tyner and others. It provides plenty of evidence that Turrentine has never simply been a soul-jazz groover, notably on a delicious version of 'God Bless the Child'.

4

MAINSTREAMERS AND REVIVALISTS
– BACK TO THE ROOTS

Mainstream has become a term with a wide currency in jazz. When it was first applied to the subject by critic Stanley Dance in the 1950s, it meant a music performed by small to mid-sized bands working in that lyrical, free-swinging territory that had become the trademark of Count Basie's musicians. But as the headlong rate of change of jazz styles continued, and the two incarnations of the music that most sharply contrasted its fiercely expressionistic and its commercial sides developed back to back – with free-jazz and jazz-rock fusion in the 1960s – 'mainstream' came to embrace ever-larger areas of the music that fell outside those categories.

But in the early 1950s, things were different. The swing era was passing, and the wreckage at first seemed considerable. Big bands had become uneconomical to run, and the shifts in jazz towards a less formally organised small-group music (the result of both postwar hardships and bebop's art-music explorations) and in popular music towards vocalists rather than instrumentalists were changing the marketplace. Rock and roll was arriving, a seductive mixture of white Southern country songs, black blues and jazz-inflected 'jump' music that made swing, its predecessor as a youth cult, seem to belong to a bygone age. Jazz clubs were emptying, big bands were breaking up – even Count Basie's, which dwindled to an octet in 1950. Yet the jazz world was still full of fine performers of this evaporating idiom wondering what they did wrong.

Impresarios like Norman Granz and George Wein (architect of the Newport Jazz Festival) still had faith in the qualities of earlier jazz – its closeness to the American songwriting traditions of the 1920s and 1930s, its rhythmic relaxation, its use of improvising styles that remained close to the shape of the original themes, its wit and warmth. So did many swing musicians, like Ben Webster, Roy Eldridge, Coleman Hawkins and Buddy Tate. Some were young, like cornettist Ruby Braff, a man of the same generation as the beboppers, yet who chose to devote his life to materials drawn from swing and blues.

With the spectacular performance by the Duke Ellington band at the 1956 Newport Festival and one of Count Basie's best albums (*Atomic Mr. Basie*) not long afterwards, an audience for forms of jazz that were neither explicitly bebop or pop-influenced gradually expanded and young musicians seduced by the airy magic of the old swing performers perfected it anew.

Allison, Mose John

(Born Tippo, Mississippi, November 11, 1927)

Mose Allison's singing, an influential triumph of artlessness (Georgie Fame has been his most respectful interpreter in this country) is rarely far from the blues. He was once a bebop pianist, accompanying STAN GETZ and Gerry Mulligan in the 1950s, but his allegiances are with simpler and earthier forms. Allison's piano-playing, a mixture of hopping, emphatic on-the-beat accents, rattling triplet runs like coaches travelling fast over points, and baleful bluesy trills, suggests a confection of saloon-bar blues pianists and the work of Ellington and Thelonious Monk. His singing is influenced by Sonny Boy Williamson and Tampa Red but with a diffident though always swinging delivery that implies private musings rather than performance.

Allison played piano as a child, and was a Dixieland trumpeter at school, but blues was an inevitable accompaniment to life in the Mississippi delta. He played throughout the region until 1956, when he moved to New York to work with Getz, Mulligan and others, but performed with his own trios from the 1960s onward, honing his unique style and expanding on a collection of brilliant original compositions including 'Parchman Farm', 'Look What You Made Me Do' and 'Everybody Cryin' Mercy'. His classic 1957 Prestige album, *Black Country Suite*, isn't available on CD.

★*Ever Since the World Ended* (Blue Note CDP 748 015-2)

Mose Allison had a lean time in the 1970s, and his signing to Blue Note for a debut album on the label in 1987 was a long-overdue recognition of his talents. Not only did this disc feature Allison's gentle perversity and ironic vision in full spate but it included some new compositions and assistance from altoist Arthur Blythe, saxophonist Benny Wallace and guitarist Kenny Burrell.

Barber, Ball and Bilk

Barber, Chris (born Hertfordshire, April 17, 1930)
Ball, Kenneth 'Kenny' (born Essex, May 22, 1930)
Bilk, Bernard Stanley 'Acker' (born Somerset, January 28, 1929)
These three musicians developed their careers quite separately, as distinctive exponents of the British revivalist music of the 1950s and 1960s, yet they are united by age, by aptitude for adapting their enthusiasms in early jazz to a commercial market in a rock-dominated period, and by the possession of far more sophisticated instrumental skills than they're often given credit for. Trombonist Chris Barber was one of the most influential figures in the British 'trad boom' of the 1950s, originally a defendent of unadulterated New Orleans playing but later the leader of a vigorous and entertaining band that intermingled rhythm & blues, Ellingtonish ensemble ideas and programmatic accounts of the early development of jazz. Trumpeter Kenny Ball began leading his own groups in 1958, and ten years later was virtually a household name with a string of pop hits from catchy tunes given a streamlined trad treatment, and regular appearance on TV. Clarinettist Acker Bilk has similarly enjoyed a career as a serious and knowledgeable exponent of early jazz instrumental skills fitfully interrupted by pop success, his biggest hit being a lilting, vibrato-packed ballad called 'Stranger on the Shore', which made Bilk the top-selling artist of the trad boom.

The emergence of the Beatles in England, and all the rhythm & blues groups that came in their wake, swept revivalist jazz aside, and these musicians and others retired to clubs and to audiences of loyal fans. They have all continued to produce good music however, often in collaboration with visiting Americans of the same inclinations.

The Ultimate (Kaz Records KAZ CD4)

Ball, Barber and Bilk in one collection that includes Ball's lively early 1960s dance-floor hit 'Midnight in Moscow', Bilk's rhapsodic 'Stranger on the Shore', and a selection of standard revivalist fare including 'When The Saints Go Marching In', 'Muskrat Ramble' and 'St Louis Blues'.

Chris Barber – Mardi Gras at the Marquee (Timeless CDTTD 5546)

A 1980s project of the energetic Barber's, whose performances were frequently historical tours around New Orleans music. But Barber has rarely been content simply to replicate early material, and in this session from the London Marquee Club, his band vivaciously rolls through a repertoire of originals by the blues singer and pianist Dr John, also present on the date.

Braff, Reuben, 'Ruby'

(Born Boston, March 16, 1927)
Cornettist Ruby Braff is the kind of jazz musician commonly overlooked because he didn't do what the rest of his generation did and thus appears to be a confused revivalist. Braff is a year younger than Miles Davis, but he plays swing. The Boston musician can play ballads with a subtlety all but lost in the post-bop compulsion to perform everything in double-time, and his tone blends the vigour of Armstrong with the bell-like sound of Beiderbecke. In his chosen field, he is one of the most evocative, hypnotic brass-playing storytellers in jazz.

Because of his avoidance of bop, Braff didn't appear in concert very much in the 1950s, but he recorded some excellent music, sometimes partnering illustrious elders such as fellow-trumpeter Roy Eldridge. Braff's warm sound and gently paced elegance make him gleam almost regardless of the playing circumstances, but particularly as a softly emotional partner of guitarist George

Barnes in the Braff-Barnes quartet. *Two by Two*, Braff's duet with pianist Ellis Larkins, deserves CD release.

★*The Mighty Braff* (Affinity AFF 757)

Superb Braff selection from the mid-1950s, unusually pitching the leader's deft and springy variations and ringing tone against a saxophone section that includes Bob Wilber. But despite the larger band, nothing distracts the attention from the full range of Braff's technique at either end of the register, which is about as well presented here as on any collection of his work.

Clooney, Rosemary

(Born Maysville, May 23, 1928)
Rosemary Clooney won't call herself a jazz singer – yet like many vocalists on the borderlines of jazz and more mainstream pop, including Frank Sinatra and Mel Torme – her inflections and timing are so coloured by jazz as to set at least some of her work in the tradition of the music. She has also frequently been at her most expressive when working with jazz musicians.

Clooney first sang with her sister Betty in the late 1940s band saxophonist Tony Pastor had formed out of the old Artie Shaw ensemble. A record deal with Columbia in 1950 produced a succession of hits, and a number of movie appearances. Personal problems all but shelved her musical career, but she returned in much jazzier guise in the late 1970s, making a series of attractive recordings for Concord.

★*Sings The Lyrics of Ira Gershwin* (Concord CCD 4112)

Clooney gives material that Ella Fitzgerald has all but defined for jazz vocalists a more considered and inhabited feel than many singers do, and the slowly-curving trajectories she imparts to songs have a compelling poise here. The band is excellent, including Scott Hamilton and Warren Vache in graceful and gracious form.

Cohn, Alvin Gilbert 'Al'

(Born New York, November 24, 1925; died Pennsylvania, February 15, 1988)

Perennially popular tenor saxophonist out of the Lester Young school (and a frequent partner of the equally respected ZOOT SIMS), Al Cohn was equally skilled as a composer and arranger. He began in the 1940s as a sideman in bands led by Buddy Rich, Woody Herman and Artie Shaw and it was the association with several leading white exponents of the Lester Young style that shaped Cohn's mature development and his long connection with Sims. Cohn exhibited a combination of raciness and relaxation often underrated, but his frequent mixture of Young-like poignancy and reserve and an occasional blaring bullishness reminiscent of Sonny Rollins gave him a distinctive identity in modern jazz.

From A-Z and Beyond (Bluebird ND 86469)

There are better Al Cohn discs than this partnership with Zoot Sims from 1956, many of them still on vinyl. But though the elegant dance of these two urbane and witty tenors can grow a little too smooth, their similarities and differences are a source of fascination, and the repertoire isn't as straight-ahead as it seems.

Connick, Harry Jnr

(Born New Orleans, 1968)

Harry Connick Jnr was one of the most unexpected near-jazz commercial successes of the 1980s. A svelte, relaxed and attractive performer with undisguised admiration for the singing style of Frank Sinatra and onstage presentation to match, Connick's elevation to the status of one of the world's big box-office draws occurred when he performed the soundtrack to the movie *When Harry Met Sally*.

For all the retro-chic of a singing style rooted firmly in the big-band swing and crooning of the 1940s and 1950s, Connick is a far more shrewd and imaginative jazz performer than he seems. He is a derivative but free-swinging pianist, with a style mingling the acerbic qualities of THELONIOUS MONK with the gleeful drive of Errol

Garner, and his insights into jazz and affection for its history are directly attributable to the inspiration in his native New Orleans of pianist, teacher and father of an influential jazz dynasty, ELLIS MARSALIS.

★*Blue Light, Red Light* (Columbia 469687)

Connick in 1991 with a big band, the setting he now prefers and which his attractive mix of musicianship and showmanship thrives in. Unlike his earlier recordings, this disc features a repertoire of Connick originals, which may disappoint some. But the band sounds fine, the textures imaginatively spliced, and the album suggests that Connick may yet have a lot of room to expand beyond his middle-of-the-road image.

Connor, Chris

(Born Kansas City, November 8, 1927)
Like June Christy, Chris Connor built her reputation on a period as a popular vocalist with the Stan Kenton band, following Christy into the orchestra in the 1950s. She had begun with arranger Claude Thornhill's vocal band, the Snowflakes, and her singing developed under the influence of the emotionally restrained, melodically subtle methods of 1950s cool jazz. Like Christy, Connor found that there wasn't room for her delicate artistry in the music business in the 1970s, but she reappeared on disc in the next decade and turned in some excellent performances on the Contemporary label.

★*Cool Chris* (Charly CDCHARLY 117)

Connor's quality is to get inside the meanings of songs rather than simply use the themes as vehicles for improvisation. She demonstrates that skill here in a fine collection of standards, including 'Lullaby of Birdland', 'Lush Life' and 'Stella by Starlight'.

Dirty Dozen Brass Band

For years visitors to New Orleans were able to witness the town's
veteran musicians playing the way they had in their youth, and
sustaining the energies of Southlands street music as both a
musical tribute and a tourist attraction. But as time took toll of
them, younger players who also loved the tradition but believed it
could be combined with more recent music began to emerge.
Though purists would continue to reject such hybrids, they were
immensely attractive to younger audiences.

One of the best examples of 'contemporary revivalism' is the
Dirty Dozen Brass Band, which was formed in New Orleans in
the early 1970s by a group of young players involved in cajun
music, street music, funk, bebop, and the kind of John Zorn-like
mischief-making that led to the inclusion of the *Flintstones* theme in
their repertoire. A delightful band in live performance, describing
its curious chemistry as 'jazz gumbo', the Dirty Dozen has made
friends wherever it has travelled, ensuring that jazz history
doesn't remain simply a collection of dusted-off museum pieces.

Mardi Gras in Montreux (Rounder CD 2052)

The Dirty Dozen as it should be heard, in live performance at the
Montreux Festival in 1985, roaring through a tireless ransacking
of many traditions. It's rightly regarded as one of the most vivid
and exciting concert recordings of the past decade.

Getz, Stanley 'Stan'

(Born Philadelphia, February 2, 1927; died 1991)
Stan Getz was one of the few top-flight jazz artists to have made
an impact in the pop charts and with wider audiences and yet
never lose the admiration of purists. His celebrated beautiful tone,
originally an adaptation of the poignant timbre of Lester Young,
made a big impact with the public when Getz was just 20, when
the 1947 recording of the ballad 'Early Autumn' (with the Woody
Herman band) engaged the ears of a jazz generation with its shy,
evaporating sound and concentration on atmosphere over notes.
Getz' ability to move mountains with very carefully edited

material worked again in the 1960s with his bossa nova recordings.

Getz began young, playing in bands led by Jack Teagarden, Stan Kenton, Jimmy Dorsey and Benny Goodman whilst still in his teens, and making his first record under his own name at 19. Joining Woody Herman, he found himself in the company of a number of young white Lester Young disciples, including ZOOT SIMS, AL COHN and Jimmy Giuffre. During the 1950s and 1960s Getz recorded extensively, many of the sessions being meetings with other imposing jazz figures – with Shelley Manne, Dizzy Gillespie (*Diz and Getz*, a session that found the saxophonist in ebullient, very nearly truculent mood), J.J. Johnson and others.

After the jazz samba period, Getz began forming bands with some of the sharpest upcoming musicians, notably a brilliant quartet with the young Gary Burton on vibes, Steve Swallow on bass and Roy Haynes on drums. He also went into partnership with Chick Corea in the late 1960s, making two albums (*Captain Marvel* and *Sweet Rain*, the latter once a CD but currently deleted) that showed how much even the guru of cool beauty could be moved by the right company.

★*At Storyville* (Vogue VG 600 093)

A live Getz date from 1951, with an excellent bebop rhythm section featuring ex-Parker pianist Al Haig, Jimmy Raney on guitar and Tiny Khan on drums. Getz is in far more dynamic mood here than the image he assumed on 'Early Autumn', charging through fast versions of 'Parker '51', 'The Song Is You', and a stream of varied choruses on 'Thou Swell'.

★*At the Opera House* (Verve/USA 831 272-2)

Six years later, Getz' mid-1950s quintet in an encounter with an instrumentalist as technically elegant as himself – trombonist J.J. Johnson. Regarded by many as displaying some of the saxophonist's most challenging, and challenged, improvising, Getz is almost fierce on 'Crazy Rhythm' and at his most poetic on 'It Never Entered My Mind'.

★*The Brothers* (Carrere 98426)

Material from Savoy recordings of the 1940s, featuring Stan Getz in company with the other white Lester Young fans of his circle – Al Cohn, Serge Chaloff, Brew Moore and Allan Eager. Getz is most substantially featured on the kind of drifting ballads – 'Indian Summer', 'Wrap Your Troubles in Dreams' – that most reflected the success of 'Early Autumn'.

★*Jazz Samba* (Verve (810 061-2)

Probably Stan Getz' most famous record. This was the first album of the 1960s bossa nova boom, and contained the hit record 'Desfinado' and the voice of Astrud Gilberto. Charlie Byrd is rich and orchestral on guitar and Getz' horn floats like a bubble over the shuffle of the rhythm. Fluffy music and no great tribute to improvisation, but only Getz, with his effortless control of dynamics, delicacy and timing, could have done it this way.

Grey, Albert Thornton 'Al'

(Born Aldie, Virginia, June 6, 1925)
After bebop, many trombonists whose styles were maturing in the 1940s tried to sound as much like trumpeters, or even saxophonists, as possible. Al Grey was one who preferred the salty, talkative vigour of the earlier practitioners in a New Orleans style, like Ellington's Tricky Sam Nanton with his expressive use of the plunger mute. Much of Grey's improvising sounds as if he's telling a musical version of a funny anecdote, and his blues playing is superb.

Grey joined Benny Carter's group after playing in a Navy band during World War II, and after Carter with a variety of swing bandleaders including Jimmie Lunceford and Lionel Hampton. In the mid Fifties Grey took the job that was at the top of the line for anyone with such an apprenticeship – the Count Basie band. Later, he toured extensively with bluesy Basieite tenorist Jimmy Forrest, and then with Buddy Tate after Forrest's death.

Al Grey Featuring Arnett Cobb and Jimmy Forrest (Black and Blue 233143)

An assortment of Grey takes from the mid-Seventies, uneven in quality but good enough on the best sessions (particularly those involving saxophonist Arnett Cobb, a player of comparably robust wit) to be an admirable representation of his best features. Cobb is wilder than Forrest, but the Forrest partnerships also involve the polished pianist Tommy Flanagan and have their own easy grace.

Hamilton, Scott

(Born New England, September 12, 1954)
If any jazz musician under 40 personifies the mainstream that idolised the sound of Ben Webster and Coleman Hawkins it's Scott Hamilton. Unlike the jazz classicists of the Marsalises generation, Hamilton has hardly sought to alter the musical legacy of his heroes at all, and has contented himself instead with perfecting a big, lazily moving sound in which the articulation of every note is important and spaciousness is crucial to melodic development. Hamilton joined Benny Goodman's band in 1977 and began recording extensively for Concord the following year, sometimes with a cornet-playing partner almost as highly thought of as a revivalist as he is – Warren Vache.

The Second Set (Concord CCD 4254)

Hamilton in live performance in Japan in 1983, with his regular group featuring John Bunch on piano, Chris Flory on guitar, Phil Flanigan on bass and Chuck Riggs on drums. Crisp, organised and as smooth as a limousine, but with the leader's gracefully scattered and rather cultivated idiosyncrasies edging it along.

Scott Hamilton Plays Ballads (Concord CCD 4386)

Hamilton in perhaps his most flattering light. An excellent thematic improviser, he develops solos by using his characteristic full-bodied tone and subtle placing of notes to stitch together a series of resonating motifs. As if to demonstrate his liberation from the shadow of Coleman Hawkins, Hamilton even applies those skills to 'Body and Soul', and makes a strikingly independent account of it.

Laine, Cleo (Clementina Dinah Campbell)

(Born Southall, Middlesex, October 27, 1927)
Cleo Laine had performed a variety of commercial music jobs by the time she auditioned for the John Dankworth Seven at the age of 25, at which point she was already possessed of a rich contralto, emotional warmth, wit and swing. She made a powerful acting debut in the 1958 Royal Court production of *Flesh to a Tiger*, developed as both a cabaret artist and an actress, collaborated with Dankworth (by 1965 a successful movie-score writer, and Laine's husband) on a musical setting for Shakespeare's sonnets that was an overnight success, and won a *Downbeat* magazine critics' poll. By the end of the decade Laine's repertoire embraced renditions of works by T.S. Eliot, Thomas Hardy and W.H. Auden, and she even earned William Walton's gratitude for a recording of his *Facade*, a musical setting for the poetry of Dame Edith Sitwell.

In 1972 a recording made at Carnegie Hall cemented Dankworth and Laine's reputation as international stars, though only peripherally jazz ones. Together, however, Laine and Dankworth have retained an enthusiasm for communicating jazz values through performance to education, with the Wavendon All Music Plan in Buckinghamshire being a project devoted to breaking down the barriers between all forms of contemporary music.

★*Cleo at Carnegie* (DRG/USA CDXP 2101)

The album for which Laine won a Grammy in 1986, with more of an emphasis on standards than on the faintly precious poetry reworkings of the 1970s. The set includes an elegant Hoagy Carmichael medley, one of her most popular ballads in 'He Was Beautiful' and jazz standards such as 'Crazy Rhythm' and 'I Want To Be Happy'.

Lyttelton, Humphrey

(Born Eton, Berkshire, May 23, 1921)
The years after the Second World War were tempestuous ones in British jazz, with fans of earlier music often particular to the point of paranoia about avoiding the slightest hint of modernism. The most prominent figure on the postwar revivalist scene (though ultimately one of the least sectarian) was old Etonian ex-Guardsman Humphrey Lyttelton, who was not only a fine trumpeter in a manner initially influenced by Louis Armstrong and later by Buck Clayton, but an energetic campaigner for jazz in general.

Lyttelton joined one of the best of the revivalist bands, George Webb's Dixielanders, in the immediate postwar years, then formed a band of his own including the excellent clarinettist and cartoonist, Wally Fawkes. Lyttelton had a hit record with 'Bad Penny Blues' in 1956, but by the end of the 1950s he was parting company with the revivalist hard-liners and began to hire saxophonists – much to the chagrin of some fans, since the only reeds in a traditional New Orleans ensemble were clarinets. With excellent saxophonists such as Bruce Turner, Tony Coe, Jimmy Skidmore, Joe Temperley and Kathy Stobart, Lyttelton broadened his scope to include Ellingtonish music, and his bands from the 1960s onwards are uniformly colourful and soloistically strong, though CDs have so far passed them by, and the Duke Ellington Classics band with Ray Warleigh and John Surman would be delightful to hear on the format. Lyttelton has also been prolific as a writer and broadcaster, and has done much to raise the profile of jazz music in Britain.

★*Back To The Sixties* (Philips 834458-2)

Terrific Lyttelton material from the early 1960s, with partners including Tony Coe and guest trumpeter Buck Clayton on three tracks. Lyttelton has by this time consolidated his conviction that anything he likes goes, so as well as more orthodox mainstream material like 'Body and Soul', Cannonball Adderley's bluesy 'Sack O' Woe' is included.

McPartland, Marian

(Born Windsor, England, March 20, 1920)
Marian McPartland is one of the finest of all mainstream jazz pianists, but her style embraces so much modern music and has evolved with such sympathy to a variety of idioms, that the category barely contains her. She swings with both exuberance and precision, and her harmonic sense reflects a rich musical education, and the ability to accommodate the styles of others enabled her to host the long-running American radio series 'Jazz Piano', in which she was frequently paired with other pianists. McPartland has also taught jazz, founded her own record label, Halcyon Records, and regularly appeared as a classical recitalist.

McPartland was born Margaret Turner in Windsor, and joined a vaudeville piano troupe after graduating from the Guildhall School of Music. Trumpeter Jimmy McPartland, a member of the 'Austin High Gang' that had followed Bix Beiderbecke and spawned Benny Goodman, heard her performing for troops in Belgium, and married her in 1944. An English woman faced a tough assignment building a career as a jazz pianist in America, but from 1946 Marian McPartland persisted with it, and from the early Fifties her trios – performing at New York nightspots like the Embers Club and the Hickory House – produced model versions of eloquent, intelligent piano jazz.

Portrait of Marian McPartland (Concord CCD 4101)

1979 trio recording, creatively augmented by Jerry Dodgion on reeds, the latter addition giving McPartland's strongest suit – a sumptuous and completely distinctive harmonic approach to familiar jazz material – an additional twist. Dodgion's flute playing particularly enhances her rich tonalities, the leader's rhapsodic and compositional skills are jointly displayed on her own 'Time and Time Again' and her shrewd choices of newer material pay off on her account of Herbie Hancock's 'Tell Me A Bedtime Story'.

Pass, Joe (Joseph Anthony Passalaqua)

(Born New Jersey, January 13, 1929)

If Joe Pass has a problem, it is that he is so comprehensively endowed with everything a bop-inclined guitarist needs to know as to have become as attractive to admirers of guitar technique as to music-lovers in general. He frequently plays unaccompanied, or in partnership with a bassist, and specialises in standards and blues, dressed in a mixture of slinky chords and walking bass lines. Pass was working in demanding company while still at high school and joined Charlie Barnet's swing band in 1947, but narcotics problems affected his career and he was in and out of music for much of the next two decades, though playing actively with jazz-oriented inmates in the Synanon Foundation Rehabilitation Centre's band in 1961. On his release, Pass's lovely sound and full technique brought plenty of offers and some that he took up included GEORGE SHEARING's, Benny Goodman's and OSCAR PETERSON's. Pass has become widely known, particularly as a festival performer (sometimes with Ella Fitzgerald) but he remains at his best in intimate surroundings where his delicacy and tonal subtleties are audible.

★*Checkmate* (Pablo CD 311-22)

A 1981 duet between Pass and the fluid, encyclopaedically knowledgeable and witty pianist Jimmy Rowles, being a valuable contrast to the interminable supplies of virtuosic solo work Pass has laid down over the years. The material is good ('So Rare', 'God Bless the Child') and the interplay is genuine.

Peterson, Oscar Emmanuel

(Born Montreal, August 15, 1925)

Oscar Peterson has often been criticised as a musician in thrall to his own runaway technique, but he remains a great virtuoso of piano jazz, and an equally effective populariser of the music among those who might otherwise not have encountered it. Influenced primarily by Art Tatum, Peterson's playing is similarly a rolling torrent of arpeggios, trills, contrapuntal tug-of-war, thundering bass figures and ignition of blazing flares of sound in every possible chink or gap in the music. Inevitably Peterson has become a phenomenon for this aspect of his work alone, with the result that the most rhapsodic or contemplative of overtures will usually turn into a roaring uptempo display before long. Yet he has a devastating rhythmic momentum, and his harmonic ear is highly developed.

A phenomenon in his native Canada, Peterson burst upon American audiences at Norman Granz' invitation in 1949 and – predominantly as a trio leader – he sustained this exhausting pressure ever since. Peterson has frequently been featured with other leading figures of jazz (Dizzy Gillespie, Roy Eldridge, Count Basie and many others) and has recorded voluminously.

Night Train (Verve 827821)

Peterson's best-known – and best – record, made in 1961. Devoted to blues, it nevertheless varies the mood considerably, and it clarifies Peterson's appeal, being a mixture of pianistic dominance and surprisingly affecting commitment. The material includes Ellington's famous 'C-Jam Blues', and more boppish departures like 'Bags' Grove' and Peterson applies a more than usually succinct force to all the material.

Compact Jazz – Oscar Peterson (Mercury 830698)

The place to start with Peterson, whose way of playing has always seemed tailor-made for the Compact Jazz concept. It features a couple of years'-worth of trio recordings with the likes of Louis Hayes and Ed Thigpen on drums plus the great Ray Brown's imperious bass-playing and is bolstered by the effusive trumpet of Clark Terry on such apposite material as 'If I Were A Bell'.

Pizzarelli, John Paul Jnr.

(Born Paterson, New Jersey, April 6, 1960)
Like other thirty-something crooner-instrumentalists (Harry Connick Jnr., A.J. Croce and others), Pizzarelli occupies a line that links Bing Crosby to contemporary balladeering pop via bop-

influenced singers like Chet Baker. Pizzarelli has a light, gracefully rhythmic style, and he breathes new life into standards more effectively than most of his better-known contemporary rivals. He is also a fine guitarist, which was the original leverage that took him into the business.

John Paul Pizzarelli Junior is the son of John Paul Pizzarelli Senior, better known as guitarist Bucky Pizzarelli, and he has a brother, Martin, who's a bassist. Bucky Pizzarelli's career began as a teenage dance-band player who later joined Benny Goodman, ZOOT SIMS and others; he also had a very successful career as a studio session-man. Following the death of Pizzarelli Senior's regular guitar partner George Barnes in 1977, father and son played together until the mid-'80s, when John Pizzarelli worked with Tony Monte's trio on New York's WNEW radio station and began to attract attention in his own right. Like his father, John Pizzarelli uses a seven-string guitar to strengthen rhythm playing, and sometimes to add a bassline. His talents have enabled him to work with such distinctive mainstream players as trumpeter Clark Terry and bassist Milt Hinton. He has recorded with a big band, but small group settings display his relaxed charm best.

Dear Mr Cole (RCA Novus 01241 63182-2)

A fine Pizzarelli set dedicated to Nat King Cole and featuring many of the songs associated with him, including 'Too Marvellous for Words', Harold Arlen's 'It's Only A Paper Moon' and 'Route 66'. But the songs and an enthusiastic atmosphere of group improvisation carry equal weight on this disc, partly because of the leader's driving, confident guitar and the presence of pianist Benny Green and bassist Christian McBride.

Shearing, George

(Born London, August 13, 1919)

One of the best-known of all British-born jazz musicians is the pianist George Shearing, a technically adroit though stylistically highly derivative performer who nevertheless developed a sizeable audience on both sides of the Atlantic for his ability to mimic and synthesise the works of many other players. Shearing nevertheless has a communicative and exciting style, and his famous original composition 'Lullaby of Birdland' is one of the most widely used of all jazz vehicles.

Shearing was blind from birth, yet his pianistic skills enabled him to quickly dominate the flourishing dance-band world of prewar London. His first jobs were with the Ambrose dance orchestra, then with Harry Parry and Stephane Grappelli during the early war years. In 1946 Shearing visited the States and decided to settle there, eventually forming an extremely popular quintet (in various forms it worked from 1949 to 1967) through which the pianist would deliver his own variations on the styles of quite dissimilar American jazz stars – from Earl Hines and Bud Powell, to Lennie Tristano, Horace Silver and Bill Evans.

★*Alone Together* (Concord CCD 4171)

Shearing paired with a more original pianist, Marian McPartland – yet finding common ground between his mix of a thumping, exclamatory straight-ahead style and plush balladeering and her subtlety of nuance.

★*Three Originals* (MPS523522-2)

A pretty fair mixture of 1970s Shearing, drawn from three discs – 'Light, Airy and Swinging', 'Continental Experience' and 'On Target'. Rather over-smoochy swinging-lovers string arrangements for the orchestral parts, but the pianist delivers some crisp variations in the small-group settings, notably with ex-Crusaders drummer Stix Hooper.

Sims, John Haley 'Zoot'

(Born Inglewood, California, October 29, 1925; died New York, March 23, 1985)

Of all the saxophonists to have taken their lead from the poetry and persuasive diffidence of Lester Young's tenor, Zoot Sims was one of the most respected and affectionately regarded. He could virtually swing in his sleep, his delivery was sleek and husky, and he conveyed an impression of both optimism and tenderness.

Sims was one of seven siblings born into a west coast vaudeville family. He took up clarinet to join a school band when he was ten, and taught himself jazz by listening to the recordings of Coleman Hawkins, Chu Berry, Lester Young, Ben Webster and Don Byas. Sims acquired the nickname 'Zoot' when he joined an LA band led by Ken Baker and happened to be occupying a music stand with 'Zoot' written on it; after a succession of local gigs he joined Benny Goodman, and then Woody Herman after army service.

It was in the saxophone section of the Herman band that Sims met a group of young reed players who were thinking as he was – Stan Getz, Jimmy Giuffre, AL COHN, Serge Chaloff among others. With Getz, Herbie Steward and Chaloff, Sims was part of the famous 'Four Brothers' ensemble sound, a popularised form of bop, since it blended the idiom's busy lyricism with the smoothness and more even accents of swing.

Sims recorded the Prestige label's first LP in the 1950s (*Zootcase*, currently deleted in all formats), made many delightful records with Al Cohn, one with violinist Joe Venuti (*Joe and Zoot*, vinyl only so far), and recorded extensively for Norman Granz' Pablo label from the 1960s on. Sims also took up the soprano saxophone in the 1970s and avoided most of its drawbacks of unpredictable pitch and sour tone. Two ebullient collaborations with the great Jimmy Rowles on piano (*Warm Tenor* and *If I'm Lucky*) are not so far available on CD, nor the Count Basie collaboration, *Basie with Zoot*.

★*Down Home* (Charly CDCHARLY 59)

Zoot Sims in 1960 with an excellent quartet including Mingus sideman Danny Richmond on drums, rolling through a selection of standards and blues on what's often taken to be one of the saxophonist's best sessions. His beat is insistent, his phrasing inventive and the general atmosphere exuberant from the opening 'Jive at Five' to the last note.

★*Somebody Loves Me* (Denon DC 8514)

Formerly *Nirvana*, a session featuring guitarist Bucky Pizzarelli and drummer Buddy Rich. Sims duets delicately with Pizzarelli on four tracks, Rich is surprisingly restrained, and the unexpected high register opening of 'Gee Baby Ain't I Good To You' and the shimmering romanticism of 'A Summer Thing' are measures of Sims' class.

5

TURNING POINT: THE 1960s
AVANT-GARDE AND BEYOND

A
t the beginning of the 1960s, 'free-jazz' sent a shock-wave
through African-American music, which reverberated
for most of the decade. For many of the players reared on
bebop and its mutations, the 1940s idiom had become a treadmill
of predictable chords and a devaluation of themes to mere
decorations, hung on the beginnings and endings of a ritual
procession of solos. Parallel to the development of the civil-rights
movement in America and a growing liberalisation of personal
politics, the free-jazz movement prized collective, collaborative
improvisation, perhaps with several horns intertwined to produce
a 'group solo' not exclusively dependent on the inclinations of any
one participant.

These weren't structurally new departures in jazz. The music's
early antecedents – like the African-derived shouts and field
hollers of the levees, railroad construction gangs and the plantations – were free, in their conversational flexibility. And since the
majority of New Orleans musicians were self-taught, their choice
of notes and intonation followed few rules. The 1960s radicals
pursued some similar courses. In many cases they attempted to
behave as if bebop intonation already existed, but the harmonic
structures it was founded on did not.

Jazz, in this period, was thus loosening its connections with
harmonic principles inherited from Europe. The musics of other
cultures were dependent on different intervals between notes,
different perceptions of rhythm, different instrumentation, and
this wider perception of how improvisation might be organised
was influential in the work of several key avantists of the era.

Saxophonists John Coltrane and Ornette Coleman were the two most prominent figures of this movement, though multi-reed player Eric Dolphy, composer/bassist Charles Mingus and pianist Cecil Taylor were highly influential too. Both Coltrane and Coleman had played in rhythm & blues bands in their youth, but while Coltrane – an obsessive student of the mechanics of music and a powerful technician – quickly gained credibility as a virtuoso, Coleman spent much of the 1950s being accused of incompetence.

In 1960 Coleman recorded the album *Free Jazz* and established its modernist credentials by featuring a reproduction of Jackson Pollack's 'White Light' on the cover. A largely free exchange for two jazz quartets working simultaneously (one, Coleman's regular group, the other a more boppish ensemble including trumpeter Freddie Hubbard), the disc inspired a generation, not just in America but across the globe.

In England, the West Indian alto saxophonist Joe Harriott was simultaneously working in a similar territory, the British Spontaneous Music Ensemble (galvanised by drummer John Stevens and altoist Trevor Watts) pursued forms of free-jazz inspired by Coleman, and similar angles were explored in Holland and Germany. And by the mid-1960s, a form of free-jazz, more dependent on explicit emotionalism, began to grip the sophisticated new rock audience in a way that Coleman's quirky lyricism had not. John Coltrane recorded *A Love Supreme*, variations on a simple, repetitive, mantra-like theme, that sold a quarter of a million copies after its release in 1965.

Many of the achievements of the 1960s avant-garde seem to have disappeared with the recent post-modernist revival of the 'classic' forms of jazz, and with many of the younger players speculating that 'self-expression' leads to indulgence if not disciplined by formal principles. But this volatile period in jazz, though it produced much erratic and ill-considered music, generated a great deal of new vocabulary for improvisers which is audible in the work of some of today's most respected classicists.

Ayler, Albert

(Born Ohio, July 13, 1936; died New York, November 25, 1970)
No one in such a short but intense musical career polarised
feelings like Albert Ayler. Appearing on a scene already split over
controversies about the merits of ORNETTE COLEMAN and CECIL
TAYLOR, Ayler, with his repertoire of earthy honks and impassioned cries, seemed even more unnerving to an unprepared
audience than they were. But just as the jazz public came to terms
with this, his music became more formal, short solos being framed
by passages of collective interweaving reminiscent of the tones of
a New Orleans band. Then Ayler changed tack again, aiming, it
seemed, for the rhythm & blues market he had once performed
for as a young saxophonist with the blues artist Little Walter.

A factor unifying all these changes was that Ayler never took
the obvious route in any direction. From New Orleans dirges and
marches to unfettered noise and then to Johnny Hodges-style
balladeering, he found inspiration in areas of black music neglected by mainstream jazz musicians. Titles from his early albums,
such as *Ghosts*, *Spirits*, *Witches and Devils* and *The Wizard*, suggest a
leaning towards the occult; he was frequently an interpreter of
spirituals as well. But even at his wildest, Ayler always paraded
the virtues of a good tune, the catchy folk-melody of 'Ghosts'
being a prime example. His background gave him an appreciation
of melody, being a saxophone player influenced from an early age
by Lester Young, Sidney Bechet and Charlie Parker; in Cleveland
his nickname was 'Little Bird'. Yet Ayler's most celebrated quote
about music was 'It's not about notes any more, it's about feelings.'

Ayler's legacy survives in the playing of Pharoah Sanders,
David Murray and others, but his was never a way of playing
readily copied. Rather he encouraged saxophone players by
example, to develop power and stamina and to work on their own
sounds rather than take those that 'come with the horn'.

★*Vibrations* (Freedom FCD 41000)

The quartet with Cherry, Peacock and Murray, recorded in
Denmark. Ayler sounds uncannily like an old-time New Orleans
performer, his tone rough around the edges and with an agitated,
quivering vibrato. Bass and drums are faultlessly and unprece-

dentedly free in this context, Murray's rat-a-tat with undulating volume ('Ghosts') – his version of the Art Blakey press-roll – and shimmering cymbals ('Mothers') being trademarks.

★*Live in Greenwich Village* (MCA/Impulse MCAD 39123)

Material from two live performances by the Ayler band in New York in 1967. The quartet is a showcase for Ayler himself, and Beaver Harris is splashily energetic on drums. While it's a fierce session at times, Ayler's ability to express a wide range of emotion with simple materials, and his immensely rich tonal palette, make his musicality clear with the benefit of over 20 years' hindsight.

★*Love Cry* (Impulse/GRP 11082)

Intriguing set from the point where Ayler signed with major label Impulse but before they encouraged him to churn out rhythm & blues records; none of it is smooth smooth jazz, but these versions of wild classics such as 'Ghosts' and 'Universal Indians' are gentler than they were before and Sunny Murray's drumming reveals why it influenced so much free-jazz percussion.

Coleman, Ornette

(Born Fort Worth, Texas, March 19, 1930)
Coleman had begun playing saxophone professionally in his teens, mostly in the blues bands popular in the black neighbour-hoods of Fort Worth. Fascinated by the timbre of the horn, he would frequently practise tone-colours on the same note all day. He thus developed an earthy, vocalised sound that had much in common with the early blues musicians, a strong, danceable beat, and a good deal of the complex solo style of Charlie Parker, but cut loose from its chords.

In the company of a number of like-minded players, including bassist Charlie Haden, trumpeter Don Cherry and drummer Billy Higgins, Coleman began to find, through constant practice, the confidence to play small-group jazz in a more flexible manner in which departures of line, rhythm and mood evolved organically, one performer picking up the ideas of another. After developing these techniques by rehearsing in a Los Angeles garage, Coleman suddenly shot to prominence as a result of two records made on the west coast, *Something Else!* and *Tomorrow is the Question*. He also attracted the attention of a number of non-jazz composers, including Gunther Schuller and Leonard Bernstein.

Coleman became a prophet of the 1960s movement known as 'free-jazz', some of which successfully interpreted his methods of ensemble improvisation, some of which was an uncommunicative din. Coleman himself performed only sporadically over the coming decade. His string quartet 'Dedication To Poets and Writers' was performed in 1962, followed by the 1965 woodwind quintet 'Sounds and Forms', and two years later Coleman won the first ever Guggenheim Fellowship for jazz composition. Moving in the other direction, towards dance music and the soul-derived funk idiom that became popular in the early 1970s, Coleman also managed to marry his spontaneous ensemble ideas (later dubbed his 'harmolodic theory') with this method of music-making too, deploying it in his electric band Prime Time. Many still regard Ornette Coleman as the greatest, and most unpredictable, genius of the blues.

★*At the Golden Circle* Vols. 1 & 2 (Blue Note CDP 784 224-2, 225-2)

Ornette Coleman's brilliant trio – with David Izenzon on bass, and Charles Moffett on drums – on its European tour in 1966. Some of the finest Coleman soloing, and the best examples of his concept of how a contemporary jazz group should function, are apparent in these sessions. Though Moffett is an odd choice, Izenzon's bass-playing is remarkable. Coleman's own creativity is displayed in most of its variations, atmospheric and evocative on 'Snowflakes and Sunshine', contemplative on 'Morning Song'.

★*Tomorrow is the Question!* (Original Jazz Classics OJC 342)

One of the early sessions that woke the jazz world up to Ornette Coleman. *Tomorrow* represents Coleman playing the way he originally envisaged it (his first recording, 'Something Else' features a pianist) and the first authentic Coleman quartet displays the power unleashed by Don Cherry (trumpet), Charlie

Haden (bass) and Billy Higgins (drums). Coleman's beautiful tone is at its most affecting on the intense 'Tears Inside'.

*_Song_ X (Geffen 924096-2)

The mid-1980s record that perplexed both Coleman fans and admirers of the guitarist Pat Metheny, though probably more of the latter than the former. Metheny had long been an admirer of Coleman's themes, and the two came together, not for a respectful skirting around their particular preoccupations, but a flat-out jam that didn't cramp Coleman and revealed the profound improvisational insights that Metheny's commercial pursuits often camouflage.

Coltrane, John

(Born North Carolina, September 23, 1926; died New York, July 17, 1967)

Though saxophonist John Coltrane devoted much of his life to extending the boundaries of music, he was always capable of reaching far beyond the jazz cognoscenti. His best-known session, _A Love Supreme_, became a cult hit with the new audiences for progressive rock when it was released in 1964. Meditative, retiring, obsessive, and in his way political (civil rights messages were often featured in his later work), Coltrane had all the credentials for artistic sainthood. Yet his work was strong and vibrant, never ethereally mystical.

John Coltrane took up alto saxophone at 15, after beginning a musical education on alto horn and clarinet. He played in local rhythm & blues bands, eventually working with r & b stars Eddie 'Cleanhead' Vinson and Earl Bostic. But Coltrane's jazz skills, influenced by the powerful style of Dexter Gordon and Charlie Parker, later Sonny Rollins and SUN RA's tenorist John Gilmore, brought him prestigious opportunities, in the Dizzy Gillespie Orchestra, then in saxophonist Johnny Hodges' group in the altoist's brief absence from the Ellington band.

In the late 1950s, Coltrane worked with Miles Davis and in a rugged, adventurous but short-lived quartet with Thelonious Monk. With records such as the 1960 classic _Giant Steps_, Coltrane took bebop as far as it could go. He also began exploring the use of the overtones of the instrument to play more than one note at a time, to release areas of the upper register previously restricted to the alto and soprano saxophones, and to explore the scale-based modal improvising of the Miles Davis group. As Coltrane's sound grew increasingly many-voiced, the critic Ira Gitler called the harmonically reverberating cry of his horn 'sheets of sound', and the name stuck.

With a new band – including pianist McCoy Tyner, bassist Jimmy Garrison and drummer ELVIN JONES – Coltrane developed some of the most adventurous small-group jazz of the era. Tyner's piano-playing was so emphatic that it carried the drummer's traditional role and allowed Jones to play texturally. The beat became more dispersed, but more brooding and tidal, and Coltrane also took up the rarely used soprano saxophone, even having a hit record with his version of 'My Favourite Things'.

John Coltrane explored new avenues for jazz with bands of various sizes. His 1965 recording *Ascension* was a storm-tossed odyssey in group texture for a larger ensemble, and these methods also affected his regular group, to the point where McCoy Tyner and Elvin Jones felt that things had gone too far, and left the band. In his final years, Coltrane ran a new band, with his second wife Alice on keyboards, saxophonist PHAROAH SANDERS (a musician influenced by ALBERT AYLER) and Rashied Ali on drums.

★*Giant Steps* (Atlantic/WEA 7813372)

Recorded in 1959, this album set the seal on the first stage of Coltrane's career. Tunes such as the blues 'Mr PC' and the ballad 'Naima' have become standards (the latter one of many Coltrane ballads that chill the spine when caressed at slow tempo) and the melodies of 'Spiral' and 'Syeeda's Song Flute' are unforgettable. *Giant Steps* (and its more aggressive blood-relative *Countdown*) provides the historical significance, with its chord-change-per-beat harmonic complexity.

★*Africa Brass 1 & 2* (MCA MCAD 420001)

A 1961 performance by a Coltrane group augmented to 14 pieces, including trumpeter Freddie Hubbard and reed player ERIC DOLPHY in addition to the regular lineup. Dolphy did much of the orchestration work for this powerful session, but Coltrane's own performances here are often regarded as being amongst his most powerful. One of the Coltrane band's most familiar devices, the repeated rhythmic figure, is the compulsive heartbeat of 'Africa'. An early outing for Coltrane's soprano saxophone is featured on 'Greensleeves'.

★*Blue Train* (Blue Note CDP 746 095-2)

One that Coltrane counted as a personal favourite. It featured the side of him audible on his work with Miles Davis, an attempt to break the stranglehold of measured bop solos over cycles of chord patterns, by packing the harmonies with ever more concentrated doses of musical high-explosive until they burst, showering the listeners with blazing cinders of notes. *Blue Train* features Lee Morgan on trumpet and one of the most swinging of all drummers, Philly Joe Jones.

★*A Love Supreme* (MCA DMCL 1505)

A Love Supreme is the album that most remember Coltrane for – a four-part devotional work featuring his finest band (with Elvin Jones, McCoy Tyner and Jimmy Garrison). On CD in particular, Jones' drum sound – a wild and elemental display of polyrhythmic playing that embraces soloists and bears them aloft – washes all over you, and its appropriateness to the mood of Coltrane at the time, a kind of manic trance, becomes more apparent than ever.

★*The Major Works of John Coltrane* (GRP/Impulse 21132 – 2 CDs)

This two-disc set includes two versions of 'Ascension', Coltrane's 1965 reaction to Ornette Coleman's *Free Jazz*. A collective improvisation for a largish group (including Pharoah Sanders and Freddie Hubbard), its methods became the model for countless free-improvising bands all over the world. Also featured are the high-pitched horns and dense percussion of the chant-like 'Om', and some superb McCoy Tyner piano variations on the more conventional 'Kulu Se Mama'.

★*Live in Japan* (GRP/Impulse 41022)

A fearsome four-disc live collection from the year before Coltrane died, including an hour-long 'My Favourite Things' (played on alto) and sustaining an atmosphere of hoarse beauty despite the general context of uncompromising free improvisation. Hardly the place to start an acquaintance with Coltrane, but certainly the place to deepen it. *Live in Japan* is a dramatic, sometimes melodramatic, example of what being at a late Coltrane show must have been like.

★*Interstellar Space* (GRP/Impulse 11102)

Interstellar Space is a fruitful duet recording for Coltrane with the looser, more textural drummer Rashied Ali. Because it's more intimate, the details of Coltrane's explorations, and the empathy he developed with Ali, are clearly audible. It also works at a far lower dynamic level, where the overtones of the saxophonist's high notes, intermingling with Ali's bustling brushwork, are compelling in their restraint.

★*The Gentle Side of John Coltrane* (GRP/Impulse 11072).

The Gentle Side is the most accessible of GRP's reissues, far more relaxed and reflective performances, with singer Johnny Hartman and Duke Ellington on piano. The upward glide of Coltrane's opening notes against Ellington's ringing chords on 'In a Sentimental Mood' are among the enduring delights of jazz.

★*Transition* (Impulse GRP 11242)

A disc from the year (1965) that followed 'A Love Supreme' and just preceded 'Ascension'. It opens with a fast blues, but one that soon reveals Coltrane's compulsion to break out of the harmonic maze and import some of the ideas being explored by unorthodox improvisors like Albert Ayler. All the Coltrane resources are firing – split notes, explosive shouts, long, roaring runs. There are also additions to the original LP, including the meditative 'Welcome' and the drum-sax duet 'Vigil' from 'Kulu Se Mama', and one subtraction, 'Dear Lord'.

Dolphy, Eric

(Born California, June 20, 1928; died Berlin, June 29, 1964)
Eric Dolphy remains the only jazz musician to stand out as a soloist on no fewer than three instruments. Even today, anyone who plays bass clarinet has to contend with him. Flautists of the calibre of James Newton dedicate compositions to him. As a saxophonist, Dolphy had what the English virtuoso Evan Parker described as 'instant access to any part of an extended range at any moment'. Time has taken nothing from the vivid expressiveness that coloured everything he touched.

Brought up in Los Angeles, Dolphy played lead alto and recorded with the Roy Porter big band in 1949. He joined Chico Hamilton's quintet in 1958 and appeared with it in the film *Jazz on a Summer's Day*. His debut as a leader, on *Outward Bound* (1960), was packaged by Prestige Records as if Dolphy were the next ORNETTE COLEMAN, though he was never exclusively involved with free-music.

Dolphy worked intimately with CHARLES MINGUS, touring with him extensively, playing a major part in his recordings. He also played on some Coltrane sessions, and with George Russell (*Ezz-thetics*), Max Roach (*Percussion Bitter Sweet*) and Oliver Nelson (*Blues and the Abstract Truth*).

Recordings of several concerts, mainly European, have been issued since Dolphy's death and add to the general perception of one of the great jazz musicians of the past 30 years. With his bird calls on flute, guttural squawks on bass clarinet and apparently impossible intervals effortlessly negotiated on the saxophone, Dolphy – by all accounts gentle and unassuming in non-musical life – comes across in music as very much larger than life.

★*At the Five* Spot Vol. 1 (Original Jazz Classics OJC 133)

A partnership that achieved a lot in a short time was the pairing of Eric Dolphy and trumpeter Booker Little. Both highly advanced in ways of music and both consummate technicians, they complemented each other because their emotional terrain was quite different. This 1961 recording also included Mal Waldron on piano, Richard Davis on bass and Ed Blackwell on drums.

★*Out to Lunch* (Blue Note CDP 746522)

Out to Lunch was Dolphy's last recording, and the sound of his flute here – particularly on 'Gazelloni' – is a reminder of how much his playing on the lighter instrument differed from his rather guttural investigations of the bass clarinet. The band is superb, the level of inventiveness startling, and the disc is an essential part of any representative collection of contemporary jazz.

Ellis, Don (Donald Johnson)

(Born Los Angeles, July 25, 1934; died December 17, 1978)
A musician and campaigner of immense energy, trumpeter, drummer and composer Don Ellis devoted his short life to stretching the boundaries of jazz and spreading the message about it all over the world. Like George Russell, Ellis was a composer who believed that much jazz writing was needlessly restricted to conservative adaptations of popular song forms and that more audacious techniques, including those drawn from non-Western cultures, could extend it. Like Russell also, Ellis adapted textural and rhythmic ideas from rock music.

Ellis played trumpet as a schoolboy and developed a technique modelled on the bebop stars, but studied composition at Boston University and began working for Maynard Ferguson as a trumpeter in the early 1960s. Shortly afterwards, he established a significant connection with George Russell and also began leading his own bands – and by the mid-1960s he was back in college, studying Indian music. Ellis initiated some of the first Indo-jazz experiments during this period, forming a big band that used time signatures unusual in Western music, electronic and percussive devices borrowed from rock, and soloing on a four-valve trumpet that could to some extent reproduce the microtonal intervals of Indian music.

*New Ideas (Original Jazz Classics OJC 431)

Ellis' best record, the 1968 'Electric Bath' isn't currently available, nor are any of the significant big band recordings. But this quintet performance from 1961 indicates the directions this restless and adventurous artist was taking, with a fine band including pianist Jaki Byard. The material veers from blues to dissonance via some unaccompanied trumpet playing that demonstrates just how quick and penetrating Ellis' technique was.

Jones, Elvin Ray

(Born Pontiac, Michigan, September 9, 1927)
Elvin Jones didn't devote the years after JOHN COLTRANE's death to the avant-garde, but he had already transformed jazz drumming, and opened up previously unthinkable choices in new percussion directions to suit a far less formal music. Jones' ability to sense a basic pulse but realise it through polyrhythmic playing that constantly seemed to be delaying or hiding crucial accents was not only the next giant step in developing the jazz legacy of Max Roach, but also in anticipating the percussive complexities of fusion music, which often required more than one drummer to get the effects that Jones could achieve on his own. Jones came from a musical family – his brothers Thad and Hank were a celebrated trumpeter and pianist respectively – and his early work included both conventional bop bands such as J.J. Johnson's and swing-tinged ones such as trumpeter Harry Edison's.

The drummer's most famous showcase was the John Coltrane quartet, for which he furnished an unbroken tumult of cross-rhythms (frequently resembling a constant solo) against which Coltrane would set his fire-sermon odysseys. But as the sax-ophonist moved ever further out into free-music in the year before his death (1966), Jones left the band. He has mostly recorded and toured with small hard boppish groups ever since, performing a sharp and forthright jazz constantly driven by that big, restless, ambiguous and inimitable beat.

★*Polycurrents* (Blue Note (CDP 784 331-2)

One of Jones' best small-group recordings as a leader, assisted by a saxophone front line almost as rhythmically insistent as he is. The band is at its best on Jones' heaving, disruptive approaches to mid-tempo playing and saxophonists Frank Foster (a direct, sinewy Basie sideman), Joe Farrell (an early Coltraneist) and Pepper Adams help the album to move as if on wheels.

Kirk, Rahsaan Roland

(Born Columbus, Ohio, August 7, 1936; died December 5, 1977) The German writer Joachim Berendt wrote that Kirk 'had all the wild untutored quality of a street musician coupled with the subtlety of a modern jazz musician'.

Kirk didn't reject bop-based jazz forms as the hard core of the 1960s avant-garde did, but his tonal palette was often as audacious, his sense of the full stretch of jazz history as a source of material as developed. This unique combination of qualities brought Kirk into CHARLES MINGUS' band, for the *Oh Yeah* album. Through the 1960s and 1970s Kirk led his own band, the Vibration Society, playing what he called 'black classical music', and delivering a repertoire that mingled blues, rock 'n' roll, bebop, New Orleans and the avant-garde. He suffered a paralysing stroke in 1975, but continued successfully to play one-handed for the next two years, until a second stroke resulted in his death. CD representation of Kirk is patchy, with no inclusion of his best albums, *Kirk's Works*, *Rip Rig and Panic*, *Rahsaan Rahsaan* and *The Inflated Tear*.

★*Soulful Saxes* (Affinity/Charly CDAFF 758)

Roland Kirk's recorded debut in 1956, when he was 20. Half of it (Booker Ervin and Zoot Sims are also on board) features the young Kirk with a piano trio, leaning heavily towards spiky, robust and distinctively abrasive interpretations of the blues. He is already capable of simultaneous three-part harmony, but also overdubs improvised duets between the tenor and manzello on 'Stormy Weather' and 'The Nearness of You'.

Live in Paris 1970 Vols. 1 & 2 (Concert Catalogue/France FCD 109 & 115)

By 1970 Roland Kirk was at full fearsome stretch, and able not only to perform contrapuntal arrangements on three horns but to improvise one line against another. This French material includes the ubiquitous 'Three for the Festival' but also a venomous version of 'You Did It', a rapturous Charlie Parker medley and the passionate 'Inflated Tear', a 1968 composition devoted to the recollection of his childhood blinding.

Lateef, Yusef (William Evans)

(Born Chattanooga, Tennessee, 1921)
Like RAHSAAN ROLAND KIRK, Yusef Lateef is a musician who widened the tonal range of jazz reeds without departing as far from the ground-rules of 1950s hard bop as the more iconoclastic performers did. Yet his openness to music outside of the jazz tradition, coupled with a perceptive intellectual grasp of African-American musical history and its modern implications, has made Lateef an influential artist, both on the experimental and the commercial and dance-oriented styles of jazz.

Lateef was raised in Detroit, then played with swing bands in the 1940s, ending the decade in the Dizzy Gillespie Orchestra. During the 1950s he led his own bands around Detroit, then performed with CHARLES MINGUS (1960) and subsequently Cannonball Adderley. Being fundamentally a strong hard-bop tenorist, Lateef was always comfortable straddling orthodox jazz and more exploratory forms, but his interest in Eastern music and philosophy significantly influenced the career of JOHN COLTRANE.

Eastern Sounds (Original Jazz Classics OJC 612)

Lateef with a piano trio led by Barry Harris in 1961. Though there are discs that highlight the leader's straight-ahead tenor playing more, this is as good as any as a demonstration of the breadth of his approach, with some oboe soloing, references to Oriental influences and two rather dated-sounding film themes (from *Spartacus* and *The Robe*). But the tenor gets a vigorous workout on the uptempo 'Snafu', and Ernie Farrow does some sterling work on bass.

Mingus, Charles

(Born Arizona, March 22, 1922; died January 5, 1979)
Outstanding both as a composer and an instrumentalist, Charles Mingus was a big man in every respect. He controlled his group performances through his own playing, bolstered at times by shouts and gestures that could alternate encouragement and threats. As a bass player, he set new levels of virtuosity, as a composer his influence on subsequent jazz composition was immense.

Mingus was brought up in Los Angeles, where he played at different times with the bands of Louis Armstrong and Kid Ory. These traditional beginnings help to explain why his mature music largely bypassed the modernistic developments of the 1940s. After making his reputation with Lionel Hampton and Red Norvo, he dropped out in the 1950s – even, it's said, being rescued from a Post Office job by the encouragement of Charlie Parker.

Various experiments reached fulfilment in his 1956 recording *Pithecanthropus Erectus*, and a string of spectacular recordings followed, their moods ranging from the satirical to the gently brooding, from unabashed gospel to unconcealed violence.

★*New Tijuana Moods* (Bluebird/BMG ND 85644)

This disc contains both the original *Tijuana Moods*, and material not issued before, mingling spliced sections and unedited originals. The subsequent versions compare very well: the leeway given to each individual more than compensates for any loss of drama in the more expanded forms. 'Los Mariachos', the most elaborate composition, benefits from an extra slice of Jimmy Knepper's impassioned trombone.

★*Black Saint and the Sinner Lady* (MCA MCAD 5649)

Mingus' major orchestral work. Recorded in 1963 with an 11-piece band and using overdubbing in ways almost unheard of for jazz albums then, *Black Saint* exorcises the debt to Ellington. The flashing brass, the gruff rumblings of the saxophones, and Quentin Jackson's growling on trombone are all Ellingtonesque, as are Charlie Mariano's echoes of Johnny Hodges. But the Mexican fanfares on 'Mode D' and the convoluted rhapsodising on 'Mode E' could only have come from Mingus, like the feverish emotional cast of it all. Mariano gives a tremendous performance.

★*Pithecanthropus Erectus* (WEA/Atlantic K781 456-2)

A high spot of Charles Mingus' recorded output, made in the mid-1950s and featuring the altoist Jackie McLean. McLean is pushed almost to distraction by the heaving, surging blurs and smears of sound that Mingus draws from his band and – though the stops and starts and restless changes of time have come to convey more indecisiveness than 'modern-life' sound effects over the years – the vigour, anger and independence of Mingus' music still blares out uncompromisingly.

Rivers, Samuel Carthorne 'Sam'

(Born El Reno, Oklahoma, September 25, 1930)
One of the most profound thinkers about jazz, as well as one of its most recognisable soloists, is reed player, pianist, viola player and composer Sam Rivers. Rivers is not only multi-talented as a player, he has explored the history of African-American music in depth as a teacher and composer too. Active in the 1960s avant-garde scene, he was, like many of its leading figures, concerned to draw all the neglected riches of black American music into the mix, to create an authentic music of pride and independence.

Rivers came from a musical family, his father and grandfather both being gospel and spirituals singers, his mother a pianist. He learned piano, then alto sax, then tenor at 12, and went to Boston Conservatory in 1947. In the 1950s, Rivers began working regularly on the jazz scene, briefly accompanying Billie Holiday and working with Herb Pomeroy's Boston band. In the next decade, the full range of Rivers' interests emerged: early in the decade he worked on the rhythm & blues scene and with soul artists (backing Wilson Pickett and B.B. King among others); in 1964 he spent six months in the Miles Davis band at the point when the trumpeter was searching for his answer to free-jazz; and in the late 1960s he began working with pianist CECIL TAYLOR, a taxing job for any horn player. During this time, with his wife Bea, Rivers opened Studio Rivbea in Harlem as a teaching and community music centre.

★*Waves* (Tomato 2696492)

In the late 1970s, Rivers' collaborations with the bassist Dave Holland were producing some of his most inventive recordings. This band is augmented by the excellent Thurman Barker on drums and Joe Daley on tuba, and its originality is a tribute both to Rivers' independence of spirit and the post-Coltrane textural adventurousness that Barker and Holland create for drums and bass. The emphasis is towards a sophisticated, non-headbanging form of free-jazz, but its melodic properties are strong.

Sanders, Pharoah

(Born Little Rock, Arkansas, October 13, 1940)
When Pharoah Sanders joined the JOHN COLTRANE group in the mid-1960s, it was taken by some as the point at which Coltrane's music sped even faster into outer space and left conventionally comprehending mortals behind. Where Coltrane was striving for a trance-like music derived from ever-more-dense compacting of jazz's harmonic complexity, Sanders took a more direct route to the same end and his sound was predominantly an abrasive, blues-drenched wail with little use of orthodox melody, influenced by ALBERT AYLER.

Like so many of the 1960s avantists, Sanders began in blues bands; he later worked in California with such artists as Dewey Redman and Philly Joe Jones and then came to New York to join SUN RA. Ayler's influence affected Sanders strongly from the mid-1960s, and he worked with Coltrane from 1966 until the great saxophonist's death the following year. Though Sanders continued to work with Coltrane's piano-playing widow, Alice, he was clearly disoriented as to how to proceed, and barely recorded in the 1970s. Latterly Sanders has discovered the textural appeal of inserting a refined version of his flame-throwing sound into conventional settings, as well as turning in some of the most affecting ballad performances of recent times.

★*Journey to the One* (Theresa TRCD 108/9)

A 1980 Sanders set, marking his return to the studio after years of indecision. *Journey to the One* seemed to represent arrival at a balancing point for Sanders and his ravishing slow tenor exploration of the ballad 'Kazuko' is a genuinely moving performance.

★*Izipho Zam* (Strata East 660-51-018)

A wild and unfettered session of late 1960s free-jazz, made just after John Coltrane's death. Like Coltrane's later music, this is a sequence of slow builds to howling intensity, its textures largely determined by percussion, its momentum by repeated two-chord vamps. Leon Thomas' free-jazz yodel was one of the truly remarkable sounds of the era, and Sanders sounds heated and impassioned. But in production terms it all sounds as if it was recorded in the bathroom.

★*Over the Rainbow* (Paddle Wheel KIC-J 136)

Much more recent and pragmatic Sanders music, featuring him in a more conventional ensemble called the New York Unit, featuring pianist John Hicks and bassist Richard Davis. But though the repertoire largely features standards, this is no exercise in post-bop nostalgia because Sanders' increasingly mellow but still highly arresting sound utterly transforms showbiz material – such as his astonishing high-register vibrancy on a version of 'Over the Rainbow'.

★*Tauhid* (GRP/Impulse 11292)

Sanders in 1966, very strongly under the influence of JOHN
COLTRANE and ALBERT AYLER, but although much of this set features
a far more abrasive Sanders than his recent fans might be used to,
there's still a groove to it that bridges the gap. Henry Grimes'
furious bass-strumming and Sonny Sharrock's sledgehammer-in-
a-bottlebank guitar provide an awesome introduction of 'Upper
Egypt'. Sanders' own mixture of piccolo playing and singing has
an eerie force, and though it's all rather approximate, its
conviction is revealing.

Shepp, Archie

(Born Fort Lauderdale, Florida, May 24, 1937)
Shepp's renowned radicalism was more verbal and political than
musical. He was famous for his denunciations of the white music
establishment, but his tenor-playing had always been a rich
mixture of forcefulness and romanticism. Shepp's influences
included Ben Webster and Coleman Hawkins, as well as Parker,
Rollins, COLTRANE and ORNETTE COLEMAN.

Shepp was raised in Philadelphia, and began playing in the
town's r & b bands as a teenager, meeting John Coltrane and Lee
Morgan in the process. In the late 1950s he studied drama, not
music, and performed in a celebrated play about jazz and
narcotics, *The Connection*. A partnership with the pianist CECIL
TAYLOR occupied the early 1960s, as did the formation of the New
York Contemporary Five, with trumpeter Don Cherry among
others. From 1965 Shepp began working with an increasingly
restless and experimental John Coltrane.

Shepp worked successfully in France in 1970, returned to the
States and brought Motown into his music in collaborations with
the singer Joe Lee Wilson. He also began a fruitful partnership
with the trumpeter and composer Cal Massey on projects that
included attempts to blend jazz and African traditional music,
teaching (drama as well as music), social work with delinquents,
and in the 1980s successful touring, revealing his commitment to
a rugged, sometimes savage version of bebop – except that Shepp

doesn't use the term, preferring the 'baroque period of Afro-American music'.

★*Fire Music* (MCA MCAD 39121)

Extended works by Shepp in interesting company (trumpeter Ted Curson and saxophonist Marion Brown are featured) including two impressive testimonies to his developing powers as a composer in 1965: 'Hambone' and 'Les Olvidados' (the forgotten ones). The former piece uses folk songs, the buoyancy and simplicity of which are repeatedly badgered and bustled by the harshness of the soloists and complex shifts of metre.

★*Goin' Home* (Steeplechase SCCD 31079)

Archie Shepp and pianist Horace Parlan in duet from 1977, the saxophonist's collaborations with this sensitive keyboard artist being fruitful, *Goin' Home* more than most. The session is devoted to spirituals, performed in a selfless and unvirtuosic manner that keeps the original simplicity intact. 'Steal Away to Jesus', 'Amazing Grace' and 'Go Down Moses' are pure Shepp, but personalised by no more than judicious quirks of intonation and phrase.

★*Archie Shepp. Black Ballads* (Timeless CD SJP 386)

A quartet standards session including 'Georgia on my Mind', 'Smoke Gets in Your Eyes', 'Lush Life' and 'Ain't Misbehavin''. Shepp isn't as steady as he was, particularly on sustained sounds, but a combination of his old assertiveness and a new vulnerability gives these songs a kind of weary defiance, particularly on 'Georgia on my Mind'.

★*On This Night* (Impulse GRP 11252)

A Shepp classic, making the best of his strengths and adding some striking assistants, such as the brilliant vibist Bobby Hutcherson, ORNETTE COLEMAN's bassist David Izenzon, and a classical soprano, Christine Spence. The set thus mixes a straight-music atmosphere, a churchy atmosphere, and blues. A bold freebop exploration, 'The Mac Man', gets several takes, as does the Ornette

Coleman-like 'The Chased', but Shepp's brilliant 'In A Sentimental Mood' almost carries off the prizes.

Sun Ra (Herman Sonny Blount)

(Born Birmingham, Alabama, May 22, 1914; died June, 1993)
Though the theatricality of his stage act (space-suits, elaborate makeup, illuminated hats, exotic dancers) has diverted attention from the substance of his work, and his own insistence that he is an astral traveller with a spiritual calling hasn't increased the sum of factual information about him, Sun Ra is one of the most adventurous and genuinely progressive of big-band leaders. From the 1950s on, his orchestral work anticipated many of the advances of the free-jazz of the next decade, and one of his regular saxophonists – John Gilmore – is commonly credited as being a direct influence on John Coltrane. The sound of his band mingles swing-era bravura (he arranged for Fletcher Henderson in the 1940s), electronic-synthesiser fury, stormy percussion and abstract horn flights, and Sun Ra himself remains one of the most imaginative exponents of the frequently treacherous synth.

Based in Chicago from the 1950s onward and counting Duke Ellington and Thelonious Monk among his disguised influences, Sun Ra collected a group of loyal musicians around him who became the nucleus of his Arkestra for years, and he also became an early pioneer of independent record production with his own Saturn label, examples of which are now collectors' pieces.

★*Solar Myth Approach* (Affinity/Charly CDAFF 760)

Good mid-period Sun Ra session from the point at which the leader had begun to incorporate electronics into an already seething soundscape. Far from overburdening the Arkestra's music, it extended an already startling stock of voicings and texture even further, and the disc (originally issued as two vinyl albums) includes Sun Ra perennials such as 'Outer Spaceways'.

*_Love in Outer Space_ (Leo CDLR 154)

Uneven but fitfully interesting and more conventional live recording made in Utrecht in 1983. The only approximate accuracy of the band's ensemble sound generally doesn't matter in the heady atmosphere of its live shows but it's more intrusive on disc. John Gilmore, however, delivers some rugged, restless solos, and the percussion effects (Sun Ra often gets virtually all his musicians to hit things at once) are dramatic.

*_Purple Night_ (A & M 75021 5324)

The Arkestra recorded in late 1989, featuring Don Cherry on trumpet and Julian Priester on trombone in addition to the usual galaxy of talent. It's a typically lurching, witty, occasionally petrifying display, with Sun Ra's keyboards passing from urbane whimsicality to wild, swirling abstractions, notably on 'Neverness', in which John Gilmore also plays a throaty, barrelling solo.

*_Live At The Hackney Empire_ (Leo Records CDLR 214/215: 2-CDs)

Chaotic, but fascinating for Sun Ra buffs. Such togetherness as the band ever has slides away after the interval on this 1990 concert, but the first half is often very gripping, and the regular members are augmented here by the London tabla player Talvin Singh, who unleashes a memorable tabla/scat solo early on. Marshall Allen's alto is evocative on 'Prelude To A Kiss', and John Gilmore pungent on 'Hocus Pocus'. Interesting, but making sense of Sun Ra isn't helped by track listings being reversed on this set.

Taylor, Cecil Percival

(Born New York, March 25, 1932)

Pianist Cecil Taylor's apprenticeship in the 1950s took in Stravinsky, Bartok and Elliott Carter inside the prestigious New England Conservatory, and Monk, Bud Powell and Duke Ellington outside it. He now belatedly receives an enthusiastic response from the academic musical establishment, but it's no more than what might have been his due a quarter-century ago. Mikhail Baryshnikov, who danced to Taylor's music in a series of concerts in the States at the end of the 1970s, spoke glowingly of the pianist revealing to him 'another dimension about dancing to music'. He has also been called 'the Art Tatum of the avant-garde'.

Taylor is of the generation of JOHN COLTRANE, ORNETTE COLEMAN, CHARLES MINGUS and ALBERT AYLER, the musicians who treated bebop as a starting point rather than a destination, and who reforged jazz history with a boldness that has not been repeated by any movement since. In some respects, because of his scalding speed, melodic density and the relentlessly high pressure of his attack, Taylor came to be regarded as the hottest potato of all. This status also meant that for years his principal employment was as a dishwasher, ironically in the very New York jazz clubs that wouldn't let him on the bandstand.

Despite early setbacks, Taylor never lost faith in the idea that what he was doing – modifying the rhythms of swing, improvising without chords, blending the timbres of jazz and some devices from European music – was right no matter what. As well as his classical influences, early Taylor reveals recognisable elements of Bud Powell, Horace Silver and Duke Ellington, and the pianist acknowledges a debt to Dave Brubeck too.

In the later 1960s, after a neglected period as an interesting curiosity, Taylor became a powerful force in New York's Jazz Composers' Guild, later working spectacularly on a Jazz Composers' Orchestra recording of Mike Mantler's *Communications*. Working more regularly with a perceptive altoist, Jimmy Lyons, Taylor's time gradually came. He also became active in jazz education, and worked with ballet dancers.

**Unit Structures* (Blue Note BCT 84237)

Some of Taylor's richest and most engaging music, as well as some of his most personal and oblique. These 1966 recordings featured Alan Silva on bass and Jimmy Lyons on alto, and the title of the album was an accurate reflection of Taylor's methods, organising his thematic material in overlapping blocks. Jimmy Lyons' alto melodies in the best track on this disc – 'Enter Evening' – highlight the empathy and intensity of the group.

Conquistador (Blue Note B21Y 84260)

This album was made in 1966 when Taylor was already a musical typhoon, but with the passage of the years much of what drove some listeners to put their hands over their ears now seems logical, bursting with energy and some of the most constructive collective interplay of the entire movement. Hardly anybody could work with Taylor – his stamina has always floored most partners, his hailstorms of notes unmatchable with complementary solos and his concept almost a personal secret – but the partners here include the perceptive Silva, Lyons and Andrew Cyrille on drums.

In Berlin '88 (Free Music Productions FMP CD – 11 discs)

Strictly for Taylor obsessives, and wealthy ones at that, but for those with the means, an extraordinary display of the riches and potential of free improvisation. The German label recorded Taylor with a variety of European improvisers, including guitarist Derek Bailey, drummers Han Bennink (an inspired collaboration) and Tony Oxley (subsequently a regular partner), cellist Tristan Honsinger and saxophonist Evan Parker. Taylor's receptiveness and encouragement of his varied partners defies much of his reputation for intransigence.

6

THE JAZZ RENAISSANCE: FUSION TO WORLDBEAT

The avant-garde badly frightened the music industry. Even steadfast jazz admirers were concerned that the demands of such unorthodox music were bewildering, or downright alienating, to a substantial slice of potential audiences. And in the 1960s, there was certainly no lack of alternatives to jazz. A new breed of virtuoso rock guitarists drew on jazz and blues. Bands such as Steely Dan and Blood Sweat and Tears used explicit jazz materials. Older notions of what jazz was didn't seem relevant any more. Though the mainstream of rejuvenated or preserved earlier styles (now including hard bop) did continue, and free-jazz protected itself and continued to develop in isolated pockets around the world, the version of jazz that made the biggest impact in the late 1960s and early 1970s was the one that made overtures to rock. The catch-all term became 'fusion'.

In 1970, Miles Davis released a key record – *Bitches Brew* – and a fusion band called Weather Report was formed from a nucleus of some ex-Davis sidemen. British guitarist John McLaughlin (who had also played with Davis) formed a more conventionally melodic and less electronic band called the Mahavishnu Orchestra. Following these, George Benson, a brilliant jazz guitarist, became a soul singer with his guitar as a sideline, and had massive hit records. Fine instrumentalists such as pianists Chick Corea, Herbie Hancock and George Duke, guitarists McLaughlin and Larry Coryell, drummer Billy Cobham, even the great saxophonist Sonny Rollins began playing funk. As had frequently been declared in the music press in earlier generations, jazz in its old guises appeared to have passed away.

But the reign of this kind of fusion hasn't lasted, at least in its original incarnations. Though 'crossover' music, as it's still sometimes known, continues to flourish (some record labels, such as GRP, are devoted to it) even its vaunted danceability and funkiness has frequently come to seem dated and corpulent by comparison with the urgent crackle of a contemporary dance form such as rap. Younger instrumentalists are developing who learn jazz and contemporary street-funk techniques simultaneously, without considering that there was ever a boundary between them. As for 'classic' jazz, salvation came with a wave of young, but tradition-conscious performers, who worshipped the heroes of the bebop era and yet were able to communicate directly with a new, unprejudiced jazz audience in the 1980s. Bebop and its forerunners are revered as classical forms. World-class jazz musicians are now appearing all over the globe.

Some inexorable creative forces of the Afro-American strand continued to flower. Miles Davis recorded a good deal during the 1980s despite illness, starting patchily with half-hearted disco music, but displaying occasional flares of his old lyricism against the breathless, restless rhythmic counterpoint of funk-based rhythm players. And the dominance of rhythmic invention as the driving force in much new jazz is confirmed by one of the brightest stars of the era, New York altoist Steve Coleman. Coleman is part of a New York group of musicians (M-Base) including pianist Geri Allen and singer Cassandra Wilson who are already making a big impression on the developing jazz of the 1990s, and particularly on many of the players of their own age emerging in Europe, including saxophonists Courtney Pine, Steven Williamson and Andy Sheppard.

The older notion of 'fusion' still thrives. It remained dominant through stars such as the highly inventive tenorist Mike Brecker and guitarist Pat Metheny until the early 1980s and Miles Davis continued to lead powerful fusion groups and make distinctive records until his death in 1991 – a loss that saddened the music-loving world and his fans old and new.

But bebop came back in the neo-classical revival of the current era, symbol of a kind of polished, technocratic elegance, but often played with real fire. Less formalised jazz can still be heard – free-improvised music still has a small but increasingly knowledgeable audience all over the planet.

Abercrombie, John L.

(Born Portchester, New York, December 16, 1944)
Abercrombie is in the front-rank of post-bop jazz guitarists, the ones whose styles evolved from the clean, swinging sound of Charlie Christian-derived bop and the later blues and rock styles of Jimi Hendrix, Eric Clapton and others. Unlike his contemporary JOHN SCOFIELD however, Abercrombie has been more impressionistic – in which respect he is closer to PAT METHENY, but with little of Metheny's folksiness and a strong exploratory urge.

John Abercrombie began on guitar at 14, played in rock bands while still at school, went to the Berklee School of Music and worked in Boston with blues organist Johnny 'Hammond' Smith. In 1969 he played in Mike and Randy BRECKER's pathfinding jazz-rock group Dreams, then with Chico Hamilton, Gil Evans, saxophonist DAVE LIEBMAN and fusion drummer Billy Cobham. But in the mid-1970s when he began recording for the German label ECM, Abercrombie flowered as an original soloist and a writer. The atmospheric *Gateway* with DAVE HOLLAND on bass is currently only available on vinyl.

★*Timeless* (ECM 1047)

Abercrombie's first ECM recording from 1974, with JACK DEJOHNETTE on drums and Jan Hammer on organ, synthesiser and piano. Wilder and rougher than Abercrombie's later work but full of his deft, economical phrasing and punchy chordwork, plus a substantial bonus in some remarkable organ-playing from Hammer, something of a special-effects player in the later fusion period but in scalding form here.

★*Animato* (ECM 1411)

After a period in the 1970s and early 1980s in which his original impact seemed to waver, Abercrombie has come back in recent times with some superb trio recordings. This one, made in 1989, features the delicate drummer Jon Christensen and synthesiser player Vince Mendoza, who has written most of the material.

Speak Of The Devil (ECM 849648-2)

A Hammond organ trio gig, but not much holy-rolling blues. Abercrombie confirms his right to be regarded as the postbop Jim Hall, weaving intricate webs of soft melody against Dan Wall's subtle organ textures. Wall doesn't go for the flamethrowing technique of most Hammondists, and some pieces here, such as the gentle 'Dreamland', almost entirely sacrifice linear playing to colour. However, there's some fast postbop too, in which Abercrombie sounds as quick and unflustered as any of his better-known guitar contemporaries.

Abrams, Muhal Richard

(Born Chicago, September 19, 1930)
One of the most influential musicians of a highly influential scene – 1960s Chicago. Abrams would be exceptional on piano alone: he is at home in a variety of styles, from ragtime and boogie, to bebop and free-music. His bands might well deliver raucous blues, or intricate abstract playing, or a blend of bebop and swing. In the latter guises he may combine light, tumbling bop melody with a stride left hand, and his material might feature Ellington, MILES DAVIS, standard songs. His early *Young at Heart* album displayed styles from James P. Johnson all the way up to Cecil Taylor, but it's only available on vinyl as yet.

Abrams has also been a leading light of the Association for the Advancement of Creative Musicians (AACM), a Chicago self-help and educational group from which the ART ENSEMBLE OF CHICAGO – to name its best-known offspring – was spawned in the late 1960s. A product of the Chicago Music College, Abrams had originally worked on the city's regular jazz scene, backing visiting soloists. But by the end of the 1950s, bebop was frustrating him. He formed the Experimental Band with Eddie Harris, ROSCOE MITCHELL and others in 1961 and it was from this nucleus that the AACM emerged, a community of musicians all living in the black districts of the South Side.

Abrams' blend of the Harlem stride he loved in childhood, bebop's rigour and free-music's impressionism has engendered a breadth of view he has taken into composition. In the 1970s

Abrams led a successful sextet (including saxophonist HENRY THREADGILL), the AACM big band, and appeared on several Chicago-based recordings including sessions with the Art Ensemble, CHICO FREEMAN and ANTHONY BRAXTON.

★*Level and Degrees of Light* (Delmark DD 413)

Abrams was preoccupied with not getting in the soloists' way and keeping the composition to pointers and atmospheric motifs on this meditative set from 1967. The session thus relied heavily on Anthony Braxton's fierce alto, Maurice McIntyre's more lissome tenor and Abrams' liquid piano figures. The twitterings of 'Bird Song' haven't survived the journey to a more pragmatic era very well, but it's a strong indication of Abrams' subsequent directions.

★*Blu Blu Blu* (Black Saint 120 117)

A 1990 session by Abrams, and much more positive than some of its predecessors, a rich mixture of African-American musical ideas further stirred by a creative big band. Dave Fiucynski's guitar howls in an authentic 1930s Chicago blues manner (the title track is a dedication to Muddy Waters) and though there are still typical Abrams oscillations between straight-ahead jazz and free-music, some of the sound effects give the whole session real impact. Joel Brandon's eerie, instrument-like whistling has to be heard to be believed.

Adams, George Rufus

(Born Covington, Georgia, April 29, 1940)
A raw and raucous saxophonist and occasional blues singer, influenced primarily by Coltrane, and by Parker, Ben Webster and Coleman Hawkins, Adams' hoarse, vocalised tone and broad-brush effects connects contemporary music powerfully to the jazz past. Adams has most frequently been seen in company with the pianist DON PULLEN in a band mixing high-energy free music and bop, as well as working with two great composer/arrangers in Charles Mingus and Gil Evans.

Like many players with his feeling for the blues, Adams played in r & b and blues bands shortly after taking up the saxophone at school, and spent the summer of 1961 (after becoming a music graduate) touring with singer Sam Cooke. In the mid-1960s Adams was working with blues and soul-jazz organ groups, then moved to New York in 1968 and began to appear with Gil Evans and Art Blakey. In the early years of the next decade he spent three educational years with Charles Mingus. The Adams/Pullen quartet is almost exclusively recorded on small European labels, with Blue Note taking a recent interest in Adams' solo albums, with mixed results.

Live at Village Vanguard Vols. 1 & 2 (Soul Note SNCD 1094/ 1144)

As good as any representation of the Adams/Pullen band on disc, these two fierce live sessions were made in 1983, and they emphasise the interdependence of the quartet. Cameron Brown on bass and Dannie Richmond on drums sustain the temperature unrelentingly, while Pullen's combination of stormy abstraction and hard-boppishness energetically complements Adams' ruggedness.

Akiyoshi, Toshiko

(Born Manchuria, China, December 12, 1929)
For a compositional style that has successfully blended the subtleties of both Gil Evans and Japanese music, Toshiko Akiyoshi gained a reputation as an unusual addition to the ranks of jazz writers. But she is also a powerful bop-derived pianist in a style closely related to BUD POWELL's, and her profound involvement with the substance as well as the technical artifice of jazz has made her work far stronger than a respectful copy.

Akiyoshi was raised as a classical music student, but grew interested in jazz on moving to Japan in 1947. Visiting Americans remarked on her talent, and OSCAR PETERSON in particular encouraged her move to the United States. Akiyoshi studied at Berklee in the late 1950s, then worked with saxophonist Charlie Mariano (her then husband) and briefly with CHARLES MINGUS. In the 1970s, Akiyoshi formed a big band with her second husband, saxophonist Lew Tabackin, and it quickly built a reputation for mixing subtlety and big-band punch in a manner that was otherwise fading as orchestral jazz diminished in popularity and economic feasibility. Many of Akiyoshi's scores were superb in their use of space, unusual textures, and percussive devices as much influenced by Japan as by African-American drumming.

*The Toshiko Akiyoshi-Lew Tabackin Big Band (Novus ND 83106)

Terrific big band record from the mid-1970s, intriguingly retaining the bite and swing of jazz without using orthodox materials, relying instead on the freshness and insight of eight Akiyoshi originals. Tabackin's tenor sax, which echoes most of the swing giants including Coleman Hawkins and Don Byas, has immense presence on this disc (with his sinewy flute playing not far behind) but it's Akioyshi's scores that drive it all, and her thoughtful use of woodwind no more detracts from the music's urge than it did for Gil Evans.

Alexander, Monty

(Born Kingston, Jamaica, June 6, 1944)
An entertaining pianist with roots in swing, Alexander possesses a considerable two-hand technique. His closest links are with Oscar Peterson, but he moderates the frequently pounding, rather stubbornly exhibitionistic qualities of the style with a reflective lyricism, the warmth of Caribbean music and sensitive accompaniment, often from a hand drummer. Alexander became popular in the States in the 1960s, often working with bassist Ray Brown and sometimes vibist Milt Jackson. The quantity of records he has made as a leader are somewhat out of proportion to his ability to vary his output, and there have been a number of recorded reunions of his Triple Treat band, with guitarist Herb Ellis and Ray Brown.

*Jamboree (Concord CCD 4359)

A return to roots by Alexander in 1988, a little different to his usual Peterson-esque fluency. On a mixture of Jamaican folk songs, calypso and reggae, the pianist appears with two steel drummers, his regular hand drummer Robert Thomas and the crackling Marvin 'Smitty' Smith on orthodox drums. Bob Marley's 'No Woman, No Cry' is one of the featured tracks.

Allen, Geri

(Born Detroit, 1959)

If you sometimes have your doubts about KEITH JARRETT, miss Bill Evans, wish PAUL BLEY still played that brooding, rainy streets piano he did in the 1960s, or that CHICK COREA had a little more bite, Geri Allen is the one. She tantalises her listeners by hanging behind the beat, then springing ahead with double-time passages ending in odd, suspended resolutions, has an enthusiasm for dissonance suggestive of both Thelonious Monk and Elmo Hope, and her rhythmic sense is magnificently wayward.

Geri Allen won the piano section as a Talent Deserving of Wider Recognition in *Downbeat* magazine four years running in the 1980s, and *Los Angeles Times* writer Leonard Feather called her 'as true an original as this decade has yet produced'. She began on piano by picking out pop tunes at seven, listened to her father's Charlie Parker records, then began jamming with friends and local musicians – including now celebrated performers like saxophonist KENNY GARRETT, bassist Bob Hurst and drummer Pheeroan Aklaff – around Detroit.

In New York from 1982, Allen met and worked with progressive musicians including saxophonists Oliver Lake and Joseph Jarman, and trumpeter Lester Bowie – connections that led to her first recordings. She also helped found Brooklyn's adventurous M-Base collective, and also began working extensively with drummer PAUL MOTIAN. Her piano influences include THELONIOUS MONK and HERBIE NICHOLS, but her musical interests run far wider.

★*Live at the Village Vanguard* (DIW 847E)

If any single record demonstrates how forcefully Geri Allen is occupying the territory currently dominated by Keith Jarrett's Standards Trio, this is it. Allen performs with her customarily low-profile clarity and intelligence, and partners CHARLIE HADEN (bass) and PAUL MOTIAN (drums) constantly indicate how many years of experience of this kind of band they have under their belts. A great record of the 1990s.

★*Maroons* (Blue Note CDP 0777 7 99493 28)

Most of Allen's recorded work has involved small-group improvisation but this is a bigger band to feature her compositions. It's a survey of several jazz styles, but no empty eclecticism, largely because her own playing is so taut. The larger pieces often suggest the dynamic MILES DAVIS band of the mid-1960s, an impression reinforced by trumpeter WALLACE RONEY's presence. An ambitious but highly varied set, and the piano improvisation is beguiling.

Apfelbaum, Peter/Hieroglyphics Ensemble

(Born California, 1961)
Multi-instrumentalist Apfelbaum and the San Francisco Hieroglyphics Ensemble have significantly helped trumpeter DON CHERRY to renewal, and Apfelbaum and bassist Bo Freeman regularly work with Cherry independently. Cherry's attitude to integrating jazz with many other styles, including reggae, African music, funk and free-improvisation, is expanded with Apfelbaum's Hieroglyphics, and the leader is a powerful force in his own right, with a throaty, Wayne Shorter-like sax sound and a mixture of the solemn and the mercurial at the piano that echoes both ABDULLAH IBRAHIM and KEITH JARRETT.

Apfelbaum has said, 'I see us . . . taking modern dance forms and using them as a basis for composition and improvisation much in the same way as Duke Ellington did with swing.' Apfelbaum began playing drums at three, joined his school jazz band at seven and took up piano at nine. Two years later he had his own school band, learned saxophone and at fifteen formed an improvising group called the Berkeley Jazz Ensemble. At college in Vermont, Apfelbaum studied with jazz musicians Andrew Hill, Jimmy Heath, Beaver Harris and Larry Young, absorbing the various concepts of these players towards bebop, free-jazz and adventurous uses of funk and blues. At 17, in 1979, Apfelbaum formed the Hieroglyphics Ensemble to put these ideas to work, and it has been his compositional and performing outlet since.

★*Signs of Life* (Antilles 422-848 634-2)

Reggae and African music provide the dominant rhythmic sensations in this band, but soul and funk are not far behind. At times it bizarrely suggests Steely Dan playing reggae, at times an African township's dance ensemble, at times even Stevie Wonder – as in Scherezade Stone's vocal 'The World Is Gifted'.

Arguelles, Julian

(Born Staffordshire, January 28, 1966)
British saxophonist Julian Arguelles surfaced in the 1980s with the cooperative big band Loose Tubes, but has since steadily developed as a lyrical saxophonist with leanings towards whimsy in his quicker tunes and reflectiveness in slower ones. His work as an improviser is significantly coupled with signs of considerable originality as a composer.

Arguelles began playing saxophone with youth jazz orchestras, including the European Community Jazz Orchestra. He moved to London in 1984, studying briefly at Trinity College of Music, then joining Loose Tubes in 1986. In the same year, Arguelles won the prestigious Pat Smythe Award, presented each year to a promising British jazz newcomer. Arguelles' sensitivity and musical intelligence has led to work with many front-rank performers, including Mike Gibbs, Django Bates, Ken Stubbs, Kenny Wheeler and CARLA BLEY.

★*Phaedrus* (AH UM 010)

Arguelles with excellent band including the great JOHN TAYLOR on piano, Mick Hutton on bass, and Martin France on drums. It's almost Taylor's disc, because his counterbalancing of textural and linear playing, awareness of his surroundings and sheer pianism are constantly absorbing. Arguelles can suggest tenor players as different as JAN GARBAREK and the late Tristanoite Warne Marsh, and the materials are engagingly offbeat.

Arguelles, Steve

(Born Sussex, November 16, 1963)
Like his saxophone playing brother Julian, drummer Steve Arguelles first came to the notice of British jazz audiences with the adventurous young big band Loose Tubes. He performed a difficult task with the orchestra, providing not only the powerful stimulus a big band drummer needs, but also quick reactions in adapting to the musicians' maverick methods, and a subtlety of shading and texture rare among percussionists.

The Loose Tubes experience marked Arguelles out on the mainstream jazz scene too, and he began to get work as a creative session drummer, often working with visiting guests at clubs such as Ronnie Scott's in the '80s. Loose Tubes encouraged him to explore composition, and to bring together many disparate areas of music – as did Human Chain, an entertainingly abstract small group in which he performed with Django Bates. Raised in Birmingham and taking up drums at school, Arguelles learned broadmindedness early, working at the age of 13 in an early Bhangra group, exploring Asian variations of pop. His enthusiasm for uncategorisable music has accelerated, and in 1992 he moved to Paris, where he developed a highly distinctive vehicle for his various interests (by now including tango and fusion as well as jazz) with local musicians in the band The Recyclers.

★*Busy Listening* (Babel BDV 9406)

Small-group music straight out of the Loose Tubes tradition of eccentric eclecticism – Hot Club accordion swing, tangos, free-jazz, tough bop, echoes of Celtic fiddle music. Tunes getting the treatment include BILL FRISELL's 'The Rag', Herbie Nichols' 'The Gig' (given an Ornette Coleman treatment) and JOHN SCOFIELD's 'Big Fun'. Highly original angles on new and old jazz.

Art Ensemble of Chicago

Bowie, Lester (born Frederick, Maryland, October 11, 1941)
Jarman, Joseph (born Pine Bluff, Arkansas, September 14, 1937)
Mitchell, Roscoe (born Chicago, Illinois, August 3, 1940)

Favors, Malachi (born Chicago, Illinois, August 22, 1937)
Moye, Famoudou Don (born Rochester, New York, May 23, 1946)

A product of the 1960s Chicago free-scene, that always displayed more inclination towards organisation than the New York one (in the Ensemble's case through theatricality and irony as much as musical structure), the band first appeared as ROSCOE MITCHELL's Art Ensemble in 1967, with Mitchell on alto, Lester Bowie on trumpet and Malachi Favors on bass. Joseph Jarman joined two years later, with Don Moye following on a trip to Paris in 1970. The band performs on many instruments, using a range of tone-colour rare for any group of its size, and it has always drawn on jazz history, incorporating snatches of marches, blues, field hollers and bebop as well as the expressionism of free-music.

However, CD issue principally represents late Art Ensemble. None of the Paris material is so far available in the format. Unfortunately neither is *Urban Bushmen*, the most complete representation of the variety of the band's styles, *Les Stances à Sophie* (with soul singer Fontella Bass), *Message to Our Folks* (featuring some sparkling bebop-playing as well as free-music) and *People in Sorrow* – all either deleted completely or only on vinyl.

★*Full Force* (ECM 1167)

More overtly sophisticated and smooth Art Ensemble, but a good indication of the band's resources. 'Magg Zelma' is a rich, colourful and collaborative piece of extended impressionism; the blues 'Charlie M' (dedicated to Mingus) is a striking example of how powerfully the Ensemble can play conventionally, with Moye's drums underpinning dynamic shifts from the stealthy to the fanfare-like and a trumpet solo from Bowie characteristically full of slurs, growls and wriggling runs.

★*The Alternate Express* (DIW 8033)

A display of many of the old Art Ensemble qualities in 1989, just when they seemed to have disappeared, and consequently a session of character and energy from one of the most inventive of all post-1960s jazz groups. It's a set that mixes the ferocious, the abstract and painterly, the reflective and the buoyant in about equal measures and much of the collective playing, notably on the grandiloquent 'Kush', is excellent.

Ballamy, Iain Mark

(Born Guildford, Surrey, February 20, 1964)
One of the new generation of distinctive British jazz musicians to have emerged in the 1980s, Ballamy is a rarity among younger musicians in that his speciality is the all but lost art of ballad-playing. As well as making his mark with the big band Loose Tubes, Ballamy has also performed a good deal with Earthworks, the unique fusion quartet led by ex-Yes drummer BILL BRUFORD.

Ballamy's own band, Balloon Man, is an attractive blend of grace and humour, lyricism and abrasiveness and above all spontaneity and structure. It is the culmination of a process of self-education that began with his piano-playing father Mark, classical lessons, discovery of Fats Waller and Scott Joplin, then hearing a saxophone player rehearsing with a band his father was in, which resulted in him changing instruments. Initially a bop and standards player, Ballamy met the unorthodox pianist DJANGO BATES in 1983, moved gradually away from an Americanised music and absorbed African ideas, gamelan, pop, brass-band sounds and free-music.

★*Balloon Man* (Editions EG EEG 63)

Excellent debut by the quirky Ballamy, with Django Bates at his formidable best on piano, like a more rugged KEITH JARRETT. In fast post-bop, offbeat tangos and even a hymn ('All I Ask Of You'), Ballamy's sax sound embraces a softly scurrying double-time low-register murmur like an overheard conversation, a cello-like mid-range and a blend of Coltraneish high-pitched split notes.

★*All Men Amen* (B & W Music BW065)

A belated 'Balloon Man' follow-up, and even better. There are the same floaty soprano rhapsodies, off-track tangos, marches-ontiptoe, canters in and out of bebop, and the compositional flair has stayed bright. The overdubbed sax solo on the enchanted Coltrane-like ballad 'Further Away' is exquisite.

Bang, Billy

(Born Mobile, Alabama, September 20, 1947)
No received wisdom about the jazz violin applies to Billy Bang. He is by generation and background disinclined to the amiable, jaunty raffishness of a Stephane Grappelli. Bang plays with the packed and tumbling intensity of a Coltraneish saxophonist, but his tunes are succinct and direct, and his variations on them pull no punches, being a constant, churning torrent of wriggling high-register sounds, curt, exclamatory chords and long, expostulatory phrases. He began in a trio with bassist John Lindberg and guitarist James Emery in the String Trio of New York, and from his earliest work it was clear that the more abrasive, fidgety and dissonant manner of free-jazz violin-playing (closer to his original mentor Leroy Jenkins) didn't exclusively appeal to him. Bang made several solo and duo albums of fitful inventiveness but his work with larger groups reveals his strengths as both a soloist and a composer.

★*Valve No.10* (Soul Note 121186)

Bang with some regular associates in drummer Dennis Charles, saxophonist Frank Lowe and bassist Sirone. This is no regular session, however, but a fierce and intense tribute to John Coltrane (including 'Lonnie's Lament') that emphasises how fruitfully the violinist adapted the saxophonist's methods. It's also highly evocative music, Bang being a fervent, emotional performer – with 'Bien-Hoa Blues' a heartfelt and atmospheric piece about his Vietnam service.

Barbieri, Leandro J. 'Gato'

(Born Rosario, Argentina, November 28, 1934)

Barbieri is a tenor saxophonist who came to general notice in the 1960s, but unlike many players influenced by the 'sheets of sound' approach pioneered by Coltrane, he placed considerable emphasis on timbre rather than speed. As a result, the Argentinian's sound is easily recognisable – a hot, tumultuous, desert-storm of a tone, but his work as a leader could incline to the obvious at times. It's thus as a partner to a succession of inventive leaders – including the trumpeter DON CHERRY and the composer CARLA BLEY – that Barbieri has been at his most effective.

Barbieri took up the saxophone at six, after hearing a recording of Charlie Parker's 'Now's the Time'. In adulthood he quickly became Argentina's leading jazz musician, and turned his back on the country's indigenous music to work in jazz and jazz-influenced popular music, notably with Lalo Schifrin. He moved to Italy in the 1960s, made two impressive albums with Don Cherry (*Complete Communion* and *Symphony for Improvisors*), then with STEVE LACY (*Nuovi Sentimenti*) and ABDULLAH IBRAHIM (*Confluence*). Barbieri's qualities of manic passion were appropriate material for the soundtrack to Bernardo Bertolucci's 1972 film *Last Tango in Paris*, for which the saxophonist won a Grammy. Later Barbieri work has moved further away from his more creative jazz roots and he has become something of a Latin-jazz MOR specialist, making *Caliente* for A & M with Herb Alpert.

★*Chapter One: Latin America* (MCA MCAD 39124)

The best of Barbieri's *Chapters* series of albums, with the saxophonist flame-throwing his way across a landscape clattering with South American percussion effects and the bandoneon playing of Dino Saluzzi. Recorded in Rio de Janeiro, 1973.

Bartz, Gary Lee

(Born Baltimore, Maryland, September 26, 1940)

In the 1960s, Gary Bartz was a saxophonist of phenomenal promise, hired by everyone who counted, including Max Roach,

Art Blakey and Miles Davis. His tone was steely yet impassioned, his harmonic imagination rich, his rhythmic inventiveness provocative. Yet the rise of fusion music in the 1970s drew him into a lucrative relationship with the disco market, and he disappeared from jazz for sixteen years. In recent times, Bartz has gone back to making orthodox jazz records, and his improvisor's touch has not deserted him.

Bartz grew interested in jazz via his father's enthusiasms, began playing alto at 11, and studied music extensively in the late 1950s. He joined Max Roach and then Art Blakey, and Miles Davis at the point of the trumpeter's deepest involvement in a mixture of black funk and modal jazz. Bartz frequently topped the sax polls in the early 1970s, toured with his adventurous band Ntu Troop, then increasingly involved himself in disco.

★*There Goes the Neighbourhood* (Candid CCD 79506)

Typical preoccupations of the Bartz method as he moves away from the dance scene, this live set (recorded at Birdland in 1990) pays court to Coltrane and to the bebop heroes – notably Charlie Parker and Tadd Dameron – about equally.

★*Shadows* (Timeless CD SJP 379)

This is Gary Bartz' fifth disc since 1988, when he began recording again as a leader. It's not quite as powerful as the live sets, but the band is good, with pianist Benny Green in grippingly heated form.

Bates, Leon 'Django'

(Born Beckenham, Kent, October 2, 1960)
Django Bates, the pianist and composer from Beckenham, undeclared star of the non-star collective band Loose Tubes, goes on proving that he is apparently immune to desultoriness and prolixity, the enemies of so much improvisation, and his playing is a constant redefinition of jazz possibilities.

Bates learned piano, trumpet and violin early on, but dropped out of music college to go on the road, and formed a band called Humans that later evolved into Human Chain. Work with saxophonists TIM WHITEHEAD and DUDU PUKWANA and with bands First House and Loose Tubes led to his selection (alongside that other 1980s British jazz star, ANDY SHEPPARD) for the prestigious George Russell UK tour of 1986. Accomplished, wide-ranging and historically aware, Bates' work can also be whimsical, anarchic, improvisationally dynamic and as likely to feature a tango, a calypso or a vintage music-hall ditty as conventional jazz. The Loose Tubes ethos of surreal eclecticism is audible in his work, but without appearing to direct it, Bates often made the occasionally unwieldy Loose Tubes sound concise, punctuated and compact. With compositions such as 'Sweet William' (dedicated to his father) and the hymnal 'Sad Afrika' Django Bates is shaping up to be a big-band composer of real vision.

★*Cashin' In* (Editions EG EEG 57)

Bates' offbeat trio Human Chain, which might begin with a sound like guitarists with very slack strings playing over neat, supper-club drumming and shift into tango-like tempos, coloured with accordion effects from the leader's synthesiser. Then comes a piano manner somewhere between the urbane folksiness of KEITH JARRETT and the faintly baleful loquacity of PAUL BLEY. Human Chain depends here on the precision of drummer Steve Arguelles and the quirky multi-instrumentalisms of Stuart Hall as well, but the keyboard player is its constant source of surprise.

★*Powder Room Collapse Orchestra – Music for the Third Policeman (AH UM 003)*

Thirteen movements by Bates intended to reflect characters and events from Flann O'Brien's surreal novel. Though the leader's jazz vocabulary underpins it, it's a definitive representation of the pianist's breadth of view. Fast bebop, odd samba patterns, gurgling reeds and jangling banjos appear, and the theme gets its most graphic imagery in the sound of a bicycle backpedalling, turning into erratic funk and then Ellingtonish sultriness.

Autumn Fires (And Green Shoots) (Polygram Jazz 514 0142)

A rarity for Bates – unaccompanied acoustic piano throughout. Some of it unleashes his substantial technique on regular bebop, some of it is reflective and preoccupied and there are references to pre-bop stride piano, South African music and even to Coltrane's 'Giant Steps', in which the tune is mostly only glimpsed, as fleeting chord riffs against stomping basslines. The KEITH JARRETT influence is apparent on the following 'Calm Steps', but mixed with quirkier, more abstract sounds.

Beck, Gordon James

(Born London, September 16, 1938)
A pianist and composer of international stature for thirty years, Beck is a bop-derived pianist, his playing founded on steely, fast-moving right-hand figures, and a harmonically active left hand, his influences including Bill Evans, Herbie Hancock and Art Tatum. His compositions reflect his improvisational imagination, being packed with melodic zigzags and unexpected twists. A self-taught musician, he was an aeronautical draughtsman at first, but launched a jazz career in 1962 accompanying saxophonist Tubby Hayes, then working in the house band at Ronnie Scott's Club, with American saxophonist Phil Woods' Rhythm Machine, and in the recording studios. Since the mid-1970s he has accompanied innumerable jazz stars, toured extensively with British guitarist Allan Holdsworth and with French violinist Didier Lockwood, worked in jazz education, and composed pieces that have entered the repertoires of such artists as Gary Burton and Phil Woods.

For Evans Sake (JMS 059)

Beck has always had a more robust, even at times impassive quality than the late Bill Evans, the object of this tribute, but the link is clear after listening to this work, with two superb partners in bassist DAVE HOLLAND and drummer JACK DEJOHNETTE. French violinist Didier Lockwood plays some fierce variations but is sparingly used, and Beck's incisive intelligence and compositional insight make this a very belated high-profile acknowledgement of his massive talent.

Beckett, Harold Winston 'Harry'

(Born Barbados, West Indies, May 30, 1935)
Barbadian Harry Beckett is one of Britain's great flugelhorn exponents. A delightfully expressive and convivial-sounding improviser, his phrasing is consistently light and buoyant, alert to partners, glowing in sound. Beckett has displayed these qualities since his arrival in Britain in the 1950s (in 1961 they won him a place in a British band led by Charles Mingus for the film *All Night Long*) and the continuing exuberance of his playing made him for a time a staple member of the Jazz Warriors, for most of whom he was an elder statesman by 30 years or so.

Beckett has played with just about every jazz band of any consequence in the last 30 years in Britain, including bassist and composer Graham Collier's, and those of MIKE WESTBROOK, STAN TRACEY, MIKE GIBBS, Ronnie Scott and many others.

★*Passion and Possession* (ITM 1456)

Typical Beckett solo devices – the latticework of softly squealed high notes, short, drumlike accents, knowing growls and sounds resembling chuckles – are all in evidence in this intriguing set of duets with pianists on the borders of post-bop and free-playing: KEITH TIPPETT, Joachim Kuhn and DJANGO BATES. This doesn't make the session inaccessible however; everyone tunes in to Beckett's warmth and wit, though tangentially in Bates' case.

Benson, George

(Born Pittsburgh, March 22, 1943)
Like Nat King Cole before him, George Benson is the consummate jazz instrumentalist whose singing voice brought him fame. In 1976 his recording of 'Breezin'' made him a pop star and there are few opportunities now (they amount to finding yourself in a New York club on whatever night Benson decides to come and

jam with old friends) to hear a guitarist whose stature in the 1960s rivalled Wes Montgomery's.

Benson sang and played ukelele as a child, and by the age of 19 was touring with organist Jack McDuff. He formed his own organ group in the mid-1960s, playing in the hard-driving jazz-funk manner popular in the period, but he also appeared on albums by other leaders (notably MILES DAVIS' *Miles in the Sky*), playing in a manner that was both highly rhythmic and which took unexpected lyrical twists. But Benson's loyalties lay with a version of jazz that was both danceable and highly communicative, and 'Breezin'' was the high point of that enthusiasm, breaking previous records for sales of an instrumental track.

*The New Boss Guitar (Original Jazz Classics OJC 460)

Benson in the old days, an organ-band recording with Jack McDuff in 1964 showing just why guitar buffs believed the new Wes Montgomery had arrived – hence the title, which is a reference to an earlier Montgomery album. Bluesy, swinging and full of crisp soloing, it's a routine format given an enthusiastic edge by the young guitarist. Fascinating as an insight into pre-MOR Benson.

*Breezin' (Warner Brothers 256199)

The 1976 jazz-funk record that made Benson's name, the infectious title track shifting him resoundingly into the pop market. But the guitarist's hard-driving, warm-toned sound is complemented here by the Stevie Wonder-like vocal technique (on Leon Russell's 'The Masquerade') which put Benson into the top spot of the US pop singles chart at the same time.

Berg, Bob

(Born New York, April 7, 1951)
Berg, who has confirmed his reputation in Britain as one of the most effective Coltrane disciples through appearances with the MILES DAVIS band and recently as a leader, is a player of immense technical command and harmonic awareness, and the resurgence

of bop-influenced music has emphasised these qualities. Berg has run against most prevailing orthodoxies. He resisted the fusion music of the 1970s and continued to develop his techniques as a bebop player during that idiom's low ebb, and combined these studies with methods he had explored as a Coltraneish free-jazz enthusiast in the previous decade. The result was that Berg evolved as a tough, precise player with a voice of his own.

From the mid-1970s to the early 1980s he worked with fine jazz pianists, including Horace Silver and Cedar Walton. In 1984 he joined the Miles Davis band and, though fusion still irked him, found that Davis' conception of the style left generous space for a player of his independence. Berg developed a successful relationship with guitarist Mike Stern through the Davis connection.

⋆*In the Shadows* (Denon CY 76210)

Nothing of Berg's on disc squares with the dynamism he sometimes displays on stage, but this session, also featuring Randy Brecker's trumpet and regular partner Mike Stern's guitar, is better than most. Both Stern and Berg play with a terse eloquence, and though the prevailing mood is fusion-oriented, 'Autumn Leaves' gets a piquant examination from the leader.

Berne, Tim

(Born 1955)
A highly original alto saxophonist, strongly associated with the New York free scene – both the earlier black-influenced jazz-based one and the newer and more eclectic version of which JOHN ZORN is a leading figure. Berne is both an inventive instrumentalist and a composer with an independent view of combining musical materials that is giving him a distinctive role in the 1990s.

Berne has dedicated himself to finding new structures in music and developing improvisation that is intimately part of the piece it develops, rather than a random addition. He draws on themes reminiscent of Ornette Coleman, and of bebop, and the sounds of contemporary urban streetlife.

★*The Ancestors* (Soul Note 1061)

Berne has had a difficult time with record companies, not being an easy artist to categorise. This 1983 live set is as good a representation as any of Berne's pursuit of a highly personal music, peppered with references to many forms including jazz, and rhythmic and dynamic surprises. The presence of drummer PAUL MOTIAN and a fine young trombonist, Ray Anderson, are major virtues.

Blackman, Cyndy

(Born Yellow Springs, Ohio, November 18, 1959)
Blackman's furious, crackling drumming is like TONY WILLIAMS with even fewer unfilled spaces (scurrying, tail-chasing cymbal patterns, bouts of shadowing the melody line, then veering off into avalanches of doubled-up snare patterns, sudden colliding, explosive sounds).

She was raised in a musical family, with both her mother and grandmother performers of the classics. Cyndy Blackman studied classical music intensively as a teenager, then took up drums, and eventually went to Berklee College. In 1982 she was in New York, and already able to work with the best in the business, including Freddie Hubbard and Jackie McLean. But she also learned valuable lessons as a street-musician, regularly playing seven-hour stretches with saxophonist George Braith's band in the open. She also joined trumpeter Ted Curson's all-nighters at the Blue Note club, which led to her wider recognition. During the mid 80s, Blackman also began to explore composition – strongly influenced by drummer/composer Tony Williams – with several of her pieces being performed by Jackie McLean's band.

★*Code Red* (Muse MCD5365)

A dedication to the late Art Blakey, this is more of a blowing session than a careful enunciation but it features a strong lineup including the fine Miles-like trumpeter WALLACE RONEY, sparring with an unlikely partner in altoist STEVE COLEMAN, and the usual high keyboard standards from Kenny Barron. Coleman's alto mixes both the implacable drive of hip-hop-era saxophonists and an attractive mellowness derived from earlier funk, and Roney's variations on 'Round Midnight' are a delight. The MILES DAVIS band of the mid-1960s is a frequent reference point.

Blackwell, Edward Joseph

(Born New Orleans, October 10, 1929; died 1991)
When jazz drummers are discussed in anything other than specialised circles, the names of Buddy Rich, Art Blakey, Elvin Jones and maybe in recent years JACK DEJOHNETTE and TONY WILLIAMS might be expected to come up. Edward Blackwell, far less likely to be referred to, is a drummer entitled to at least as much consideration. An inspired explorer of the timbre of drums and a master of perfectly placed (and tightly edited) accents across the main pulse, Blackwell was a sophisticated innovator of post-bop drumming.

Blackwell performed around his native New Orleans in the late 1940s, with Marsalis Sr (pianist Ellis Marsalis) among others. He met the saxophonist Ornette Coleman there, and by the 1950s both men were getting work in r & b and blues bands. Coleman's interest in a harmonically looser music than bop, wide-ranging melodically but anchored by a steady yet vital pulse, suited Blackwell, whose hustling, short-volley left-hand accents contrasted crisply with a flowing cymbal beat, and whose timbral subtlety reflected his interest in African drum principles. He worked in New York after 1960, with Coleman, Coltrane, DON CHERRY and for a while Thelonious Monk, also appearing with Eric Dolphy on the famous '*Live at the Five Spot*' session. Blackwell taught from 1972, though his health was poor, worked in the Old and New Dreams band devoted to Ornette Coleman's compositions, and worked fruitfully with trumpeter Don Cherry.

★*El Corazon* (ECM 1230)

Don Cherry visited Morocco in the mid-1960s, at the beginning of his world-music explorations and Ed Blackwell joined him there for a year. The intensity of that musical relationship, and the adventurousness of their explorations of timbre and time emerged on *Mu* but is still reflected in this session of ten years later, using unadorned and folksy acoustic melodies, wooden flutes and assorted percussion. Cherry is bubbling, whimsical, at times plaintive, Blackwell as light and springy as a dancer.

★*Old and New Dreams* (ECM 1154)

A celebration of Ornette Coleman's compositions with Cherry, Blackwell, bassist CHARLIE HADEN and tenorist Dewey Redman. All four Coleman alumni were by this stage of their careers immersed in global musical enthusiasms of their own, so the disc ranges over musical exotica and Coleman classics such as the compellingly dirgey 'Lonely Woman'.

Blanchard, Terence

(Born New Orleans, March 1962)
Blanchard is another famous graduate of the Art Blakey Jazz Messengers school, but also a young native of New Orleans, and therefore in danger of eclipse by that city's most famous recent jazz son, fellow-trumpeter Wynton Marsalis.

Blanchard took up the trumpet at eight, joined a New Orleans classical orchestra as a teenager, and was turned on to jazz as a result of teaching by pianist Ellis Marsalis (the MARSALIS brothers' father) at the New Orleans Centre for Creative Arts. Blanchard went to New York to finish studying in 1980, learning classical music and jazz simultaneously and developing fast enough to be hired by Art Blakey when Wynton Marsalis left him in 1981. As might be expected for a musician in the neo-traditionalist mould, Blanchard admires Freddie Hubbard, Clifford Brown, MILES DAVIS and, less predictably, Clark Terry.

★*New York Second Line* (Concord CCD 430-02)

Blanchard's debut in 1983, recorded with a brilliant assortment of players on the rise at the start of the 1980s: the distinctive and unorthodox Donald 'Duck' Harrison on alto, Mulgrew Miller on piano, Lonnie Plaxico on bass and Marvin 'Smitty' Smith on drums. The repertoire mingles new material with earlier work (such as 'I Can't Get Started') and is crackling, businesslike, straight-between-the-eyes nouveau-bop.

Bley, Carla

(Born Oakland, California, May 11, 1938)

Like Gil Evans and GEORGE RUSSELL, Carla Bley is an innovative jazz composer and orchestrator who by a mixture of intention and accident avoided absorbing orthodoxies of composition save those engendered by her own wayward curiosity; she has quoted Erik Satie and the Beatles as significant influences, and pianist PAUL BLEY, composer Charles Mingus and George Russell have left their mark too. She remains one of the most idiosyncratic figures on the contemporary jazz scene.

Carla Bley (originally Carla Borg), the daughter of a Swedish immigrant living in California, studied piano as a child, grew up with church music, and dropped out of school at 15 to work with a folk singer and play the piano in bars. Growing interested in jazz, she went to New York at 19, worked as a cigarette girl at Birdland, and met (and soon married) the Canadian virtuoso pianist Paul Bley. Carla Bley began to write jazz music, soon displaying a quirky melodic sense not enslaved to jazz orthodoxies. Paul Bley began to record her, as did Jimmy Giuffre, George Russell and trumpeter Art Farmer. It was Carla Bley's extended suite, *A Genuine Tong Funeral*, for vibraharpist GARY BURTON, followed by work on bassist CHARLIE HADEN's Spanish-flavoured *Liberation Music Orchestra* album and then the opera *Escalator over the Hill* for the Jazz Composers' Orchestra that secured her reputation.

With her second husband and musical partner, trumpeter MIKE MANTLER, Carla Bley campaigned vigorously for independent production and distribution of creative music, formed Watt Records, and continued to compose jazz-derived work. She also moved towards composed music plus a single soloist (3/4 with a classical orchestra and KEITH JARRETT on piano). In the late 1970s and early 1980s Carla Bley's own music took turns both towards a wacky, vaudevillian presentation and pop, plus her taste for tango and Kurt Weill, but in more recent times jazz has resurfaced, her bigger bands at times reminiscent of Charles

Mingus and Gil Evans. She has also recorded and performed in a duo with bassist Steve Swallow.

Escalator over the Hill (ECM 839 310-2)

Carla Bley's landmark of the 1970s, the jazz/pop opera *Escalator over the Hill*. The CD set even has the original box and accompanying photographs. Bley's odyssey, based on the poetry of Paul Haines, is clearly of its time. But her writing, particularly in the sumptuous and dramatic overture, in which Roswell Rudd's trombone winds up drifting over the evaporating chords of the orchestra with a gleam like a moon over snow, is consistently rich and the improvising of a raft of star guests, including trumpeter Don Cherry, John McLaughlin and country singer Linda Ronstadt, demonstrates Ms Bley's capacity for pulling that extra percentage from musicians who've heard it all.

Night-Glo (Watt 16 827 640)

Carla Bley tightened her grip on improvisers through the 1980s, moving instead towards more carefully controlled pieces that achieved their effects through jazz intonation rather than lyrical spontaneity. But since electric bassist Steve Swallow has evolved a sound that is the closest to the human voice this frequently uncommunicative instrument has come, extended soloing isn't missed. The mood is reflective, even melancholic, but full of Bley's skewed charm.

Fleur Carnivore (Watt 21 839 662)

Terrific big-band session from 1988, featuring Bley's multi-national lineup that also includes British saxophonist ANDY SHEPPARD. This band was something of a return to Bley's jazz roots, a reflection of her growing interest in jazz education. It's no formal display but a spirited and creative extravaganza for offbeat improvisers, under the wing of one of the most offbeat composers currently at work.

★*Go Together* (Watt 24 517 673-2)

Just Bley's piano and Steve Swallow's singing, poetic bass sound in variations on their own pieces, with Bley's writing unsurprisingly having the edge. Her piano-playing is no virtuoso display, but is as wry and subtly angled as her compositions. And since the latter include, on this set, classics such as 'Sing Me Softly of the Blues', 'Mother of the Dead Man' and 'Fleur Carnivore', it's more of a head-start than most piano players have, however fast their fingers move.

Bley, Paul

(Born Montreal, November 10, 1932)
Pianist Paul Bley has never sounded happy inhabiting a well-defined idiom. Though he had demonstrated early on the technique and grasp of regular jazz materials to be a straight-ahead player (he inherited Oscar Peterson's drummer and bassist when his fellow-countryman went to the States in 1949), Bley has rarely strayed far from experimental situations. It was possibly his tendency to explore in a muted rather than a ferocious manner that made him less of a cause célèbre in the avant-garde upheavals of the 1960s. But it was a band led by Bley that put Ornette Coleman on record for the first time, and it wasn't a coincidence.

Bley went to New York to study in the early 1950s, and by 1954 was playing at Birdland. He went to the west coast later in the decade, and Ornette Coleman and DON CHERRY began to work with him in 1958. Bley then collaborated with composer GEORGE RUSSELL (in partnership with Bill Evans on *Jazz in the Space Age*), with Jimmy Giuffre and Sonny Rollins. A series of superb albums by Paul Bley trios followed through the 1960s (often interpreting the distinctive tunes of his first wife Carla) and in the next decade Bley turned to the emerging electronics revolution.

★*Footloose* (Savoy SV 0149)

Quite brilliant Bley trio recordings from 1962 and 1963, the better for being hitched to CARLA BLEY's songs. The pianist's melodic originality, subtlety in shifting harmonies and clipped, nervous timing (he occasionally suggests what Bill Evans might have sounded like as an avantist) never flag, and bassist Steve Swallow and drummer Pete LaRoca are magnificent.

★*Open, to Love* (ECM 1023)

Unaccompanied Bley, displaying the pianist's cool and candid touch, spacious sense of design and rich left-hand work on a series of compositions perfectly suited to him, including Carla Bley's hypnotic and unsettling 'Ida Lupino'.

★*Fragments* (ECM 1320)

The first of two CDs of Bley's mid-1980s band, including JOHN SURMAN on reeds, BILL FRISELL on guitar and PAUL MOTIAN on drums. Predominantly restrained in mood, but the material (furnished by all the players and thus embracing Frisell's warped-rock leanings, Surman's faintly rural wistfulness as well as the leader's rainy streets poignancy) is needling and compulsive.

★*Bebop* (Steeplechase SCCD 31259)

Everyone seemed to be going back to bebop as the 1980s wore on, but on Bley's track record it was always likely that he wouldn't just run down the chord changes. This is another trio album, and on the face of it it's straight-ahead jazz on a string of bop standbys, such as 'Ornithology' and 'Now's the Time'. But Bley shakes them to their roots, in an astonishing display of improvisation.

★With John Surman, Steve Swallow, Tony Oxley. *In The Evenings Out There* (ECM 1488)

Further Bley extension into the European improvising scene (like his contemporary piano innovator, Cecil Taylor). However, this excellent disc doesn't bring all the protagonists together much, but features them in duos and trios. Surman is often soft and romantic rather than bombastic on the baritone, Oxley mixes his inimitably disruptive vision of swing with dramatic sound-effects, Peacock is supple and lyrical on bass. It's mostly quiet, but the production is very clear, and Bley makes every overtone of the piano sing.

*With Evan Parker and Barre Phillips. *Time Will Tell* (ECM 1537)

Bley even deeper inside the Euro-free-jazz ballpark. This is generally very quiet and detailed improvising, mixing the abstract and the structured, and hardly for amazing your friends at parties. Parker, often fierce on tenor, takes on a bleakly romantic role here and there, though he cuts loose on a remarkable display of angry buzzing, harmonics-fireworks and breathless speed at the end. Bley gathers pace from minimalist beginnings to thick, clustered music later, and Phillips is his usual musical self. Twenty-first century chamber music.

Blythe, Arthur Murray

(Born Los Angeles, July 5, 1940)

Like CHICO FREEMAN and DAVID MURRAY, Blythe is a saxophonist who grew up dominated by the brief but brilliant flare of John Coltrane across his sky. Blythe has absorbed a great deal of saxophone history, and exhibits a subtle understanding of everybody from Johnny Hodges to Albert Ayler and Coltrane.

He grew up in San Diego, and studied with Jimmie Lunceford and saxophonist Kirtland Bradford as a teenager. In Los Angeles at the beginning of the '60s, he worked with Horace Tapscott, and they were both founder members of the Union of God's Musicians and Artists Ascension in 1961. Blythe then moved to New York, where he played with Chico Hamilton (1974–7) and GIL EVANS (1976–80), as well as performing in lofts with his own groups. From 1978 to 1980 he regularly turned up in Lester Bowie's bands, and with JACK DEJOHNETTE's Special Edition.

A broadminded performer, Blythe has experimented with jazz-funk and pop, and also led bands that have explored traditional and free-jazz materials – the latter including the guitarists James 'Blood' Ulmer and Kelvyn Bell, musicians influenced by the approach of Ornette Coleman. In 1984 he was part of a supergroup, The Leaders.

★*Retroflection* (ENJA 8046-2)

A live recording at the Village Vanguard, with the superb John Hicks on piano and in which Blythe's appetite for rubbing free-music up against earthy bluesiness is strikingly portrayed. The ensemble playing frays a bit at the edges, but the leader's slightly fraught lyricism is delectable on 'Light Blue', whilst his celebrated original 'Lennox Avenue Breakdown' has just the right degree of raucous, faintly paranoid energy.

Brackeen, Joanne

(Born Ventura, California, July 26, 1938)
Joanne Brackeen an eloquent, dynamic pianist who at times performs like a less ruminative Bill Evans too, but whose style has also been associated with CHICK COREA's. She is capable of performing with a compulsive, foot-tapping energy (qualities essential to sustaining a three-year tenure with Art Blakey's Messengers) but her own material is personal, devoid of cliché and whimsical without preciousness.

California-born, and largely self-taught, Brackeen moved to New York in the mid-1960s having enjoyed an active career in west coast bop from 1958 with leaders such as Dexter Gordon and Harold Land. In 1970 she joined one of the most famous bands in jazz – Art Blakey's Jazz Messengers – and followed a two-year stint with employment by two of the finest saxophonists, JOE HENDERSON and Stan Getz. Now Ms Brackeen mostly performs her own material. A 1982 album, *Special Identity* (on Antilles with JACK DEJOHNETTE and Eddie Gomez), deserves CD release.

★*Fi-Fi Goes to Heaven* (Concord CCD 4316)

Terrific Brackeen record made in 1986 with TERENCE BLANCHARD on trumpet, BRANFORD MARSALIS on reeds, Cecil McBee on bass and Al Foster on drums. Despite such illustrious partners, Brackeen discreetly dominates from the keyboard, and is at her graceful best on 'Stardust' and most eloquent on the title track.

Braxton, Anthony

(Born Chicago, June 4, 1945)

In a period in which experimentation in jazz is in eclipse, Anthony Braxton remains unshakeably devoted to bending the rules. An awesome technician on a multiplicity of instruments (he plays most of the saxophone and clarinet family), he acknowledges influence by John Coltrane, Ornette Coleman, Eric Dolphy, Karlheinz Stockhausen, John Cage, unfashionable improvisors such as the late Warne Marsh and Paul Desmond, Egyptian mysticism, physics and astrology.

Anthony Braxton went to school with two other prominent Chicago jazz artists, ROSCOE MITCHELL and Joseph Jarman, who later came to prominence through the ART ENSEMBLE OF CHICAGO.

Like other members of Chicago's Association for the Advancement of Creative Musicians (AACM, see Muhal Richard Abrams) Braxton decamped for Paris at the end of the 1960s, and also formed a short-lived but adventurous band called Circle, including pianist CHICK COREA, during his brief flirtation with the avantgarde. Braxton's work has continued in astonishing variety since. He has written for chamber orchestras, for ballets, for electronics, performed in sensational duet with one of bebop's founding fathers, drummer Max Roach (see Max Roach) and received numerous awards and citations for his work. In 1985 Braxton became Professor of Composition at Mills College, Oakland, and he continues to tour and perform with his own band which includes the exciting young pianist MARILYN CRISPELL.

In the Tradition Vol. 2 (Steeplechase SCCD 1045)

The second of Braxton's 1974 Copenhagen sessions devoted primarily to mutated bebop. Reforging of classic materials with such panache as to make most of the neo-traditionalist movement sound somnambulant, Braxton rattles his way through Parker's 'Donna Lee', MILES DAVIS' 'Half Nelson', as well as 'Body and Soul' and 'My Funny Valentine'.

★Six Monk Compositions (Black Saint 120116-2)

Most interpreters of Monk try to find an equivalent to his crabby ambiguity, but Braxton typically takes the opposite stance and swarms all over the music. Moreover his Monk choices are tough ones, which the saxophonist mostly decides to play at hair-raising speed. It's Mal Waldron, the pianist, who retains Monk's canny, flinty percussiveness. The set includes 'Brilliant Corners', played alternately like a ghostly tea dance, and in a flying double-time high register oddly reminiscent of Art Pepper.

★Seven Compositions (Trio) 1989 (Hat ART CD 6025)

Recorded in France in 1989, this represents the Braxton trio that also visited Britain on tour. It was almost indecently well endowed, avoiding melodic or rhythmic cliché, displaying intelligent articulacy even at the craziest tempos, a sense of an evolving jazz tradition in reworking both regular themes and swing, and a sizzling group empathy. There is a dynamic combination of independence and sensitivity from drummer Tony Oxley, though he can at times be an overwhelming player.

★Anthony Braxton Quartet: Coventry 1985 (Leo Records CD/LR 204/205)

The Braxton Quartet's 1985 British tour has already been pretty exhaustively documented by Leo Records (Birmingham and London precede this one) but for deeply committed Braxton followers further documentation simply provides more insights into how different this thrilling group's performances were – including pianist Marilyn Crispell – and for newcomers it benefits from an informative, informal and often humorous discussion between Braxton and his biographer Graham Lock.

★Braxton/Parker/Rutherford: Trio (*London, 1993*) (Leo Records CD LR 197)

Not strictly appropriate for a Braxton namecheck alone – it was a truly equal exchange – but these unscheduled performances preceded Braxton's concerts on the 1993 London Jazz Festival, when Anthony Braxton jammed with saxophonist EVAN PARKER and trombonist Paul Rutherford. There were no rules or scores, but the music sang with conviction and virtuosity, drawing on an immense spontaneous sound palette that suggested storms, stampedes, ghostly string sections, and even episodes of Cool School poise. The very best of free jazz.

Brecker, Mike

(Born Philadelphia, March 29, 1949)
Asked who they admire, most fledgling saxophone players soon get to the name of Mike Brecker. A discreetly virtuosic amalgam of the styles of John Coltrane and the rounder, more embracing sound of the soul saxophonists and southern blues players, Brecker is also the most extensively recorded, since he has performed with John Lennon, Yoko Ono, Eric Clapton and James Taylor. If there is a secret to Brecker's success it is that he has found a polished and sophisticated equivalent for every innovation: a softened abrasiveness from the 1960s avant-garde, a blues-sax raunchiness without coarseness, and an extensive awareness of the jazz past.

Brecker comes from a musical family – his father was a skilled amateur jazz pianist, and his older brother Randy is a fine trumpeter. The two brothers formed a highly influential jazz-rock band called Dreams, with drummer Billy Cobham. With vibraharpist Mike Mainieri he formed Steps Ahead in 1978, an intelligent fusion band that occupied him for nearly ten years.

★*Collection* Vol. 2 (Novus ND 83076)

Catalogue of early Brecker brothers outings in the 1970s, featuring in addition the likes of DAVE SANBORN, Don Grolnick, Harvey Mason and others. The graceful funk of the Crusaders is influential, as is the more raucous of MILES DAVIS' fusion styles, plus elements of Weather Report atmosphere and the reverberating bass guitar vamps of Herbie Hancock's Headhunters.

*Michael Brecker (MCA 5980)

Brecker's debut album as a leader, which took him until 1987 to get around to. It was one of the strongest albums of that year, confounding expectations that the chameleon Brecker would have nothing to say for himself, and it featured a sensational band including CHARLIE HADEN on bass, JACK DEJOHNETTE on drums, Kenny Kirkland on piano and PAT METHENY on guitar. Inspired by Metheny's *80/81* album, on which Brecker played, it's a session of composure and independence.

*Brecker Brothers: *Out of the Loop* (GRP 97842)

Backbeat-jazz, with lots of funky horn figures, though more of an influence from the '80s MILES DAVIS sessions like 'Amandla' than formerly. The Breckers wanted this set to be looser and more spontaneous, and it is, with Randy's Milesian trumpet and the ever-astonishing Mike's accumulating tenor marathons always compelling. But they never sound as if they're leaving anything to chance, even when they are. It's the price of such expertise.

Brotzmann, Peter

(Born Remscheid, Germany, March 6, 1941)
One of the loudest and most fearsome saxophone players on the European avant garde, Brotzmann is a legend among the performers who emerged there in the wake of the activities of JOHN COLTRANE, ALBERT AYLER, ORNETTE COLEMAN and others in the States. Brotzmann's sound on tenor is an abrasive exploration of saxophone texture of formidable intensity suggestive of Ayler and Pharoah Sanders, and a remarkable stamina enables him to play in this mode over lengthy sustained performances.

Brotzmann played in a New Orleans style in the late 1950s, but was a free player by the middle of the next decade, often working with bassist Peter Kowald. He then worked with Carla Bley and her trumpeter husband of that time, Mike Mantler, with the revolutionary free-playing Globe Unity Orchestra, and became a founder of the FMP (Free Music Productions) record label. Also in 1969, Brotzmann worked with pianist Fred van Hove and drummer Han Bennink in an influential synthesis of American jazz and European folk roots. Brotzmann has worked with most international free players of significance since, notably in the powerful quartet Last Exit, with guitarist Sonny Sharrock, bassist Bill Laswell and drummer Ronald Shannon Jackson.

★*Last Exit* (Enemy EMY 101)

There are many Brotzmann recordings of considerable interest under his own name, but as an introduction to his sound and to recent minglings of rock and free-music this ferocious band does the business. Jackson's drumming is a staggering display of polyrhythmic playing, Laswell and Sharrock aggressively redefine bass and guitar, and Brotzmann's howling horn finds one of its most suitable settings. This is a live recording, and Sharrock's presence adds a tantalising flavour of the blues.

Bruford, Bill (William Scott)

(Born Sevenoaks, Kent, May 17, 1949)
Bill Bruford is an original and broadminded drummer who emerged in the late 1960s and made his reputation in the art-rock movement, with bands such as Yes and King Crimson. He grew interested in jazz at school, being out of step by preferring Mingus to the Rolling Stones or the Beatles; and he initially tried to push Yes towards jazz.

Since 1986, Bruford has been working extensively with his fusion quartet Earthworks, featuring two prominent Loose Tubes Voices in DJANGO BATES (keyboards) and IAIN BALLAMY (saxophone). During King Crimson's comeback period of 1980–4, Bruford experimented with the electronic drums, and the expanded range of sound effects available encouraged his enthusiasm for musical travelogues, re-creating the melodic sound of West African drums or the guttural drone of a didgeridoo.

★*Dig!* (EG EEGCD 60)

Bruford in powerful partnership with Django Bates and Iain Ballamy. Bates' musical restlessness and impatience with recycled formulae suits Bruford's own, and the repertoire on *Dig!* shifts from calypso to a bizarre, melancholy, Nordic version of the Petula Clark pop hit 'Downtown', to a mélange of New Orleans and Coltrane-like music on Bates' 'Dancing on Frith Street'.

Burton, Gary

(Born Indiana, January 23, 1943)
In the 1960s the vibraharpist Gary Burton seemed to have solved many of the problems confronted by practitioners of the instrument. He avoided the clipped, hollow tone of many vibists, colouring his sound through a remarkable chordal technique (using several mallets at once) and a slurred, bent-note effect that had previously seemed beyond the instrument's scope.

Burton surfaced as a 17-year-old, on an early 1960s bebop outing with country guitarist Hank Garland. Stan Getz subsequently hired Burton, but later in the 1960s he became interested in jazz-rock, working with up-and-coming guitarists LARRY CORYELL and PAT METHENY.

Burton's sublime sound and song-like thematic constructions made him superficially similar to KEITH JARRETT, but he could often play at his best in unfamiliar settings, such as CARLA BLEY's provocative writing on *A Genuine Tong Funeral*. Burton has remained interested in jazz education, preserving his connection with Boston's Berklee College, has successfully recorded with Jarrett and CHICK COREA, and explored semi-classical ventures.

★*The New Quartet* (ECM 1030)

The 1973 quartet with Mick Goodrick on guitar, among others. Burton returned to form with this band, discovering an impetus he had lost, through bustling group give-and-take on pieces by Carla Bley, Keith Jarrett, MICHAEL GIBBS and others.

★*Artists' Choice* (Bluebird ND 86280)

A 1963–8 compilation of Burton's music for RCA, during his first and most energetic phase. There are tracks from work with George Shearing and Stan Getz, as well as the quirkier presence of saxophonists STEVE LACY and GATO BARBIERI, and two tracks from *A Genuine Tong Funeral*. The multi-tracked 'Norwegian Wood' isn't enlivening, but otherwise it's often quietly spirited music.

Camilo, Michael

(Born Santa Domingo, Dominican Republic, 1954)
A one-man street-party of a pianist, whose dancing, Caribbean-dominated music puts him in the same category for pianistic resourcefulness and rhythm-driven accessibility as CHICK COREA was in the 1970s. He began as a classical pianist, but took to studying jazz in New York, working from 1983 to 1985 with saxophonist Paquito D'Rivera's group. In the late 1980s, Camilo began working around New York on his own account, and his shows began to take off with the press. A pianist of unself-conscious exuberance with a drummer-like forcefulness, who is never far from fiesta-like displays of pounding chordwork, Camilo is still a resourceful improviser.

Why Not? (Electric Bird K28P 6371)

Why Not?, a 1986 recording featuring Camilo with excellent support including Lew Soloff's trumpet, is a delightful session, invaluable both for a party or an hour in the armchair. Soloff delivers a lot of street-festival trumpet, balanced by Briton Chris Hunter's slightly over-intense bop figures; not all the music is as good as the title track.

Carr, Ian

(Born Dumfries, April 21, 1933)
Ian Carr is not only one of the most distinctive British interpreters of MILES DAVIS' sound, a pioneer of jazz-rock fusion from the earliest days of the idiom and a prolific composer, he's also a journalist and a jazz academic. A biographer of both Miles Davis and KEITH JARRETT, Carr has always been intrigued by widening the accessibility of jazz, from his days with his organist brother Mike in a

Tyneside bebop band called the Emcee Five, which occasionally featured the then undiscovered guitarist JOHN McLAUGHLIN.

Coming to London in 1962, Carr formed one of the most respected of 1960s British bop bands with saxophonist Don Rendell, and subsequently worked with saxophonists Joe Harriott and Barbara Thompson, pianist Michael Garrick and composers Neil Ardley and MIKE WESTBROOK. Inspired by the work of Miles Davis and Herbie Hancock, he launched Nucleus in 1969, and took it all over the world. He continues to write, teach and play.

★*Old Heartland* (MMC 1016)

Fusion of a different kind – that between Carr's Nucleus-based jazz musicians and a string orchestra – in a programmatic piece based on the Northumbrian countryside. It blends a drifting contemplativeness with punchy bass-lines and intricate ensemble writing – and though it isn't wholly successful, nor some of the string themes more than routine, it's a bold sally by Carr on which his trumpet sounds fine.

Carter, Betty

(Born Flint, Michigan, May 16, 1930)
A supreme jazz singer capable of reinventing songs in ways that enhance the already precious ones and wickedly caricature the worst of Tin Pan Alley. Her work alternates between sounding unfinished and restless, skidding away from notes half-formed, a rhythmic bounce as infectious as a drummer ('What a Little Moonlight Can Do'), and a kind of sensuous assertiveness when she stops running, as on the brooding 'Make It Last'.

Carter was born Ella Mae Jones and appeared onstage with Charlie Parker in Detroit in the 1940s, disguising her age to frequent clubs presenting bebop, which obsessed her. She maintained a stormy relationship with the Lionel Hampton band for a couple of years – Hampton dubbed her 'Betty Bebop' which she hated – but though she was a fine big-band singer, and later an inspired and inspiring collaborator with artists such as MILES DAVIS and Ray Charles, it has always been in small groups that she has been at her most inventive. In such situations she can wind together and pick apart a tapestry of vocal invention that is quite unlike both the wide-screen, heart-on-the-sleeve emotionalism of the torchy jazz singers, or the metallic, disembodied scatting of bop vocalists who pretend to be instruments – a practice she nowadays dislikes. Like the late Art Blakey Betty Carter relishes working with musicians much younger than herself, and up-and-coming young musicians such as pianist Benny Green and drummer WINARD HARPER have been dynamic additions to her group in recent years.

★*Finally – Betty Carter* (Roulette EMI CDP 795333)

Despite winning a Grammy in 1989, the exciting *Look What I Got* was quickly deleted. This session, from 1969, is a worthy CD addition however, a live performance of ten pieces (including two medleys combining 'Body and Soul', 'I Didn't Know What Time It Was' and 'All the Things You Are') performed in New York. Carter's ability not only to reforge the most familiar materials, in her own image, but even to reforge them several different ways in the same account, is on brilliant display here – skidding, diving and sliding through 'Seems Like Old Times', tantalisingly drawn out on 'I Remember You', glowing on 'Blue Moon'.

★*Droppin Things* (Verve 843991)

Carter in 1990, and with a fine collection of guests including trumpeter FREDDIE HUBBARD and pianist GERI ALLEN. As she moved into her sixties, Carter's emotional range deepened so much that comparisons with BILLIE HOLIDAY weren't unreasonable, and her improvising skills and confidence in delaying or sustaining effects became utterly hypnotic. Even with powerful individuals like Hubbard and Allen on board, Carter's oblique forcefulness makes the group sound typically, tantalisingly, tight.

★*Feed The Fire* (Verve 523 600-2)

Betty Carter with a superband at the Festival Hall in 1993. Nothing quite catches the barging intimacy she has with her young accompanists in a club, and partners of the stature of GERI ALLEN on piano, DAVID HOLLAND on bass and JACK DEJOHNETTE on drums aren't as malleable as she's used to. But she frequently picks up on their interventions just the same, especially Dave Holland's voluble bass-lines. Geri Allen's solo on 'If I Should Lose You' is one of the set's memorable breaks, and the general improvising level is something else.

Chase, Thomas 'Tommy'

(Born Manchester, March 22, 1947)

British drummer Tommy Chase spent part of the 1980s being a hit with British dance audiences. Chase won Best Group and Best Album awards from the readers of Britain's *Wire* magazine in 1986. His albums have punchy, bullish titles such as *Hard!* and *Drive!* and he is devoted to hard bop, particularly to the backbeat-driven bop funk popular with organ-led groups int he 1960s.

Chase was raised in Worsley, on the outskirts of Manchester. Like many British kids in the early 1960s, his enthusiasm for jazz was an oddity to be shared only with one or two other converts. He was turned on to jazz by hearing trumpeter Clifford Brown on record (the fact that the local fish-shop was run by a man called Charlie Parker, and the local optician was Clifford Brown was a joke Chase could rarely share at school) and was a professional drummer at 17, playing summer shows and cruises. He began forming his own bands in the mid-1970s in London, supported visiting Americans, and dedicated himself to a salty danceable jazz repertoire, though still with considerable space for improvisers.

★*Rebel Fire* (Mole Records MRTC 002)

A 1990 Chase album, mostly a celebration of effects such as raucous soul saxophone, churning organ and whiplash backbeat. More of a club DJ's disc than a feet-up-at-home session it nevertheless has a good organist in Gary Baldwin and a powerful saxophonist in the impassioned Ben Waghorn.

Cherry, Donald E. 'Don'

(Born Oklahoma City, November 18, 1936; died October 18, 1995)

Trumpeter Don Cherry was an indisputable one-off in jazz. Originally a bebop trumpeter, he was as likely to perform a John Lee Hooker blues played on a Malinese hunting guitar (the doussn'gourni) as a post-bop trumpet variation on an Ornette Coleman theme. He worked with musicians of the stature of Ornette Coleman, Sonny Rollins, GATO BARBIERI, CARLA BLEY and Lou Reed. He also worked onstage with his pop-star stepdaughter Neneh Cherry, whom he claimed as a significant influence.

Cherry's arrival on the world's jazz stage began in the winter of 1958 when the revolutionary Ornette Coleman quartet rehearsed in Cherry's mother's garage in Watts. He was a deserving recipient of the nowadays almost obligatory title 'world-musician' by around 1966. It was then that he left the States for Stockholm (having met his second wife Moki, a painter, and Neneh's mother, while on a European tour with Sonny Rollins) and spent the early months of his new life in that city's Ethnographic Museum, studying ethnic instruments. Cherry then took his new family in a camper through Africa, the Middle East and India, sitting in with village musicians on three continents. He formed an audacious small group with Argentinian tenorist Gato Barbieri, producing classic albums such as *Complete Communion* and *Symphony for Improvisors*, worked with ethereal ingenuity with Carla Bley and the Jazz Composers' Orchestra on the Indian-influenced *Escalator Over The Hill*, and explored Tibetan and Japanese music with the late sitarist Collin Wallcott in the band Cordona.

★*Art Deco* (A & M 395 258-2)

A distinctly jazzy recording with two of Cherry's most creative partners – bassist CHARLIE HADEN and drummer Billy Higgins – plus Texas saxophonist James Clay, an early collaborator with Ornette Coleman but who missed out on Coleman's revolution and spent much of his life as a sideman in the Ray Charles band. Clay has some of the broad tone of Sonny Rollins, and some of the unfinished, squawky quality of the late Warne Marsh.

★*Multi-Kulti* (A & M 395323)

A strongly ethnic-flavoured 1990 session, finding the trumpeter with a variety of interesting associates (including the soulful altoist Carlos Ward, and the west coast multi-genre Hieroglyphics Ensemble) who together perform a repertoire that draws on western pop, free-jazz, Middle-Eastern and African music, and many of the other ingredients that Cherry had absorbed since the 1960s. Nods to salsa, funk and hard bop.

Coe, Anthony George 'Tony'

(Born Canterbury, Kent, November 29, 1934)
Since the mid-1950s the great English reed player Tony Coe has performed mainstream jazz, bebop, classical music, free-improvisation – even been offered a job by Count Basie. He is a brilliant clarinettist, a luxuriant tenorist, and a thoughtful composer, able to draw materials from inspirations as diverse as Debussy and Louis Armstrong.

Coe's father was a clarinettist, and the boy learned the instrument formally, but taught himself the saxophone. He studied composition with a variety of teachers and contemporaries, including Richard Rodney Bennett, and performed with Humphrey Lyttelton's mainstream band in the early 1960s. Coe worked with JOHN DANKWORTH during that decade and then with the European/American Kenny Clarke-Francy Boland band; but also during the 1970s he extended himself into free-improvisation with guitarist Derek Bailey's Company.

★*Canterbury Song* (Hot House HHCD 1005)

Attractive and unassuming set by the lustrous Coe in collaboration with American members of the Paris Reunion band: Benny Bailey on trumpet, Horace Parlan on piano, Jimmy Woode on bass and Idris Muhammad on drums. The group wreathes effortlessly through a selection of classy compositions, including the MILES DAVIS vehicle 'Blue in Green', 'I Guess I'll Hang My Tears Out to Dry' and *Return to Forever*'s sensuous 'Sometime Ago'.

Coleman, Steve

(Born Chicago, 1956)
The saxophonist Steve Coleman can be a neo-bop altoist of a
force, fluency and freedom that reveals a creative indebtedness to
Charlie Parker, but also a musician raised with the street-beat of
the 1980s.

Coleman was born on Chicago's South Side, and grew up
listening to funk and rock. His father was a Charlie Parker fan,
however, but it wasn't until he was a student at Wesleyan
University that he rediscovered Parker as the route to learning to
improvise after some years of playing alto with house and funk
outfits. Once bitten, Coleman started to absorb experience from
some of Chicago's veterans – notably one of jazz's greatest
underrated saxophonists, Von Freeman. In 1978, Steve Coleman
moved to New York, then joined the Thad Jones/Mel Lewis big
band, and later ensembles led by Slide Hampton, Cecil Taylor and
Sam Rivers. Coleman wanted nothing less than to find a
contemporary equivalent for the breakthrough Charlie Parker
had made in the 1940s. But he wanted to use hip-hop and rap and
other black-derived pop materials of the 1980s and 1990s as
elements to combine with bop. With that in mind, Coleman
started the band Five Elements, while working for a highly
virtuosic but more down-the-line jazz band led by bassist DAVE
HOLLAND.

★*World Expansion* (JMT 872010)

Featuring Coleman with an early New York busking associate,
Mark Johnson, on drums, plus the excellent Robin Eubanks and
GERI ALLEN on trombone and piano respectively, and CASSANDRA
WILSON (a more abstract version of BETTY CARTER) on vocals. This
was a 1986 outing for the Five Elements band, enterprisingly
developing a group sound of fertile overlaps, dancing rhythms
and collective spontaneity – but it's still troubled by the contradic-
tions of splicing dance grooves and probing improvisation.

★*Drop Kick* (Novus 01241 63144-2)

A warmer, more accessible version of Coleman's search, with a punchy backbeat but a tight, sinewy ensemble sound, rather reminiscent of an all-saxophone band. Less hard and frantic than other Five Elements discs, it points more fruitfully towards Coleman's future, though Cassandra Wilson fans will find her appearance fairly perfunctory.

★*Black Science* (Novus PD 83119)

More explorations of funk for the head and bop for the feet. *Black Science* is the Coleman album that best integrates New York, Africa, formal development, improvisation and a groove. The time-signatures change a lot, and there's a dedication to formal preoccupations that can blunt its exuberance, even some rather dated-sounding poetry and jazz.

Company

In the mid-1970s, when he first thought of the idea of a variable repertory company of improvising musicians of no fixed persuasion, the spirited British guitarist Derek Bailey (born Sheffield, January 29, 1930) opined that bands were interesting until they 'discovered their music', after which they hardened a style and became less interesting improvisationally. Since the late 1960s, Bailey has been largely true to these principles himself. Originally a nightclub and session performer in the north of England (his father was a professional musician) Bailey collaborated in a free-jazz group along Coltrane lines in Sheffield.

In an attempt to combat the tyranny of style, Bailey conceived of Company, an international group of musicians dispersed by geography, language, musical training and personal tastes, united only by an interest in occasionally making unrehearsed music in the company of irregular partners or even total strangers. Over the years the list has included musicians as distinct from one another as the brilliant modern classical trombonist Vinko Globokar and one of the most piquant and distinctive voices of the cool jazz movement of the 1950s, Lee Konitz.

★Once (Incus CD04)

Cool school sax star LEE KONITZ participates in the improvising repertory group Company (on an Incus CD taken from the 1987 season), Konitz straightfacedly draping 'It Ain't Necessarily So' over the drifting cello and arco bass (Tristan Honsinger and Barre Phillips). The unfamiliarity of larger free ensembles makes Konitz hesitant at times, and it doesn't sound like a situation he would spend the rest of his life trying to repeat. But *Once* is nevertheless an empathetic set of musical conversations, with a high level of dynamic variety. Guitarist Bailey's frosty, gleaming harmonics and skittering runs, and virtuoso bassist Barre Phillips' restless sonorities are powerful features.

Corea, Armando Anthony 'Chick'

(Born Massachusetts, June 12, 1941)
Of all the genuinely gifted musicians to have appeared in jazz over the past 30 years, pianist Chick Corea has been one of the most inconsistent. By the end of the 1960s it seemed clear that he, KEITH JARRETT and HERBIE HANCOCK were not only the leading pianists of their generation, but were sufficiently visionary and artistically ambitious positively to redirect the course of jazz. But though Corea has often played beautifully and contributed several catchy compositions to the music, his work has equally been repetitious.

Corea was classically trained, playing piano and drums before he was ten. He worked with funk and Latin bands led by Herbie Mann and Mongo Santamaria, and he gained a reputation as a lyrical acoustic pianist with a penchant for Latin idioms. In the late 1960s he joined Stan Getz as a pianist and composer, then MILES DAVIS. But Davis' version of jazz-rock could allow abstraction among the melody players if the pulse was secure. This taste of freer music led Corea and the band's British bassist, DAVE HOLLAND, to leave and form a semi-free band – Circle – which was closer to the European improvising scene.

Corea then formed the Latin-influenced Return to Forever (including singer Flora Purim), which started light and flexible but became more ritualised until it broke up in 1980. Corea returned to jazzy acoustic playing, work with Herbie Hancock and vibist

GARY BURTON, flirtations with classical music, and writing his own piano concerto. In 1986 he also formed a heavier Elektric Band with drummer Dave Weckl.

*_Now He Sings Now He Sobs_ (Blue Note CDP 790 055-2)

Corea's 1968 acoustic piano album with drummer Roy Haynes and bassist Miroslav Vitous, and the best early indication of the richness of his resources, drawn from Horace Silver, Bud Powell and Bill Evans. There is the delightful waltz 'Windows', which Corea originally wrote for Stan Getz, and enough stretching and twisting of materials to suggest the pianist's brief but intense fascination with the avant-garde.

*_ARC_ (ECM 1009)

Corea with Circle partners Dave Holland (bass) and Barry Altschul (drums). Fascinating insight into how far the fundamentally conservative Corea was prepared to go, and how taut and inventive the Holland/Altschul team was. Pieces include the band's uniquely deconstructivist version of the WAYNE SHORTER/ Miles Davis vehicle, 'Nefertiti'.

*_Light as a Feather_ (Polydor 2310247)

The first Return to Forever album, from 1972, and the best by miles. The songs featuring Flora Purim (notably 'What Game Shall We Play Today' and 'Sometime Ago') have an airy and playful quality that is never coy. Corea's electric piano is delicate, propulsive and as yet devoid of electric-keyboard conveniences, while Stanley Clarke's bass is springy and agile and the late Joe Farrell's grainy tenor lends a necessary grit.

*_Three Quartets_ (Stretch Records GRS 00032)

Half of this disc is a 1982 set with Eddie Gomez on bass, MIKE BRECKER on tenor and Steve Gadd on drums, set up to produce a three-part mood piece reflecting Ellington and Coltrane. It's pleasant enough, until you get to the previously unreleased second section, featuring the same band enjoying itself in spare studio time. Corea says on the notes he thought originally the difference was too startling to put them out together, and Brecker certainly sounds untrammelled, cutting loose on Charlie Parker's 'Confirmation' as if he didn't have an image to protect.

Coryell, Larry

(Born Galveston, Texas, April 2, 1943)
Larry Coryell is a well-equipped guitarist uncertain of what to do with his skills, but he did deliver (notably with his band Eleventh House) some of the more convincing fusion guitar displays of the early years, as well as some inventive low-volume explorations, notably with the late EMILY REMLER.

Coryell studied journalism, but he had performed in teenage bands as a guitarist influenced by the country style of Chet Atkins. After he graduated, he took guitar lessons, moved towards Latin and rock music, and eventually worked with percussionist Chico Hamilton, flautist HERBIE MANN (on the influential *Memphis Underground*) and vibist GARY BURTON.

Coryell's feverish, but often exciting Eleventh House band (including a tempestuous drummer, Al Mouzon, and trumpeter Randy Brecker) toured the world, but later Coryell turned back to acoustic music, and more jazz-based electric guitar outings.

★*Spaces* (Start Records VMCD 7305)

Excellent 1970s session, teaming Coryell with fellow-guitarist JOHN McLAUGHLIN, plus CHICK COREA on piano, Miroslav Vitous on bass and Billy Cobham on drums. Fluent, conversational and undemonstrative exchanges between McLaughlin and Coryell run throughout the disc with a sensitivity otherwise rare for either man at the time.

★*Toku Du* (Muse MCD 5350)

Like many good musicians who had a cultish reputation at one time in their lives, Coryell entered middle life interested in just playing. This fine band, with Stanley Cowell on piano, Buster

Williams on bass and Beaver Harris on drums, playing a mixture of standards and Coltrane-era themes, finds him doing just that.

Crispell, Marilyn

(Born Philadelphia, March 30, 1947)
Despite the whirlwind arrival of Cecil Taylor on the jazz scene at the beginning of the 1960s, most pianists have followed the routes established by McCOY TYNER, or HERBIE HANCOCK, or KEITH JARRETT. Marilyn Crispell is a fitting inheritor of Taylor's mantle. She is as inclined as Taylor to zipping ascents and descents, rippling, atonal arpeggios and banging, dissonant chords but has a tendency to be less declamatory and unforgiving, giving the sometimes brutal Taylor legacy a communicative air.

Crispell took up the piano at seven, and studied piano and composition at Boston's New England Conservatory. But she dropped music during this period and took up medicine, only returning to playing six years later – as a blues singer. Hearing Coltrane's 'A Love Supreme' and the piano-playing of Thelonious Monk and Cecil Taylor drew her to jazz. She studied the music from then on, mostly at the Creative Music Studio in Woodstock, meeting many inventive musicians, ANTHONY BRAXTON among them, during this time. She has been one of Anthony Braxton's most suitable partners.

★*Gaia* (Leo Records CDLR 152)

A trio album, featuring Reggie Workman on bass and Doug James on drums. It is Crispell's most balanced recording, intense and shapely improvisation without a formal structure (nor with much recourse to jazz time on the part of Workman or James) yet it is the most compelling and orderly of free sessions. Crispell's Taylorisms are clearly audible, yet these are about the only elements that qualify as 'references' in a taut, selfless and powerful three-way dialogue. One of the handful of pathfinding records of the 1980s, but a pointer to the 1990s too.

Crusaders

The Crusaders pre-dated the jazz-rock fusion boom of the 1970s. The central figures in the band were its pianist Joe Sample (born Houston, February 1, 1939), saxophonist Wilton Felder (born Houston, August 31, 1940) and drummer Nesbert 'Stix' Hooper (born Houston, August 15, 1938); other saxophonists, bassists and trombonists came and went. Emerging as the Modern Jazz Sextet in Texas in 1958, the outfit then moved to the west coast, having changed their name to the Nighthawks, and they eventually released an album in 1961, by which time they were known as the Crusaders. The band's sound was more plush and relaxed than the hard and metallic sounds of jazz-rock. It was created from catchy bass-riffs, warm-toned ensembles and Wilton Felder's steamy, wide-angle tenor sound in particular. As they became more popular, their work was appropriated by admirers, such as the Average White Band.

The best Crusaders records were made in the 1970s during the period when the graceful guitarist Larry Carlton was a member. The eclipse of jazz-rock affected the Crusaders, but they had considerable popular success through partnerships with singers such as Randy Crawford and Bobby Womack.

★*Freedom Sound* (Pacific CDP7 96864-2)

The Crusaders' 1961 debut, with a repertoire of pieces by trombonist Wayne Henderson and saxophonist Wilton Felder, save for the theme from *Exodus* (which everybody took a crack at in those days), which they just about avoid getting kitsched by. Two alternate takes pack the original out to a CD without adding much, but that plush and amiable Texas blues sound has already acquired its lazily rolling charm.

★*The Golden Years* (GRP 50072)

Three-disc set, covering 31 tracks and 20 years from 1962 to 1982, from albums such as *Southern Comfort, Free as the Wind, Chain Reaction* and *Street Life*. As the insert says: 'They were funky by their origins in Texas, so nobody had to tell them to put a back beat on the bebop.' 'Stomp and Buck Dance' from the *Southern Comfort* album is vintage Crusaders, solos easing coolly in and out of those tightly freewheeling ensembles. All the later singers and orchestras are neither here nor there, and B.B. King doesn't sound transported on 'Royal Jam' but nothing, not even a symphony orchestra, can simmer down that Texas gospel.

Dankworth, John Philip William

(Born Essex, September 20, 1927)
John Dankworth is probably the best known of all British jazz musicians who have remained based in the UK – even including Ronnie Scott – because Dankworth has been successful in America, written music for films, and collaborated in light classics and pops repertoires with symphony orchestras all over the world. Dankworth's singer wife Cleo Laine, more internationally celebrated than he is, has helped sustain his reputation.

Dankworth's skills always lay in composition and arrangement, and a mischievous sense of what could be borrowed and adapted from other idioms. Within 15 months of taking up clarinet as a teenager he won a dance-band soloist's award in the 1940s, began to run Goodmanesque bands of his own, graduated from music college and discovered Charlie Parker. Pilgrimages on the transatlantic liners to New York followed, and in the 1950s his seven-piece, strongly influenced by the MILES DAVIS' *Birth of the Cool* band, had pop hits with such themes as 'Experiments With Mice', and later played the Newport Festival. Dankworth has composed a number of film scores, notably for Karel Reisz' *We Are the Lambeth Boys* and *Saturday Night and Sunday Morning*.

★The Vintage Years 1953–59 (Sepia RSCD 2014)

Big-band Dankworth from the 1950s, reflecting the British jazz scene's uneasy straddling of the world of the Mecca Ballrooms and creative music. But there's enough of a flavour of Dankworth's particular reworkings of jazz favourites to give an impression of why he was in the front rank of European jazz at the time.

★*Generation Big Band* (Jazz House JHCD 029)

The effect of an injection of youth led by Dankworth Jnr. (bassist Alec) and newcomers like trumpeter Gerard Presence and saxophonist Andy Panayi, although John Dankworth preserves his luxuriant orchestral subtleties and retains storytelling swing soloists (like the excellent tenorist Jimmy Hastings) to play a repertoire that includes JOE HENDERSON's 'Black Narcissus', CARLA BLEY's beautiful 'Ida Lupino', as well as Gershwin, Johnny Mandel, Cole Porter and originals. Excellent big band music.

Davis, Anthony

(Born Paterson, New Jersey, 1951)
Immensely talented pianist whose roots lay in Duke Ellington, Thelonious Monk and Cecil Taylor but whose contribution has been largely to a contemporary music occupying a territory between jazz and the chamber group. Davis was a classical piano student who went to Yale and while there met many of the most adventurous jazz avantists of the 1970s, including trombonist George Lewis. In 1974 Davis joined trumpeter Leo Smith's band and a year later ran his own quartet, with Jay Hoggard on vibes, Mark Helias on bass and Ed Blackwell on drums. Work with ANTHONY BRAXTON and CHICO FREEMAN followed, and in 1978 Davis recorded his first album as a leader, *Song for the Old World*.

During the 1980s Anthony Davis began appearing regularly with the flautist JAMES NEWTON, and the pianist's music increasingly turned to composition. With his octet Epicene, Davis further explored ensemble-writing, and the arrangement of other composers' work. In 1985, Davis' opera X, based on the life of Malcolm X, was performed in the States.

★*Middle Passage* (Gramavision GRCD 8401)

Davis displaying most of his post-1970s virtues single-handed. This solo piano set finds him in persuasive instrumental form, working with materials largely from outside orthodox jazz. The title piece was written for the pianist by the contemporary straight composer Ursula Oppens, and 'Particle W' is a piece by Earl Howard for piano and electronics.

Davis, Miles

(See page 149 for earlier biography)

Following his early 1980s comeback after illness, Miles Davis passed through a painful stage of rebuilding his confidence and technique, via the comparatively relaxed re-entry of *You're Under Arrest* (featuring, among other things, the work of Cyndy Lauper) and then, coinciding with a break from CBS to WEA, the electronically orchestral *Tutu*. Though Davis seemed to have shrunk in his compelling solo power, the disc demonstrated that he and bassist/composer Marcus Miller were a substantial force. Miller brought lyricism back to Davis to weave around the rhythmic animation that had characterised his electric bands, as well as writing and arranging a rich repertoire of jazz and funk that has a contrapuntal variety as demanding as anything the trumpeter has worked on.

Davis the dazzling lyrical soloist became a musical persona in short supply as the 1980s went on, but his bands continued to be highly rhythmic, and exhibited a freshness in handling electronics that often testified to the trumpeter's continuing taste. He was aiming his music at the black pop radio stations through most of the decade, but in his last years began to turn, quite unexpectedly, towards an overview of his earlier work – even performing with Quincy Jones at Montreux on remakes of some of the old Gil Evans orchestral pieces.

★*Amandla* (Warner Brothers 925873)

Amandla splices the lazy mid-tempo funk groove that Davis grew so fond of with a feel for the raw materials of the instrumentation that makes the set full of sudden splashes of colour (guitars are several times used simply as explosive sound effects), and a graceful melodic strength. There is an infectious energy to the pulse on 'Big Time'. Reminiscences of Weather Report emerge in the gently dancing 'Jo-Jo' and the convoluted bass-and-synths riff that underpins the seething 'Jilli'.

*_Aura_ (CBS 463 351)

Scandinavian trumpeter Palle Mikkelborg's concerto for his hero, recorded in Copenhagen to accompany Miles' receipt of the Sonning Music Prize, a prestigious tribute whose earlier recipients have been Stravinsky, Leonard Bernstein and Isaac Stern. Harps echo John McLaughlin's scalding guitar figures, synthesisers unleash cascading peals of sound like church bells, sustained low trombone sounds throb beneath the horn and guitar-like sensations from a distant engine-room. On the last side's 'Violet', a reworked blues with references to Messiaen in it, some of Miles Davis' most exquisite slow playing is to be heard over slurred, sliding chords and the kind of empty space that he seldom tolerated later in his career.

*_Doo-Bop_ (Warner Brothers 7599-26938)

Close to being a hip-hop session, and unfinished at the time of Davis' death. A collaboration with the young dance producer and rapper Easy Mo Bee, it was completed by building two of the tracks around a couple of unused Miles solos from the 1980s. In some respects, the trumpet work sounds like the mixture from _You're Under Arrest_ – plaintive muted figures resembling 'Time After Time', or fast sections such as 'High Speed Chase' with background noises of car-horns and barrelling organ sounds. But it all gives an intriguing insight into Miles' take on new black dance. The lyrics of the raps are vain in a way he never was on his own records though.

Dean, Elton

(Born Nottingham, England, October 28, 1945)
A fine English reed player who came up with the jazzier end of the British free scene in the early 1970s, often associated with the brilliant west country pianist Keith Tippett. Dean doesn't need much in the way of structure to be inventive, and his warm and rounded sound leavens the abrasiveness of some of the less forgiving exploits into 'high-energy' collective improvisation. His band of the late 1970s, Ninesense, was one of the most inventive

in Britain, and would have been more widely recognised as such but for the tough time that any form of jazz other than fusion was facing in that period.

Dean came to jazz via rhythm and blues at first, working with the singer Long John Baldry – then with Keith Tippett in 1968. He joined the art-rock improvising group Soft Machine for three years, and through the 1970s appeared in a variety of bands involving Tippett and the talented South African emigrés in London including drummer Louis Moholo.

★*All The Tradition* (Slam 201)

A superb example of the way in which some contemporary improvisors approach traditional jazz elements without the deference that hampers creativity. This session was co-led with pianist Howard Riley, a resourceful explorer of contemporary musical languages inside and outside jazz, and though it's not a fair representation of the regular material used by either player – standards like 'Naima' and 'I Remember Clifford' are on it – the mixture of approaches from both chromatic and free improvising styles is so seamlessly achieved as to make this disc a triumph.

Dedication Orchestra

(Formed New Year, 1992)

The dedication is to a remarkable, but tragically short-lived group of exiled South African jazz musicians who helped galvanise the British scene of the 1960s and 1970s – Dudu Pukwana, Chris McGregor, Harry Miller, Mongezi Feza and Johnny Dyani among them, members of the original Blue Notes group which had evolved in South Africa to play a mixture of local music and modern American jazz.

The Blue Notes arrived in London in the mid-1960s, and immediately made an impact with their irrepressible energy and fearless assault on jazz borders at that time largely erected along the lines of bebop. Pukwana, an altoist influenced by both JOHNNY HODGES and ORNETTE COLEMAN, exhibited a conversational spontaneity that recalled much earlier jazz, and pianist McGregor was inspired by both CECIL TAYLOR and DUKE ELLINGTON. These creative opposites most resoundingly combined in 1970, when McGregor formed the Brotherhood of Breath big band, a thrilling mixture of Ellingtonesque luxuriance and African townships dance.

All the Blue Notes except the great drummer Louis Moholo died young, but they influenced not only the generation of British jazz performers who worked with them, but younger players.

★*Spirits Rejoice* (Ogun OGCD101)

The Dedication Orchestra echoes the exciting blend of Duke Ellington, townships' jive and free-jazz that was pianist and composer Chris McGregor's Brotherhood of Breath ensemble. But the updated version features younger stars of the British scene, including pianist DJANGO BATES and trumpeters Claude Deppa and Guy Barker as well as those who came up on the London scene alongside the original South Africans, such as saxophonists EVAN PARKER and Alan Skidmore, pianist KEITH TIPPETT and trumpeter HARRY BECKETT. Parker is irresistible in a gruff but warmer and less dissonant guise, altoist Elton Dean is passionately lyrical and the last surviving Blue Note, drummer Louis Moholo, cracks his customarily imperious whip.

★*Ixesha* (2 CDs Ogun OGCE 102/103)

'A living volcano, and right inside such pretty tunes – a rhythmic urgency not just dancing in your head, but rocking your socks off,' writes singer Robert Wyatt in the notes to this follow-up double disc. Raw and loose once again, but immediate as ever – with the repertoire including the late Dudu Pukwana's joyous, churning 'Mra', the laid-back swing of 'Angel-Nomali', the roaring bop of 'Bird Lives', and the osmotic shift from writhing free playing to a street march on 'Wish You Sunshine'. Louis Moholo is a powerhouse on drums throughout.

DeJohnette, Jack

(Born Chicago, August 9, 1942)
A one-time pianist turned drummer, Jack DeJohnette has become a highly sought-after musician, with a direct, insistent style and

boundless energy in accompaniment, as well as a sensitivity to his partners that endeared him to a succession of celebrated leaders: Charles Lloyd, Bill Evans, Stan Getz, and eventually MILES DAVIS. Davis and DeJohnette worked together during the most dynamic period of the trumpeter's patchy relationship with jazz-rock fusion and the new drummer's crackling accents (as emphatic as a ringmaster's whip), furious one-footed rolls on the bass drum and boiling cymbal work were a crucial contribution to sidestepping the rhythmic predictability of so much fusion music.

DeJohnette studied classical music initially, which established his piano technique, and attended the American Conservatory of Music in Chicago where he began playing drums. He moved to New York in the mid-1960s, joined organist John Patton, then altoist Jackie McLean, and singer BETTY CARTER. But it was DeJohnette's membership of saxophonist Charles Lloyd's group that established his reputation.

In more recent times DeJohnette has pursued a creative duo partnership with the English multi-instrumentalist JOHN SURMAN, with whom he made an excellent all-electronics album *The Amazing Adventures of Simon Simon* for ECM in 1984. He also created an inventive multi-idiomatic outfit called Special Edition, the vehicle for a string of successful albums for ECM. Latterly DeJohnette has continued to distinguish himself as a straight jazz time-player mixing uncanny empathy with propulsive force, notably in Keith Jarrett's Standards Trio.

★*Special Edition* (ECM 1152)

DeJohnette's debut with the Special Edition band in 1979; the searing Arthur Blythe on alto, and the equally heated DAVID MURRAY on tenor. A triumph, thanks to DeJohnette's ability to create a context for his musicians through engineering the unexpected both in his arrangements and from his percussion. Blythe and Murray struck sparks, and the session wound up as one of DeJohnette's finest.

★*Music for the Fifth World* (EMI/Manhattan CDP 0777 7
99089-2 9)

Plenty of electric guitar (JOHN SCOFIELD), choir-like vocals, keyboards and synthesisers. Its 'world-music' repertoire is truly
global – African and aboriginal music, rock, reggae and blues. It
opens with a typical DeJohnette drum avalanche on 'Fifth World
Anthem', then into an African chant, a powerful Miles Davis
tribute using part of a theme from 'In a Silent Way', a reggae-
flavoured vocal blues about media manipulation ('Deception
Blues') and a mesmeric investigation of overlapping patterns from
keyboards, drums and bass on 'Aboriginal Dream Time'.

★*Tin Can Alley* (ECM 1189 517 754-2)

A fusion classic rightly reissued. 'Tin Can Alley' was a Special
Edition record from 1980, featuring CHICO FREEMAN and John
Purcell on reeds, and Peter Warren on bass, and it's one of
DeJohnette's most progressive and exciting, Ellington-like ensem-
ble sounds. Free-jazz boldness, funk and imaginative drum
improvisation have rarely been more successfully combined.

Dennerlein, Barbara

(Born Munich, 1964)
In the 1960s, accompanying the enthusiasm for strongly soul- and
blues-flavoured small-group jazz, the Hammond organ enjoyed a
boom in the hands of Jack Macduff, Jimmy Smith, Wild Bill Davis
and others. One of the most sophisticated contemporary practitioners of this earthy music-making is the young German
organist Barbara Dennerlein. Not only is she a vigorous exponent
of organ blues, she is also a writer of attractive compositions that
use funky elements but complicate the melodic materials.

Dennerlein was given her first organ when she was 11, and two
years later she was playing in public, appearing at the Munich Jazz
Festival when she was 15. She has accompanied many visiting
stars in Germany and played with Jimmy Smith when he toured
that country. Dennerlein's albums have been prizewinners, and

she has appeared extensively at German festivals. She is certain to be a prominent figure in European music during the 1990s.

★*Hot Stuff* (Enja 6050-2)

A 1990 recording by a Dennerlein quartet, featuring Britain's ANDY SHEPPARD and Mark Mondesir on tenor and drums, with Mitch Watkins on guitar. The tunes are mostly originals and not all of them are memorable, but the rolling groove of the title track and the irresistible mid-tempo bluesy feel of 'Wow' which alternates a lazy, insinuating swing with hard-hit accents on top of the beat (Mark Mondesir crackles compellingly throughout the disc) are delightful.

Freeman, Earl 'Chico' Jr

(Born Chicago, July 17, 1949)
Chico Freeman is the son of one of the world's great underrated saxophone eccentrics, Von Freeman. Like most modern Chicago musicians, Freeman Jr was influenced by the town's composer/ pianist MUHAL RICHARD ABRAMS, and also by offbeat bandleader Sun Ra. From the mid-1970s he began working in New York, though by reputation he was still associated with the avant-garde, and in particular the methods of John Coltrane. Freeman has worked with the brilliant drummer Elvin Jones, and led many bands of his own, but a sustained independence, worthy of his skills, still just eludes him.

★*Freeman and Freeman* (India Navigation IN 1070)

Freeman Jr and Sr in partnership, with a fine group including Muhal Richard Abrams and the driving drumming of JACK DEJOHNETTE. As well as a good opportunity to hear just how different the two front-line performers are, a standards-based repertoire inspires some of their finest commitments to disc.

Frisell, William Richard 'Bill'

(Born Baltimore, Maryland, March 18, 1951)

Bill Frisell's reputation for playing the guitar for everybody from PAUL BLEY to Marianne Faithfull, his spectacular thrash-meets-bop concerts with the energetic New Yorker JOHN ZORN, and record company promises of 'a radical guitar hero for the 1990s' have all helped build what is now a substantial reputation. And inasmuch as Frisell's remarkable sound is not classifiable with that of any current mainstream guitarist in pop or jazz, he deserves his reputation for radicalism – he has the softness of a cerebral mainstream player such as Jim Hall, but couples it with the fire of Jimi Hendrix at times. The material can be a patchwork of doctored country intros, lopsided blues, 1950s rock and film music.

Frisell was a reed player originally, but took up guitar and had private lessons with Jim Hall. By the time he graduated from Berklee Jazz School he was an award-winning player, and the presence of composer Mike Gibbs on the Berklee staff ignited Frisell's recording career. He worked with Europeans EBERHARD WEBER and JAN GARBAREK, and very fruitfully with the ground-breaking ex-Bill Evans drummer PAUL MOTIAN.

Rambler (ECM 1287)

Frisell in 1984 with Paul Motian, British-based trumpeter KEN WHEELER and others. Frisell's various influences, curiously inter-woven, are more clearly audible here than in later recordings, and this was the session that secured his status as a guitar revolution-ary – the level of organisation is high, but so are the leader's improvisational skills.

Lookout for Hope (ECM 1351)

Two years later, and the impact of Zorn and his cohorts is obvious, not least through the presence of Zorn sidemen Joey Baron (drums) and Kermit Driscoll (bass). The music has moved away from the faintly wistful abstractions of earlier work to a more bitingly sardonic flavour, indebted to Zorn's incorporation of elements of postwar popular culture into his music. There is, therefore, a raucous and nervy account of 'Hard Plains Drifter' with Frisell's warped country sound stitching it all together.

Ganelin Trio

Ganelin, Vyacheslav (born Kraskov, former USSR, 1944)
Chekasin, Vladimir (born Sverdlovsk, former USSR, 1947)
Tarasov, Vladimir (born Archangelsk, former USSR, 1947)
The band that first woke up the west to a dynamic contemporary jazz scene operating in pre-glasnost Russia. The Ganelin Trio consists of three classically trained musicians who developed a part-free, part-composed music out of a combination of the influences of western records (notably Cecil Taylor, Ornette Coleman, John Coltrane) and their own experiences as film-music writers, orchestral players and teachers. When the trio performed at the 1980 Berlin Jazz Festival they astonished many of their listeners with their forceful independence, and the German critic Joachim Berendt, in an influential quote, called it 'the wildest and yet the best organised and most professional free jazz I've heard in years'. The state label Melodiya slowly began to release Ganelin records, and with the thawing of the political atmosphere, the band began to tour abroad – including Britain and the USA.

Leader Vyacheslav Ganelin is a graduate of the Vilnius Conservatory, a writer of operas and film scores. Vladimir Chekasin, an improviser who at times recalls both Rahsaan Roland Kirk and Albert Ayler, began as a violinist, moved to saxophone at 18, and has latterly been both a teacher and the director of a conservatory orchestra. Vladimir Tarasov is also the drummer with the Lithuanian State Symphony Orchestra.

The Ganelin Trio was a composer's band, however explosive and reflexive its performances seemed. Their shows involved parodies of programme music, early jazz forms, children's songs, and their underground status endured into more open times.

Non Troppo (hat Art CD 6059)

The piece performed by the Ganelin trio on their debut appearance in London in 1984, a chilly, wintry episode made all the more haunting and baleful by Vladimir Tarasov's static conception of percussion, but which refers to a conventional jazz theme, 'Too Close for Comfort'. The song, however, is used only as a motif, and not structurally. Ganelin himself is a mixture of influences that could only have come together in the unique circumstances of pre-Gorbachev Russia, sometimes sounding as if George Shearing and Cecil Taylor are fighting for dominance.

★*The Eighties Document: New Music From Russia* (Leo Records 801/8)

The Ganelin Trio feature – separately and together – on the final disc of this massive collection of improvised and abstract Russian music of the 1980s. The trio performance is a feverish, sometimes crabbily swinging, sometimes lyrical, sometimes outlandish version of 'Old Wine, New Bottles', recorded on their tour of Britain in 1984. The other discs include vocalist Valentina Ponomareva, Russia's equivalent of Cecil Taylor in pianist Sergei Kuryokhin, and many others. It's costly, the sleeve notes need a microscope, and for those unfamiliar with free-music some of it sounds dolorous and tentative. But Russian improvisation has become a powerful force in developing jazz, and these are the musicians at work on it.

Garbarek, Jan

(Born Norway, March 4, 1947)

The Norwegian saxophonist Jan Garbarek is a unique performer of a mix of bleak north European romanticism and the poignant and sometimes desolate sound of John Coltrane. But for all his initial inspiration from Coltrane, Garbarek is one of Europe's few undisputed jazz originals, once described by the eminent American orchestra leader George Russell as 'just about the most uniquely talented jazz musician Europe has produced since Django Reinhardt'.

Garbarek took up the saxophone at 14, after hearing Coltrane on the radio, but knowing nothing of jazz. Now he is internationally known in jazz, has worked with its leading artists (notably KEITH JARRETT), and is a celebrity in his native country. Absorbing the Afro-American line of jazz into a music strongly suggestive of northern Europe, Garbarek has composed and improvised using materials intimately meaningful to him, setting the works of poet Tomas Transtromer to music, composing for Norwegian productions of *Brand* and *Peer Gynt*. But Garbarek's ear for musical material doesn't extend only as far as the cattle-calls of Norway – it includes also the incantatory music of Bali, or native Indian music of North America. Garbarek has also recorded and performed with Indian fusion violinist L. Shankar, on the 1984 album *Song for Everyone*. In recent times his bands, with local folk singers and the ex-MILES DAVIS percussionist MARILYN MAZUR, have taken on a new vigour and urgency.

★*Works* (ECM 823266)

A wide range of Garbarek's atmospheric exploits, dating from the beginning of his recording career with ECM in 1970. The saxophonist's involvement with the more urgent side of his Afro-American inspirations is audible in his vocalised sound and busier delivery on 'Beast of Kammodo', the delicate upper reaches of his tenor sound are haunting on 'SkrikHyl', as is his use of space on 'Passing'. Garbarek also displays his interests in eastern music in the Indian flavour of 'Saije'.

★*Wayfarer* (ECM 1259)

One of the most distinguished of all Garbarek groups in rather more animated action in 1982 with BILL FRISELL on guitar, EBERHARD WEBER on bass and Michael Di Pasqua on drums. The presence of Frisell has an interesting textural impact on a Garbarek group, preserving the contemplative atmosphere here, but purging it of its frequently fey quality.

★*Madar* (ECM 1515)

Quite a pushy and animated set for the sometimes becalmed Garbarek, and in interesting company, with Anouar Brehem's guitar-like oud and Ustad Shaukat Hussain's tabla – both of them pushing at Garbarek with contrasting lines and rhythmic challenges, whilst the Norwegian hits back with timbres closer to his distant African-American origins. The tabla playing is very varied and expressive, and it's a jazz world-music triumph.

Officium (ECM New Series 1525 445 369-2)

Almost *the* jazz news story of 1994. This set is a collaboration between Garbarek and the British early-music Hilliard vocal ensemble, who have recorded Tallis and Perotin, as well as Arvo Part and Gavin Bryars for ECM. The disc features fifteen pieces from the early Gregorian repertory up to sixteenth century polyphony, and the moonlit flicker of Garbarek's soprano sound against the sibilance of the voices, or the urgency of his tenor welling up above the ensemble, make this sound an ideal venture for him. The most effective vehicles are the polyphonic pieces, which enable him to improvise within the ensemble rather than comment on its statements; the least effective are the folk-songs that corral him with their beat. Guillaume Dufay's 'Ave Maris Stella', the soprano drifting like smoke among the harmonies, is quite magnificent.

Gibbs, Michael Clement Irving 'Mike'

(Born Harare, Zimbabwe (then Salisbury, Rhodesia), September 25, 1937)

Michael Gibbs' background, education and subsequent career touched too many places to make it useful to pigeonhole him with citizenship. He grew up in pre-independence Zimbabwe (then Rhodesia), studied in the USA, flourished as a composer in Britain, then returned to America. But wherever he belongs, Gibbs is a composer and arranger to rival CARLA BLEY, and even the late Gil Evans, in glowing sonority, open-mindedness, and power to surprise with a thematic ambiguity rare in jazz. Gibbs' writing, for brass particularly, is an ever-recognisable rising fanfare, his melodies brooding or jubilant, his materials most explicitly drawn from Gil Evans, Olivier Messiaen and MILES DAVIS.

Gibbs learned piano from the age of seven, then the trombone as a teenager; he went to Berklee in 1959, then to the Lenox School where he studied with Gunther Schuller and GEORGE RUSSELL. Berklee was Gibbs' link with the vibraharpist GARY

BURTON, and the two began a musical association that lasted many years. Gibbs also continued his studies, exploring classical composition with teachers such as Aaron Copland, Iannis Xenakis and Lukas Foss. From 1965 he worked in London and formed a big band to flesh out the songs he had written for both Gary Burton and Stan Getz.

Gibbs went back to the States in 1974 as Composer in Residence at Berklee. In the 1980s he began working exclusively as a freelance, operating in America and Europe with artists including Peter Gabriel, Joni Mitchell, Carla Bley, MIKE MANTLER and John Dankworth, also orchestrating a film score by PAT METHENY, a guitar concerto by JOHN McLAUGHLIN and a number of ballet scores of his own. Gibbs' early recordings are probably too little known for CD release, but his first Decca/Deram album, *Michael Gibbs*, deserves to be, despite a few moments of unconvincing ensemble playing.

★*Big Music* (Venture CDVE 27)

Mike Gibbs' first album as a leader in over a decade, but still revealing the alertness to the contemporary scene that first marked him out as a composer. Miles Davis and Gil Evans influences are strong, there is excellent guitar work from a trio of JOHN SCOFIELD, BILL FRISELL and Kevin Eubanks, and the integration of soloists with texture is more successful than on any Gibbs album apart from the unavailable *In the Public Interest*.

★*By The Way* (Ah Um 016)

A reprise of some of Gibbs' most successful pieces, including 'To Lady Mac', 'Something Similar', and the fanfare 'Just A Head', all first heard on long-unavailable records. There are some awesome improvisors on it, including KENNY WHEELER, JOHN TAYLOR, CHARLIE MARIANO, Steve Swallow and EVAN PARKER, with Parker firing his atonalisms past the peals of 'Just A Head'. The soloing and the ensembles don't quite grow out of each other as used to occur in the bands of Gibbs' hero Gil Evans, but these themes represent some of the most exciting scoring for a British jazz orchestra before the coming of Loose Tubes.

Gismonti, Egberto

(Born Carrio, Rio de Janeiro, December 5, 1947)

A virtuoso exponent of many musics including jazz, Brazilian and African. Gismonti now belongs firmly in the wider 'world-music' frame, though he often performs at jazz festivals and has worked with two of the most inventive of contemporary jazz artists in bassist CHARLIE HADEN and saxophonist JAN GARBAREK. Gismonti's resources as a musician have been extended by his experimentation with an eight-string guitar and alternative tunings.

Originally a classical student, Gismonti studied in Paris with Nadia Boulanger, worked in Brazil as a freelance arranger, and then developed an interest in a form of funky Brazilian pop (*choro*) followed by investigation of jazz and rock guitar through the inspirations of Jimi Hendrix, Wes Montgomery and JOHN McLAUGHLIN. Gismonti spent a period in the Amazon jungle working with Indian musicians to gather material for his first ECM album, *Danca Das Cabecas*. He continues to tour extensively, and has composed and performed the music for several films.

Duas Vozes (ECM 823640)

A brilliantly inventive duo session between Gismonti, on both guitars and piano, and the percussionist NANA VASCONCELOS. In fusing Brazilian percussion effects (Vasconcelos can produce an entire rainforest of background noises on his own) with jazz piano on 'O Dia, A Noite' and jazz/flamenco on 'Dancando', Gismonti effected a fusion that cheapened none of the ingredients. The session is emotive and emotional without cloying exotica on the Amazon Indian song 'Tamarepeba', delicate overdubbing of voices and percussion still sustaining the disc's lyrical simplicity.

Grolnick, Don

(Born Long Island, 1947)

You can trawl a lot of jazz reference books without finding Don Grolnick's name – which, considering he's in his late forties now and has been respected for a couple of decades by some of the leading figures in the music, is an interesting omission at the least.

Grolnick isn't in the books because he has spent much of his life as a studio arranger for the likes of Bonnie Raitt, James Brown and Steely Dan's Fagin and Becker, and has hardly recorded on his own account. But treating jazz – for which he appears to have had a startling natural facility since his teens – as a hobby hasn't cramped either his improvising flair as a pianist or his ingenuity as a composer.

★Nighttown (Blue Note CDP 0777 7 98689 2 6)

Both as a fine bop pianist and as an ingenious composer of themes that sit somewhere between TV cop show atmospherics and a lissome and witty jazz with allegiances to the mid-'60s Miles Davis band, CARLA BLEY, Bill Evans and Charles Mingus, Grolnick is a late-flowering star. The harmonic movement across the instrumentation in his bands have a laconic drive that marks him out, and he's capable of sounding convincing and convinced with anything from a meticulous chamber jazz to Latin blues. Soloists including JOE LOVANO, Randy Brecker, STEVE TURRE and DAVID HOLLAND don't do any harm either.

Gurtu, Trilok

(Born Bombay, India, October 30, 1951)

Trilok Gurtu is a remarkable blend of the methods of Indian classical percussion and the polyrhythmic jazz playing of Elvin Jones, as captivating to watch as he is to listen to, seated at a hybrid kit of Western trap-drums and tablas whilst kneeling on a rug, his sound by turns evocative of wildlife at night, waterfalls, firework parties. But for all his textural ingenuity, Gurtu can put a driving swing behind a blues as forcefully as any drummer down a straighter line of the African-American tradition.

Born in a musical family, Gurtu studied classical tabla – accompanying his mother and siblings at home from the age of six – and taught himself jazz in his teens, leading a percussion group in 1965 influenced by MILES DAVIS and JOHN COLTRANE. Gurtu visited Italy with an Indian fusion band in 1973, staying for two years, and then visiting the States to perform with a variety of the more broadminded of jazz musicians including Charlie Mariano and

Don Cherry, Karl Berger and Archie Shepp. Gurtu replaced the late Collin Wallcott in the folk-jazz group Oregon, and has latterly worked extensively with the guitarist John McLaughlin.

*Living Magic (CMP CD 50)

A fast-moving, garrulous record featuring Gurtu's astonishing percussion virtuosity and JAN GARBAREK's lonely saxophone largely as a special effect. But however withdrawn Garbarek tries to be, Gurtu's gargling drum sounds and bustling cymbals push him outwards. This is an extraordinary display of percussion skills (the echoing steel-drum sounds against handclaps and monsoon-like cymbals on 'Transition' is a good example) and of open-mindedness, since the influences are Indian music, NANA VASCONCELOS's Brazilian ruralisms and an offbeat version of rap.

*Crazy Saints (CMP CD 66)

A world-music odyssey, featuring Gurtu alongside his classical-singer mother Shoba, and with compositions by Joe Zawinul and PAT METHENY. There's a lot of rapid-fire improvising conversation drawn as much from Indian music as jazz, but the most successful parts of a generally adventurous and creatively eclectic album are Gurtu's duets with Zawinul's keyboards, percussion rain landing in rich harmonic pools.

Guy, Barry John

(Born London, April 22, 1947)
British bassist Barry Guy has, from his early twenties, been as accustomed to performing the works of Xenakis or Berio (or even early English music) in chamber orchestras as he has jazz-derived free-music and contemporary composer Pierre Boulez has written specifically for him. He worked with the leading players on London's 1960s avant-garde, including drummer John Stevens and saxophonist Trevor Watts in the Spontaneous Music Ensemble. But as the 1970s dawned, Guy was moving away even from a form of free-music driven by jazz. His composition studies at the Guildhall School convinced him that some of the raw materials of

contemporary straight composers could be effectively extended by jazz improvisers. He also emerged as one of the country's great bass virtuosi in any idiom.

In 1970 Guy formed the 21-piece Jazz Composers' Orchestra. He regards the current period as the 'third phase' of the orchestra's life, moving from the initial point of complex and highly detailed ensemble writing (increasingly involving non-improvising players), through a stage of restoration of responsibilities to the interpreting musicians, and back again to firmer direction from Guy himself, though with the addition of distinctly jazz-based horn-players in Simon Picard, Paul Dunmall and Pete McPhail. The Zurich-based Intakt record label has helped the orchestra considerably, and put out a double album of some concert work in Switzerland in 1988.

★*Harmos* (Intakt Records CD 013)

The London Jazz Composers' Orchestra's second venture for Intakt, revealing Guy's 'third phase' in a tighter dependence on organisation, and structural methods raising the profile of exuberant jazz elements against the more preoccupied conservatoire experimentalism the band has exhibited in the past. More harmonically elegant and resolved than the earlier *Polyhymnia*, as if the improvisers and the writer have collaborated to beat a fiery, white-hot metal into a sculpture of poise and resolution.

★*Double Trouble* (Intakt CD 019)

Originally a double concerto for two of the most formidable pianists of the European avant-garde, Briton Howard Riley and German Alex Schlippenbach. Riley carries the piano role himself here, with a blazing solo early in this 50-minute piece, setting the pace for a variety of solos and sub-groupings pulled together by all 17 members supplying ensemble parts that superficially sound like free squalls but have been written by Guy to the last detail. Rugged, dissonant, demanding and adventurous orchestral music, within which a ferocious improvising trio (saxophonist EVAN PARKER, drummer Paul Lytton and Guy himself) reveals how powerful the momentum of the 1970s-derived European free-scene still is.

★*Arcus* (Maya MCD 9101)

Free-improvised duos recorded without production frills in a French church, with Guy and the equally remarkable Barre Phillips. Guy is fiercer, but 74 minutes of intense spontaneous interplay shift between the gracefully abstract on 'Prophesies' and something not unlike a percussive swing on 'Sundance'. Two bass masters at work.

★*Theoria* (Intakt CD 024)

The London Jazz Composers' Orchestra in a concerto featuring the great Swiss avant-garde piano virtuoso Irene Schweizer. *Theoria* is one of Barry Guy's most exciting pieces, mingling orthodox jazz (much of it furnished by Henry Lowther's graceful trumpet) and acerbic dissonance. Schweizer's palette of fast arpeggios, Cecil Taylorish ferocity and drumlike sounds mingle with Paul Dunmall's guttural, Pharoah Sanders-like howls, or Evan Parker's high, circular-breathing soprano harmonics enhanced by Schweizer's sustained high trill. The orchestral figures can sometimes be a little bludgeoning, and it won't convert Buddy Rich fans, but it's truly contemporary music.

Haden, Charles Edward

(Born Shenandoah, Iowa, August 6, 1937)
One of the indisputably great bassists of the jazz of the past three decades. Haden emerged in association with the revolutionary saxophonist Ornette Coleman, and learned through Coleman's music to unfold counter-melodies related to the pulse of the piece, but without dependence on a progression of chords.

As a boy, Charlie Haden sang on his parents' radio show, but he began working with west coast jazz musicians in the 1950s, playing with Art Pepper, Elmo Hope and Hampton Hawes. He began performing with the adventurous Canadian pianist PAUL BLEY in 1957, whose band first recorded Ornette Coleman. In the 1960s, Haden was associated with the New York Jazz Composers' Orchestra Association (which also included CARLA BLEY), and it was from the membership of this organisation, and in partnership with Carla Bley, that Haden put together his Liberation Music Orchestra, using the songs of the Spanish Civil War to reflect liberation movements of the 1960s. Thereafter Haden appeared with pianist Alice Coltrane, with KEITH JARRETT, and later with the Old and New Dreams band, reviving the best compositions of Ornette Coleman. Haden resurrected the Liberation Music Orchestra in 1982, and has also lent his brooding, dramatic sound to the music of Europeans JAN GARBAREK and EGBERTO GISMONTI.

★*Liberation Music Orchestra* (MCAD 39125)

Heated, declamatory orchestral music, arranged by Carla Bley, and extensively using Republican songs of the Spanish Civil War, which the tenor saxophone of GATO BARBIERI perfectly complements in its searing intensity. Though this album was a critical hit when it emerged, and it contains one of Haden's most moving compositions in 'Song For Che', it hasn't worn as well as Haden's work with Ornette Coleman from the same period.

★*Ballad of the Fallen* (ECM 1248)

The Liberation Music Orchestra comeback of 1982. Though it was verbose and ill-controlled in live performance, the conciseness of the recording brought the best out of a more varied and idiosyncratic set of themes (Spanish Civil War again, plus pieces from Nicaragua and El Salvador) and Carla Bley's arrangements once more burst with life. DON CHERRY was present again, plus Dewey Redman on saxophones and the scorching Gary Valente on trombone.

★*Quartet West* (Verve 831 673-2)

Much more modest small-group jazz album dedicated to Haden's adopted Los Angeles, performing standards, two originals, and pieces by PAT METHENY and Ornette Coleman. A little low-key by comparison with Haden's more impassioned activities, but intelligent and subtle music, with a bass solo on the leader's dedication to his parents, 'Taney County', displaying his ability to make the bass sing with a mixture of rich tone-colour, time changes and storytelling skill.

Hancock, Herbert Jeffrey 'Herbie'

(Born Chicago, April 12, 1940)

Hancock, a MILES DAVIS sideman from 1963 to 1968, already had an illustrious career behind him before he joined the great trumpeter at 23. He had played Mozart's D Major piano concerto with the Chicago Symphony Orchestra at the age of 11, and became virtually house pianist of the Blue Note record label in the early 1960s, as well as writing a pop hit – 'Watermelon Man' – which has been recorded by more than 200 artists. Hancock's playing with the Davis group combined exactly the agility of bebop and the harmonic inventiveness that the trumpeter wanted for a band operating in a period in which hard bop and free-form were both pulling at the loyalties of jazz fans. As a pianist his touch was light and deft, his timing perfect, his themes mostly catchy enough to register after one hearing.

After leaving Davis, Hancock explored some of the atmospheric compositional territory he had investigated in the Blue Note days, then had considerable commercial success (notably with the funk band Headhunters, whose first album became the best-selling jazz record ever) followed by a return to the '63/'64 Davis group sound with the VSOP band in the 1970s.

Herbie Hancock now successfully operates in many fields: as a fusion artist, a devastating jazz piano improviser with a still-torrential stream of fresh ideas, and as a composer.

★*Takin Off* (Blue Note CDP 746506)

Hancock's impressive 1963 debut as leader, when he was only 23, heralded as one of the most mature beginnings to a recording career in all jazz. The album was a near-perfect blend of Hancock's clean, dancing piano sound, blend of funk and bop construction, classy pop-oriented composition and ideal assistance in the shape of Dexter Gordon on tenor and Freddie Hubbard on trumpet. It was also the debut of the funky 'Watermelon Man'.

★*Maiden Voyage* (Blue Note CDP 746339)

One of the most influential and compositionally sophisticated Hancock records, this time with sidemen who became the foundation of one of the best Miles Davis bands, notably Ron Carter on bass and TONY WILLIAMS on drums. The title track and 'Dolphin Dance' are among Hancock's most enduring originals.

Hargrove, Roy

(Born Chicago, 1971)
One of several very young performers to have hit the headlines in recent years, Hargrove is a trumpeter who is already finding his name mentioned in the same breath as an established 1980s hero such as WYNTON MARSALIS. Unlike many of the technocratic newcomers, however, Hargrove is interested in shape and design more than blazing virtuosity. Musically he is currently rooted in the neo-bop movement, a situation in which personal development is difficult.

Hargrove was only 16 when he won a prestigious music scholarship and, with the prize-money he was making from competition successes, he financed studies at Berklee. Hargrove was simultaneously appearing on stage with Marsalis, with resurrected west coast bop altoist Frank Morgan and with the dynamic ex-Blakey saxophonist BOBBY WATSON.

*_The Vibe_ (BMG PD 90668)

A big improvement over Hargrove's debut, if still a little like a sampler. It all hangs on Hargrove's relationship with the young altoist Antonio Hart, and blues and bop are its primary colours. The former quality gets the backup of David 'Fathead' Newman and the organist Brother Jack McDuff on a couple of tracks, aided by saxophonist BRANFORD MARSALIS. Hargrove puts a forthright, jostling edge on 'Milestones' and the rhythm section is terrific.

*_With The Tenors Of Our Time_ (Verve 523 019-2)

Twelve bebop vehicles and an excuse to let a glitzy group of tenorists loose on them, including Johnny Griffin, JOE HENDERSON, BRANFORD MARSALIS, JOSHUA REDMAN and Stanley Turrentine. But everybody sounds a bit subdued by being dropped into a situation in which they're supposed to blow the paint off, and Griffin is generally the most convincing on 'When We Were One' and the funky 'Greens At The Chicken Shack'. Joe Henderson sounds vague, but Joshua Redman grabs his two tracks and shakes them.

Harle, John

(Born Newcastle upon Tyne, England, September 20, 1956)
John Harle is a British classical saxophone player, but his inspirations and enthusiasms have so consistently been drawn from jazz that distinctions between styles become meaningless. Contemporary composers Luciano Berio, Harrison Birtwhistle and Dominic Muldowney have written pieces for Harle's unique saxophone sound, and his own repertoire can include Bartok, Satie, PAT METHENY and Duke Ellington.

A classical saxophonist by training, Harle's original inspirations were Duke Ellington's Johnny Hodges and a superb British classical clarinettist, Jack Brymer. The jazz influence on Harle helped rescue classical saxophone from the cloying tone it has frequently displayed, and his impact has been such that it's inconceivable that the instrument will continue to be taught in progressive conservatoires in the old way. But though he loves the spontaneity of jazz, Harle is very particular about the details of his work. He is also devoted to Duke Ellington for his refusal to be bound by the simple riff-forms and song structures previously central to jazz composition.

In the Shadow Of The Duke (EMI CDC 7 542 98-2)

John Harle plays Ellington's 'Caravan' with a jazz group, and over a fast four-four beat here, but he doesn't really sound like an orthodox jazz saxophonist. The solo is a yielding swirl of sound instead, distinctive in its own right. He also captures a luxurious, Ben Webster-like vibrato for the insinuating, suggestive 'The Mooche'. On this collection of familiar and less familiar works of Duke Ellington's, the saxophonist sheds a new light on jazz materials, and only Richard Rodney Bennett's soupy scoring for strings takes the softness of the method too far. The STAN TRACEY band puts back the muscle with the thumping version of 'In a Mellotone'.

Harper Brothers

Winard Harper (born 1962); Philip Harper (born 1965)

The Harper brothers have run their own band together since 1985, and are generally treated together in the current accolades greeting the new generation; *Time* magazine accorded them a prominent place in its autumn 1990 survey of 'The New Jazz Age'. But Winard – a drummer of precocious poise and sense of dynamics – had been seen on the circuit a good deal before the brothers worked together, notably in bands led by singer BETTY CARTER and tenorist Dexter Gordon. Trumpeter Philip has worked with jazz-blues organist Jimmy McGriff and with Art Blakey's Jazz Messengers. Both men have studied extensively with an older-generation altoist devoted to inspiring new talent – the great Jackie McLean.

★*Remembrance* (Verve 841723)

Partly aided by the encouragement of live performance, and partly by an unambiguous commitment to a feverish Blakeyesque manner almost all through, the Harper Brothers' second disc does get close, if not to eloquence, then certainly infectious enthusiasm. Eleven out of the 12 tunes were written either by members of the band or specifically for them (a bustling Clifford Brown tribute was contributed by Scotland's own Bobby Wellins), which helps the band establish both the idiomatic and dynamic resemblance to a Messengers approach it favours and yet sound as if it's doing much more than genuflecting.

Harrell, Tom

(Born Urbana, Illinois, June 16, 1946)

A considered and deliberate trumpeter in the Clifford Brown mould who has been working steadily and unobtrusively as an excellent sideman for two decades, Harrell has only recently emerged as a leader in his own right, and his pensive originality of phrasing has marked him out. Harrell first appeared as a member of the late Woody Herman's band, and subsequently worked with

Bill Evans, GEORGE RUSSELL, LEE KONITZ, Gerry Mulligan and through the 1980s as a member of altoist PHIL WOODS' group.

*Stories (Contemporary C14043)

Fine Harrell lyricism and good support from strong partners including saxophonist BOB BERG and guitarist JOHN SCOFIELD. One of Harrell's best discs, though still exuding a faintly unresolved quality, it nevertheless encourages fine contributions from the band, and highly original shaping of phrases from the leader.

Hemingway, Gerry

(Born Connecticut, March 23, 1955)
Hemingway's father had dreamed of being a composer (he studied with Hindemith) but was diverted by the family business. As a teenager, Gerry Hemingway listened to classical music and Jimi Hendrix and took up drums, but heard jazz at New York's Slug's club (Sun Ra and Weather Report among others) while at high school, and was transfixed by it. He advertised in *Rolling Stone* for a pianist, and found ANTHONY DAVIS, who opened him up to jazz history.

Hemingway enrolled at Berklee, but disliked the academic teaching of jazz, and quickly left. He formed a band with Anthony Davis, and through the 1970s unofficially attended Yale composition classes, studied drums with Dave Brubeck's Alan Dawson, and founded his own record label. The 1980s saw a downturn, and Hemingway moved away from jazz towards electronics and new percussion ideas. But in 1983 he joined ANTHONY BRAXTON and has since been able to draw together his many interests, both inside Braxton's band and outside it.

*Special Detail (hatART CD 6084)

Not merely a repetition of ANTHONY BRAXTON's ensemble methods, but a mixture of that crucial influence on Hemingway, with bluesy interchanges reminiscent of Charles Mingus, free-playing and some fine soloing against deep, complex harmonies. Wolter Wierbos on trombone and the excellent Don Byron on reeds are both full of ingenuity, but the standout is Ernst Reijseger on cello, a virtuoso of twisted lyricism, aggression, musical gags and openness to partners' ideas. Forward-looking music.

Hemphill, Julius Arthur

(Born Fort Worth, Texas, 1940)
Like ORNETTE COLEMAN, Julius Hemphill is a Fort Worth-born saxophonist steeped in the blues, who worked in pop music before becoming involved with free-jazz. Hemphill has often walked a line between experimentation and highly accessible music, but his surprisingly romantic and poignant saxophone sound has also been a long-time feature of one of the most respected of all-saxophone groups, the World Saxophone Quartet. Hemphill is also a subtle and original composer.

Hemphill was a clarinettist at first, then worked on the Texas rhythm and blues scene in the 1950s, at one time touring with Ike Turner's rock show. In 1968 he became a member of the Black Artists Group (BAG) in St Louis, and worked with Anthony Braxton in the next decade – in Chicago, and in Europe. Hemphill has often worked programmatically, devoting complex collages of music, dance and poetry to social and philosophical themes. He was a founder member of the World Saxophone Quartet in 1977.

Fat Man And The Hard Blues (Black Saint 1201152)

Sextet extension of Hemphill's work with the World Saxophone Quartet, featuring an all-reed lineup without a rhythm section. As with the WSQ, the personal metronomes of the members prevent drums and bass from being missed, and Hemphill's organisation of the resources imparts weight and luminescence to very subtle shifts of detail. Intriguing modern music.

Henderson, Joseph A. 'Joe'

(Born Lima, Ohio, April 24, 1937)
Henderson's stock has considerably risen in recent years. He is now almost universally held to be one of a handful of sax-

ophonists in jazz with a sound like a signature, and record company interest is leading to a succession of recording projects devoted to the work of great jazz creators.

Henderson first appeared in a 1962 band of trumpeter Kenny Dorham, following it with a stretch with Horace Silver, then co-leading the Jazz Communicators with Freddie Hubbard, joining HERBIE HANCOCK from 1969 to 1970 and working for four months with the r & b band Blood, Sweat and Tears. His Blue Note session-playing was usually powerful and concise (he appears on Lee Morgan's classic *Sidewinder* album among many others) but explorations of fusion in the 1970s didn't enhance Henderson's initially glowing reputation in the long run. His early and recent work with tight, boppish groups demonstrates that this is his ideal environment.

Henderson is fundamentally a bebopper, his playing extensively founded on Sonny Rollins and Coltrane, but he has absorbed all his influences and made their voices his own. He is also one of the few practitioners of his instrument to eschew high volume and high register as a means of conveying heightened intensity, preferring to maintain an even, hollow, faintly mournful tone, and develop his improvisations almost entirely by new melody. Usually happy with standard jazz forms, Henderson frequently unfolds his thoughts in a mixture of muttering double-time, oblique resolutions, and deft but minimal use of the modern saxophonist's favourite prop of fast repeated phrases to convey rhythmic momentum – and he can be devastating on a blues.

★*Our Thing* (Blue Note B21Y 84152)

An early Henderson collaboration with the erudite and unconventional pianist ANDREW HILL, with Kenny Dorham on trumpet. 'Pedro's Time', a compelling Latin groove, brings the best out of all the sidemen.

★*State of the Tenor – Live at the Village Vanguard* Vols. 1 & 2 (Blue Note CDP 746296/746426)

Ideal listening circumstances for Joe Henderson, in a trio with Ron Carter (bass) and Al Foster (drums), bristling with ideas on pieces mingling neo-bop, Latin music and abrasive reconstructions of soft-centre music such as 'All the Things You Are'.

★*Lush Life* (Verve 511 779-2)

The start of Henderson's projects devoted to jazz heroes, beginning with Billy Strayhorn. This disc won a Grammy, and put Henderson right on the map as the most likely inheritor to Sonny Rollins' mantle for originality, alertness, unconventionality of phrasing and avoidance of clichés. Henderson's tenor sounds like a flute on 'Isfahan', or a swing player on the hurtling 'Blood Count'. WYNTON MARSALIS puts in three tracks of refreshing trumpet bop into the bargain.

★*So Near So Far: Musings for Miles* (Verve 517 674-2)

Not quite as integrated as the Strayhorn disc, a little more straddled between Henderson's own preoccupations and a band that might have reflected MILES DAVIS' later interests, thus giving the fine guitarist JOHN SCOFIELD almost as much space, but slightly blurring the clarity. Not that this is a tribute to the material that the Davis band played after the 1960s – it revolves around older classics such as 'Miles Ahead', 'Flamenco Sketches' and a lesser-known forerunner of 'Milestones'.

★*The Blue Note Years* (Blue Note CDP 0777-7 89287 2 0)

The Blue Note years for Henderson are 1963 to 1967, much of it work on other people's sessions, like Kenny Dorham's 'Una Mas', Horace Silver's 'Song for My Father', episodes with Larry Young, McCoy Tyner and Lee Morgan, and his own 'Mode for Joe' and 'State of the Tenor' albums. Henderson has had his fallow periods, but this was where his present massive vocabulary came to maturity, and most of the great hard-boppers of the period are on this set too, if it needed extra marketing.

★*The Milestone Years* (Milestone 8MCD-4413-2)

The period that followed on Milestone is represented here in a massive eight-cd collection with all the informational trimmings.

Henderson still played a lot of hard bop in this era, but was taking in funk and free music too. There's the astonishing impromptu set with a furiously dedicated Japanese trio from the 1971 *In Japan* album (notably on the blistering 'Junk Blues') and a fine live exchange with the late trumpeter Woody Shaw, a man with much of Henderson's audacity of line and pacing.

Double Rainbow (Verve 527 222-2)

Henderson's 1995 tribute-project, this time to Brazilian 'jazz-samba' genius Antonio Carlos Jobim, who was scheduled to appear on it, but died before the sessions. It's really two records pretending to be one, half being for a Brazilian quintet including Eliane Elias on piano and former Jobim guitarist Oscar Castro-Neves, that gently grooves but allows Henderson to coast a little. But the second suite ('Joe/Jazz/Jobim') wakes up under the coaxing of Herbie Hancock and Jack DeJohnette, a display of effortless empathy and inventiveness. Henderson and Hancock's duet on the langourous 'Photograph' is wonderful.

Hill, Andrew

(Born Port Au Prince, Haiti, June 30, 1937)
Like Thelonious Monk, Andrew Hill has always remained in a piano school of his own. Like Monk, Hill has stripped down conventional jazz materials and explored rhythmic dislocations.

Hill was born in Haiti but raised in Chicago, working in blues bands and then with the leading Chicago musicians, including Von Freeman and Johnny Griffin. In the 1960s Hill – because of his obvious hard-bop leanings – became a regular figure on the Blue Note roster, extending that label's experimentalism as far as it went towards more unorthodox jazz, and seeming to establish a bridge between the eccentric accessibility of Monk and the storming spaceflights of Cecil Taylor. Latterly Hill has taught more than he has played in public.

★*Black Fire* (Blue Note BCT 84151)

Powerful 1963 debut for Hill, in a demanding trio format also featuring Richard Davis on bass and Roy Haynes on drums. *Black Fire* established the leader's inclination towards a rattling, percussive music full of sudden rhythmic zigzags and odd intervals – and also that his harmonic extension of regular jazz materials was as audacious and visionary for his generation as Monk's had been 20 years before.

★*Point of Departure* (Blue Note B11E 81467)

Hill's great early album, this time for a sextet including Kenny Dorham on trumpet, JOE HENDERSON and Eric Dolphy on reeds. Though Hill had not much explored a larger group format before, he revealed through this session one of the most valuable qualities in jazz: combining the unorthodox and the supportive in sufficient balance to awaken hidden powers in soloists.

★*Shades* (Soul Note 1113)

One of Hill's most impressive later records, a 1986 quartet session with the magisterial Clifford Jordan on tenor, Rufus Reid on bass and Ben Riley on drums. 'Monk's Glimpse' is a fascinating insight into the similarities and differences (the latter being principally measured in greater intensity and volubility) between Hill and his departed mentor.

Holland, David

(Born Wolverhampton, October 1, 1946)
Dave Holland is not only one of the world's leading bassists, but a musician for whom a dream came true. Originally a student at London's Guildhall whose clean articulation and unwavering, percussive beat quickly established him on the local jazz circuit of the 1960s (and whose free-ranging imagination established him with the London avant-garde as well), Holland was noticed at Ronnie Scott's in 1968 by MILES DAVIS and invited to the States. He worked on the powerful Davis fusion albums *In a Silent Way*, *Bitches*

Brew and *Filles de Kilimanjaro*, then left to join CHICK COREA's advanced acoustic trio. A variety of work with legendary jazz artists (among them Thelonious Monk) and with members of the avant-garde followed, including a productive partnership with saxophonist Sam Rivers on *Conference of the Birds*. Holland also recorded some devastating unaccompanied bass and cello improvisations on *Emerald Tears* and *Life Cycle*.

★*Jumpin' In* (ECM 1269)

The debut of the excellent free-bop ensembles that Dave Holland put on the road in the 1980s; this recording dates from 1983, and includes the British trumpeter KEN WHEELER, Julian Priester on trombone, Steve Coleman on alto and Kenny Washington on drums. Holland left a lot of space to his musicians, but his devotion to Mingus, both in the jostling bluesiness of the compositions and his own extraordinarily propulsive bass lines, is apparent.

★*Triplicate* (ECM 1373)

A trio set for Holland with JACK DEJOHNETTE on drums and Steve Coleman on saxophones, with the latter delivering his best-ever playing with the band. The detail in the music is enthralling, Coleman playing the concluding theme statement of Holland's 'Quiet Fire' as an ascending series of silvery breaths, accompanied by tiny pings from DeJohnette's kit and a final, gentle shower of cymbal sound.

Hussain, Zakir

(Born Bombay, March 9, 1951)
Zakir Hussain is an Indian tabla player who has effected some of the most creative and genuinely communicative links between Indian music and jazz. Like his fellow-countryman TRILOK GURTU, Hussain has worked with the expatriate British guitar virtuoso JOHN McLAUGHLIN.

Hussain was the student of the famous tabla player Alla Rakha, who not only played traditional Indian music but worked with Buddy Rich, Elvin Jones and Yusef Lateef, so the boy was familiar with jazz from his early years. He heard Charlie Parker when he was 12, and found it easy to assimilate jazz and Indian music side by side. Hussain recorded with pop-jazz saxophone star John Handy, with Ali Akbar Khan, and then became a member of John McLaughlin's Indo-jazz band Shakti in the mid-1970s.

★Making Music (ECM 831544)

One of the most successful albums of east-west collaboration, featuring Hussain on tabla with McLaughlin on acoustic guitar, flautist Hariprasad Chaurasia and Norwegian saxophonist JAN GARBAREK. Garbarek's ghostly tone and long, hooting lines blend atmospherically with the flute and the reserved sway of the rhythm, and McLaughlin cuts down on speed and the banter of exchanging phrases he sometimes goes in for, in favour of substantial support of the ensemble. Thoughtful, softly glowing world-jazz.

Ibrahim, Abdullah (Dollar Brand)

(Born Cape Town, South Africa, October 9, 1934)
With the trumpeter HUGH MASEKELA, Abdullah Ibrahim has become the most prominent exponent of South Africa's unique version of jazz music in the world. Originally recording as Dollar Brand, Ibrahim gained a devoted following for a music that was moving, dignified and exuberant, and he was equally acclaimed as a pianist (with some clear allegiances to Duke Ellington and Thelonious Monk) and as a composer of themes that frequently combine the edgy immediacy of jazz and the composure and unity of church music.

The latter, plus indigenous dance music were central to Ibrahim's culture as, in the 1940s, was American jazz – picked up over the radio, and on expensively imported records. Ibrahim's first professional jobs were in vocal groups performing American pop and spirituals, then in dance bands. But when he and Hugh Masekela formed the Jazz Epistles in 1960, which became the first black group to record an album in South Africa, Ibrahim's future was transformed. After the Sharpeville massacre, he left South Africa to work first in Europe and then in the States. His work so impressed Duke Ellington that Ellington arranged for him to record, and Ibrahim even took the piano chair with the Ellington band on tour. Influenced extensively by the free-scene of the 1960s, Ibrahim nevertheless reverted to more song-like, accessible music following his conversion to Islam in 1968.

★*African Piano* (Japo 60002)

One of the best early 1970s examples of Ibrahim as a solo pianist, full of resonating chordwork, evocative hymnal sounds, and constantly patient use of space.

★*The Mountain* (Kaz Records KAZ CD7)

Ibrahim with his fine small band, Ekaya, formed in 1983. The individuality of such instrumentalists as Carlos Ward (alto) and Ricky Ford (tenor) isn't cramped by Ibrahim's rich and distinctive settings, and the music (much of which was drawn from an earlier recording, *Water From an Ancient Well*) is powerful, emotional, and among the leader's best group work of recent times.

Jackson, Ronald Shannon

(Born Fort Worth, Texas, January 12, 1940)
Drummer Ronald Shannon Jackson spectacularly merges the density and polyrhythmic virtuosity of the post-1960s jazz drummers with a Texan feel for the blues, and has frequently worked with ORNETTE COLEMAN, a purveyor of much the same blend of earthiness and originality of form.

Jackson played professionally in Texas from his mid-teens, then worked with CHARLES MINGUS, BETTY CARTER, JACKIE McLEAN, McCOY TYNER and others in New York. But he moved towards free-jazz in 1966, working with ALBERT AYLER, then retiring for half of the 1970s to study and reorientate his music. When he returned it was to help Ornette Coleman develop his own ideas for a union of funk and free-jazz with Prime Time. Jackson's power and energy has also been the fuel for groups of his own extending the Prime Time thesis (Decoding Society) and for the volcanic free-funk ensemble Last Exit (see PETER BROTZMANN).

★*Taboo* (Virgin CDVE 47)

Disturbing but revealing and sometimes majestic mix of jazz, rock, electronics and open improvisation with a powerful horn section and a fascinating fluidity of movement between abstract noise, thrashing free-bop exchanges and big, churning contemporary big-band sounds. Jackson's drumming rumbles and thunders around it.

Jarreau, Al

(Born Milwaukee, March 12, 1940)

Jazz documentation rarely credits singer Al Jarreau with giving much back to jazz, which has formed the basis of his vocabulary and his immense vocal resources. But although his records don't always reflect it, Jarreau in live performance is a fascinating improvisor, threading into the expectations of commercial soul-funk shows an adventurousness that takes his variations to the borders of free-music. Jarreau's palette of sounds can take in mimicry of musical instruments from violins to Brazilian or African percussion, and a wide sweep of human vocal expressiveness as well, from the urbane to the maniacal – and his material frequently includes jazz standards.

In the 1960s Jarreau was an academic and a youth worker in San Francisco, but began a career in music after amateur successes in local clubs with a style indebted to the vocalese approach of Lambert, Hendricks and Ross. The predominance of fusion music and soul-inflected jazz in the 1970s led to a string of hit discs in the idiom, but Jarreau is a true improvisor, and still shows it.

★*Heaven and Earth* (East West Records)

Jarreau's talents are well represented on one of his most recent albums, displaying a return to his jazz inspirations by making a feature of the famous MILES DAVIS theme from 'Kind of Blue'. The singer delivers this haunting melody as a slow, high weave around the keyboards at first, and his delicacy and fluency of nuance are neatly captured by it. Jarreau's marketplace demands a great deal of easy fusion, but there's nothing easy about the options he takes as a vocalist.

Jarrett, Keith

(Born Allentown, Pennsylvania, May 8, 1945)
Pianist Keith Jarrett prefigured New Age romanticism and 1980s eclecticism by a decade and a half, and his European romantic leanings and adaptation of music other than jazz have brought him both rapturous audiences and some critical disapproval. But at its strongest Jarrett's music represents genuinely adventurous improvisation, vaulting over bar-lines and chorus patterns with a spontaneous symmetry that fitfully puts him in the league of jazz piano giants.

Jarrett was a child prodigy, taking up piano at three, giving lengthy solo recitals at seven, and touring as a child with a repertoire of his own pieces and classical standards. Jarrett studied in Paris with Nadia Boulanger, went to Berklee for a year, and then left to start his own band. In the late 1960s Jarrett played with Art Blakey's Jazz Messengers, then with saxophonist Charles Lloyd's popular early fusion quartet. When Jarrett left Lloyd he formed his own trio, operating at times in territory close to one of his principal influences, Bill Evans. But it was the association with MILES DAVIS in 1970–1 that lifted Jarrett's reputation. In the 1970s he was mainly associated with the German ECM label, virtually securing the company's financial future with the sales of one live recording in particular, the 1975 *Köln Concert*. Jarrett also successfully continued with small-group music in America.

To more traditional jazz listeners, some of Jarrett's most satisfying music has been delivered by his Standards Trio (with JACK DEJOHNETTE on drums and Gary Peacock on bass), a vehicle for classic materials of an older jazz repertoire, often operating very close to the sound of the Bill Evans trio.

★*Belonging* (ECM 1050)

One of Jarrett's finest recordings with his European quartet, of Jan Garbarek (reeds), Palle Danielsson (bass) and Jon Christensen (drums). Of the six Jarrett originals, two are ravishing ballads, the remainder display a more abandoned, rhythmically driving aspect of the leader that's engagingly reminiscent of his early and less self-preoccupied work. Garbarek, his tone austere and hypnotically tranquil, almost steals the show.

Köln Concert (ECM 1064/5)

A 1975 solo gig, and vintage Jarrett. From the opening dew-drop melody through the passages of roaring riffs and folksy, country-music jauntiness, Jarrett is one hundred per cent on the case, with the brake firmly applied to the sentimentality and archness he sometimes falls for.

The Survivor's Suite (ECM 1085)

The 'American band' (tenorist Dewey Redman, bassist CHARLIE HADEN, drummer PAUL MOTIAN) in 1976, on one of their best-ever recordings and before the steam ran out the following year. It's an integrated piece, but it never sounds as if the form is sitting on top of the contributors, who are all in spirited shape.

Standards Live (ECM 1317)

The Standards Trio of Jarrett, Jack DeJohnette and Gary Peacock in urgent mood on a 1985 live performance from Paris. Jarrett recovers his lightness and fluency on the standards material, not least because he's being propelled by two of the best rhythm-section players in jazz, and the band breezes gracefully through material including 'Stella by Starlight', 'Falling in Love with Love' and 'The Way You Look Tonight'.

At The Deer Head Inn (ECM 1531)

A 1992 return for Jarrett to the place where he played his first piano trio gigs, with Paul Motian – with whom Jarrett hadn't worked for sixteen years – substituting for JACK DEJOHNETTE on drums. It's almost all standards playing, but Jarrett is much less circumspect than he can sometimes be, and some of his improvisations with their impatient ascending key-changes are as good as anything in the Standards Trio library. 'Basin Street Blues' has a gospel air, 'You Don't Know What Love Is' borders on the Moorish, and 'You And The Night And The Music' and 'Bye Bye Blackbird' are typically unquenchable Jarrett odysseys. The recording picks up a bit too much of his vocal chattering to himself, the only snag.

Jordan, Sheila (Sheila Dawson)

(Born Detroit, November 18, 1929)
Sheila Jordan must be the most skilled and imaginative bebop vocalist never to have been seriously discovered until she was 34, and then remaining largely out of public view for most of the last 20 years. She was a student of music theory with the ascetic pianist Lennie Tristano in the 1940s, a devoted Charlie Parker enthusiast (she even formed a vocal trio to put lyrics to Parker tunes) and an associate of the revolutionary composer GEORGE RUSSELL. Out of this apprenticeship she has evolved an undemonstrative style without bravura, emotionalism or coyness, unsurprisingly (given the Tristano experience) reliant on cool and careful melodic improvisation, mostly in a kind of quiet mid-register yodel, very attentive to the meaning of lyrics and sometimes even spontaneously concocting new ones. She was mostly in obscurity, married to the bebop pianist Duke Jordan, during the 1950s, but was discovered by George Russell (recording a memorable version of 'You Are My Sunshine' with Russell's band), making her debut LP *Portrait of Sheila* for Blue Note in 1963.

★*Portrait of Sheila* (Blue Note CDP 789 002)

Sheila Jordan's best album of her earlier years, made in 1962 and featuring the singer with Barry Galbraith's guitar, Steve Swallow on bass and Denzil Best on drums. Jordan's instrumental technique as applied to the voice is much in evidence here, but she is never remote and always spontaneous, tender on 'If You Could See Me Now', abandoned on 'Let's Face the Music and Dance'.

★*Lost and Found* (Muse M5390)

All the subtleties, ironies and concentration of Sheila Jordan's memorable recent live performances are captured in this superb studio disc from 1990, featuring the singer with Kenny Barron on piano, Harvie Schwartz on bass and Ben Riley on drums. The material is ambitious and follows no rules except Jordan's own wayward, private meticulousness and melodic ingenuity.

★With Mark Murphy. *One For Junior* (Muse Records MCD 5489)

A bit whimsical and Greenwich Village-bohemian, but Jordan is paired here with a singer after her own heart on a collection of ballads and breezy bebop in the company of Kenny Barron on piano among others. Like a long-united couple, they mutter and banter their way through a tribute to Jordan's mentor Charlie Parker, and on a dense and pensive George Gruntz/Amina Baraka song 'Aria 18', they jointly fuel the atmosphere like one voice. A bit self-consciously Beat-Culture, but very classy jazz singing.

★*Heart Strings* (Muse MCD 5468)

Jordan has searched for material rarely unearthed here, including Loesser's 'Inch Worm' and 'Look For The Silver Lining', plus a typically shrewd and sometimes caustic 'Haunted Heart'. There are fitful contributions from a string quartet, but the most effective collaborations are between Jordan and the great drummer Marvin 'Smitty' Smith.

Joseph, Julian

(Born London, 1965)
Britain has produced many fine jazz pianists over the decades – George Shearing, Victor Feldman, STAN TRACEY, GORDON BECK, Mike Pyne and JOHN TAYLOR are just a handful – and Julian Joseph is the latest of the line. He can play with the heat of McCOY TYNER, but also with a subtlety and swing echoing HERBIE HANCOCK, one of his first and most enduring heroes.

Jazz got under his skin at 12, and he won a grant for private jazz lessons, and later a scholarship to the Berklee Jazz School in Boston. He met the Marsalis brothers through this connection, joined saxophonist BRANFORD MARSALIS' band and toured widely with it. But his roots have remained in London, and he performs with an excellent quartet.

★*The Language of Truth* (East West 90317 51222)

A guided tour to Joseph's interests, but rarely far from the Herbie Hancock/WAYNE SHORTER piano/saxophone combination of the mid-1960s. The band is excellent, with Alec Dankworth on bass, JEAN TOUSSAINT on saxophones and a whirlwind drummer, Mark Mondesir. Jean Toussaint's horn lines wriggle engagingly over Joseph's always probing accompaniment. There are some soul vocals as well, to leaven the mix for new fans.

King, Peter John

(Born Surrey, August 11, 1940)

Peter King appeared at the end of the 1950s as a Charlie Parker disciple who nevertheless delivered his accolades with a swing and sureness of phrasing rare for non-American jazz players at the time. Age has certainly not withered King, who in recent times – partly through adding some of Coltrane's innovations to Parker's – has improved on even his own impressive record, his phrasing on the fastest themes still sounding like the best of a number of competing options all racing neck-and-neck in his brain.

King's first major appearance was at the opening of Ronnie Scott's Gerrard Street club in 1959. The assurance of his performances quickly marked him out, and he began to find work with prestigious bands, including JOHN DANKWORTH's, Maynard Ferguson's, and Tubby Hayes'. Through the 1960s and 1970s Parkerish bebop was his forte, and he appeared in such contexts with innumerable British bands and in the company of visiting Americans such as Zoot Sims and Hampton Hawes, as well as joining the Ray Charles Orchestra for a European tour.

★*Brother Bernard* (Miles Music MM CD076)

An augmented version of the 1989 LP, four new tracks including a dazzling unaccompanied version of Jerome Kern's 'Yesterdays'. Other high spots are the racing bossa nova version of Stevie Wonder's 'Overjoyed', and an eloquent and intricate account of 'But Beautiful', an overplayed song that it takes a resourceful improvisor to genuinely enhance. Tenorist Alan Skidmore is as combative and bustling as ever on the finale.

Knitting Factory

Despite the 1980s revivals of older jazz forms, some musicians have continued to swim against the tide, developing unusual compositional methods, using unfamiliar instrumentation, seeking untried settings for improvisation. A highly successful home for such activities has been the Knitting Factory at 47 East Houston Street in New York's Greenwich Village. The Knitting Factory has been run by an enterprising promoter, Michael Dorf, and it has played host to a variety of (mostly younger) musicians from avant-garde jazz, experimental rock and pop, and straight music.

★*Live at the Knitting Factory* Vols. 1 & 2 (Enemy EMCD 111/112)

Eclectic blend of experimenters and oddballs including the Jazz Passengers, a septet mixing scrambling violin passages, fitful stretches of breezy jazz time and bricks-through-windows electric guitar eruptions; violin-led trios that play as lyrically as if they were trying to sell Elgar to East Side street-gangs; soloists who improvise on Albert Ayler tunes country-style on a steel guitar; plus electronics, banshee chanteuses and much more. The second volume, featuring the jagged sound of guitarist Sonny Sharrock and the inventive British expat Fred Frith, is more abstract but more dramatic than the first.

Konitz, Lee

(Born Chicago, October 13, 1927)
Lee Konitz is the best-known of those white jazz musicians to emerge concurrently with the rise of bebop in the 1940s, but whose version of it was dominated by the influence of the pianist, teacher and rigorous theoretician Lennie Tristano rather than by Charlie Parker. Tristano was a fellow-Chicagoan whose impatience with what seemed to him the irrational pursuit of basing a melodically and rhythmically sophisticated improvised music on the materials of Tin Pan Alley standards led him to develop a linear, low-volume, dynamically narrow but melodically complex music without the bluesy emotionalism of orthodox bop.

Konitz began working around Chicago in the mid-1940s, joined the superior dance band led by Claude Thornhill, and performed on the plush, sumptuously orchestrated *Birth of the Cool* recordings, a sound significantly influenced by Thornhill's ensembles. Konitz' ethereal sound inevitably became more muscular after a stint with the Stan Kenton Orchestra in the early 1950s, and some of his records with Gerry Mulligan, and another brilliant Tristanoite saxophonist, Warne Marsh, deservedly became classics.

Latterly, Konitz' preoccupation with strictly musical values has been reflected in the tough improvising situations he has put himself into. But a Konitz solo always displays its originator's inimitable trademarks – fast, whirling runs descending into breathy low sounds, flute-like slow ascents vibrating with puffs of air, long notes plumbing the depths of the silence around them.

*_Motion_ (Verve 821 553-2)

Konitz is often thought of as a player of intellectualised refinement, but this 1961 session pitches him against a musician of very different inclinations – the tumultuous drummer Elvin Jones, who stings the saxophonist into performances of both grace and intensity on a selection of standards including 'All of Me', 'You'd Be So Nice To Come Home To' and 'I Remember April'. Konitz' forthrightness on 'Foolin' Myself' reveals how far the saxophonist had come from the shy sound of the *Birth of the Cool* era.

★*Konitz Meets Mulligan* (Pacific Jazz CDP 746 847-2)

Lee Konitz' 1952 stint with the Stan Kenton Orchestra made him more upfront, and an exuberant session of the following year with baritonist Gerry Mulligan demonstrates it. Konitz' long, fluting lines and wry inflections contrast vividly, with Mulligan's throaty robustness on baritone, and the electric vitality of their musical repartee and intimacy on 'Too Marvellous For Words' has rightly made it a classic.

★*Rhapsody* (Paddlewheel KIJC 174)

Konitz is a veteran now, but shows no signs of losing his taste for adventure. A big-scale operation, this, with very productive conversations generated between Konitz's economical horn lines and guests including Gerry Mulligan, vocalist Helen Merrill, and sharp-end operators like JOE LOVANO, BILL FRISELL and PAUL MOTIAN. Konitz shares cool-jazz delicacies with Lovano, and often resembles a rather cultured-sounding free player on his own. Mulligan isn't always happy with the looseness of structure, but there's a fine dialogue with vocalist Judy Niemack on 'All The Things You Are'. Sometimes a little impassive, but very musical.

Kuhn, Steve (Stephen Lewis)

(Born New York, March 24, 1938)
Steve Kuhn is an underrated master. He was briefly pianist in JOHN COLTRANE's first quartet, but his musical interests embrace almost every incarnation of jazz piano, from stride and swing (Fats Waller and Art Tatum were among his early influences) to BUD POWELL and BILL EVANS.

Kuhn began playing piano at five, first performed professionally at thirteen, and by his early twenties was appearing in bands led by trumpeters KENNY DORHAM and ART FARMER, and saxophonists STAN GETZ and John Coltrane. Briefly working with the bass genius SCOTT LAFARO in Getz's band substantially influenced Kuhn's conception of accompaniment and group interplay. In the late 1960s Kuhn lived in Sweden and worked throughout Europe with a trio, returning to the States in the 1970s and developing a fruitful musical relationship with the singer Sheila Jordan, with whom he still appears.

★*Porgy* (Jazz City 66053012)

Excellent example of the mature Kuhn style, recorded in 1988 and featuring Buster Williams or Eddie Gomez on bass, and Al Foster on drums. The pianist's handling of the Gershwin title track is a delicious instance of the range of effects at Kuhn's disposal, and Gomez further enriches them. Laura Ann Taylor's vocals don't dispel the atmosphere of intelligent unorthodoxy and Foster's drumming is as deft and creative as ever.

Lacy, Steve (Steven Lackritz)

(Born New York, July 23, 1934)
Like his inspiration Sidney Bechet, Steve Lacy is a virtuoso soprano saxophone specialist. Yet he isn't primarily a bebop player or a performer of fiddly tunes and dazzling runs, but his four-octave range and tonal purity are highly expressive. He is as subtle an architect of delicate, glancing effects as anyone in jazz.

Lacy first emulated the swing, intensity and passion of Sidney Bechet, missed bebop and moved straight to the complex thematic improvising style of the pianist Cecil Taylor. At the time, Taylor's closest piano relative was probably Thelonious Monk, but the younger man also possessed an immense technique, packed with fast-moving classical references. Lacy and Taylor associated until the late 1950s, at which point Lacy developed an obsessive interest in Monk, learning all his tunes and eventually joining his band for a season in 1960. Later he worked in Rome for three years with the straight experimental electronics group Musica Elettronica Viva, then moving to Paris.

Since the 1980s Lacy has frequently been featured with a quintet playing a remarkably integrated synthesis of stark, fragmented composed music, wry, slippery improvisation (his own soprano sound is predominantly a high-pitched, inquisitive sound) and collective interplay reminiscent of the methods of Cecil Taylor. Lacy has also participated in highly attractive

European dedications to the work of pianists Thelonious Monk and Herbie Nichols.

★*The Door* (BMG PD 83049)

Excellent introduction to recent Lacy (1988), featuring his restless, needling, endlessly reconstructing soprano style in collaboration with varying permutations of his regular group, including Steve Potts on alto and Kent Carter on bass.

★*Straight Horn of Steve Lacy* (Candid CCD 9007)

The best CD version so far of Lacy in his earlier and more orthodox guise, working here in 1960 with drummer Roy Haynes and performing three challenging Monk tunes, some Cecil Taylor material and the bebop classic 'Donna Lee'. His solos are effervescent and artfully constructed passages of snaky boppish lines and sidelong jazz inflection. Even at this stage though, the contrast between Roy Haynes' unhesitating rhythmic propulsion and Lacy's instinct for sidestepping the beat gives the session a quality unique to the leader.

★*Anthem* (BMG/Novus PD 83079)

Further Lacy exploration of territory populated by jazz and contemporary straight music, partly put together at the request of the French government for the 200th anniversary of the Revolution. There are sounds like Greek bouzouki music, Lacy's singer wife Irene Aebi's solemnly unjazzy vocals, a recital of a revolutionary text (ending in a boiling collective interplay) and an echoing of the piano style of Lacy's old partner Cecil Taylor by the powerful Bobby Few.

Lake, Oliver

(Born Marianna, Arkansas, 1944)

Altoist Oliver Lake is best known for his role as one-quarter of the World Saxophone Quartet, but he leads a vigorously independent musical life as well. Brought up in St Louis, Lake was originally a percussionist, starting on alto saxophone at 16. In the 1960s, with the civil-rights movement and black liberation politics strongly affecting the sound of American free-jazz, Lake became part of the Black Artists' Group in St Louis, and for much of that period was associated with the avant-garde. He moved, as did the Art Ensemble and several other experimental bands, to Paris in the early 1970s, but in 1977 in the States he was a founder member of the World Saxophone Quartet.

★*Otherside* (Gramavision 188901-2)

Lake in a 1988 collaboration with a highly gifted recent partner, pianist GERI ALLEN, with tracks featuring both small groups and a big band. Following a Lake tradition on his own albums of dedications to his alto inspiration Eric Dolphy, *Otherside* features a Dolphy dedication, and a challenging collection of his typically knife-edge balancing acts between waywardness and offbeat lyricism.

Laws, Ronnie

(Born Houston, Texas, October 3, 1950)
A bluesy, exciting saxophonist who displays the broad tone and leisurely gait so familiar to Texas horn players, but whose undoubted talents have been masked by the formulaic disco styles on many of his records. In the late 1970s, Laws became the highest-selling debut artist ever to have recorded for Blue Note when he made the album *Pressure Sensitive*, astutely produced by the Crusaders' trombonist Wayne Henderson.

Most of the members of Laws' family have been musical. His grandfather was a harmonica player, his mother a gospel pianist and his brother Hubert a successful flute player. Laws studied music, then moved to Los Angeles at 21, joining rock band Von Ryan's Express and, later, Earth Wind and Fire.

★*Classic Masters* (Capitol CDP 746 585-2)

The original *Pressure Sensitive* CD has been deleted, but this moderately varied selection of Laws' fusion work at least includes

'Always There', the standout *Pressure Sensitive* track, with the saxophonist mixing a tenor sound both plaintive and exuberant over an irresistibly propulsive keyboard figure.

★*Deep Soul* (101 South 101 S 7125-2)

A recent Laws set, confirming his class despite all the pop compromises. He's economical with his strong points, lets the rhythm fill the spaces, and the fills he slides between many of the fusion devices are often deeply rooted in the most subtle jazz-sax phrasing. 'Always There' is featured, and a good blues called 'Blues in the 5th Ward'.

Liebman, David

(Born New York, September 4, 1946)
Even the most occasional jazz listener quickly loses count of the number of Coltrane admirers there are. New Yorker Dave Liebman is a saxophonist whose style is founded on Coltrane but who has added, by accident or design, a fragile, tremulous quality to his upper-register playing on soprano that is quite distinctive.

Liebman explored improvisation with one of its most eccentric masters, Lennie Tristano, in the 1960s, then began to work with the rock band Ten Wheel Drive and eventually with the early MILES DAVIS fusion ensembles. He shifted exclusively to the soprano saxophone ten years ago, and through the 1980s was principally absorbed in developing Quest, an adventurous quartet exploring collective improvisation.

★*Quest 2* (Storyville/Moss Music/USA STCD 4132)

Quest in 1986, with Liebman and pianist Richie Beirach plus Ron McLure on bass and Billy Hart on drums. Sharp, weaving, seat-of-the-pants contemporary jazz, reflexive and fast-moving, developing spiky themes in unexpected ways, an object lesson in fresh phraseology.

Homage to John Coltrane (Owl/France LC 046)

Paddlewheel's *Tribute to John Coltrane* might have been a better choice for a CD reissue, but *Homage* is almost as strong and wilful, with Liebman showing how resourcefully he can improvise at length over repeated figures – an attribute of Coltrane's that most of his disciples, unlike Liebman, lack the harmonic knowledge to pull off.

Loose Tubes

(Formed 1984, dissolved 1990)
Loose Tubes was a London-based big band that, by blending African hi-life music, bebop, soca, funk, rock 'n' roll, sambas, marches and bursts of crazed electro-pop, broke most standard big-band rules and gained a wide following in Britain in the 1980s.

Loose Tubes was born in early 1984. Graham Collier, a highly-regarded British composer who had been running bands of various sizes since 1964 and was also a teacher at the Guildhall School of Music and Drama, set up a workshop orchestra for adventurous up-and-coming jazz musicians. The project soon became Loose Tubes, and often featured material by pianist DJANGO BATES which sounded like somebody flipping stations on a radio, with strong echoes of Charles Mingus, Don Ellis and CARLA BLEY. The collective energy generated by the band galvanised the careers of many of its individuals, and it was the competing commitments of sidemen such as Bates, IAIN BALLAMY, Mark Lockheart and others that hastened its demise.

Open Letter (Editions EGED 55)

Loose Tubes' third and best album. The South African influence is a particularly strong feature (the full title is *An Open Letter to Dudu Pukwana*, the late great Port Elizabeth altoist who had lived in London), and it offsets the Tubes' occasional tendency to musical fidgetiness with its warmth, rhythmic exuberance, and song-like directness. The session was cut in London but produced by the prestigious American jazz recording guru Teo Macero. The soloing doesn't always gleam as much as the band en masse, though the mercurial (and on this showing, surprisingly Eric Dolphy-like) Iain Ballamy and the fierce Dave DeFries make up most of the difference.

Lovano, Joe

(Born Cleveland, Ohio, 1953)

After a long career as a sideman in the bands of famous leaders, saxophonist Joe Lovano came into his own as he was approaching middle age, through exposure in the successful bands of guitarist John Scofield. In an era in which the sound and harmonic approach of JOHN COLTRANE has dominated saxophonists' conceptions, Lovano can be both as ruggedly and unsentimentally inventive as any postbop performer and as warm and delicate as the sax romantics of an earlier era, like Lester Young.

Lovano was raised in a jazz household, among jazz musicians of the swing and early bop era, whose relaxation and concentration on tonal subtlety he still reflects, and he learned to play fast duets with his father in the Gene Ammons-Dexter Gordon style. In 1971 Lovano went to the Berklee jazz school, where he met guitarists Scofield and Bill Frisell, and the musicians pursued the elusive objective of a jazz-based sound, able to work off standards, but nevertheless reflecting the popular musics of the day. Lovano learned about funk and rhythm-and-blues in organ groups such as Jack McDuff's, then gained invaluable big band experience, from 1976 and 1979 in WOODY HERMAN's saxophone section, then MEL LEWIS's, CHARLIE HADEN's and CARLA BLEY's, later pursuing small-band music with drummer PAUL MOTIAN and BILL FRISELL.

★Landmarks (Blue Note CDP 796108)

Lovano's debut as leader for Blue Note, and a disc that turned up on many commentators' lists of the best jazz albums of 1991. All the experience the saxophonist had been building over nearly twenty years in the business came together in an arresting blend of Monkish composition, Coltrane-influenced group sound and hard funk, with guitarist John Abercrombie performing the Scofield role with less quirkiness but more feverishness. But it's

Lovano's unfashionable translucency on the ballads that gives this excellent disc an extra twist.

★*Universal Language* (Blue Note 0777 7 99830-2-5)

Widening Lovano's considerable net – this time to include some contemporary classical references via his singer wife, soprano Judi Silvano. The set opens Monkishly, and splicing the sounds of the soprano voice and some Miles Davis-like trumpet from Tim Hagans is a startling piece of texture that characterises the session. Coltrane in pensive mood, the bigger Monk groups, and Jan Garbarek's combinations of saxophone and voice are also recalled here and there.

★*Rush Hour* (Blue Note CDP 7243 8 29269 2 4)

Further splicings of jazz and classical influences, this time into a pairing with the composer and jazz academic Gunther Schuller. It initially rings the purists' alarm bells with its big string sections, classical singers and tricksy charts. But the saxophonist soon sets the mind at rest. The material includes pieces by Charles Mingus, Thelonious Monk, Duke Ellington and Ornette Coleman, and though the string writing is sometimes a little glutinous, Schuller makes a great job of an almost imperceptibly mobile 'Crepuscule with Nellie', and Lovano boils with enthusiasm and intelligence.

McFerrin, Bobby

(Born New York, March 11, 1950)

The son of an opera singer and a classical soprano, McFerrin had been taught piano as a child, and developed a jazz style on the instrument close to KEITH JARRETT's; but in 1983 he turned to singing, encouraged by the successful bop vocalist of the 1950s and 1960s, Jon Hendricks. McFerrin quickly indicated that he was not simply a singer with an attractively light, buoyant tone, but an uncanny mimic too, able to sound like most members of an entire band by himself. Though his early successes were on tours with George Benson, Grover Washington and HERBIE HANCOCK (and he appeared on the 1982 Young Lions concerts alongside WYNTON

MARSALIS), it was as an unaccompanied performer that McFerrin was to make a special mark. He dazzled audiences with a technique that used indrawn breaths and chest beating with the mike held close to represent percussion sounds, with low, gargling noises resembling funk bass figures and synthesiser effects – in which respect McFerrin was probably the first 'instrumental' jazz vocalist to sound like electric rather than acoustic instruments.

★*Simple Pleasures* (EMI/Manhattan CDP 748 059)

McFerrin's most commercially successful album. But though the audacity of some of his live shows with jazzier partners is passed over, McFerrin's expertise, swing and choice of songs (the album includes 'Suzie Q' and 'Sunshine of Your Love' as well as the chart hit 'Don't Worry Be Happy') makes much of it a pleasure, and sometimes a marvel, to listen to.

★*Medicine Music* (EMI/Manhattan CDP 792 048)

McFerrin in 1990, displaying two further developments in his approach: more lyrics, and a kind of hip piety as befits his religious interests and endorsement of traditional family values. Some of this highly eclectic album is irritatingly devout, but the ensemble sound that McFerrin achieves through overdubbing, plus some support from the vocal group Voicestra, is remarkable. Idioms touched on are American Indian, African and gospel music. The more abstract sound-effects pieces, such as 'The Train' and 'He Ran All The Way', may appeal more to McFerrin's pre-pop fans.

McLaughlin, John

(Born Yorkshire, January 4, 1942)
Nobody can accuse guitarist John McLaughlin of jumping on the world-music bandwagon. Following an illustrious stint with MILES DAVIS at the end of the 1960s, McLaughlin's subsequent Maha-vishnu Orchestra (one of the most successful of all the jazz-rock fusion bands of the early 1970s) was inspired by the leader's fascination with the east. His next group, Shakti, featured three

Indian musicians, and tried to unite western jazz and pop with traditional Indian forms.

McLaughlin was raised in a musical family but was mostly self-taught on guitar. He played blues on it at first, and then fell under the spell of Belgian Django Reinhardt. Playing at first in r & b and bebop groups around Newcastle, he moved to London in the early 1960s and took part in the British r & b boom of that era. McLaughlin attracted the attention of the Miles Davis circle, initially worked for Davis' talented drummer TONY WILLIAMS, then for the trumpeter himself on landmark fusion albums such as *Bitches Brew* and *In a Silent Way*.

From 1975 to date McLaughlin has moved back and forth between revamped Mahavishnu bands, acoustic groups and straight-ahead bluesy trios with organist Joey Defranco.

★*Extrapolation* (Polydor 841598)

It took a very long time for Polydor to realise what a classic they had in their vaults and get around to reissuing this British-made McLaughlin session from 1969. It's a must for anybody who likes McLaughlin's unusual mixture of Django Reinhardt-like flourishes and punchy bluesiness but who wishes he didn't play so many notes – and it features a superb British band of the day in the young John Surman on baritone sax and a devastating Tony Oxley on drums. Oxley's sudden tom-tom roll on the opening of the stalking, displaced-blues 'Binky's Beam' is one of the great moments in jazz.

★*The Inner Mounting Flame* (Columbia 31067)

Made under the name of the Mahavishnu Orchestra, the love-and-meditation band McLaughlin formed after his encounter with the Indian guru Sri Chinmoy in 1971, this first disc by the group was by a long chalk its best. A blend of electric rock drive and volume, and a jazzy subtlety of harmony and complex time, it was a landmark in early fusion.

*With Free Spirits. *Tokyo Live* (Verve 521 870-2)

McLaughlin with his current road band, a back-to-basics organ trio with the juggernaut drummer Dennis Chambers and the shrewd and distinctive young Hammond player Joey DeFrancesco, who is also a dab hand at muted Miles Davis trumpet. Everybody sprays notes all over the place, but this kind of stuff is an infectiously die-hard idiom, and when they all dig into uptempo bluesy bebop (like 'No Blues', an old Miles Davis vehicle) you have a hard time stopping the feet from tapping.

Mann, Herbert Jay Solomon 'Herbie'

(Born Brooklyn, April 16, 1930)
A technically adept and commercially opportunistic performer on a distinctly marginal jazz instrument – the flute – Herbie Mann didn't simply make waves in the 1960s as an unusual voice on a little-used instrument, but as one of the closest things to a pop star the jazz world throws up. He had a major hit with one of the seminal fusion albums, *Memphis Underground*, in the late 1960s. For years afterwards Mann topped the press polls as everybody's favourite jazz flautist.

Mann was originally a clarinettist, and worked for three years with a US army band in the early 1950s, following that up with successful studio work on the west coast. The music of other cultures interested him, and in the early 1960s he toured both Africa and Brazil with his own group. Later in the decade he became more rock-oriented, and in the following decade he investigated both reggae and disco music.

Memphis Underground (WEA 7567 81364)

A virtual definition of Herbie Mann's particular alchemy – a powerful, headlong blend of two quite dissimilar guitarists (the harmonically subtle LARRY CORYELL and the bludgeoning SONNY SHARROCK) plus funky vibraharpist Roy Ayres and a swinging Memphis rhythm section.

Maria, Tania

(Born Sao Luis, Brazil, 1948)

In the 1970s, when the world already knew of Astrud Gilberto and Flora Purim, singer/pianist Tania Maria was still building the foundations of what was to become her mature style. She was invited to work in a Paris nightclub on a three-month contract, and wound up staying in Europe for the next seven years, recording several albums powerfully highlighting her Brazilian roots for the French Barclay label. During her European stay, she continued to make the occasional impact in the States – performing on the same bill as Sarah Vaughan at the 1975 Newport Festival. By 1981, through the encouragement of Charlie Byrd (a guitarist who had long sought to further the Brazilian connection, and who had played on the Getz/Gilberto samba classics of the 1960s) Tania Maria had cut an American album, *Piquant*, and moved to New York City to live. She made a number of successful albums for Concord during the 1980s, though in the latter part of the decade her work has lost much of its reckless bravura and is beginning to adopt the kind of showbiz polish that she was once such a refreshing change from. Live, she can still be sensational.

★*The Real Tania Maria – Wild* (Concord CCD 4264)

One of the few Tania Maria albums to capture her true flavour, this 1984 recording was a live set that included some of her most famous tunes, including the rat-tat-tat uptempo scat classic 'Sangria', the driving 'Yatra-Ta', and percussion displays likely to set even the weariest of feet on the move.

Mariano, Charlie (Carmine Ugo)

(Born Boston, November 12, 1923)

A creative and original reed player, far more highly regarded by his colleagues and musical partners than by the public – originally a bebop altoist in the Charlie Parker mould, later affected by Coltrane and by the music of the east, which he has intelligently absorbed and adapted.

Mariano was taught piano as a child, later playing in an army band and then studying saxophone at the Berklee School. He spent part of the 1950s working in the Stan Kenton band, and performing with various of its sidemen around Los Angeles. In 1959 he married and also formed a jazz quartet with the Japanese pianist and composer TOSHIKO AKIYOSHI, later working in Charles Mingus' group. He has extensively studied the oboe-like South Indian nagaswaram. Mariano has also worked a good deal with European musicians, notably the composer of gentle fusion tone-poems, German bassist EBERHARD WEBER.

★*Jyothi* (ECM 1256)

Mariano in his Indian incarnation, a 1982 collaboration in Bangalore with the Karnataka College of Percussion. The leader reveals the depths of his commitment to Indian music in his weaving, wraith-like lines on the nadaswaram; a richer collaboration between cultures than many more celebrated recent examples of such hook-ups.

Marsalis, Branford

(Born New Orleans, August 26, 1960)

The saxophone-playing member of the dominant family in contemporary jazz – the Marsalises. Branford Marsalis is a brilliant reeds player who personifies the best of the 'neo-classical' period of jazz in which post-bop styles are being re-examined and redeployed. His recent preferences have been for the collective agility and rhythmic ambiguity of the pre-electric MILES DAVIS bands of the mid-1960s. Marsalis is no copyist, however. His bands have a quirkiness, wit and subtlety of their own, and his saxophone-playing is frequently Sonny Rollins-like in its mixture of bristling runs and sudden indignant squawks, but at other times even has echoes of Lester Young in passages of light, skittering, nearly evaporating phrases, like someone absently doodling. Branford Marsalis is also a movie actor of promise as well.

In the late 1970s, Branford Marsalis was at Southern University in Baton Rouge, studying clarinet with a legendary New Orleans traditionalist, Alvin Batiste. He then went to Berklee, and from there straight into Art Blakey's Jazz Messengers, eventually playing in that band side by side with his younger brother Wynton on trumpet. In 1983 Branford Marsalis made his debut album, later joining pop singer Sting's backing band.

★*Trio Jeepy* (CBS 465134)

A trio album for Branford Marsalis plus the remarkable poly-rhythmic drummer Jeff 'Tain' Watts and octogenarian bassist Milt Hinton. The result is a session of vitality and wide-ranging references, with a spaciousness deriving from the trio format and the directness of Branford's approach that enables the improvisatory talents of all three to flower. Marsalis plays a dazzling fast solo on 'Three Little Words' (an old Sonny Rollins favourite) without a repetition or a cliché, and there's hardly a dull moment on the disc.

Marsalis, Delfeayo

(Born New Orleans, 1966)
It might have seemed a tough task to follow in the footsteps of the older members of the Marsalis family – most notably trumpeter Wynton and saxophonist Branford. But trombonist, composer and record producer Delfeayo Marsalis has managed it without cloning his ideas off anyone, inside his family or out. Delfeayo's name got around as a producer first (he performed the role for his brothers, and for HARRY CONNICK JNR, COURTNEY PINE, MARCUS ROBERTS and others), but when his debut disc *Pontius Pilate's Decision* emerged, it was a mature work of thematic jazz that firmly established his credentials as a player and leader.

As a trombonist, Delfeayo Marsalis owes much of his fleetness of execution and clean sound to J.J. Johnson. Like all the Marsalis children, Delfeayo was raised with jazz around him, growing up in the key city of the music's history. Since graduation, he has produced many records, toured with ART BLAKEY, RAY CHARLES and FATS DOMINO, and worked on the soundtracks to such movies *Do The Right Thing* and *Mo Better Blues*.

*_Pontius Pilate's Decision_ (Novus PD 90669)

Four Marsalises here, on a concept work devoted to major New Testament events. Unexpectedly, this isn't a solemn set but features the leader's languidly affecting trombone sound, some bouncy post-boppish episodes that seem hard to fit into the scheme of things, and an arranging style that suggests Charles Mingus, but that a shrewd young sensibility has adapted.

Marsalis, Wynton

(Born New Orleans, October 18, 1961)
This strikingly gifted young trumpeter took the jazz world by storm in 1980, when he was just 19 years old. He was one of six sons born to pianist Ellis Marsalis, named in honour of the pianist Wynton Kelly. Wynton, Ellis and saxophonist Branford have been known to perform in each other's company, as on the album _Fathers and Sons_. Wynton, almost inevitably in such an environment, learned music early, studied classical trumpet, and was playing solo on the Haydn Trumpet Concerto with the New Orleans Symphony Orchestra by the age of 14. Three years later the New Orleans-born musician arrived in New York to study at the Juilliard School, supplementing his allowance by playing in the Broadway pit band for _Sweeney Todd_. During this period that indefatigable talent scout Art Blakey heard him play and soon Wynton Marsalis had joined that glittering array of trumpet stars who have fronted the Jazz Messengers.

From 1983 onwards, Wynton Marsalis was beginning to work virtually on his own terms, in that year winning Grammies for both his second album, _Think of One_, and a collection of classical trumpet concertos. He toured with Herbie Hancock's VSOP band, which was devoted to sustaining the style of the classic MILES DAVIS group of the early and middle 1960s, and the Davis sound of that era was clearly a powerful inspiration. With the release of _Standard Time_, Wynton Marsalis firmly demonstrated the mixture of dedication and respect for the past that shapes his music.

★*Standard Time* (Columbia CK 40461)

Twelve lyrical, lovingly burnished jazz evergreens performed by the quartet of Marsalis plus MARCUS ROBERTS on piano, Bob Hurst on bass and Jeff 'Tain' Watts on drums. 'Caravan' is delivered like a long cackle and dipped briefly into salty dissonance, 'Cherokee' appears in two versions with a stunning muted solo over Jeff Watts' scurrying brushwork in the first, the coda taking the form of ever more urgent ascents of the register, finishing abruptly on a ledge as if suspended in space.

★*Live at Blues Alley* (Columbia G2K 40675)

One of the loosest Wynton Marsalis records, made in 1986 and featuring the trumpeter with the same quartet that made *Standard Time*. Most of the regular criticisms of Wynton Marsalis – uptight orderliness, brilliant but disengaged coasting on favourite jazz and classical phrases, solos sounding like exercises, unwillingness to leave spaces – are despatched by this album.

★*The Majesty of the Blues* (Columbia CK 45091)

Marsalis with a tribute to his New Orleans roots, full of growls, wah-wahs, jangling vibrato and chugging rhythms of early jazz. *The Majesty of the Blues* isn't a straight pastiche. The group continues to flavour its reminiscences with modernisms, particularly from the piano and reeds. The 20-minute spoken sermon on the 'noble sound' of jazz is a stirring, Luther King-like delivery imparted to a ploddingly banal text.

Martin, Claire

(Born London, September 6, 1967)
Since her emergence in the early 90s, Claire Martin has been recognised as one of Britain's most promising singers in years. Her debut album *The Waiting Game* became one of the biggest selling British jazz records of 1992, and the following year she came out with *Devil May Care*, a compilation that took in material

from Patsy Cline to Rodgers and Hart. She won a Rising Star award at the British Jazz Awards in April 1994.

Though still in the early stages of her career, Claire Martin is a widely experienced singer, taking in studio work, club-work and the international cruise liners. She has a profound, and often witty, understanding of a wide range of songs from all eras, frequently discovers good material rarely aired, and she works with some of the best performers on the British jazz scene.

Old Boyfriends (Linn Records AKD 028)

Claire Martin's best record, testing her strengths in shading and dynamics, by which she massages new meanings from old lyrics. Mostly a ballad set, reviving good neglected songs, as she often does. The band plays things rather on-the-nose, though Mark Nightingale's trombone almost steals the show. Guitarist Jim Mullen isn't far behind.

Masekela, Hugh

(Born Witbank, South Africa, April 4, 1939)

Trumpeter Hugh Masekela is nowadays probably the best known of the black South African jazz musicians to have merged townships dance music and the Afro-American traditions. His music is jubilant, phlegmatic and defiant, at one moment political satire, at another a celebration of the sunshine, or an impassioned rendition of Bob Marley's 'No Woman No Cry'. Yet Masekela began firmly in the jazz lineage, doubly famous for blowing a trumpet given to him as a teenager by Louis Armstrong.

Masekela formed the Jazz Epistles, the first black band to make an LP in South Africa, but left the country in 1960 after the Sharpeville massacre, coming first to London to take up a Guildhall Music School place fixed for him by JOHN DANKWORTH, then going to study in New York. Since the 1960s Masekela has variously lived in America, Britain, Zimbabwe and Botswana, and some of his American albums – in seeking to blend jazz-rock fusion and South African music – have blurred the distinctive identity he originally had.

★*Uptownship* (BMG/Novus PD 83070)

Good representation of late-1980s Masekela, performing a mixture of music with a strong African flavour and his later American influences from western dance music and funk. Though the disc does have a faintly formulaic quality, and it's no substitute for hearing this magnetic performer live, there is still a strong enough sense of his band's exuberance and the dancing quality of his trumpet phrasing.

Mazur, Marilyn

(Born New York, Jan 8, 1955)
For her ability to switch between abstract, kaleidoscopic percussion effects, either alone or in accompaniment, and orthodox rhythm playing of immense assurance and energy, Danish drummer Mazur built a reputation in America and Europe during the 1980s as a performer of selfless creativity in what was often a supporting role. She became better-known during the latter part of the decade for her work with the MILES DAVIS band, and since the trumpeter's death as a galvanising element in the sometimes rather remote bands of saxophonist Jan Garbarek.

Mazur was born in the States but moved to Denmark with her parents when she was six. By her mid teens she was composing, and learned percussion instruments. From the beginning of the Eighties she appeared in a variety of bands, including Danish pianist Finn Savery's, Pierre Dorge's and with her own quartet, through which she displayed a fast-maturing compositional breadth. In 1984 she worked in the Primi Band, a group of ten women, then performed with Miles Davis, Wayne Shorter, and later Jan Garbarek.

★*Future Song* (veraBra Records vBr 2105-2)

Mazur's own project, recorded in Denmark. It's a punchy mix of MILES DAVIS-like funk (trumpeter Nils Petter Molvaer provides the Miles echoes), a use of north European folk singing rather similar to the way Mazur's employer JAN GARBAREK uses it, and some bristling and highly imaginative drumming. Slightly meandering at times, but Mazur herself lends sparkle to almost all of it.

Metheny, Pat

(Born Kansas City, Missouri, August 12, 1954)
Guitarist Pat Metheny has, since the 1970s, enjoyed a worldwide reputation as a dealer in some of the most melodic of fusion music – atmospheric, often sustained over long suite-like pieces, highly evocative of rural landscapes and country music as well as jazz. But there is a side of Metheny sometimes submerged in his carefully wrought programmatic music: the spontaneous improvising guitar player who assiduously studied Wes Montgomery's guitar bop as a child, but was growing up in an era in which it couldn't be disconnected from the new influences of the Beatles and Jimi Hendrix.

Metheny took up the guitar at 13, learning so fast that he was a skilled guitar teacher as well as sophisticated sitter-in in Kansas City clubs before he had even gone to music college himself. He joined vibist GARY BURTON's group at 19 and then established such an instantly recognisable composer's trademark with his own albums that he began veering between the release of 'blowing' jazz records with the likes of MIKE BRECKER and Dewey Redman, and largely composed works that almost inevitably led to movie scores. But with the scorching and largely soloistic *Song X* session of 1985 (Metheny in partnership with an old idol, saxophonist Ornette Coleman; see Ornette Coleman) the young guitarist proved that he hadn't deserted his earliest loves.

★80/81 (ECM 1180/1)

One of Metheny's most productive recording dates, made when the title suggests, and bringing together the talents of saxophonist Mike Brecker and drummer Jack DeJohnette, plus two celebrated alumni of Ornette Coleman in tenorist Dewey Redman and bassist CHARLIE HADEN. Metheny's affection for Coleman's skewed lyricism is well known, and Brecker's urbane eloquence and Redman's quirkier style make an effective contrast with each other.

★*As Falls Wichita, So Falls Wichita Falls* (ECM 1190)

Made around the same time as *80/81*, this was a total contrast. Spacious, less explicitly jazzy, and full of big country musical imagery, it is an imaginative, texturally rich collaboration between Metheny and pianist Lyle Mays, that took the guitarist's work to the borderline with easy listening. It nevertheless retained a poignancy and tonal adventurousness that set it apart from New Age music.

★*Offramp* (ECM 1216)

One of Metheny's most enduringly popular and attractive records features the leader on guitar synthesiser (on which he achieves a sound mingling charisma and whimsy, like a violin section crossed with a choir of harmonicas) proceeding through a repertoire of inventive and laid-back funk, with occasional bursts of near-abstract wildness.

★*Secret Story* (Geffen 24468)

Metheny's mid-life crisis on disc. This programmatic piece, a five-year project featuring a string orchestra and various guests, is the closest thing to *As Falls Wichita, So Falls Wichita Falls*. Though some of it sounds indistinguishable from other Metheny records, his improvised playing is unexpectedly devastating here, and some of the writing, notably on the serpentine 'Antonia' and the lustrous 'The Truth Will Always Be', is as good as anything he's ever done.

★*Rejoicing* (ECM 1271)

Superb Metheny trio album, presenting the guitarist in the guise in which his more jazz-oiriented listeners would always rather hear him. The other members of the band are Charlie Haden (bass) and Billy Higgins (drums), the title track is ORNETTE COLEMAN's, and HORACE SILVER's 'Lonely Woman' gets a wistful but never coy performance out of the leader.

★*The Road To You – Recorded Live in Europe* (Geffen 24601)

Maybe an attempt to get some of *Secret Story*'s investment back, this is a pick from recent live shows with all his fave raves, like the freewheeling 'Have You Heard', plus 'Letter From Home' and many others. Not as fresh as some Metheny live material, or as good as the 1982 *Travels*, but a memento for those who attended, or who didn't.

Minton, Philip

(Born Wales, 1940)
One of Europe's foremost improvising vocalists, though not always explicitly drawing on jazz. But Minton often works with jazz musicians, and his timing and feel go to the fundamentals of the music. A mixture of a folk singer, a blues singer, a torch singer and a free-improviser, Minton's early influences included Count Basie's vocalist Jimmy Rushing, but also Japanese traditional singing, Lapp folk music and West African sounds. In improvisation he can be devastating in range, with a palette of percussive noises, high-pitched mutterings, exclamatory sounds, exhortations and demands, furious falsetto stutterings, exclamations, admonitions, pleadings, demands.

He is descended from a family of Welsh choral singers, but grew up in the West Country. Though he regularly works with composer Mike Westbrook, Minton nevertheless pursued free-improvisation as the route to his own music and eventually pursued this course far more extensively, often in the company of international performers including New York avantist JOHN ZORN, the great jazz pianist PAUL BLEY, German saxophonist Peter Brotzmann and many others. He has also worked fruitfully with the British pianist and composer Veryan Weston.

★*Ways* (ITN 1420)

Duets between Minton and a frequent associate, pianist Veryan Weston. This exposed setting makes the extremes of Minton's interests more demanding than the fine *Berlin Station* (only on FMP vinyl) but it also establishes how wide his emotional range can be, and how detailed his command over the intricacies of high-class vocal improvisation.

Mitchell, Roscoe

(Born Chicago, August 3, 1940; died 1995)
A multi-reed player best known for his association with one of the most communicative of all 1960s avant-garde descendants, the ART ENSEMBLE OF CHICAGO. As well as a visionary composer, Mitchell was a virtuoso saxophonist, particularly on alto, but he eschewed most of the styles by which jazz musicians sell records, and his skills have thus been neglected.

Though primarily a free player, Mitchell intimately familiarised himself with bop through work in army bands in the 1950s, and early in the following decade he participated in hard-bop groups. Later in the 1960s he led his own bands, and participated in the Association for the Advancement of Creative Musicians (AACM) which led to the formation of the Art Ensemble. With albums such as *Congliptious* and *Sound* Mitchell revealed a hushed and dramatic version of the avant-garde, widely spaced sounds wheeling in dark spaces.

★*LRG/The Maze* (Chief Recs CHIEFCD 4)

LRG is a trio featuring Mitchell plus trumpeter Leo Smith and the revolutionary trombonist and computer-music innovator George Lewis, and these recordings of its intricate and faintly precious work were made in 1978. 'The Maze' is an unhurried and compelling extended piece for eight percussionists, and Mitchell also plays a long solo soprano feature ('S II Examples') which doesn't display his improvising talents at their best. Not ideal Mitchell, but better than nothing.

Montoliu, Vincente 'Tete'

(Born Barcelona, Spain, March 28, 1933)
Brilliant blind Catalan pianist, whose technique blends the tumbling single-note manner of bop with the rich harmonic

support of an Errol Garner or even a Tatum. Montoliu was immersed in jazz records from childhood and by 1956 had recorded with Lionel Hampton and later with Roland Kirk and the avantist ANTHONY BRAXTON. He has worked extensively throughout Europe, visited the States, and recorded excellent duo sessions with tenorist George Coleman and fellow-pianist CHICK COREA. Montoliu is an outstanding unaccompanied performer however, working both with orthodox jazz material and the folk music of northern Spain.

★*Tete!* (Steeplechase SCS 1029)

One of the best of a very large number of Montoliu trio recordings in the catalogue, cut in 1974. The accompanists are NIELS-HENNING ORSTED-PEDERSEN on bass and ALBERT 'TOOTIE' HEATH on drums, and the two represent an ideal combination of punch and etiquette for the leader's quick-thinking ruminations. Excellent keyboard bop.

Moreira, Airto

(Born Itaiopolis, Brazil, August 6, 1941)
Moreira has been a dominant force in Latin-American percussion for 30 years, as a phenomenal technician, an imaginative bandleader, and as a formidable authority on ethnic percussion instruments. He was one of the first from his country to significantly influence the American jazz scene of the fusion era, bringing the authentic vitality and colour of Brazilian music to jazz – aspects hitherto somewhat obscured by the laid-back qualities of the bossa nova fad that had preceded him. Moreira's unaccompanied percussion displays on tambourine alone regularly brings club audiences to their feet.

An early starter, Airto Moreira was at work in music by his early teens, and by his twenties had formed an adventurous band, Quarteto Novo, with multi-instrumentalist HERMETO PASCOAL, which toured all over Brazil. Moreira married singer Flora Purim, moved to the States in 1968 and found the depth of his absorption in Brazilian rural music so much in demand that he was soon working with MILES DAVIS, STAN GETZ and CANNONBALL ADDERLEY, and helping to found the original Weather Report and Return to Forever bands. Moreira now works regularly in Fourth World, a fusion band with dominant Latin percussion textures he leads with Flora Purim.

★*Fourth World* (B & W Records)

Fourth World is consistently a big success in clubs and this debut disc by the band captures much of its vivacity and fire. The combination of Moreira's tempestuous percussion and Purim's increasingly rugged and powerful vocals would be an unusual centrepiece for any group, and guitarist Jose Neto and saxophonist Gary Meek compound the energy with strong contributions of their own. Turn the volume up and clear the furniture.

Motian, Stephen Paul

(Born Providence, Rhode Island, March 25, 1931)

Many drummers are spectacular, but musical ones are harder to find, and those that do exist are often undervalued. Paul Motian is one such. Motian's originality has not always made his music the most accessible in the world, but his work generally emphasises the most conversational and detailed aspects of freer jazz, even when his settings and partners don't always observe orthodox tonality.

Motian's most famous job was accompanying the late Bill Evans from 1959 to 1964, in which situation – like bassist Scott LaFaro – he helped further emancipate the rhythm section to operate in virtually a contrapuntal partnership with the leader. Motian had formerly been a crisp bop performer whose partners in the 1950s included mainstream tenorist Zoot Sims, and following the stretch with Bill Evans, he spent almost a decade in KEITH JARRETT's band, forming a close association with the innovative bassist CHARLIE HADEN in the process, and via him mingling with the younger radicals of the 1960s New York avant-garde. The extent of Motian's open-mindedness was indicated by his choice of the young sound-effects guitarist BILL FRISELL for his group in 1980.

★*It Should've Happened a Long Time Ago* (ECM 823 641-2)

Ambiguous and fascinating performance from the early 1980s by a Motian trio featuring Bill Frisell on guitars, and JOE LOVANO on reeds. Some of Frisell's most effective forays have occurred in Motian's company, and Lovano's playing is altogether a more satisfying mixture of patience and impulsiveness than is usual among most of his saxophone contemporaries.

★*Monk in Motian* (JMT 834421)

One of the best collaborations between the drummer and the pianist GERI ALLEN, who appears here for two THELONIOUS MONK tunes ('Off Minor' and 'Ruby My Dear') and makes a fine account of both with her superb control of dynamics and rhythmic contrast. Motian uses the whole group to explore Monk's originality of line, almost as if all the musicians were representing the way Monk would sound unaccompanied – so it's abstract compared with a straight-bop record, but very indicative of Motian's insight and intelligence.

★*Bill Evans* (JMT 834445)

A performance devoted to some of the more obscure compositions of pianist Bill Evans, with Joe Lovano, Bill Frisell and Marc Johnson. Motian understood Evans intimately, and Frisell used the pianist's ideas in developing his approach to guitar style. There's little probing swing in the original Evans sense, but Motian exposes his old boss's talents by more circuitous means.

★*Conception Vessel* (ECM 519 279-2)

A small-scale version of the Charlie Haden Liberation Music Orchestra in which Motian participated, with such linking elements as guitarist Sam Brown's free-jazz/flamenco excursions. KEITH JARRETT appears on two tracks, intriguingly exploring a kind of impressionistic and romantic free-improvisation that he later abandoned.

*Electric Bebop Band: *Reincarnation of a Lovebird* (JMT 51 4016-2)

Nouveau-bop. The bop standards repertoire ('2 Bass Hit', 'Ornithology' and 'Round Midnight') shaken to the bone by BILL FRISELL-like guitar noises and chattery counterpoint, with Motian, sophisticated altoist Chris Potter, Wolfgang Muthspiel on guitar, Steve Swallow on bass and Don Alias on percussion. Essential relief for all those who like the tunes, but will explode if they hear another '50s clone-band.

Mseleku, Bheki

(Born South Africa)
In 1987 in London, saxophonist and club-proprietor Ronnie Scott, a shrewd judge of new talent, told every jazz-lover he could to come down and hear a young South African emigre, Bheki Mseleku, play piano and saxophone in a style that seemed to embrace townships music, church music, eastern and oriental meditative music and straight-ahead jazz. Many regard him as the most powerful and imaginative jazz musician to have come out of South Africa since ABDULLAH IBRAHIM (Dollar Brand).

Through his work in London, Mseleku came to the attention of young American performers Marvin 'Smitty' Smith (collaborator with the New York M-Base group and bassist Dave Holland's band among many others) and bassist Michael Bowie. These musicians, and later bassist Charnett Moffett, took the unusual step of returning to London specifically to work and record with Mseleku. He counts as his influences McCoy Tyner as a keyboard virtuoso (whose sound is the closest allegiance his piano playing displays), and John Coltrane, Pharoah Sanders and Sun Ra for musical/spiritual inspiration. Bheki Mseleku's father was a political activist, a multi-instrumentalist who played guitar, saxophone and violin, but it was through accidental work with a pop band that the boy discovered his musicality.

Celebration (World Circuit Records)

Debut group disc for Mseleku, revealing how much more extensive his affection for bebop and Latin American jazz is than for many of his jazz compatriots. It features New Yorkers Marvin 'Smitty' Smith and Michael Bowie, plus London performers including tenorist Jean Toussaint, ex Loose Tubes flautist Eddie Parker, Courtney Pine, Steve Williamson and others. The pianist's scything, seamless lines and hammering chordwork drives the Latin theme 'Angola' and the intense 'Blues for Africa', and Smith's drumming is a delight.

Mullen, Jim

(Born Glasgow, 1945)
One of Britain's most relaxed and swinging guitar players, at home with either bebop or funk. Like Wes Montgomery, Mullen plucks the strings with his thumb rather than a pick, and his phrasing has a chunky, solid, percussive quality. Having begun to play the guitar at ten, and finding work in his teens as both a guitarist and a bassist, Mullen came to London at the end of the 1960s and worked with a variety of jazz and blues-influenced groups. In the 1970s he worked in the States with the Average White Band and flautist HERBIE MANN, and for a decade from the mid-1970s he was involved in the Morrissey-Mullen jazz-funk band with tenorist Dick Morrissey.

*Soundbites (EFZ 1003)

Recent Mullen, influenced increasingly by the jazzier sound of the JOHN SCOFIELD band, but still displaying the old relaxation and resonant sound. A mid-tempo, easy-going funk dominates it though, with plenty of Brecker/Sanborn saxophone sensuousness provided by the promising young British player Dave O'Higgins.

Murphy, Mark Howe

(Born New York, March 14, 1932)
Like many fine jazz artists whose stars appeared to have waned for no better reason than changing tastes, singer Mark Murphy's skills were belatedly appreciated by the new club audiences in the

1980s and his musicality and single-minded pursuit of his own methods began to receive their due. Murphy is an original singer whose work takes in swing, vocalese and scatting, bebop, and a sensitivity to the best qualities of good songs, and he doesn't affect an earthiness or rootiness that isn't part of his background.

He began performing in his teens and was an early success, touring the States in his twenties and appearing on TV. Murphy moved to Europe in the 1960s where he continued to tour and record, then returned to the States in the next decade with his career in apparent decline. Now that the kind of mix of standards and more complex jazz that he has long espoused has returned to favour, it may be that many long-disappeared Murphy discs will resurface on CD.

Beauty and the Beast (Muse M 5355)

Good Murphy session from the mid-eighties, with a brisk band (including Bryan Lynch on trumpet and Joey Baron on drums) and a display of his skills on a typical confection of bop and standards like 'I Can't Get Started'. Murphy's headlong dive into the melodic zigzags of Sonny Rollins' 'Doxy' might be the standout for straight-ahead jazz fans.

I'll Close My Eyes (Muse MCD 5436)

Excellent recent session, effortlessly bringing together ballads, latin music, straight-ahead jazz and an Al Jarreau vehicle too. Murphy is partnered by the Brazilian trumpeter Claudio Roditi and pianist Pat Rebillot, and everybody sounds animated, to the extent of giving it all much of the casually dangerous edge of a Murphy live show.

Murray, David

(Born Berkeley, California, February 19, 1955)
Bridging the periods of rejection of earlier styles that erupted in the 1960s and the re-evaluation of the tradition that returned at the end of the 1970s, is the saxophonist David Murray. Murray has been a fierce avant-garde improviser, an organiser of

adventurous big bands, leader of an enthralling octet that sounded like a free Ellington group, a lyrical soloist in the tradition of the swing masters of the 1930s, even a re-creator of the famous Duke Ellington 1956 Newport performance of 'Diminuendo and Crescendo in Blue'.

Murray's tenor-playing went back to childhood, and he learned harmony from his mother, a church pianist. He studied music at college in Los Angeles (having already led his own r & b groups) and by the age of 20 had moved to New York to lead his own bands. Free-music interested him, and he performed with Cecil Taylor and ANTHONY BRAXTON initially, though he quickly moved towards balancing abstract improvisation with regular structures. Murray has also appeared with JACK DEJOHNETTE's Special Edition and in the World Saxophone Quartet.

★*Home* (Black Saint BSR 0055)

A 1981 octet, with some of Murray's best compositions on it, including 'Last of the Hipmen' and '3D Family' as well as the title track, 'Home', a ballad, a mixture of frankness and off-register probings. Murray's chemistry of vigorous contrapuntal work and rhythmic surprises in his ensemble writing gives the entire session an integrated quality that both makes already vivid compositions shine, and makes the band sound bigger than it is.

★*Morning Song* (Black Saint BSR 0075)

Murray's quartet in 1983, featuring John Hicks on piano, Ray Drummond on bass and ED BLACKWELL on drums in 1983, including a brilliant rendition of 'Body and Soul' that shows how close Murray perceives himself to be to the great lyricists such as Coleman Hawkins and proves himself entirely worthy of the responsibility with his sureness of touch at the extremes of the register, variation of dynamics and melodic adroitness.

★*The Hill* (Black Saint BSR 0110)

A more phlegmatic and musing Murray, but on music no less vibrant for that. This is one of his most integrated achievements, in the company only of Joe Chambers on drums and Richard

Davis on bass, and the overwhelming feeling is one of consolidation. Murray shows he is as inventive with a standard such as 'Chelsea Bridge' as he is with more contemporary resources, and his bass clarinet work here is magnificent.

Music Improvisation Company

The Music Improvisation Company, a quartet at times mutually supportive, at times antagonistic, featured guitarist Derek Bailey, saxophonist EVAN PARKER, percussionist Jamie Muir (who subsequently joined King Crimson) and sometime Stockhausen collaborator Hugh Davies on electronics.

During its brief but intense life this abrasive, demanding, wilful group put intense pressures on the resources of its members, and sometimes on audiences too. Its music betrayed no associations with any familiar idioms, except by accident. The sound of any given performance would often be determined by a 'leader' who emerged organically in the course of an improvisation, sometimes to retain that role over a period of months. But though stressful and challenging, the Music Improvisation Company was invaluable experience. EVAN PARKER said later: 'Being part of the group through this period opened me to the point where, when the wind's in the right direction, I'm ready to play with anyone.'

*_Music Improvisation Company 1968–1971_ (Incus CD 12)

No tunes, no chords, and no rehearsals come to that, but a lateral development out of John Cage and John Coltrane. Hugh Davies knew nothing of jazz, but he diverted the others into unexpected tonal refuges. Jamie Muir's percussion alternates between ghostly rattlings and admonishing rolls, Bailey sometimes glows, sometimes glowers and Parker phrases in fearsome multiphonic wails. Tough but salty music.

Newton, James

(Born California, 1953)

Composition has always been a thorny issue in jazz, though less so for those jazz composers (notably Ellington and Mingus) whose works were intimately related to the sounds that jazz soloists already made. But some performers who have shown considerable interest in jazz have been as powerfully drawn by classical music, and sought to unite techniques associated with both. Flautist James Newton has fruitfully explored this delicate territory.

Newton is not a saxophonist who plays flute but a specialist with a delectable tone and such delicate control over his sound that he is able to use unusual intervals as well as audaciously expanding the vocabulary of voice and flute-playing simultaneously – even to the extent of being able to sing one theme and improvise an instrumental one independently. Eric Dolphy was his inspiration, though he had formerly been a rock musician in school bands. At college he was comfortable in both classical and jazz groups, and after graduation he began working regularly with ANTHONY DAVIS.

★*African Flower* (Blue Note 746292)

One of Newton's finest, a 1985 recording (it made 'Record of the Year' in the 1986 *Downbeat* critics' poll) featuring the impassioned alto of Arthur Blythe with Jay Hoggard on vibes, Anthony Davis and the excellent violinist John Blake. The album is devoted to Ellington's music and makes shrewd and graceful work of 'Black and Tan Fantasy', 'Cottontail', 'Sophisticated Lady' and others.

Oregon

A pioneering and sophisticated 'world-music' outfit exploring many folk forms. Oregon was formed in 1972, to combine the talents of guitarist Ralph Towner, reed player Paul McCandless, violinist, flautist and pianist Glen Moore, and tabla player and percussionist Collin Walcott. Towner had already developed large-scale orchestral effects as well as subtle detail from a 12-

string guitar, McCandless and Moore had worked extensively with Indian musicians, and recorded with MILES DAVIS. Walcott's breadth of view was such that he could not only play Indian classical music on the sitar, but also sound like a jazz bassist or a guitarist on it, and his talents were so sharply missed by Oregon when he was tragically killed in a road crash in Europe that the band folded afterwards, and has only recently re-formed.

Music of Another Present Era (Vanguard VSD 79326)

Excellent early Oregon set, dominated by Towner and McCandless but nevertheless dependent for its textural strength on equal contributions from everyone. For all its reputation for wistful meanderings, Oregon could be both abstract and hard-swinging, and this disc captures just how powerful Walcott's percussion influence on the group was.

Osborne, Mike (Michael Evans)

(Born Hereford, England, September 28, 1941)
When MIKE WESTBROOK, Chris McGregor, JOHN SURMAN, DUDU PUKWANA, Alan Skidmore and the other major figures of the British jazz generation that emerged in the late Sixties dominated the universe here, Mike Osborne was the saxophonist to whom they all raised an eyebrow, which is a big accolade in the jazz business. Illness took Osborne out of regular public performance in 1982, but his searing tone, distraught-sounding whirls into the upper register and sudden crunching descents into the alto's basement sounds, and his ability to negotiate the most intense free-music without repetition or bluster made him the English Eric Dolphy, and his early retirement was an irreplaceable loss.

Outback (Future Music FDR CD07-031994)

One of Osborne's best records, a '70s set reproduced here down to the original artwork, even the misspelling of his name. A tumultuous, abrasive, unrelenting display of the cutting-edge jazz of the era – straight-ahead mixed with African music and Ornette Coleman – with South African exiles Louis Moholo (drums),

Harry Miller (bass) and Chris McGregor (piano) in hot support. Harry Becket's trumpet leavens the sometimes dark atmosphere with typical bouyancy and Osborne's shrill, hard sound sounds as fresh as it ever has.

Osby, Greg

(Born New York)

Greg Osby is one of the most striking of the M-Base players, that group of young virtuosi (STEVE COLEMAN, GERI ALLEN, CASSANDRA WILSON are others) whose absorption in bebop and then evolution from it has given some of them the freedom to try those harmonically driven skills against quirkier rhythmic and orchestral ideas drawn from funk, hip-hop, rap, and bits and pieces of contemporary straight music. Osby graduated from Berklee in Boston in 1983, and joined the quintet of trumpeter Jon Faddis, following that with a stint with JACK DEJOHNETTE's Special Edition, Dizzy Gillespie, PAT METHENY, McCOY TYNER and others.

But it has been the M-Base collective, and Steve Coleman in particular, which has involved Osby the most. As with Coleman, it has been other leaders' work that seems to have loosened up Osby the improviser, and his own sessions – though intriguing – have yet to take wing.

★*Mind Games* (JMT 834422)

An Osby session from 1988, featuring the great pianist Geri Allen. At its best, it offers a freshness of ensemble sound that is an encouraging change from the classic jazz movement, but some over-deliberation aimed at the development of new jazz structures (a constant challenge for most of the M-Base artists) prevents the improvisers from altogether finding their feet.

★*Season of Renewal* (JMT 834 435-2)

More hallmarks of the M-Base style here – shuffling, staccato rap-like pieces such as 'For the Cause', a piece that quickly shifts into its solo sax mode (against a tambourine and occasional rimshot clatters) after a spine-chilling soprano wail and then STEVE LACY-like high blipping sounds interweaving with the rhythm. The essence, as with so much of the genre, is rhythmic counterpoint. Bursts of funk patterns culminate in cymbal splashes, against repeated scurrying keyboard figures, legato vocals, horns diving between them. An ambitious, patchily compelling session.

Papasov, Ivo

(Born Kardjali, Bulgaria, February 16, 1952)
Some are already comparing the impact of Ivo Papasov on jazz with that of Django Reinhardt in the 1930s. They shared Romany origins, they were both preoccupied with hybrids of jazz and the indigenous music of their own communities, and both delivered music of immense excitement and panache. Papasov is the beneficiary of relaxed cultural connections between east and west, and his choices have been shaped by a combination of the traditional Balkan wedding music of his locality, the music of Charlie Parker and Benny Goodman that has influenced his reed-playing, and the international language of funk, which has affected his rhythm section. Wedding Band or stambolovo music is the dance music of rural Bulgaria, but Papasov's interest in jazz has startlingly modified it.

Orpheus Ascending (Hannibal HNCD 1346)

Papasov's British record debut, with a feverish, whirling display of jazz-influenced improvising pitched against the complicated dance rhythms of traditional Bulgarian music. It's mostly high-energy collective playing, but Papasov's unique bitter-sweet intonation and interspersing of hurricane runs against solemn, declamatory passages compounds the all-round amiable freneticism.

Parker, Evan Shaw

(Born Bristol, England, April 5, 1944)
Of all the saxophonists originally inspired by the example of John Coltrane, Evan Parker is one of the most unusual. Now an internationally respected virtuoso improviser with explicit jazz

inclinations, Parker came to prominence in the 1970s as a purely abstract player. He went much further than his idols, or most other British free players, in recording and performing technically remarkable researches into harmonics, split-note formation, playing of chords on the horn and two or more lines at once, very little of it referring to regular jazz structure or tempo. Over 20 years, he has worked with the most inventive improvisers in the world.

Atlanta (Impetus IMPCD 18617)

A formidable 1986 recording with bassist BARRY GUY and drummer Paul Lytton, vividly representing the collaborative, texturally rich, sometimes austere music of this school.

Conic Sections (ah um 015)

Evan Parker's first unaccompanied recording on CD, and a remarkable exposition of his talents. Parker's achievement is to create a saxophone soundscape of completely personal materials, with little or no references to orthodox idioms, yet deliver it with such intensity – and sometimes ferocity – as to make its vocabulary and syntax utterly logical. In recent years his tone has mellowed, with occasional echoes even of 1950s cool-sax artists, which adds to this music's richness.

Pascoal, Hermeto

(Born Lagoa da Canoa, Brazil, June 22, 1936)
Hermeto Pascoal, a man as visually charismatic as he has been musically influential (bearded, and with flowing white hair, he makes Robinson Crusoe look like a police cadet), has been a model for the careers of many Latin-American musicians, notably percussionist AIRTO MOREIRA and singer Flora Purim, and is also sometimes quoted as one of the less obvious influences on MILES DAVIS' post-1972 exploits.

Pascoal plays a variety of instruments including flutes, keyboards and a huge tusk-like horn that sounds like an elephant announcing dinner. Sometimes the themes have depended on a churning, repeated-pattern flavour that sounds like a cross between circus music and old Frank Zappa records, but they never become lost in this maze because there are always sudden breaks into the sunny clearings of straight-ahead Brazilian swing. Pascoal has even been known to enlist the services of a live piglet onstage, inducing the unlikely improviser to squeal at key moments – an innovation for which he found the RSPCA joining his audiences on his last British tour. Long, obscure spoken monologues may unfold over wild, concertina-like electric keyboard improvisations, but Pascoal is also fond of slow, drifting, trance-like pieces for guitars. His music represents a refreshingly idiosyncratic aspect of a now highly commercialised and transformed idiom.

★*Festa Des Deuses* (Philips 510 407-2)

A sampled goose and a sewing machine are apparently included in the instrumental mix on this typical Pascoal brew. There are other unlikely samples too, including the voice of the Brazilian president, and the regular Pascoal band is augmented by an assortment of more conventional guests. Saxophonist Carlos Malta, so often a striking performer on live shows, plays a dominant role.

Peacock, Annette

(Dates unknown)
An artist unclaimable by the entertainment corporations is Annette Peacock, the vocalist and synthesiser player. Her music is unsentimental, devoid of orthodox lyricism, monochromatic, and taut as toned muscles. Her voice is clear, but razor-edged rather than rounded, often working over jumps of wide intervals, and is sometimes surprisingly slight and withdrawn, rather as Blossom Dearie might sound if she'd worked for John Zorn. Peacock's keyboard-playing is spare but telling, in both its quirky melodic shapes and its tonal variation: a pioneer user of the synthesiser, having been presented with a 1968 version by R.A. Moog himself, Ms Peacock gives her short, needling figures the texture of vibes, strings or acoustic pianos.

Annette Peacock's association with the jazz community began with her relationship with the brilliant bassist Gary Peacock, with whom she moved to New York in the 1960s. She became involved with the psychedelic movement of the period, and with one of its gurus, Dr Timothy Leary, and then began to contribute highly personal themes to the piano repertoire of PAUL BLEY, much as Carla Bley had done before her. She has performed with many of the most original musicians in Europe and the States, and in 1987 toured with Karlheinz Stockhausen.

Skyskating (Ironic IRONIC 2CD)

Annette Peacock's first album for her own Ironic label, a selection from her own solo live shows in which she handles all the instrumentation and yet maintains an intensity that derives from the impassive conviction of her work.

Petrucianni, Michel

(Born Montpellier, France, December 28, 1962)
An explicit admirer of the work of Bill Evans, KEITH JARRETT and McCOY TYNER, French pianist Michel Petrucianni is one of the most striking of the new generation of non Afro-American jazz-influenced virtuosi who are of the right age, background, independence and open-mindedness to bend jazz history their way.

Petrucianni was discovered at 18, by the *International Herald Tribune*'s Mike Zwerin (himself a musician) and a French tour with LEE KONITZ followed. Two years later, Petrucianni was adopted by a once-fashionable jazz saxophonist who had devoted 15 years to retirement and transcendental meditation – Charles Lloyd, who was sufficiently inspired to come out of retirement and hire Petrucianni himself. Two years later, at impresario George Wein's instigation, Petrucianni was playing a solo concert at Carnegie Hall, to acclaim in *Time* magazine and the *New York Times*.

The pianist came from a musical family, and was inspired to take up piano at the age of four when he saw Duke Ellington on a TV show. He also enjoyed drums, partly as therapy for the wasting disease that has resulted in his minuscule physical stature. Petrucianni's triumphs over the practical obstacles to being a jazz pianist are, however, aspects he prefers to play down.

Power of Three (Blue Note CDP 746427)

A 1986 Petrucianni live session from the Montreux Festival, with the pianist and an excellent partner in the guitarist Jim Hall, a discreet and oblique contrast for Petrucianni's flooding exuberance. Wayne Shorter joins the band for a spacious workout on 'Limbo', for Hall's calypso 'SRO', and for Petrucianni's rich and evocative 'Morning Blues'.

Promenade with Duke (Blue Note 0777 7 80590 28)

Petrucianni pays his tribute to his original inspiration, Duke Ellington, with wit and style. Some of his piano devices become familiar (octave shifts to vary the same figure particularly), but he changes the character of 'Caravan' with some brooding chordwork, delays harmonic changes with spaces or endlessly jangling trills, while the headlong version of 'C Jam Blues' is an astonishing virtuoso display over a stomping left-hand pattern.

Au Théâtre Des Champs-Elysées (Dreyfus Jazz FDM 36570-2. 2 CDs)

A double-CD, recorded live in Paris in November 1994 – an unaccompanied $1\frac{3}{4}$ hours, of which forty minutes is devoted to the opening medley (Ellington, Hancock, standards, blues). But it's all so joyous and good-humoured that it hardly ever palls. Later on, there is a rock-breaking 'I Mean You', a coy 'Round About Midnight', and an overwhelmingly crowded 'Caravan'. One of Petrucianni's best ever firework displays.

Pine, Courtney

(Born London, 1964)

Though many players of distinction have recently emerged from the fervent expansion of jazz enthusiasm among Britain's young black population, Courtney Pine remains the most prominent and a rallying point. Originally a funk and reggae saxophonist, Pine was taken under the wing of Mac Tontoh, who ran a successful African rock band called Osibisa. Then Pine heard Sonny Rollins'

1950s album *Way Out West* and decided to commit himself to jazz. Though his friends mostly liked Bob Marley and Stevie Wonder, Pine stuck with it, joined a class run by drummer John Stevens, and began working regularly. With his wife June, he formed Abibi Jazz Arts, a west London workshop designed to show his contemporaries that jazz could be British black music too.

Out of Abibi Jazz Arts, Pine encouraged the foundation of an orchestra, the Jazz Warriors. With this band and with his own Coltraneish small groups, often featuring fast-learning young sidemen such as pianist JULIAN JOSEPH and drummer Mark Mondesir, Pine gained an international reputation. He has also worked with American musicians including orchestra leader GEORGE RUSSELL, the late Art Blakey, Elvin Jones, and the MARSALIS brothers' mentor, piano-playing father Ellis Marsalis.

★*Journey to the Urge Within* (Island CID 9846)

Pine's debut album in 1986, a tour around his musical interests and skills that has over the years shifted the astonishing total of over 100,000 copies. Though it touched on many idioms, early 1960s Coltrane was its principal inspiration, particularly those incantational aspects of Coltrane; Pine confirmed his preoccupation with this music, and his technical sophistication as well, in the tunes 'I Believe' and 'Peace'.

★*The Vision's Tale* (Antilles ANCD 8746)

Although the least adventurous (and despite the leader's slight discomfort with the open spaces of ballads), *The Vision's Tale* was one of the more satisfying Pine albums, not least because of the confident restraint of a highly original American rhythm section including Ellis Marsalis on piano and Jeff 'Tain' Watts on drums. The material includes 'In a Mellow Tone', 'God Bless the Child' and (in a nod to Rollins) 'I'm an Old Cowhand'.

★*To the Eyes of Creation* (Antilles)

The most focused work Pine has recorded so far, a blend of the music of Africa, the Caribbean, America and Europe without simply seeming like tourism. It includes a ska track ('Eastern

Standard Time'), and Bob Marley's 'Redemption Song', but through it all Pine performs with the commitment and drive that he has applied to all his other assignments.

Ponty, Jean-Luc

(Born Avranches, Normandy, September 29, 1942)
Ex-classical violinist Jean-Luc Ponty has spent much of his career attempting to camouflage the effects of his musical upbringing, yet his breadth of view and lyricism still demonstrate a strong connection with it. He is of the generation of jazz violinists who grew up with the sound of Coltrane in their ears, and who therefore tended to eschew the jaunty swing or kaleidoscopic bop styles of earlier practitioners in pursuit of a denser and more impacted manner, seeking powerful emotional effects from sustained energy levels and electronic effects.

Ponty's parents were both music teachers and the boy was a star student on classical violin. In the early 1960s, though working with a straight orchestra, he became increasingly involved in jazz, and began to make an impact in the idiom at festivals in Europe, and eventually at Monterey in the US. During the 1970s Ponty took to working in America with his own fusion bands and with eccentric rock artist Frank Zappa's adventurous Mothers of Invention, notably on the great *Hot Rats* session.

Aurora (Atlantic 19158)

Good 1975 session by Ponty, revealing how successfully he has kept the electric violin from destroying the tonal virtues of the acoustic instrument. Pianist Patrice Rushen fronts a capable band, but it's really Ponty's session, and the themes are more striking than is common for the genre.

Porter, Art

(Born Little Rock, Arkansas)
Because the young Arkansas-born saxophonist Art Porter is one of the most skilful of the new generation of players, with an

almost violin-like sound on ballads, he has become one of the busiest saxophonists in the music. He makes an exciting and theatrical pop-jazz that appeals to a wide audience.

Art Porter was raised in a musical family, in Little Rock, Arkansas, where his father still runs his own piano trio. The boy played drums first, then became the bassist in his father's group, switching to saxophones in his teens. He studied with Ellis Marsalis at Virginia Commonwealth University, has featured with bands led by Pharoah Sanders, Brother Jack MacDuff and Clark Terry, and has won many awards as a saxophonist. His debut album, *Pocket City*, is a typical Porter package – mid-tempo funk, gliding ballads, and blues-flavoured bop.

*_Pocket City_ (Verve/Forecast)

Inevitably strong influence of disco and super-smooth production values, and it isn't the same as witnessing Porter's irrepressibly energetic stage-act, but a deft compilation of pop tunes and dance-grooves overlaid with the leader's fleet saxophone lines. There's no feeling of grup interplay because the background is static, but that's what this kind of idiom is about.

Pukwana, Mututuzel 'Dudu'

(Born Port Elizabeth, South Africa, July 18, 1938; died London, June 29, 1990)
Dudu Pukwana, the South African altoist who lived in London from 1966 until his premature death in 1990, was one of the most formidable of the Cape's powerful complement of jazz musicians. He admired the work of Ornette Coleman, but also the luxurious, romantic styles of the swing players. His playing thus veered between wild swoops of sound ending in cantankerous honks, tender, vibrato-laden rhapsody, raucous guffaws turning into sly, knowing seductiveness, and tantalising displays of quivering romanticism.

Initially a pianist, it was as an altoist and composer that Pukwana helped white pianist Chris McGregor form the Blue Notes – a band that became famous not just for the vigour of its music, but for its then unique mixed-race lineup, which led to its exile from South Africa. In the 1970s in England (after successes with various McGregor groups including the spectacular Ellington-meets-kwela big band Brotherhood of Breath) Pukwana began to form groups of his own. One of his first, Spear, toured South Africa with HUGH MASEKELA, and then toured the States. Pukwana also liked reggae, and even the distinctly unsonglike sounds of the European free-improvisers. In 1978 Pukwana formed Zila, a sometimes ragged but unfailingly exhilarating band with which he worked until his final illness.

In the Townships (Earthworks/Virgin CDEWV 5)

A reissue of a typically headlong and uneven Pukwana session, recorded with his ensemble Spear in the 1970s. There are seven tracks, and the African flavour dominates the set, but the leader's improvisational flair, both in violent abstract playing and in moods of manic tenderness, display Pukwana's rich jazz awareness.

Pullen, Don Gabriel

(Born Roanoke, Virginia, December 25, 1944; died April 1995)
Pianist and organist Don Pullen's dramatic keyboard style is often compared to Cecil Taylor's, and in its complexity, mercurial variety, bursts of hammering dissonance and tightly packed phrasing it resembles it, but Pullen is less Europeanised than Taylor, and less unforgiving. Pullen can be boppish, rhapsodic, or even resemble a bop-gospel organ player.

Pullen's family was musical, and his most valuable apprenticeship was served with the Chicago avantists in the 1960s, most notably MUHAL RICHARD ABRAMS. He established a creative partnership with the drummer Milford Graves, their recordings together being mostly independently produced free-music, but in the 1970s Pullen began to work with more high-profile artists, including NINA SIMONE and Art Blakey. It was as a member of the Charles Mingus band between 1973 and 1975 that Pullen most firmly established himself, his percussive style being ideally suited to the forceful Mingus manner. Through that experience, Pullen established a fruitful partnership with the tenorist GEORGE ADAMS.

★*Sixth Sense* (Black Saint BSR 0088)

Powerful lineup for Pullen's mid-1980s band, with Olu Dara on trumpet, Donald 'Duck' Harrison (late of Art Blakey's Messengers) on alto, Fred Hopkins on bass and Bobby Battle on drums. Powerful, improvisationally resourceful music, complete with one of the most imposing of all modern bass players in Fred Hopkins.

Rava, Enrico

(Born Trieste, Italy, August 20, 1943)
Enrico Rava is the Italian trumpeter who has for years been one of the most attractive European interpreters of the 1955–65 MILES DAVIS manner. He has added a Mediterranean warmth and light to that poetry of curling long notes, tantalising pauses and unexpected accents that have made up Davis' most expressive and economical style.

Rava was self-taught, though his mother was a pianist. Miles Davis, Chet Baker, Coltrane and Ellington figure among his influences. In the mid-1960s he played with Argentinian saxophonist GATO BARBIERI, then with STEVE LACY and later with trombonist Roswell Rudd, and in more recent times both with prominent European experimentalists (such as drummer Tony Oxley) and the legendary American avantist Cecil Taylor.

★*Secrets* (Soul Note SN1164)

Some of Rava's best music still lingers on vinyl, but this 1986 set featuring the superb British pianist JOHN TAYLOR is a good enough representation of Rava's remarkable range of moods – from the ethereal to a shimmering Mediterranean heat.

Rebello, Jason

(Born London, 1969)
Jason Rebello didn't wait to hit twenty before he began making waves on the British jazz scene. He possessed a piano technique

equal to most idioms, including classical playing and many styles of jazz, and he was both profoundly aware of the musical traditions he was inheriting and creative enough to extend them.

Rebello was a soul and funk fan in his teens, and already a student of classical piano, but a new world of musical ideas were opened up by hearing Herbie Hancock and Charlie Parker. Rebello went to London's Guildhall School of Music as a classical student but was already working with leading British jazz players including saxophonists Tommy Smith and Steve Williamson. Before long Rebello's reputation spread, and he was invited to tour with star American saxophonist WAYNE SHORTER. Rebello has also worked as a TV presenter on the BBC's arts show *Artrageous*. In 1995 he announced his retirement to a Buddhist monastery.

★*Keeping Time* (Novus 7432112904-2)

Not really a typical example of Rebello's jazz talents, but a return to his soul and funk origins. Soul singer Jocelyn Brown helps out with a simpler, more direct version of jazz-fusion, and though some of it's bland, Rebello's promise and taste still show.

Redman, Joshua

(Born Berkeley, California, 1970)
One of a handful of rising stars of the early 1990s who has really looked the part of a saxophone giant of the decade, Joshua Redman is the son of tenorist Dewey Redman, long-time associate of Ornette Coleman. As soon as he emerged, Redman looked like the young postbopper who really made everything that he played count – with a debut album raved over around the world, and a series of live performances that were astonishing for their fertile maturity.

Redman was invited to attend both Harvard and Yale, but left student life after winning the 1991 Thelonious Monk International Saxophone Competition, judged by Benny Carter and BRANFORD MARSALIS among others. There is strong flavour of Sonny Rollins in his playing, but also of an older generation including Ben Webster, Coleman Hawkins, Lester Young and

Dexter Gordon. Always sounding composed, even at the fastest tempos, Redman's relaxed blending of many approaches to the saxophone is a substantial part of his appeal.

★*Wish* (WEA 9362453652)

Superb Redman debut, in the company of such stars as PAT METHENY, CHARLIE HADEN and Billy Higgins. Redman demonstrates here that, like JOE HENDERSON, he hardly ever repeats himself, and in the manner of the great soloists, seems able to foresee the development of a solo over long stretches than most mortals. Good material, great improvisations.

Reeves, Dianne

(Born Detroit, 1956)
Dianne Reeves is a gifted and formidably equipped singer (a contralto with a three-and-a-half-octave range) who has so far narrowly missed making the mark at the more improvisational end of jazz that it once seemed she might. Her voice is rich, and strong at the extremes of her range, but her talents have so far been obscured by flashy production and a good deal of unsuitable material. With more modest projects and simpler support she may yet achieve the distinctiveness that is currently eluding her.

Dianne Reeves was discovered as a teenager by the trumpeter Clark Terry, working with his band until her move to Los Angeles, when she began working with Sergio Mendez and Harry Belafonte. Reeves brought the house down at a Monterey Jazz Festival performance with Tito Puente, and made two albums for the Palo Alto label before being taken up by Blue Note/ EMI. Her first disc for the company, *Dianne Reeves*, produced by pianist George Duke, made the album charts in the States.

★*Dianne Reeves* (Blue Note)

Although this album isn't as accurate a representation of the singer's onstage power as it might have been, and over-schmaltzy production muddied it, it was still an impressive debut. Reeves ranges widely in idiom, but she has a strong feeling for jazz and it's the underpinning of the session.

Remler, Emily

(Born Englewood Cliffs, New Jersey, September 18, 1957; died Australia, May 4, 1990)
Emily Remler was a superb exponent of a swinging bebop guitar style based on the work of Wes Montgomery and modernised by the ideas of PAT METHENY; had she not died at the age of 32 she might well have expanded on her antecedents a lot more.

Remler was another Berklee student, but she moved to New Orleans in 1976 and worked there with singers Nancy Wilson and Astrud Gilberto, and later trumpeter WYNTON MARSALIS and vocalist BOBBY McFERRIN. She also met a veteran bop guitarist, Herb Ellis, who got her a record deal. The result was the 1982 session, *Firefly*, for Concord. By the mid-1980s the music-business pressures that led her to alcoholism began to interrupt her work but by 1988 she appeared to be back on line. Her death was one of the more acute of several jazz losses during 1990.

Retrospective Vol. 2 (Concord CCD 4463)

Pieces of Emily Remler's from several Concords, including the albums *Catwalk*, *Transitions*, *Take Two*, *Firefly* and a little of *East To Wes* too. Remler's warm, flowing sound ideally suits Latin dance pieces such as 'Nunca Mais', and her Wes Montgomery outings (on 'Blues for Herb', 'The Firefly' and 'East to Wes') are as good a tribute to the boss as anyone has come out with, full of that breezily funky swing and singing sound.

Tony Remy

(Born London, August 13, 1962)
Tony Remy, like John McLaughlin in the late Sixties, is the new British guitar-export capable not only of blasting improvisation and jazzy swing, but also of pop-angled ideas that broaden his audience. That's why GRP have signed him up, though in some

ways 'Boof!' says more about GRP than about a guitarist whose mixture of feline rhythmic touch and sudden eruptions of spontaneous energy make him such a hypnotic performer.

★*Boof!* (GRP 97362)

Being GRP, this is a disc aimed at the crossover and jazz-soul market, its landmarks including Stevie Wonder-like vocals, busy hip-hop and occasional ballads with a Pat Metheny tinge. Remy's stage act is punchier than this, but the use of electronic layering is inventive, and the guitarist's duet with the excellent drummer Pete Lewinson gives a hint of the real thing.

Roberts, Marcus

(Born 1963)

For some years pianist Marcus Roberts was in the odd position of being one of the most interesting elements in the WYNTON MARSALIS band, a young guardian of the traditions exhibiting both the smooth swing of Wynton Kelly and the crabbiness of Thelonious Monk. As his solo career blossomed, this promise wasn't entirely upheld, but Roberts remains a keyboard artist of considerable stature and encyclopaedic knowledge, who also exhibits a vim and vitality about his work often missing from neo-classical jazz. Roberts studied at Florida State University and in the early 1980s began to win piano competitions. He joined Wynton Marsalis in 1985, and the comprehensive sweep across the entire jazz piano firmament that he would demonstrate in his unaccompanied sections soon led to recording opportunities.

★*Truth is Spoken Here* (BMG/Novus PD 83051)

Marcus Roberts' debut album of standards, originals that sound like standards, and tributes to Monk, and a session on which his sometime group leader Wynton Marsalis also appears. Roberts' easy migrations between stride piano and the borderline of abstraction are undeniably impressive.

Robinson, Orphy

(Born London, 1964)

Vibes and marimba player and composer Orphy Robinson was raised in North London, studied music at school and discovered the xylophone in a prizewinning student band, good enough to appear on exhibition performance at the Albert Hall and Wembley. Robinson eventually found himself in a studio-based funk band called Savannah, but began to tentatively contact jazz by tracing the roots of famous funk stars like saxophonist Grover Washington. In the mid-1980s, when the London saxophonist Courtney Pine led the emergence of a young generation of black and Asian jazz performers, and formed a big band called the Jazz Warriors to act as their performing workshop, Robinson found himself catapulted into a jazz improvising situation, and learned on the job. A vibrant, free-swinging performer whose swing and relaxation sometimes recall an earlier generation of vibists, Robinson can also be thoughtful and formally audacious, as he demonstrates with his own band Annavas.

★*When Tomorrow Comes* (Blue Note CDP 7985812)

Despite Robinson's origins in funk, this is an ascetic, almost cerebral debut. It has echoes of GARY BURTON with KEITH JARRETT, minimalist modern classical music, even the eerie, spacious impressionism of the Nordic music of such artists as JAN GARBAREK. Robinson's band Annavas features vibes, flute, piano, cello, bass and drums, and pianist Joe Bashorun is the co-composer.

★*The Vibes Describes* (Blue Note 7243 8 29223 2 2)

Not a sensational follow-up, and by the mid-'90s, Robinson was having trouble clarifying what road he wanted to go down. Brazilian percussionist NANA VASCONCELOS makes a welcome appearance here and there, but the worldbeat burble of percussion, hushed, stealthy chanting, and general tone-poetry with a backbeat (though, unexpectedly, there's the Stranglers' 'Golden Brown') isn't quite enough to make Robinson's future clear.

Roney, Wallace

(Born 1960)

As if to prove that younger trumpet players in thrall to earlier MILES DAVIS shouldn't be dismissed out of hand, Wallace Roney has been consistently demonstrating through the 1980s that he has grasped the elusive essence of Davis as well as that oblique, muted, tightly edited sound. Like Davis, Roney's use of space and delay not only creates more dramatic and involving music but it also makes rhythm sections more creative.

Roney recorded with CHICO FREEMAN first, in 1982, then Art Blakey's Jazz Messengers. Roney's sound was ideal for drummer Tony Williams' return to a measured, reserved acoustic ensemble sound in the manner of the mid-1960s Miles Davis band, and after 1986 Roney appeared regularly with Williams. In 1991, shortly before Davis' death, Roney performed alongside his hero with Quincy Jones' band at Montreux, playing the more technically taxing parts in a re-creation of some Gil Evans scores. He also worked in the Miles Davis Tribute Band featuring former Davis sidemen that toured in 1992.

★*Obsession* (Muse Records MCD 5423)

Not much doubt about what the obsession still is: Roney is the best interpreter of Miles Davis' achievements in the business, and drummer CYNDY BLACKMAN is one of the best at the explosive Tony Williams drumming style that was so much a part of the 1960s Davis picture. Gary Thomas' Wayne Shorterish tenor helps confirm the atmosphere, and an earlier Miles era – the 1950s one with Coltrane and Red Garland – even beckons on 'Alone Together' and a speeding 'Donna Lee'. But it's certainly a loving and consummately musical form of worship – except in the sleeve notes, which mention Miles, in passing, only once.

Rosnes, Renée

(Born Canada, 1962)

'Imagine Rachmaninoff writing for and jamming with the Nat Cole Trio,' says Robert Doershuk in the liner notes to this set by

417

Canadian pianist Renée Rosnes, and he's got a point. Rosnes, a fluid and delicate, conservatoire-trained pianist, loosely resembles Bill Evans and has been accompanist to some distinctly heavyweight saxophonists including JOE HENDERSON.

★*Without Words* (Blue Note CDP 0777 7 98168-2-8)

Rosnes with a classical string group plus her acoustic trio. The pianist's Bill Evans roots are strongly confirmed by the coherence of her solos as narratives, her ability to accelerate casually dramatic episodes out of almost absent-minded interludes, and Evans-related material like 'You and The Night and the Music', 'I've Got You Under My Skin', and Miles Davis's 'Solar'. Robert Freedman has imaginatively scored the ensemble charts, and made the fiddle-section as jazzy as it could be. But Rosnes unimpeded is just fine.

Russell, George

(Born Cincinnati, Ohio, June 23, 1923)
Composer and arranger George Russell's music bursts with life, and a colliding, ricocheting life informed by the leader's intellectual and emotional grip on bebop, African rhythmic ideas, western modern classical devices, and orthodox big-band swing. He may slowly fan a 15th-century madrigal into a rhythmic inferno, or free-sounding slitherings and wrigglings between the ensemble sections into sustained blasts of uptempo rock time and blazing trumpet riffs abandoning melody for sheer energy and driving tempo.

As a child Russell heard jazz on the riverboats, and by his early twenties was a drummer good enough to get an invite to join Charlie Parker in New York. But though the tuberculosis that plagued him in the 1940s kept him from the gig, he began writing for Dizzy Gillespie's big band ('Cubana Be/Cubana Bop' was his most celebrated contribution to it) and was not much more than 25 when he wrote 'A Bird in Igor's Yard', a marriage of bebop phraseology with rhythmic textures closely related to the 'Rite of Spring'. Russell eventually published a complex theoretical work in 1953, *The Lydian Chromatic Concept of Tonal Organisation*, which extensively influenced the shift from chordal to modal (scale-based) playing during the 1950s, the underpinning of the most independent work by MILES DAVIS and John Coltrane. Russell's writings indicated ways they could be used to reconcile soloists at various points with the given key or the harmonic activity of the rhythm section – but not all the time, as was the case with bop.

Since the late 1950s, Russell has extensively taught as well as played, but during the 1960s he regularly led sextets (at times featuring the great reed player Eric Dolphy) that audaciously blended free and structured materials, and the success of these groups in Europe led Russell to live in Sweden for five years. Russell's ideas have extensively influenced musicians on either side of the Atlantic: notably CARLA BLEY and Eric Dolphy in the States, JAN GARBAREK, Palle Mikkelborg and latterly British saxophonist ANDY SHEPPARD in Europe. In 1989 Russell won the MacArthur Prize, one of the most prestigious American tributes for services to intellectual and cultural life.

★*Jazz Workshop* (Bluebird/BMG ND 86467)

One of the best of all Russell discs, *Jazz Workshop* represents the most consistent of his early efforts to splice improvisation and complex organisation. It was recorded in 1956, and features pianist Bill Evans and trumpeter Art Farmer, among others, in bands perfectly attuned to the complex demands of the composer. Russell's Lydian Concept not only offered fascinating alternatives to improvisers but also reshaped the nature of jazz melody, and 'Jack's Blues' and 'Night Sound' both exhibit a needling unorthodoxy and subtle transformation of blues materials that came as a breath of fresh air in an era dominated by bop.

★*New York Big Band* (Soul Note SNCD 1039)

1982 performance by Russell's revived New York Big Band, typically dense and intense, but well served by an illustrious assembly of contemporary musicians. There's a superb version of 'Cubana Be, Cubana Bop' and a beautiful version of the famous Eric Dolphy vehicle, 'God Bless the Child'.

*_Living Time Orchestra: The London Concert_ (Label Bleu LBLC 6527/8)

This double-CD set was recorded live at Ronnie Scott's Club in 1989 with a mixed American and British band. It begins with Russell's adaptation of a madrigal (which erupts into free-jazz and thunderous rock after a while) and ends with his delightful arrangement of Miles Davis' famous 'So What' trumpet solo, orchestrated as a long theme. Fine representation of the tidal sound of a Russell band in performance.

Sanborn, David William

(Born Tampa, Florida, July 30, 1945)
Dave Sanborn has helped shape the techniques of a generation of saxophone players, as well as lending his talents to innumerable recording sessions. But though he's fleet, inventive and in most respects the complete virtuoso, Sanborn remains the most direct of players. He took up the saxophone as respiratory exercise after childhood polio, passed through rhythm & blues (working with the Paul Butterfield band from 1967, when he was 22) and the soulful sound became a permanent feature of his playing that led to work with Stevie Wonder in 1972.

Sanborn listened closely to the most blues-derived of musicians such as Ray Charles and saxophonist Hank Crawford, as well as the most subtle and complex yet forthright blues saxophonist of all, Charlie Parker. Sanborn's wailing eloquence made him a regular partner of the late composing and arranging genius Gil Evans, but the same penetrating voice has also appeared on the work of many soul and pop artists, such as James Taylor ('How Sweet It Is') and David Bowie ('Young Americans').

*_Voyeur_ (WEA 256 900)

Typical setting for Sanborn's burning tone and dancing momentum, _Voyeur_ is a 1981 collection of funk and bluesy music that won a Grammy for the saxophonist. Exuberant, direct and earthy music, and Sanborn varies the disco-funk atmosphere with some delicate alto sketches on such tunes as 'All I Need Is You'.

★*Another Hand* (Elektra Musician 7559-61088)

An unexpected Sanborn disc that went back to some of his earlier preferences in a thoughtful and jazzier session that frequently resembled the sound of the Gil Evans band in its ensemble passages. It isn't an unqualified success, and Sanborn occasionally sounds a shade lost, but the music is ambitious and the band includes some illustrious personnel including BILL FRISELL, Marcus Miller and CHARLIE HADEN.

★*Upfront* (Elektra 7559-61272)

Back to the earlier formula, but though it echoes the 1980s Miles Davis band it's more surefooted with the idiom, there's some spikily Ornette Colemanish Sanborn alto on a crunching organ blues ('Full House') and the leader at his most swoopingly elegiac on a Ray Charlesian 'Soul Serenade'. 'Bang-Bang' is just noisy let's-party music, but the funky version of Ornette Coleman's magical 'Ramblin'' is a triumph.

Sanchez, David

(Born Guaynabo, Puerto Rico, 1968)
Of the many young musicians whose careers were advanced by the interest of the late Dizzy Gillespie, the Puerto Rican saxophonist David Sanchez has proved to be one of the most distinctive and promising. Sanchez now regularly turns up close to the top of the saxophone polls in magazines such as *Downbeat*, and his particular chemistry of North American, Latin American and Caribbean music has a unique flavour.

Sanchez took up the conga drums at eight, and the saxophone at the age of twelve, and grew up listening to a mixture of Afro-Caribbean, Puerto Rican and Latin classical music. He eventually became fascinated by the work of MILES DAVIS and Billie Holiday. Sanchez first studied psychology, then committed himself to music. He moved to New York, where he was soon playing with most of the city's Latin-jazz celebrities, joining Dizzy Gillespie's United Nations Orchestra in 1990. Sanchez is also a regular member of the Philip Morris Superband, and has cut a follow-up to his debut disc 'The Departure' with 'Sketches of Dreams', a mix of standards, Afro-Caribbean music, and bop.

★*The Departure* (Columbia COL 476507 2)

A really noticeable debut. The flight to the past has resulted in so many clones of earlier styles that Sanchez risked being overlooked as another from the same mould at first (there are the usual references to the '60s Miles Davis band, '80s street-funk, and Latin music. However, the overall tone of this set exhibits a restraint, timing and economy missing from many of the rest. TOM HARRELL makes his usual wise and subtle trumpet contributions, and Danilo Perez is an attractively Monkish pianist who is a good foil for Sanchez' full, eager lines.

Sandoval, Arturo

(Born Cuba, 1949)
A showman to the tips of his toes, and about as nonchalantly in command of the resources of the trumpet as anyone in jazz, trumpeter Arturo Sandoval's whistling, accurately pitched high notes, bull-charging runs, tiptoeing muted figures, machine-gun bebop and tongue-in-cheek showband finales shower over his listeners, and if the effect is sometimes dazzling to the point of saturation, Sandoval nevertheless delivers it all with an exuberance that is highly communicative in itself.

Sandoval originally came to the attention of Americans and Europeans through his work with the exotic Cuban ensemble Irakere. He was already a music teacher at the Havana Conservatory, adept on piano and trumpet and fluent in the classical repertoire as well as jazz. Sandoval played with Dizzy Gillespie – his original primary influence in jazz – from the beginning of the 1980s onward, and became a prominent feature of Gillespie's United Nations big band.

★*I Remember Clifford* (GRP 96682)

Sandoval's second disc for GRP was a tribute to a hero, not the usual collection of Latin dance grooves. This bop-based gesture to the memory of Clifford Brown shows the best side of Sandoval, and he has the invaluable help of Kenny Kirkland on piano, Ernie Watts and others. As if one Sandoval wasn't enough, the record features several of his solos overdubbed to form a trumpet choir belting through famous Brown solos.

Scofield, John

(Born Ohio, December 26, 1951)

In the 1960s the jazz and the blues tributaries in electric guitar were fused by a group of artists including PAT METHENY, JOHN McLAUGHLIN and John Scofield. Scofield, a gifted Berklee student who worked with Chet Baker, funk drummer Billy Cobham, Charles Mingus, vibist GARY BURTON and the imaginative saxophonist DAVID LIEBMAN, came to big-time fame with MILES DAVIS' comeback to playing in the early 1980s, when he and fellow-guitarist Mike Stern collaborated in helping the long-laid-up Davis back to form.

Scofield's work, both in composition and improvising, constantly suggests bebop, but the sound he applies to it takes into account B.B. King as well as Jim Hall, Muddy Waters as well as Pat Martino. Scofield sounds moody, glowering, his vocabulary full of reverberating, fiercely struck low notes and arching treble sounds. He even sounds like this on old pop tunes such as 'Secret Love', imparting to them an ironic, cantankerous quality straight from the sassiest of blues. A succession of discs in the early 1990s, often in partnership with the fine saxophonist JOE LOVANO and mingling rock, bop and a compositional style reminiscent of Charles Mingus, have been Scofield's best records, and some of the best of the era so far. His sound unites the implacable expertise of bebop and an ungroomed, teenage, three-chord clang that makes an engaging combination.

*_Flat Out_ (Gramavision 188903-2)

A 1988 session of Scofield in his jazz-funk incarnation, almost everything he plays turned into something like blues, though with tunes such as 'All the Things You Are' he is beginning to demonstrate a revised interest in older jazz forms and away from thunderous funk. Dated, but exhilaratingly unpretentious.

★*Time on my Hands* (Blue Note CDP 792 894-2)

Scofield's best ever album. The blues intonation is still strong, and there are insinuating hints of rock 'n' roll hovering around it, but as a blend of his influences it's a delightful record with barely a slack moment. The presence of JACK DEJOHNETTE on drums and the excellent Joe Lovano on saxophones helps a lot, Scofield's writing is consistently good, and the Mingus influence that informs some of the ballad-playing (distinct echoes of 'Goodbye Pork Pie Hat') imparts a new poignancy to his work.

★*Grace Under Pressure* (Blue Note CDP7 98167-2)

Muscular blues-bop from Scofield and spacey sound-effects guitar from BILL FRISELL on this fine disc. It's quite different to *Time on my Hands*, with a wider spread of thematic sources – suggestions of CARLA BLEY, rhythm & blues, Pat Metheny, soul music – and drummer Joey Baron is one of the current scene's most lateral-thinking yet hard-driving performers. The swaggering, shouting blues-funk track 'Twang', with a judiciously-applied horn-ensemble backup, is worth the disc.

Sharrock, Sonny

(Born New York, August 27, 1940; died April 1995)
Sharrock was not the kind of guitarist who devoted himself to tripping arpeggios and rippling chords. He was a cross between punk, free-jazz and 1970s 'jazz-rock', but he was playing like this before punk was invented and his sound, though it has a kind of ghetto-rhetoric, is primarily an attempt to sidestep all the generations of bop-dominated pluckers in jazz who have made guitar solos sound like fingering exercises. Sharrock sounds like skyrockets bursting, brakes squealing, an arcade of video games. Sharrock was unexpectedly hired by the fusion flautist HERBIE MANN for the band that made the commercially successful *Memphis Underground* album but in the 1970s he toured with a semi-

abstract band featuring his singer wife Linda. In the 1980s he was involved in the formation of the ferocious free-electric ensemble Last Exit – also featuring drummer Ronald Shannon Jackson, saxophonist Peter Brotzmann and bassist Bill Laswell.

★*Guitar* (Enemy EMY 102)

Sensational, terrifying exercise in abstract sounds, fragmented blues, feedback and slide-guitar splinterings, that is nonetheless one of the most effective antidotes to the prim and studiedly dramatic conventional jazz-guitar performances on the circuit. By Sharrock's standards, this is also a return to his roots, with the sounds of blues and gospel evident all over it.

Shaw, Ian

(Born Wales, 1965)
The young British vocalist Ian Shaw's inspirations were Mel Torme and Madeleine Bell, and his range of interests is just as wide as the difference between those two singers, if not wider. Shaw sings jazz, raps, scats, hits a chorister's high notes, sometimes ironically (and sometimes not) resembles a Las Vegas torch singer, sometimes a Motown soul artist. He is regarded by many as the most distinctive jazz-based male singer to have emerged in Britain since PHIL MINTON.

Shaw grew up in north Wales, playing cornet in brass bands, studied music in London, then travelled around Europe singing and listening – to Mel Torme (whom he met in Amsterdam), to Nancy Wilson, British soul star Dusty Springfield, and jazz musicians such as Bill Evans and JAN GARBAREK. He worked on the alternative cabaret scene in London, then met a young pianist, Adrian York, who introduced him to the British jazz scene.

★*Ghost Songs* (Jazz House Records JHCD 025)

Just about as eclectic a selection as might be expected from Shaw, recorded live at Ronnie Scott's in 1990. 'Danny Boy' is there, but with none of its usual mawkishness and its beautiful tune highlighted. So are jazz vehicles such as 'I Remember April', a medley of Ellington songs including 'Sophisticated Lady', and 'I Got It Bad and That Ain't Good', and the 1970s rock classic 'Spinning Wheel'. Not always evenly performed, but an imposing solo debut.

★*Taking It To Hart* (Jazz House JHCD 036)

A demanding tribute to Rodgers and Hart, revealing Shaw's strengths (via soul music and saloon-bar emoting as well as jazz) in slow, torchy features like 'Little Girl Blue'. There's a nice duet with Mari Wilson on 'My Romance', and a superb Iain Ballamy tenor solo on 'I Didn't Know What Time It Was', but Shaw isn't so happy with the faster, twistier stuff.

Sheppard, Andy

(Born Bristol, January 18, 1957)
Andy Sheppard is one of Britain's foremost new saxophone stars of the 1980s. Whilst almost inevitably indebted to both John Coltrane and Sonny Rollins, Sheppard's combination of whimsy, abrasiveness and danceable swing is distinctive. Apart from the Americans Coltrane and STEVE LACY, Sheppard counts British players such as Don Weller, Art Themen and the avantist EVAN PARKER among his saxophone influences, as well as highly individualistic pianists Geoff Williams and KEITH TIPPETT.

Unusually, Sheppard – a former choirboy – didn't discover jazz until he was 19, but quickly absorbed the idiom and was soon playing with Sphere and then with the French performance-art group Urban Sax. He came a highly-rated second in the Shlitz Young Jazz Musicians' contest in London in 1986, after which his career blossomed. Sheppard has now made a number of good small-group albums and an ambitious orchestral record with a multinational big band. He has also become a regular member of groups led by American composer/arrangers of the stature of CARLA BLEY and GEORGE RUSSELL for their European tours.

★*Andy Sheppard* (ANCD 8720)

Sheppard's first album, a 'blowing' session with a strong boppish feel and a powerful presence of John Coltrane. 'Coming Second' was a breezy exploration of driving bop, and the American trumpeter Randy Brecker made some deft and glossy interventions.

★*Introductions in the Dark* (Antilles ANCD 8742)

Sheppard's second disc, stretching his writing more, and ranging beyond the jazz tradition. Much of the disc is devoted to a suite, 'Romantic Conversations', which includes the ensemble's ingenious African percussionist, a frequently returning mid-tempo Latin-flavoured saxophone theme that is graceful but a bit obvious, and some impressively funky contributions from Sheppard's vibraharp player, the effortlessly swinging ORPHY ROBINSON.

★*Soft on the Inside* (Antilles ANCD 8751)

Sheppard's ambitious multinational big band. Though it innocently begins with some disarming west coast studio-style low trombone licks and wide-grin trumpet figures, the dedication to Carla Bley is appropriately sardonic, with reverberating low trombone sounds against paint-blistering trumpets giving way to a James Bond riff; the first part of 'Rave Trade' is pure Gil Evans, the second part a gospelly tribute to Mingus, ending in a wild drum thrash.

★*In Co-Motion* (Antilles ANCD 8766)

This was Sheppard's electric band, set up to play funk and featuring a waspish, darting Claud Deppa on trumpet, Sylvan Richardson from Simply Red on bass, and one of the most inventive of synthesiser explorers in Steve Lodder. Deppa's phrasing in this context suggests the growls and slithers of funk-jazz MILES DAVIS, but the moods jump restlessly.

Shorter, Wayne

(Born Newark, New Jersey, August 25, 1933)
When he arrived on the jazz scene, Shorter was a Coltraneish performer who nevertheless didn't sound like a copy, with a clipped, gritty Humphrey Bogart rasp and a fast, staccato manner of phrasing. He was also shaping into a peerless composer for small jazz groups, which he demonstrated with Art Blakey's Jazz Messengers and then with MILES DAVIS.

Shorter learned his craft as a university student and then in the army, joining Blakey in 1959 and Miles Davis five years later. With Davis, Shorter blossomed as a soloist, since all the melodic originality he had been refining in the previous years was shaken into new shapes by the rhythmic openness of that remarkable band that also included Ron Carter, HERBIE HANCOCK and TONY WILLIAMS. Several of Shorter's compositions (notably 'ESP' and 'Nefertiti') became regular features of the Davis repertoire, and the saxophonist extended his imaginative contributions into the electro-funk Davis era, adopting the soprano horn for 'In a Silent Way' and delivering haunting, beautifully structured solos on it. Shorter collaborated in the formation of Weather Report in 1970, but though the band inventively used electronics orchestrally, Shorter's own playing became mainly textural. He has, however, continued to lead attractive small groups since, and his compositions remain unique. The Art Blakey bands containing Shorter (see page 136) are good instances of his early originality as both soloist and composer.

★Super Nova (Blue Note B21Y 84332)

This album represents Wayne Shorter moving closer to Miles Davis' fusion position after the release of *In a Silent Way* and *Bitches Brew*. It features the obligatory guitars (but an interestingly abrasive blend in JOHN McLAUGHLIN and SONNY SHARROCK) and multiple percussion; Shorter plays soprano throughout, on which his curling lines are intermittently delicious.

★*Speak No Evil* (Blue Note CDP 746509)

Shorter with trumpeter Freddie Hubbard, too brash and direct a trumpeter really to mesh with the saxophonist's ambiguities and ambivalencies. There are, however, sublime ballad performances on 'Dance Cadaverous' and 'Infant Eyes', the latter a tightly edited and faintly unnerving set of melodic variations well supported by Herbie Hancock's piano.

Simone, Nina (Eunice Waymon)

(Born Tryon, North Carolina, February 21, 1933)
Brittle, unpredictable, yet a great entertainer and at times appropriately bracketed under 'jazz' for her reworking of familiar materials and the gospelly drive of her piano-playing, Nina Simone came back to popularity with British audiences in the 1980s.

Simone's background was in both gospel and classical music. She sang in the local choir as a child, but she went on to study music and became a piano teacher. Her voice, however, had an incisive, unforgiving bite that was her true calling card. In 1959 she had a hit with her version of 'I Loves You Porgy', and through the 1960s she was successful both in the States and in Europe with a string of gospel-tinged songs, some strongly influenced by her involvement in the civil-rights movement. Simone celebrated the work of poets such as Paul Dunbar and Langston Hughes in her work, and songs of black politics such as 'Mississippi Goddam', 'Backlash Blues' and 'To Be Young, Gifted and Black' became staples of her repertoire. Her bruised integrity continues to fascinate and awe audiences.

★*My Baby Just Cares For Me* (Charly CDCHARLY 6)

Nina Simone's first album from 1959, that brought her to fame. It includes her hit song of the period 'I Loves You Porgy', a great deal of exploration of the possibilities of 'My Baby Just Cares For Me', 'Mood Indigo' and a mixture of standards and blues. More defiant and spring-heeled, not fractured and doubtful like later Simone, but with the same imperious dignity then as now.

★*Live at Ronnie Scott's* (Hendring HEN 6017Y)

Nina Simone's series of club performances in the mid-1980s were theatrical and spine-chilling affairs, and though her British drummer Paul Robinson is a little inclined to hot Billy Cobhamish tom-tom licks, this album brings them instantly back to life. 'See Line Woman' and 'God God God' locate Simone at her baleful best, and 'My Baby Just Cares For Me', imparts a characteristic suspicion to a usually jaunty vehicle.

Smith, Thomas 'Tommy'

(Born Luton, Bedfordshire, April 27, 1967)
A consummate technician, Scots-raised saxophonist Tommy Smith mastered the fundamentals of bebop saxophone by the age of 15, and his precocity has enabled him to move away from that garrulous style towards the haunting, understated manner of Norwegian JAN GARBAREK, and thus probably closer to his own sympathies.

Smith took up the saxophone at 12, and made national TV in a trio with pianist GORDON BECK and bassist Neils-Henning Oersted Pedersen at 15, recording two albums for Scottish labels shortly afterwards. Smith went to Berklee two years later and formed a band called Forward Motion there, joining vibraharpist GARY BURTON in 1986. Smith made his debut recording for Blue Note in 1988 and has also appeared in a variety of pop contexts, notably with the Scots band Hue and Cry.

★*Step By Step* (Blue Note CDP 791 930-2)

Smith's debut for Blue Note, accompanied by the kind of illustrious partners increasingly becoming obligatory for the first recordings of newcomers. Drummer JACK DEJOHNETTE, bassist Eddie Gomez and guitarist JOHN SCOFIELD all took part, but though Smith's playing successfully demonstrated his growing tonal sophistication the disc didn't altogether avoid the trap of sounding like a high-class demo.

★*Paris* (Blue Note 0777 7 80612 29)

Much more coherently realised, this is Smith's best band at work on disc, including Jason Rebello on piano, Guy Barker on trumpet and JULIAN ARGUELLES on tenor in addition to a brisk rhythm section. The mood evoked by the title (Smith recently spent a year there) is caught by some of the more reflective episodes, but otherwise it's an exercise in fast-moving tempo changes and sharp dynamic shifts between busy ensembles and open swing. Rebello is excellent, and Smith sounds as if he's coming into his own.

Stevens, John William

(Born London, June 10, 1940; died London, September 13, 1994) When the British drummer John Stevens died suddenly at the age of 54, European contemporary music and improvisation was deprived of a dedicated and highly influential artist. Players, bands, listeners, teaching institutions, and broadcasting and arts-funding establishments have all been affected by his restless devotion to new music, and his vision about its power.

Stevens was a brilliant drummer who had absorbed the approaches of all the giants, but particularly Ornette Coleman's principal accompanists ED BLACKWELL and Billy Higgins, and the British drum hero of the '50s and '60s, Phil Seamen. Stevens could play straight-ahead swing that would awaken the most preoccupied soloists, or sometimes reduce his kit to a small snare and a cymbal in the more ascetic free-improvising contexts. But as well as being a percussion original, Stevens also fought tirelessly to create a free-improvising culture in Britain. Inspired by Ornette Coleman and Albert Ayler, he founded a constantly changing free-group called the Spontaneous Music Ensemble, and ran London's Little Theatre Club as a regular home for left-field jazz players in the '60s and '70s.

John Stevens was a gifted teacher and talent-scout. He spotted up-and-coming young British performers like COURTNEY PINE, Byron Wallen and CLAIRE MARTIN when they were little known, and helped to encourage their careers. Stevens developed his own methods for inducing students to improvise, often based on rhythmic chanting, and influenced by the music of the east, as well as America.

Stevens was the son of a tap-dancer, who took up drums at seventeen. He disciplined his early enthusiasms in an RAF band in 1958, and met saxophonist Trevor Watts in the service, who was to become a regular partner. He worked on the regular jazz scene (with Tubby Hayes, Ronnie Scott, JOHN MCLAUGHLIN and others), but wasn't happy in it and developed his own parallel jazz culture outside. An unstoppable campaigner, Stevens helped to induce the BBC to start broadcasting free jazz, and though his later career was rarely materially rewarding, he worked with many of the most adventurous performers in Britain, including pianist STAN TRACY, saxophonists DUDU PUKWANA, John Tchicai and EVAN PARKER, even John Lennon and Yoko Ono. He won a Thames TV Award for his community-music work in 1972, and directed the former Jazz Centre Society's Outreach Community Music Project from 1983. Until his death, he was as active as ever as a player, and in his work for London's Community Music project.

★*Re-Touch and Quartet* (Konnex KCD 5027)

The 1971 version of the Spontaneous Music Ensemble (including singer Julie Tippetts, formerly Julie Driscoll) and an electric band including Allan Holdsworth, then a fusion star in the making, who plays with more warmth than usual against Stevens' surging, impulsive percussion. There are some ferocious bass solos from BARRY GUY, and on the fast jazz-time episodes Holdsworth has rarely sounded better. Julie Tippetts is haunting on the Albert Ayler dedication.

★With Evan Parker. *Corner to Corner* (Ogun OGCD 005)

All excess baggage is jettisoned on this unpremeditated set between saxophonist Parker on soprano throughout, and Stevens on a kit with no bass drum and just a child's snare and two hi-hats. It begins with free-jazz call-and-response of squirty sax phrases and exclamatory drumming, but evolves into a music of foxy pauses, ecstatic simultaneous playing, and brooding laments.

★*A Luta Continua* (Konnex KCD 5056)

A wide span musically here, recordings from 1977 to 1981 including the big Dance Orchestra, which delivers a kind of free r & b, and a free electric bebop band that unleashes a memorable tribute to the memory of three British bop pioneers, Derek Humble, Phil Seamen and Tubby Hayes.

Surman, John Douglas

(Born Tavistock, Devon, August 30, 1944)

Like ANDY SHEPPARD in the 1980s, John Surman was a West Countryman who arrived like a whirlwind on the British jazz scene of the mid-1960s. He was, like most of his contemporaries all over the world, devoted to the saxophone technique of John Coltrane – an intense, seamless tumult of variations on arpeggios and modes – but he was doing it on the baritone saxophone, a cumbersome instrument usually used in a more sedate manner.

Surman's involvement with jazz had begun at school in Plymouth, when he attended workshops run by a local jazz talent applying new sounds to Ellington, MIKE WESTBROOK. In the early 1960s, Surman and Westbrook went to London, where the saxophonist's fire and energy and his mentor's blend of Ellingtonian sophistication and art-school subversiveness marked them out as the coming jazz generation in Britain. Surman then joined forces with an American drummer and bassist (Stu Martin and Barre Phillips) to form the Trio, a spontaneous outfit.

In 1970 Surman took the World Expo in Osaka by storm with a firebreathing performance with the European Francy Boland Band, and throughout the following decade he endlessly experimented: with electric guitars (Morning Glory), with all-saxophone ensembles (SOS), with brass (John Surman Brass Project) and briefly with the German trombone genius Albert Mangelsdorff (MUMPS). In more recent times he has increasingly devoted his energies to unaccompanied playing (assisted by electronics), but has also enjoyed a fruitful free-improvising partnership with American drummer and pianist JACK DEJOHNETTE. Rescuing one of Surman's early, Westbrook-oriented sessions (*How Many Clouds Can You See?* for Decca/Deram) and The Trio double-LP for CD would be a service to the proper documentation of European jazz.

★*Amazing Adventures of Simon Simon* (ECM 1193)

Duet performance by Surman and Jack DeJohnette, which won plaudits in America and Europe. Though it's informed by Surman's long-term interest in English folk music, the interplay between the musicians is motivated by the jazz tradition.

★*Private City* (ECM 1366)

About half of the music here was written for a ballet of the same name which premiered at Sadler's Wells. The title is faithful to the music, a computer-aided solo project full of Surman's affection for song-like melody, avoidance of transatlantic jazz clichés and sax-romanticism. Without prodding from partners, the solos do take on a preoccupied air occasionally, but Surman is as affecting and inventive at this kind of music as anyone currently at work.

★*Adventure Playground* (ECM 1463)

A first-class band – PAUL BLEY on piano, KEITH JARRETT's trio partner Gary Peacock on bass, and the superb and unpredictable Briton Tony Oxley on drums. The music is a mixture of gliding contemplation and a softly persuasive swing. Jazzy pieces such as Bley's 'Pigfoot' get deliciously clangy, bluesy introduction from Peacock, and Oxley's inimitable version of a straight-ahead beat, with Surman surging and lurching over Bley's propulsive chords.

Taylor, John

(Born Manchester, England, Sept 25, 1942)
One of the finest jazz pianists in Europe over twenty years, John Taylor's reputation is widely known to musicians and fans, though his pursuit of his own music has not won him a wide following. Initially basing his methods on a broad synthesis of the styles of McCOY TYNER and HERBIE HANCOCK, Taylor's work has latterly become more personal, poignant and rich – but he can still

participate in a neo-bop jam with as much vigour and energy as any pianist currently active.

Taylor surfaced on the British jazz scene with the generation that included soloists John Surman and Alan Skidmore. He partnered singer CLEO LAINE in the 1970s, joined Ronnie Scott's group, and increasingly began composing his own material – culminating in the formation of the atmospheric and lyrical trio Azimuth, with his singer wife Norma Winstone and trumpeter Kenny Wheeler. During the 1980s, Taylor's skills were in demand throughout Europe, for sessions with JAN GARBAREK, GIL EVANS, LEE KONITZ and others. He has also taken to composing larger-scale pieces for full-sized orchestras.

*Ambleside Days (ah um 013)

John Taylor and an old associate, JOHN SURMAN, in reflective communion, using jazz methods to express a repertoire hardly linked thematically to conventional jazz roots at all. It's an elegiac project about places that mean a lot to Taylor – so the poignant 'Coniston Falls' and the joyous, jig-like 'Clapperclowe' both have a distinct and personal clarity, and invite a textural form of improvising that particularly suits latter-day Surman. But the special place jazz has in the sensibilities of both these virtuoso players is audible in the bluesy coda to the rumbling 'Scale Force', and some of the interplay borders on empathetic free-music.

*Azimuth (ECM 1546-48 523010-2)

Belated CD release for the three best Azimuth albums of the late '70s – 'Azimuth', 'Touchstone', and 'Depart', the last one featuring Ralph Towner's vibrant acoustic guitar. Norma Winstone and trumpeter Kenny Wheeler circle each other with such under-standing that it sometimes seems like telepathic free music, sometimes it's as slow and spacey as JAN GARBAREK. There's probably a new audience for Azimuth with the ambient-music fans, but this is more demanding than that.

★With Palle Danielsson/Peter Erskine. *Time Being* (ECM 1532)

Superb acoustic piano trio music to match Jarrett's Standards trio, GERI ALLEN and others. The themes are very good (a relief from the usual standards and 'classics' format) and reached by tantalising diversions and delays. There is fast swing and Latin effervescence amid the contemplation, and it's true ensemble music without a pecking order. Great.

Taylor, Martin

(Born Harlow, Essex, 1956)
One of the few British jazz guitarists to have won an international reputation, Martin Taylor specialises in a warm, relaxed blend of the methods of swing players and the post-Charlie Christian beboppers.

Taylor took up the guitar at the age of four (his father was a dance-band musician) and he made his professional debut at eight. By his mid-teens he was working the cruise ships as an entertainer, at 16 even sharing a *QE2* voyage with the Count Basie band and sitting in with it. But Taylor's big break came when he was invited to begin a long and successful partnership with the veteran violinist Stephane Grappelli. Taylor also appeared with many mainstream jazz musicians including clarinettist Buddy de Franco and cornettist Ruby Braff, and with non-jazz figures such as Yehudi Menuhin and Nelson Riddle. Taylor won the 'Artist Most Deserving of Wider Recognition' and 'Jazz Guitarist of the Year' categories of *Downbeat* magazine readers' polls in 1987 and 1988.

★*Artistry* (Linn Records)

Taylor's ability to play lead, rhythm and bass simultaneously and to generate musical vitality rather than simply technical fireworks are spectacularly exemplified on his latest disc. There are eleven pieces here, with composers as different as Duke Ellington and the Beatles, and material specially furnished by Taylor's celebrated sometime partner Stephane Grappelli.

★*Spirit of Django* (Linn Records AKD 030)

Martin Taylor's playing is always a tribute to Django Rheinhardt, camouflaged or not, but this is the explicit one. But Taylor is original enough to have avoided the nostalgia trip, and instead has recreated the feel of Django's immense contribution within a postbop band in which the young saxophonist Dave O'Higgins plays superbly and Jack Emblow's accordion is a discreet delight.

Thompson, Danny

(Born London, February 4, 1939)
The credentials of British bass player Danny Thompson extend from employment by the late Tubby Hayes and the young JOHN McLAUGHLIN, via Pentangle (the successful British folk-pop ensemble of the late 1960s), Kate Bush and all the way up to his recent resonant blend of Swedish and English folk music, Charles Mingus' magisterial bass sound and the one-touch receptivity of the best small-group jazz.

From the late 1960s to the mid-1980s, Thompson was all but invisible on the British jazz scene despite continuing to appear sporadically with excellent musicians including drummer John Stevens and pianist Stan Tracey. But Thompson's pop assignments kept him busy until his decision to form Whatever in 1987.

★*Whatever* (Hannibal HNCD 1326)

Whatever's first record, and an immensely classy debut, the melodic strength of the band being utterly accessible, amenable to jazz improvisation, and yet for the most part utterly different from the jazz tradition. The first repertoire included the folk-jazz hybrids of the late Swedish musician Jan Johannsen, English traditionals such as 'Lovely Joan', dedications to Scottish folk singer Alex Campbell, and a strong underpinning of swing.

Threadgill, Henry Luther

(Born Chicago, February 15, 1944)

A creative explorer of compositional methods appropriate to free jazz is the Chicago saxophonist and composer Henry Threadgill, a powerful improviser whose style drew on Sonny Rollins, Ornette Coleman and the blues tradition. Threadgill was a prominent member of Chicago's Association for the Advancement of Creative Musicians (AACM, see Muhal Richard Abrams) in the 1960s, who produced some of the most original improvising to have emerged from the movement, as well as attractive syntheses of free-playing with the music of Scott Joplin and Jelly Roll Morton in the trio Air.

Threadgill had been formally trained, but worked with gospel groups and blues bands in the early 1960s, before becoming involved with AACM and also working as a music teacher. In recent times Threadgill's work as a composer has become a more prominent feature of his career, and he has deployed audacious configurations – including all-bass and saxophone bands – and consistently celebrated the early jazz past.

Air Lore (Bluebird/BMG ND 86578)

Air's sixth album, made in 1979, representing Threadgill, bassist Fred Hopkins and drummer Steve McCall at their most sweepingly mature, spinning rich variations on material by Scott Joplin and Jelly Roll Morton. Unlike many of the retreats into the archives by contemporary jazz musicians, this set both illuminates the originals and emphasises the remarkable empathy that the trio had established by this time – and Hopkins' bass is in full imperious flow.

Rag Bush and All (BMG PD 83052)

Threadgill's augmented group, a sextet recorded in 1988 – retaining both the group interplay of Air and the balancing of expressionism and classicism that the leader had been refining through the decade. In the later stages of Air's work, Threadgill's writing had grown increasingly dolorous, and the sextet session was a welcome lightening of the atmosphere, as well as enhancing his reputation for independence from jazz fashions.

Tippett, Keith

(Born Bristol, August 25, 1947)
In an era of highly technical jazz keyboardists specialising in linear improvisation, West Country pianist Keith Tippett is a rare exception – a consummate textural pianist whose hailstorms of bright, spangly sound or the dark, pounding rhythms of his low-register playing mark him out, and since he is able to maintain rhythmic drive for long periods by the sheer density of fast arpeggio playing (rather like Cecil Taylor), he is often his own percussionist. Tippett formed one of the first British jazz-rock bands with Long John Baldry sidemen Elton Dean and Marc Charig, and the leviathan 50-piece orchestra Centipede, which included musicians from the classical, rock and jazz spheres. But for much of the 1980s Tippett's career was quiet, especially in Britain, though he went on developing out of all proportion to his reputation, recording extensively for the German label FMP. In recent times, Tippett has performed regularly with the sensational improvising quartet Mujician.

★*Couple in Spirit* (EG EEGCD 52)

Much of this has a soulful, unadorned, pentatonic quality obliquely suggestive of both gospel music and English folk songs. The rich, chanting vocals of the pianist's wife Julie Tippett (formerly R & B singer Julie Driscoll) bring a solemnity and calm to the proceedings, and though there is a fey and sometimes faintly unconvincing children-of-nature guilelessness about *Couple in Spirit*, its musicality and originality are indisputable.

★*The Dartington Concert* (EEG 2106-2)

A phenomenal live solo piano set, dedicated to the late DUDU PUKWANA, a free-jazz virtuoso blend of tumbling runs over thunderous chords, constant changes of tone-colour so that long, high-register trills change character. Free-music it may be, but it's accessible to any audience.

★With Howard Riley. *The Bern Concert* (Future Music FMR CD08)

Tippett's power, intensity, and sense of abstract detail has a good foil in a more restrained but creative fellow-Briton, Howard Riley. Two improvising pianists sometimes bury each other, but Riley's patient examination of the materials and careful harmonic manipulation is so different to Tippett's way of working that they don't. Genuine dialogue, and a clear live recording.

★*Mujician-Poem About The Hero* (Cuneiform Records Rune 62)

A great free-jazz small-group, playing a suite in five parts – dissonant and free-associative, but with a shapeliness provided by an underlying dynamic rhythm and the familiarity of the players with each other. Saxophonist Paul Dunmall is one of the best European celebrators of the Coltrane legacy, Paul Rogers plays bowed bass like a cathedral organ, and drummer Tony like a Mujician gig.

Toussaint, Jean

(Born Aruba, Antilles, July 27, 1960)
Saxophonist Jean Toussaint has become a prominent performer on the new British jazz scene since he settled in England in 1987 after appearances with Art Blakey's Jazz Messengers. Toussaint proved himself to be a hard-swinging, vigorous and inventive saxophonist in the line of John Coltrane, Wayne Shorter and Sonny Rollins, and his tonal range has also made him an eloquent interpreter of ballads – a rarity among young post-bop performers.

Toussaint was attracted to the London scene when DJ Paul Murphy introduced him to a club world in which young fans danced to classic Jazz Messengers records. He took a teaching post at the Guildhall School and began working regularly with London players including Jason Rebello, drummer Winston Clifford and pianist Julian Joseph.

*What Goes Around (World Circuit WCD 029)

Two Monk tunes, 'Autumn Leaves' and some good lateral-bop originals from the Anglophile American saxophonist. There's also an interesting spread of London musicians appearing in the variety of bands on this disc, including the pianists JULIAN JOSEPH, Bheki Mseleku and JASON REBELLO. A 1960s MILES DAVIS feel to the best track, the fast 'Rice Head', gets an excellent group performance, 'Ruby My Dear' is given a slow, searching treatment and only 'Autumn Leaves' sounds ill-conceived.

Towns, Colin

(Born London, May 13, 1948)
A highly talented British composer and arranger, who appeared as a pianist on the local scene in the '70s, then disappeared into studio and TV work. Towns re-emerged in 1994 with his Mask Orchestra, a powerful and imaginative band using some of the best British players, and drawing on ideas from inside and outside the world of jazz, reflecting Towns' rich experience of music of all kinds, and his understanding of drama and surprise.

Towns began learning piano at seven, played in jazz bands during his teens, then joined with Ian Gillan, and co-writing and playing keyboards with his band for ten albums and until their split in 1983. Following that change, Towns began writing film scores, including the music for 'Full Circle', with Mia Farrow and Tom Conti. His work has subsequently included 'Vampire's Kiss', 'Wolves of Willoughby Chase', 'Between the Lines', and the BBC costume drama 'The Buccaneers'. But jazz has always been his first love, and following the death of his wife, who had always encouraged this pursuit, he has thrown himself into it with resounding effect.

*Mask Orchestra (The Jazz Label TJL 001CD)

Excellent debut for Towns' audacious Mask Orchestra, featuring such premier-league British modernists as JOHN SURMAN and Alan Skidmore on saxophones, Henry Lowther on trumpet, and JOHN TAYLOR on piano, with trumpeter Guy Barker and saxophonist

Nigel Hitchcock bringing up the younger generation. Towns' seesawing Stravinsky-like drama, constant time-changes and restless manipulation of the ensembles behind soloists makes his band very distinctive, with GEORGE RUSSELL's its nearest relative – though some of the use of insistent bass grooves and rock drum lines, and skidding brass patterns shot through with sudden flares, also have similarities with MIKE GIBBS. A telling debut.

Tracey, Stanley William 'Stan'

(Born London, December 30, 1926)
After working with the British pianist Stan Tracey in the 1960s, Sonny Rollins asked in the music press, 'Does anybody here know just how good he really is?' Too few people did.

Tracey was a forces entertainer during the latter years of the Second World War, became a full-time professional in the 1950s and worked both in the insular and dedicated world of British modern jazz and in the commercial sphere during that decade, most notably as the pianist in Ted Heath's famous dance orchestra. Though Tracey is recognisable within the first few bars, his percussive, rumbling piano style always suggests links with Thelonious Monk and with Duke Ellington. It is a method of working that has endeared him to several generations of musicians and listeners – he has worked with this country's most resourceful avantists, as well as those of more orthodox persuasion – and even led to a successful recording (*Playing in the Yard*) with the American saxophonist Charlie Rouse, a partner of Thelonious Monk's for nearly a decade. Tracey has a different kind of clout as a composer, and one that is closely related to the methods of the late Duke Ellington, but with an infectious rhythmic impact also reminiscent of Count Basie.

Stan Tracey – Portraits Plus (Blue Note CDP 780 6962)

A set of dedications by Tracey to musical heroes – Duke Ellington, Thelonious Monk, Sonny Rollins and Gil Evans – and featuring a major league British octet including Pete King on alto, Don Weller on tenor and Guy Barker on trumpet. The Rollins-angled piece, 'Newk's Fluke', pulls together a set of dislocated styles – Caribbean music, folksy barn-dance jauntiness, straight-ahead swing – in a manner uniquely Tracey's yet suggestive of its inspiration.

★*Under Milk Wood* (Blue Note CDP 789 4492)

One of the classics of British jazz, originally recorded in the 1960s, and featuring Tracey with his quartet of the time, including the brilliant and romantic Scots tenorist Bobby Wellins. A collection of typically quirky Tracey compositions devoted to the Dylan Thomas play, it's delightful combination of writing originality and improvisation, with Wellins' dark, sighing tenor solo over Tracey's tolling chords on 'Starless and Bible Black' a great jazz performance.

★*Duets* (Blue Note International 0777 7 89450 2 4)

A collection of Tracey's duo work with the pianist KEITH TIPPETT and the saxophonist JOHN SURMAN from the '70s, meetings that helped to reactivate his career. Surman is a little cramped by the pianist's ceaseless shunting and bumping, and the slow pieces between them work best, even allowing for Surman's slightly clunky early synthesiser. Tracey and Tippett try to fit around each other less, and exhibit a level of frantic energy that isn't always conversational but often thrilling.

★*Live At The QEH* (Blue Note 7243 8 31139 2 7)

One of the best of Tracey live shows, with seven bands including his own solo performance, celebrating fifty years in the music business in 1993. Some of the best music of the night came from the duo set between the pianist and the young trumpeter Gerard Presencer, notably on a quicksilver dialogue on 'Easy Living'. PETER KING plays superbly too, but Tracey's unaccompanied 'Sophisticated Lady' at the end says exactly what his methods are all about.

Turre, Steve

(Born Omaha, September 12, 1948)

Turre is a superb trombonist, adept equally as a fast, precise bop-oriented soloist or as the trenchant underpinning of a big-band brass section. He is also an original as a leader and composer, as his recent work has demonstrated.

Like many musicians whose skills came to fruition in the 1960s, Turre was restless with pigeon-holing or narrow definitions of jazz. He studied music formally, but worked with the rock band Santana in San Francisco, and with Rahsaan Roland Kirk around 1968. Touring work with the Ray Charles orchestra followed, then with Art Blakey's Jazz Messengers and the Thad Jones-Mel Lewis band. All this was invaluable experience for Turre, both in solo opportunities and insights into arrangement. With trumpeter Woody Shaw in the mid-1970s, Turre's solo voice can be heard gaining in assurance and by the 1980s he was arranging for Slide Hampton's World of Tombones band, and for Max Roach.

Right There (Antilles 314 510040-2)

One of the best discs of 1991, this session led by Turre includes guest appearances by WYNTON MARSALIS and Benny Golson (Golson's arranging style affects Turre strongly) and Billy Higgins' zingy cymbals impart an extra lift to everything. There are two bands featured, one coloured by strings (the excellent John Blake on violin, plus cello), the other one a straight jazz ensemble. Turre's earthy, deep-down sound and early jazz wah-wah unleash the blues in 'Duke's Mountain', but he's also as deft and agile as a bop player.

Tyner, McCoy Alfred

(Born Philadelphia, December 11, 1938)

McCoy Tyner is one of the most widely imitated pianists in modern jazz. In the famous John Coltrane quartet in the 1960s, Tyner appeared to have turned the piano – an instrument usually used in bebop-derived music for either harmonic support in a group or melodically complex soloing over a minimal chord framework – into something closer to the drums.

Tyner came up in the Jazztet, an excellent, tightly knit outfit led by trumpeter Art Farmer and saxophonist Benny Golson. He moved straight from there to the Coltrane group in 1960. Coltrane's music required stamina as well as inventiveness from accompanists, and Tyner, a muscular player with an immense finger-span, could hammer out the same trance-like pattern under sustained improvisations that could run for an hour.

Tyner left Coltrane in 1965, as the saxophonist moved further out into the territory of free and atonal music. The first years were tough, but in a series of recordings for Blue Note and then Milestone, Tyner discovered an independent appeal to the public again, and with the Milestone recordings that included *Enlightenment*, *Atlantis*, and *Sama Layuca*, he reforged the furious and unrelenting Coltrane style with a lyricism that still recalled his old allegiances to Bill Evans and an interest in ethnic music outside the immediate orbit of jazz. The excellent earlier Milestone albums aren't available on CD.

Live at the Musicians' Exchange (Kingdom CDGATE 7021)

Tyner's trio in 1988, at its feverish best (Avery Sharpe is on bass and Louis Hayes on drums) in a pyrotechnic display of tidal arpeggios and avalanche chords which nonetheless strives for the spiritual content of the material rather than simply bouncing technicalities off it. The material includes an attractive 'Lover Man' and 'You Taught my Heart to Sing'.

Uptown/Downtown (Milestone M-9167)

A big, plush, highly varied big-band recording, cut over two nights at the Blue Note in New York in 1988. The thumping chordal pivot of 'Love Surrounds Us' firmly establishes that this is a Tyner set, soon engagingly shot through with spears of trumpet sounds. On the fast, high-stepping 'Uptown', the horns are constantly rubbing against each other, brass flares dying away, wild riffing ending in explosive crescendos – but the highlight is a Tyner classic – 'Genesis' from the old *Enlightenment* session – given a mysterious, diffuse quality by Robin Eubanks' arrangement.

445

*With Bobby Hutcherson *Manhattan Moods* (Blue Note CDP 7243 8 28423 2 3)

A fruitful occasional partnership, between Tyner and the great vibraharpist and marimba player Bobby Hutcherson. Largely a standards repertoire, but both players have such vaulting harmonic imaginations that they can grow spectacular blooms on familiar ground. Hutcherson memorably performs 'Blue Monk' on the marimba, there's a standout version of 'I Loves You Porgy', and Mal Waldron's 'Soul Eyes' finds them both remaking the tune as their own.

Vasconcelos, Nana

(Born Recife, Brazil, August 2, 1944)
The reputation of that graceful coiled-spring of a Brazilian percussionist, Nana Vasconcelos, has been built over 20 years on collaborations with other employers – and the Brazilian's breadth of view is embodied in the diversity of his partners, who have included Milton Nascimento, B.B. King, Talking Heads, PAT METHENY and DON CHERRY.

Vasconcelos came into the music business as a bongo player during the samba boom, and was brought to New York by the Argentinian tenorist GATO BARBIERI. He toured Europe with Barbieri, remaining in Paris afterwards to play and to work with handicapped children, and also occasionally performing with trumpeter Don Cherry – a liaison that has continued into the 1990s. He has also specialised in the berimbau, an African-derived instrument used to accompany martial arts in Brazil, and which looks like an enormous bow and arrow with a gourd on one end. Whether evoking the sound of a jew's harp, dice on a wheel, clattering drumbeats or ghostly voices, there is always a driving rhythm behind all Vasconcelos' work.

*Bush Dance (Antilles ANCD 8701)

Vasconcelos' typical sound-forest forays of the mid-1980s, but of a highly communicative kind – rhythmic, highly textured, supported by an empathetic quartet, and blending north-western and

Latin-American influences in the creative manner for which the percussionist's name has become a byword.

Vesala, Edward

(Born Mantyharju, Finland, February 15, 1945)
Like a fellow Scandinavian, Jan Garbarek, drummer-composer Edward Vesala makes a jazz-derived music out of local materials and the conviction that merely repeating the time-honoured patterns of jazz is pointless. Vesala has run his own orchestra, Sound and Fury, not simply as a band but as a way of life for years, and his iconoclastic attitude to new music – mixing contemporary classics, rock, and folk idioms, including the Finn's unexpected relish for the tango – is a lifetime crusade to him.

He studied orchestral percussion in Helsinki at first, but grew impatient with it. During the 1960s he became a bandleader, and in 1972 regularly worked with the Norwegians JAN GARBAREK and Arild Andersen. Throughout the decade he worked with trumpeter Tomasz Stanko, and supported visiting musicians including PAUL BLEY, CHICK COREA and Archie Shepp. In 1980 Vesala recorded the album 'Heavy Life' in New York with Stanko, and through the 1980s he ran clinics, unorthodox music schools (the Sound and Fury lineups were drawn from these pupils) and increasingly pursued his own distinctive muse. He has written music for theatre, including the Finnish national epic 'Kalevala'. In 1994 he toured the UK for the first time.

★*Ode To The Death of Jazz* (ECM 1413)
A 1990 Vesala session that just about sums up his approach. It remains one of the most telling journeys down the road toward banishing hot licks and bolt-on jazz expediencies, though clear references to the music's history to emerge amid the collages of contemporary classical references and Finnish folk music. Some of it intriguingly echoes Gil Evans; there is some engaging tango music, and tongue-in-cheek bebop charges against dancefloor electronics, thrash guitar and collective wails like a Mingus band. Fascinating.

Watson, Robert Michael 'Bobby'

(Born Lawrence, Kansas, August 23, 1953)

Saxophonist Bobby Watson is one of the few recently emerged performers (a young veteran of bands led by Art Blakey, George Coleman, even Panama Francis) who can, in Rollins fashion, silence a room with unaccompanied alto expeditions uncannily reminiscent of the fluid eloquence of the late Cannonball Adderley, but with jolting contrasts of spinning, repeated motifs against yawing flights across the register, modulations of key and interweaving of glossy semiquavers against offpitch sounds and bluesy smears that avoids Adderley's glibness.

The son of a saxophonist, Watson studied music at the University of Miami, having already organised and orchestrated for his high-school band. Watson's skills as an arranger as well as a soloist won him the musical director's position in Art Blakey's Messengers between 1977 and 1981 and he worked with a variety of groups afterwards, including those led by saxophonist George Coleman and drummer Charlie Persip. In 1983 Watson co-formed the 29th Street Saxophone Quartet with Rich Rothenberg (tenor), Jim Hartog (baritone) and Ed Jackson (alto).

★*The Inventor* (Blue Note CDP 791 915-2)

Watson's second record for Blue Note (June 1989) and an excellent collaboration between the saxophonist and the young pianist Benny Green, plus Melton Mustafa on trumpet. Watson's soaring alto takes off with an assurance he has more usually displayed in his work with the 29th Street Saxophone Quartet.

★*Underground* (Antilles 422 848 415-2)

One of the wittiest, slickest and loose-sounding of all saxophone bands, the 29th Street Saxophone Quartet has this time varied the mixture with some additional instrumentation – HUGH MASEKELA makes a guest appearance, there's an occasional vocalist, and some drums and percussion. Apart from Pamela Watson's rather anonymous soul-jazz singing, much of the material retains their usual panache (the sassy, streetwalking drive of much of their work oddly recalls _West Side Story_), and there's a crackling version of Dizzy Gillespie's 'Manteca'.

Weber, Eberhard

(Born Stuttgart, January 22, 1940)
Originally a virtuoso bop bassist occasionally involved in free-music too, Eberhard Weber moved towards a kind of pastoral, electronically symphonic music heavily dependent on synthesisers and multi-tracking. In solo recital, his preferred performance vehicle, Weber will develop contrapuntal structures by electronically delaying an earlier phrase and threading it in a few seconds later, after which he will then improvise against it, often with slurred sitar effects in the upper register.

In the 70s, Weber moved into his more impressionistic territory with his own invention of the 'electrobass', a skinny upright instrument electronically designed to sustain notes as if they were bowed and to produce exotic textures. Weber recorded with GARY BURTON, then formed his own imaginative ensemble Colours, with saxophonist CHARLIE MARIANO. He has also regularly appeared with Norwegian saxophonist JAN GARBAREK, for whom his slightly dolorous romanticism is entirely appropriate.

★_Colours of Chloe_ (ECM 833 331-2)

Weber in 1973 in partnership with keyboardist Rainer Bruninghaus and a classical cello section, achieving the beginnings of effects that Weber would eventually find ways to concoct on his own. Very spacious, graceful music, and entirely accessible (it won prizes and much critical acclaim on its appearance), though the improvisational content is strictly subservient to the material.

★_Orchestra Solo Bass_ (ECM 837 343-2)

An impression of Weber's unaccompanied performances, though a brass section collaborates here and there. Sonorous, liquid melody lines, arching sustained sounds and reverberating chords confirming Weber's status as one of the great contributors to the bass vocabulary.

Westbrook, Michael John David 'Mike' and Katherine Jane 'Kate'

(Mike Westbrook born Buckinghamshire, March 21, 1936; Kate Westbrook born Surrey)

Mike Westbrook's band dominated the British jazz scene of the late 1960s and early 1970s, an unruly and imaginative collection of the best of the younger local players of the period, having much the same impact as Loose Tubes was to do in the 1980s. Westbrook was an art student who loved jazz and was mainly self-taught on piano and trumpet. In Plymouth in 1960 he ran a jazz workshop and formed a six-piece that included a precocious young saxophone talent in JOHN SURMAN. The band came to London, and quickly expanded, influenced primarily by Ellington, but also by the free-scene. Westbrook was also intrigued by theatre, joining forces with the group Welfare State for mixed-media shows, and by the notion of street performances using a completely mobile brass-band instrumentation.

Kate Westbrook was also a painter originally, and worked as a performance artist in the States in the 1960s. She joined Mike Westbrook's Brass Band in 1974 and devoted herself entirely to music, performing as a jazz-cabaret vocalist and English horn player with Westbrook, as a solo artist with radio orchestras in Europe and in partnership with the oboeist and composer Lindsay Cooper. Separately and together, the Westbrooks represent some of the most independent musical thought and unique transformations of jazz to have been achieved in Britain.

★*On Duke's Birthday* (Hat Hut ARTCD 6021)

One of Westbrook's most triumphant recordings, a project commissioned in France in 1984 to feature the leader's 11-piece band. Dedicated to Duke Ellington, Westbrook's compositional inspiration, it intelligently seeks Ellington's essence in textural richness, subtle settings for the soloists' particular qualities and ensemble unity rather than replicating 'classic works'.

★*Citadel Room 315* (Novus ND7 4987)

A Westbrook classic from 1975, with John Surman on saxophones, and Henry Lowther and KEN WHEELER among the trumpets. Westbrook moved creatively between the inspirations of Duke Ellington and Gil Evans, jazz-fusion, and free-music, making the elements sound at home with each other, and inciting spectacular performances from soloists. John Surman performs on this selection almost as if the piece were a concerto for him, and it's one of his most inventive exploits on disc.

★*The Cortege* (ENJA ENJ 7087-22)

One of Westbrook's most magnificent achievements, now reissued as a double-CD. Of all the composer's dramatic fusions of jazz, traditional song, poetry, street music and theatrical vividness, this piece for voices and big-band, drawing on materials from Lorca, Rimbaud, Blake and others is perhaps the most overwhelming and imaginative.

Wheeler, Kenneth 'Kenny'

(Born Toronto, Canada, January 14, 1930)

A brass virtuoso, Canadian-born Kenny Wheeler has appeared in virtually every kind of jazz band in Britain since his arrival in the country in 1952, performing with dance bands, then the JOHN DANKWORTH Orchestra, the free-playing Spontaneous Music Ensemble, the Gil Evans-influenced MIKE GIBBS band and the American avantist ANTHONY BRAXTON's group. Wheeler has a cool, spare sound, but he displays a controlled athleticism in careering runs and wide leaps of intervals that make his work a blend of rigour and tantalising hints at abandon; MILES DAVIS, Booker Little and Art Farmer are among his trumpet heroes. A diffident and modest man, Wheeler has rarely believed in his own talents and therefore did not lead his own bands until comparatively late in his career. When he did, he revealed that his embrace of all music, regardless of degrees of abstraction from regular rules, produced an orchestral sound close to that of Gil Evans but which combined mainstream and free-playing soloists in intriguing juxtaposition.

Wheeler's talents are now widely recognised in America and elsewhere in Europe.

★*Gnu High* (ECM 825 591-2)

Wheeler's debut as a group leader for ECM, an event that helped bring him to the notice of American musicians subsequently. It's a typically oblique, rather reserved session, and thus synonymous with exactly those qualities in the trumpeter's own playing. But Wheeler's clear, soaring sound and distinctive phrasing are well supported by a fine American band that includes KEITH JARRETT (piano) and JACK DEJOHNETTE on drums.

Whitehead, Tim

(Born Liverpool, 1950)

Saxophonist Tim Whitehead was cut out to be a classical clarinettist at first, but the Beatles and Motown music, and later the work of Frank Zappa and Soft Machine diverted him. Whitehead sought a music of more direct appeal that nevertheless offered the freedoms of improvisation, and the synthesis of these forces is audible in the fluent eclecticism of his work.

In 1976 Whitehead switched from a prospective career in law to full-time music. He formed his own band, Borderline, including pianist Django Bates and drummer Nick France. Whitehead became a founder member of Loose Tubes in the mid 1980s, a mutually fruitful relationship.

★*Authentic* (Jazz House JHCD 017)

A live set from Ronnie Scott's in 1992, and although on the face of it it's a familiar enough mix of small-group Latin music, postbop and a rather meticulous funk, Whitehead's own sound transforms it. His clarity at high registers gives his ballads a shivery relish, and his relaxation at mid-tempo is neatly complemented by Pete Jacobson's piano. But on top of all that, he can slip into Sanbornish soul-sax charges, or Coltrane-like intensity with ease. Unpretentious, but high-class.

Williams, Anthony 'Tony'

(Born Chicago, December 12, 1945)

Along with Elvin Jones, Tony Williams was the colossus of jazz drumming from the 1960s onward, and he has retained much of his impact today. Like Max Roach, who was an early influence, Williams' style is constantly active, even hyperactive: his four limbs display astonishing independence even in the most complex figures, his constant eruptions and clatters of sound link spaces in the music or emphasise soloists' phrasing, his accompaniment is an orchestration rather than a timekeeping exercise, and his sense of where the beat is is so acute that he can accelerate or delay it with unerring accuracy.

Tony Williams' father was a saxophonist, and the boy began on drums at ten, studying with Dave Brubeck's drummer, Alan Dawson. By his teens Williams was playing with the avant-garde saxophonist Sam Rivers, and in 1962 he was working with altoist Jackie McLean. At 17 Williams was with MILES DAVIS, and the combination of the young drummer, pianist HERBIE HANCOCK and bassist Ron Carter made the rhythm section of that band the envy and wonder of the jazz world. After he left Davis in 1969 Williams formed a raucous and experimental fusion band (Lifetime, with JOHN McLAUGHLIN on guitar and Larry Young on organ) which broke up too early, and by the late 1970s he had reverted to celebrating the 1960s Miles band without Miles in the popular VSOP ensemble. He has also recorded with rock musicians.

★*Angel Street* (Blue Note CDP 748 494-2)

A delightful 1988 blend of the intense, brooding, edge-of-darkness sound of the pre-electric Miles band and an irresistible rhythmic bounce. 'Dreamland', with its chiming funky piano and driving horn lead could have figured on a 1960s Herbie Hancock disc, and is worth the album on its own. Williams' compositional strengths are considerable by this point, and the solo and collective contributions of saxophonist Billy Pierce, trumpeter WALLACE RONEY and pianist Mulgrew Miller illuminate and amplify them.

Williamson, Steve

(Born London, 1956)

Like COURTNEY PINE, his more celebrated contemporary, Steve Williamson's lineage is Britain's West Indian community. He emerged as part of the wave of young black music that reinvigorated the British jazz scene in the 1980s, initially as a clarinet player and an enthusiast of the soul sound of Al Green, Marvin Gaye and James Brown. When he turned to saxophone, Williamson was initially inspired by funk horn players such as Grover Washington and Wilton Felder – until he heard Charlie Parker.

On tenor, Williamson's sound has always crackled with a fierceness and urgency that suggests John Coltrane and WAYNE SHORTER, but his affection for the rhythmic grooves of dance patterns gives him an enthusiasm for the more direct and convivial style of an artist such as Sonny Rollins, with elements of the reverberating funk of Ornette Coleman's Prime Time also apparent in earlier periods of his work.

★*A Waltz For Grace* (Polydor Verve 843 088)

Debut album of immense alertness and sophistication and rhythmic variety. It was recorded in both Britain and America and the session thus included key figures from the British scene such as the brilliant young drummer Mark Mondesir, and powerful New York sidemen such as Art Blakey's bassist Lonnie Plaxico. Funk, African, jazz and blues.

★*Rhyme Time* (Verve 511 235-2)

British saxophonist Williamson's transatlantic recording band, with M-Basers Dave Gilmore (guitar) and CASSANDRA WILSON (vocals). It's a more relaxed music than its predecessor, and Williamson has taken considerable care of dynamic details, such as the contrast of a chopped-off slide guitar sound against sudden fusillades of chords or typically mobile, restless sax lines.

Wilson, Cassandra

(Born Mississippi, 1963)
That group of radical young black New Yorkers going under the collective name of M-Base (currently producing some of the most unexpected departures from the long traditions of jazz and the shorter ones of hip-hop and rap) includes in its ranks one of the most powerful emerging talents in the world of jazz singing in Cassandra Wilson.

Cassandra Wilson debuted in New York in 1982, quickly revealing allegiances to BETTY CARTER and Abbey Lincoln, but also a flexibility that enabled her to work successfully in adventurous contexts, such as saxophonist/composer Henry Threadgill's band in 1983. She resembles at times a less fanciful and more muscular Betty Carter, with an abrupt and spine-chilling mid-register fierceness that even suggested NINA SIMONE, and these qualities have been easier to detect in more conventional contexts than in the collectivised sound of the STEVE COLEMAN Five Elements group.

★*Blue Skies* (JMT 834419-2)

A 1988 Wilson recording of jazz standards, delivered in her intriguingly displaced, reflective style, with bursts of emphatic, exclamatory scatting and sudden four-wheel skids on the accents. She's accompanied by an excellent trio of Mulgrew Miller (piano), Lonnie Plaxico (bass) and Terri-Lyne Carrington (drums).

★*Blue Light Till Dawn* (Blue Note CDP 0777 7 81357 2 2)

Wilson's roots record, an acoustic album concentrating on blues and ballads – including two Robert Johnson scorchers. Much of the disc features Brandon Ross's buzzy, pliable-sounding acoustic guitar, and some of it Olu Dara's bold and painterly cornet, and there's also an ethereally superb percussion band led by hand-drummer Vinx. The material ranges wide, including Van Morrison's 'Tupelo Honey' and the production is very plush – but though it's a retreat from the sharp end, it's one of Wilson's best displays of her strengths.

Woods, Philip Wells 'Phil'

(Born Springfield, Massachusetts, November 2, 1931)

Woods was invariably labelled a Charlie Parker clone in the 1950s, but he has always been an intelligent and sensitive one, modifying the pure style with the atmospherics of earlier jazz in vocalised growls and bent notes. In recent years he has devoted himself to fresh and thoughtful variations on acoustic bebop (even to the extent of turning the microphones off in many live situations), avoiding technical displays and bravura. Woods played with guitarist Jimmy Raney in the mid-1950s, then joined Dizzy Gillespie's orchestra, following that up with a key role with Quincy Jones. He then moved to Europe and broadened his original bop specialism with a looser and more accessible band, the European Rhythm Machine; when he returned to the States in the early 1970s, however, it was to a more straight-ahead bop with a fine quartet including Hal Galper on piano.

★Birds of a Feather (Polystar J33D 20003)

Fine Woods quartet session from the early 1980s, revealing the extent to which the altoist's tone had deepened and strengthened since his early associations with the Cannonball Adderley school of Parker variation. 'Star Eyes' is a measure of the intensity and collective momentum of the band. 'Goodbye Mr Evans' is a ravishing ballad display.

Zorn, John

(Born New York, 1954)

Zorn is the New York composer and improviser who erupted to public notice (after nearly 15 years underground with the avantists and performance artists of the Lower East Side) with a captivatingly personal interpretation of the movie music of Ennio Morricone (the memorable spaghetti western themes of *A Fistful of Dollars* and others were his) in 1987.

Zorn is a tireless beachcomber of contemporary culture and his reference points are movies, the line of jazz and blues that runs into pop, and urban soundscapes. He is devoted to Japan because he admires that culture's openness about borrowing and remixing ingredients from elsewhere. His own playing (he is an excellent saxophonist, but perversely camouflages it) mixes bop alto, duck calls, heavy metal music and pounding, horror-movie clichés. His first musical interests were in Cage and Ives, but a period of his life spent in St Louis attracted him to jazz, particularly bebop and the post-bop avant-garde.

Big Gundown (Nonesuch 979 139-2)

Zorn's extraordinary Morricone tribute, a display of bebop, funk, blues, free-music and musical collagism that not only calls on the leader's regular repertory company of off-the-wall players but also blues guitarists and even the legendary harmonica-playing composer Toots Thielemanns.

Spy Vs Spy (Nonesuch K960 844-2)

Ornette Coleman's early themes – some of the most beautiful jazz tunes since the bebop era – merged bop lines, free-improvisation and a rough-hewn early New Orleans intonation, but often delivered in a superfast, blurted, jerky fashion quite different to the lava flow of bop. Zorn here plays 17 tracks spanning much of Coleman's extensive composing career. The first half of this album is performed as frantic thrash-jazz, the remainder is more open, bluesy and yearning, closer to Coleman's original conception. Crazed, affectionate, headbanging elegance.

INDEX